From the Earth to Our Hearts . . .

MORE WAYS TO CELEBRATE THE CYCLES OF
THE SEASONS AND OUR LIVES

- Acknowledge the gifts of winter by making snow candy
- Bring the loving influence of extended family into your children's life
- Celebrate water by walking in the rain
- Create sacred space in your home with an altar
- Bake Summer Solstice cupcakes
- Say a Teacher's Blessing
- Read the story "The Nahua Creation of the Sun and the Moon"
- Include stepchildren in a new household or marriage with a simple ritual
- Sing the "Spiral of Life" song

And many more creative, fun family activities

BANTAM BOOKS
New York Toronto London Sydney Auckland

CIRCLE ROUND

Raising Children in Goddess Traditions

Starhawk

Diane Baker

Anne Hill

Illustrations by
Sara Ceres Boore

This edition contains the complete text
of the original hardcover edition.
NOT ONE WORD HAS BEEN OMITTED.

CIRCLE ROUND

PUBLISHING HISTORY
Bantam hardcover edition published November 1998
Bantam trade paperback edition / February 2000

ISBN 0-553-37805-8

Published simultaneously in the United States and Canada

Bantam Books are published by Bantam Books, a division of Random House,
Inc. Its trademark, consisting of the words "Bantam Books" and the portrayal
of a rooster, is Registered in U.S. Patent and Trademark Office and in other
countries. Marca Registrada. Bantam Books, 1540 Broadway, New York, New
York 10036.

PRINTED IN THE UNITED STATES OF AMERICA
FFG   10 9 8 7 6 5 4

Dedication

I dedicate my work with love to Vivian and Brigit who rooted me in family life and inspired this book, and to my husband Todd, partner in the magnificent and the mundane
—*Diane Baker*

To my wonderful children old and new, Bowen, Lyra, Johanna, Alex, and Rose; to Ross, for being a great partner as well as a great father; and to the children of the future, for whom Goddess tradition will be as natural as breath and as normal as breathing, making this book entirely unnecessary
—*Anne Hill*

For Marie Cantlon, and for Kore Margaret Simpich
—*Starhawk*

Contents

PART TWO:
CYCLES OF THE MOON AND SUN   41

Chapter Three

Moon Cycle   46

Chapter Four

Sun Cycle   67

Chapter Five

Samhain   71

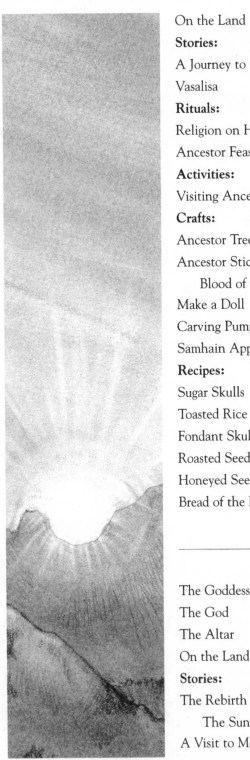

Chapter Six

Yule/Winter Solstice   95

Chapter Seven

Brigit 124

Chapter Eight

Eostar/Spring Equinox   148

Chapter Nine

Beltane   171

Chapter Eleven

Lughnasad/Lammas   231

Chapter Twelve

Mabon/Fall Equinox   253

Recipes:

PART THREE: THE LIFE CYCLE   281

Chapter Thirteen

Beginnings   287

Chapter Fourteen

Growth   301

Chapter Fifteen

Coming of Age: Adolescence   311

Chapter Sixteen

Coming of Age: Rites of Passage   321

Chapter Seventeen

Life Transitions   334

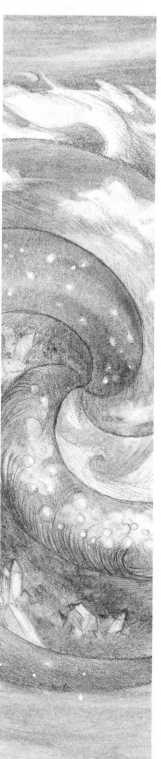

Acknowledgments

First we want to thank the extended Reclaiming community, both in the Bay Area and around the country, for being a great storehouse of energy and experiences. Many of the customs, rituals, insights, and practices found here arise out of our collective celebrations and mutual explorations. Our grateful thanks go to the many families of Goddess tradition who shared with us their struggles, their successes, and their commitment, and whose voices we hope are reflected in these pages.

We especially thank Marie Cantlon, who helped us develop the concept and structure of this book. For over two decades, Marie has shaped and guided many of the germinal works on feminist and earth-based spirituality, including almost all of Starhawk's books. Her skills and commitment have been a true gift to the Goddess movement, and we are grateful for her long and always interesting friendship, her steady vision, and her endless patience.

We also thank our editor at Bantam, Beth de Guzman, who shepherded this book to completion, and the wonderful staff at Bantam responsible for the book's design, copyediting, and production.

Our illustrator, Sara Boore, worked selflessly to create the charming illustrations that bring these stories alive. We are grateful, too, to those who contributed the magical tales told here, those who enriched this book by sharing personal experiences and stories from their own families, and those who took time to respond to our survey of the Pagan community.

Alice Medrich and Glenn Mitchell shared their baking expertise. Leane Sebastian contributed great craft ideas.

We are indebted to Francesca De Grandis for coining the term "The Third Road" to designate both her Faery Wicca teachings and the road to Faery in Thomas the Rhymer, thus bringing this concept to our attention.

Our agent, Ken Sherman, has been an unfailing support throughout this process. Jonathan Kirsch contributed his legal expertise.

No mother gets this much work done without helpers. Diane thanks her wonderful friends Indiana Guiterrez, Rachel Bethune Jackson Richardson, Kathryn Novaes, and Annie Altberg, who helped her and loved her children; her life support system Emily Marks, who's always ready to walk, talk, and listen; her great neighborhood blood-pact clan; the children's circle Scarlet Cord, and her ritual sisters, Olivia and Paula.

Anne's parents and sisters Martha and Sarah gave her encouragement even when what she was doing mystified them. She thanks her circlemates past and present for many years of great magic: Cybele, Cynthia, Marian, Karen, Paula, Jody, Reya, Patti, Thorn, and Oak.

Starhawk thanks her husband, David, her stepdaughters Juanita, Skye, Amie, and Juliana, her stepgrandchildren Emily Sunrise and Leif, her extended family the Black Cats: Rose, Bill, Donna, Jeanne, April, and also Kore; Bethany, Delaney, and Síannon, for whom many of these rituals were first conceived; and the other wonderful children who enrich her life: Florence, Ami, Allison, Casey, Aidan, and Colin.

How This Book Came to Be

One darkening October evening the day before Samhain, also known as Halloween, I (Diane) was standing in my kitchen. My husband was traveling. I had a major work project due. The children needed Halloween costumes. I was overwhelmed with household chores. And I had to create a religious celebration that would convey the essence of Samhain to my children in a meaningful way.

Leaning against the stove, I screamed inside, *Why isn't there just a book I could open?* I fantasized about this book. It would explain the holidays in language I could read to the children. There would be activities, stories, menus. It would answer my children's questions. It would make me feel connected to all the other families raising their children in Goddess tradition. It was then that I resolved to be the last person to feel so desperately alone in my faith.

I decided the children would eat boxed macaroni and cheese for dinner and hard-boiled eggs the next day. I threw in the laundry, turned on a video for the kids, and got on the telephone to Marie Cantlon, a longtime friend and book editor. She loved the idea. "But I think Starhawk is writing something about children. You should talk to her."

I caught up with my old friend Star the next day and asked whether she was writing the book I was waiting for. "Anne Hill and I talked about doing something. Let's write it together," she suggested.

So began the next three years of writing, meeting, listening to other families, trying out ideas on our children (Anne says she felt like a field anthropologist in her own home) and children of friends. And all this time we've kept that person in the kitchen in mind. She's not alone anymore.

How to Use This Book

Our goal for *Circle Round* is to support families building their own spiritual tradition, by bringing you celebrations, explanations, activities, and the experiences of other families. Our definition of family for this book is broad: loving people who join together in the hard and important work of raising children. Children and families need love and support. We hope you find both in the pages of this book.

In our practice of Goddess traditions, celebrations and rituals come from our creativity and our needs. The rituals in this book are examples, not liturgy or dogma. Our goal is for you to enjoy inventing your own family traditions. But as realistic members of our busy society, we know that most families have little time for creating new celebrations and we offer ours to share. This book is not meant to add more obligations to families, but to create nourishing energy that everyone can draw upon for renewal.

We have aimed for explanations clear enough to be read aloud to young children or read independently by older children. You may also wish to paraphrase our discussions in your own words, or use them to sharpen your own thinking. You may disagree with our ideas, and may sometimes tell your children, "The women who wrote this book say thus and such, but I believe _____."

Three of us wrote this book. Although in general Starhawk wrote most of the stories, Anne and Diane most of the rituals, Anne most of the music, and Diane most of the crafts and recipes, we each had input into the whole. Just try to stop any one of us from expressing an opinion! We are all involved in raising children, both our own and others'. Because our views are so intermingled, we didn't sign each segment, but where a writer refers to a personal experience, her name appears in parentheses, so our readers get a sense of the variety and diversity of our homes.

The Goddess Tradition: Where We Fit In

The thealogy and practices described in this book are those that arise from the Reclaiming community in the San Francisco Bay Area and beyond. Reclaiming is a community of women and men who have been working together, teaching and creating public rituals, for almost two decades. We encompass many different circles and covens, and over the years we have created our own evolving tradition. We have several roots: in the Faery tradition of Wicca as taught to us by Victor and Cora Anderson, in nonviolent direct-action politics of groups such as the Abalone Alliance, and in the ongoing experimentation and creativity of our community.

The Goddess tradition itself is composed of many circles that may overlap but are not identical. Here is a brief overview of these intertwined strands, and our relationship to them:

⚲ Feminist spirituality includes people who range from initiated Witches to Christian ministers and rabbis. All share a concern with the role of women in religion and with the role religious images play in shaping our possibilities and opportunities as women.

⚲ Earth-based spirituality includes people drawn to traditions of the sacred that put the earth at center, ranging from Native American elders to Witches to creation-centered Christians, including most of the indigenous peoples on the planet.

⚲ The New Age/human-potential movement is concerned with expanding the narrow definition of reality to include not only what is quantifiable but also possibilities of consciousness that move beyond the rational. It often draws from the insights of Eastern religious traditions as well as indigenous traditions worldwide.

ⓖ *Paganism* is the term for the revival of the earth-based sacred traditions, particularly of Europe and the Middle East. One of those Pagan traditions is Wicca or Witchcraft, which itself has many branches. (Witchcraft is sometimes referred to as the Craft.) We are Witches; that is to say, we have each made a deep, lifelong commitment to the Goddess, been initiated into our tradition, and serve as her priestesses.[1] We identify with the line of women and men martyred in the Burning Times and with the traditional healers and practitioners of magic.

ⓖ *Shamanism* is a word that originated with the indigenous healers of Siberia and has come to be broadly used for anyone exploring wider dimensions of consciousness with some guidance from an indigenous tradition. The Witches were the shamans of Europe. We prefer not to lay claim to this word, and rather reserve it for indigenous healers working within their own communities and intact traditions.

ⓖ The twelve-step programs (Alcoholics Anonymous and so on) have been a big influence on our community over the last decade. As we have become more aware of the pervasiveness of addictions in our culture, we have moved away from the use of wine or other forms of alcohol in our rituals. Aside from caffeine, chocolate, and herb tea, we do not use any mind-altering substances in our magical practice and certainly do not recommend doing so when children are present.

The native peoples of this continent have thousands of years of experience in living on this land. We have received much from them—many of our major food plants, for example. Many people of European ancestry are attracted to the practices and teachings of these indigenous traditions.

We want to state clearly that we are not Native Americans, nor do we teach any Native American traditions or ceremonies or make any claim to do so. Our rituals originate from native European roots and our collective creativity and experimentation. They have some similarities of form to many Native American traditions—for example, we all work within a sacred circle and honor the four directions. We share with indigenous peoples everywhere a strong commitment to protect the earth and her sacred places and to support the rights of indigenous peoples to their own lands and to self-determination.

Note: The word *theology* is rooted in the Greek *theos*, the male form for God. We use thealogy, from *thea*, Goddess.

Families in Goddess Tradition

Who are we, these families raising our children to love and revere Earth and Goddess? First, we're people who have enough faith in the future and enough stability in the present to bring children into the spiral of life or nurture children who are not born to us. In this, we join everyone who has raised children before us, all who have connected deeply to a child. Second, we are people conscious of the complex web of which we're part, who feel the vibrating wholeness of life and call that Goddess. Finally, we're people caught up, or ground down, by the daily routines of living as we move through each day, each cycle.

We don't look any different from any other people in our culture, unless we choose to do so. Like most families, we typically don't discuss religion with neighbors or casual friends. Our homes might show our religious orientation, if at all, through a simple symbol or a small altar tucked in some corner. Visions of haunted houses, complete with spider webs and esoteric symbols, belong to our detractors, not our supporters.

No census includes "Pagan" or "Goddess worshipper" among its categories, but we estimate over 500,000 people in the U.S. identify with some aspect of earth-based spirituality. More of us are women than men, but we do include many men and boys. We are all ages, from newborn to very old.

Our tradition is of European origin, so we naturally attract people of European ancestry. But our community includes and welcomes people of all races and many different ethnic and religious backgrounds. Our occupations range through the economic and educational spectrum. We include secretaries, managers, entrepreneurs, farmers, lawyers, mechanics, welfare recipients, business owners, social workers, teachers, healers, artists, university professors, high-school dropouts, ambulance attendants, military personnel, psychotherapists, prisoners, prison guards, and just about everyone else, including more than our fair share of computer programmers and others who work in high-tech fields.

We define family as a bond of choice as well as blood, and our families come in many forms, including extended families, "traditional" nuclear families, intentional communities with multiple parents, single-parent families, lesbian and gay families, and families living with housemates who share parenting, to name just a few. The three of us (Starhawk, Anne, and Diane) live in three different examples of Pagan families: Diane lives with her husband and children, in a diverse neighborhood that includes Jewish, Hindu, Sufi, and Baptist neighbors; Starhawk lives in a multiracial, urban collective household that includes adults, teenagers, and a toddler; Anne and her extended family live on rural property, with two houses for her partner and three children, teenage nephew and niece, and in-laws.

If we in the Goddess tradition share any one thing in common, it is a resistance to dogma. The tradition we have adopted is a highly creative one that values spontaneity and accepts change. Our rituals are often works-in-progress, changing as our needs and interests change and our insights deepen.

Of course, it is all very well to value ambiguity and mystery, right up until the moment a five-year-old with a logical mind asks us to explain what we believe. Children can't be deflected with vague esotericisms. In framing these explanations and stories, we've necessarily made statements that are sometimes more definitive than we ideally prefer to be. We hope you will take this book in the spirit of an offering, not a prescription. Every family is different, and each of us must ultimately be our own thealogian.

The gifts and challenges of raising children in our diverse family settings are a source of richness that deserve to be shared by all of us. Though we realize that there are many topics that deserve fuller treatment than we are able to give, we hope with this book to provide a starting point for the sharing and discussion that will nourish the growth of our tradition for generations to come.

PART ONE

WELCOME TO
THE CIRCLE

CHAPTER ONE

Goddess Tradition and Children

What Is Goddess Tradition?

NOT LONG AGO I (Starhawk) was part of a circle of women celebrating the First Blood ritual of my Goddess-daughter Shannon. We walked a labyrinth cut into a meadow on a ridge of the coastal mountains; we strung necklaces of blessings and beads; we bathed her in a clear stream trickling through a grotto of moss-covered rocks. The ritual felt as ancient as the spirals we traced on her back and shoulders with henna paste, and at the same time as contemporary as the self-tanning cream her mother added to the paste to make the designs last longer. In that way, our ritual was a perfect expression of the old/new character of the Goddess tradition itself: primeval as the big-bellied sculptures of Paleolithic cave dwellers, modern as the thousands of Pagans linked on the Internet.

Goddess tradition is indeed both the oldest and youngest of spiritual paths. For as long as human beings have existed, the numinous powers of conceiving, birthing, feeding, and bleeding have stirred the imagination wherever people lived in close relationship with the earth. For generations, the European-based expressions of that long tradition were suppressed or forgotten. But over the last twenty years, as our ecological and social crises have deepened, more and more women and men have been newly drawn toward a spirituality that puts the earth at center.

Most Pagans, therefore, have come to the Goddess in adult life. We are faced with the challenge of rearing our children in traditions in which we ourselves were not raised. The heart of our ritual for Shannon, for example, was the time we spent telling stories about our own first menstruations, which were *not* celebrated with gifts and magic. Our tales were charged with the awkward feelings and embarrassment of the women of our generation, born at midcentury into a world in which rituals such as Shannon's were mentioned only in anthropology texts. We stand between two worlds: the world of our parents and grandparents, in which rituals such as Shannon's are unthinkable, and the world of our daughters and sons, grandchildren, and Goddess-children, for whom we hope such celebrations will become the norm.

How, then, do we answer our children when they ask questions about life and death, about causes and origins, about right and wrong?

In this section we present the basic worldview and some of the core myths of the Goddess tradition. If you are brand-new to Goddess tradition, the following discussion will help you understand the concepts and values that underlie our stories and rituals. If you have many years of experience creating ritual on your own,

what follows will clarify our interpretations. If you identify strongly with some other spiritual tradition, or with none at all, you will find here both differences and points of similarity with your own beliefs.

The stories and explanations that follow are meant not as gospel but as a workable framework for rituals and traditions that we hope will develop many unique expressions reflecting your own encounters with the sacred and the needs of your own community.

Goddess Tradition: Explanations for Children

Who Is the Goddess?

The earth is a living being whom we call the Goddess. Everything around us is alive and part of her living body; animals and plants, of course, but also some things that may not ordinarily seem to be alive, such as rocks, mountains, streams, rivers, stars, and clouds.

Even though we are separate people, all of us are part of her, just as each of your fingers is a part of your hand. And the earth herself is part of the larger living body of the universe, just as your hand is part of your arm, and your arm is part of your body.

Each living being is important and sacred, the way each part of your body is important to you. When something is sacred, we must take care of it and respect it. Human life is sacred to us, and so are the plants and the animals and all the elements that make life possible. If one thing is hurt, it hurts us all—just as when you cut even the tip of your little finger, you feel the pain all over.

The Goddess is always close to us. You touch the Goddess whenever you hug somebody, climb a tree, smell a flower, or pet a cat. The water we drink, the food we eat, and the ground we walk on are all part of the Goddess.

We also believe in many different Goddesses and Gods, whom we call by many different names. They are all spirit parts of the living universe, and there are many beautiful stories about them. To Pagans, each Goddess and God is a different way of trying to understand the universe. The universe is so enormous that our minds cannot understand it all at once, only in parts. We know that different people have different names they use for Goddesses and Gods, and that's good. The universe-being is like a great jigsaw puzzle. Each of us has a piece of the puzzle, and the more pieces we place together, the more we can understand about the whole. No one group or piece has all the picture; no one idea is right for everybody. The Goddess tradition teaches us to respect other beliefs and ways of thinking.

The Goddesses and Gods can help us in different ways. When we call on a particular Goddess or God, it's as if we stepped into that piece of the jigsaw puzzle. In the movie *Mary Poppins*, the children step into a chalk picture and it comes alive and takes them into another world. Calling on a particular Goddess or God is a bit like

that. In our imagination, that piece of the puzzle comes alive for us, and we learn something only that Goddess or God can teach us. In this book, the many stories about different Goddesses and Gods are like magic pictures we can enter.

The Circle of Life

Life is a circle. We are born, we grow up, and we die. But death too is part of the circle, not a final end. When we die, we are told, our spirit goes to a place where we can rest and grow young again, and be with the Goddess and the old Gods. We call this place Summerland, or the Isle of Apples, or the Land of Youth, and we imagine it as a beautiful land across a dark sea, outside of ordinary time. There we can think about what we learned in this life and what we might do in our next life. When we are ready, we are reborn in some new form. When someone we love dies, we are sad because we can't see them and talk to them in our daily lives anymore, and we will miss them. But we are not afraid for them, because we know that they will be in a place of peace and love and beauty.

We can't see the dead, or talk to them, except in our minds, but some of us do have dreams or visions of the dead. Sometimes we receive very clear messages from them. Some of us remember other lifetimes or know things that we learned in other lives. But mostly we know that life is a circle because we see how everything in nature moves in circles.

The moon is born as a silver crescent, grows to be round and full, and wanes away

Spiral of Life[1]

Words and music by Diane Baker

Oh the spi-ral of life goes on and on In a

cir - cle, but ne - ver go - ing back

to darkness, only to be born again. The seasons change from warm to cold and back to warm, or from rainy to dry to rainy. Baby plants grow up as green shoots from the earth, grow tall, blossom, set seed, and die. The seed falls to the earth and goes underground, only to rise again in the spring.

Magic

Pagans practice magic. That doesn't mean we can just wave a wand and turn mice into horses. We wish we could! If you listen to the word *magic,* it sounds a lot like *imagine.* Magic is a way of training our imagination to make pictures and sounds and feelings and even smells in our minds that are so clear they almost seem to be real. When we say we practice, we're not kidding, because it takes a lot of practice, just as it does to become a good dancer or baseball player. Luckily imagination is something kids are naturally good at, better even than grown-ups.

Magic can't turn straw into gold. But with magic, we can change the way we feel about things, and sometimes that can change things outside us too. Magic can change the energy around us, and when energy changes, new things can happen. And magic can help us remember that we are part of the Goddess, that we are important and sacred and loved.

We use magic for healing, and for helping things go better in our lives and in the world around us. We believe that using magic to harm somebody is not only wrong but stupid. Whatever you send out with magic, whatever you create, that same kind of energy will return to you three times over. So if you use magic for good, for helping and healing, good will come to you. But if you use it to gain power over others, or in harmful or greedy ways, you are asking for harm to come to you.

The Elements

The four elements—air, fire, water, and earth—are especially sacred, because they are the things all life depends on. We all need air to breathe. Even the fish who live underwater need oxygen to survive. We all need water to drink. All life and growth on earth feeds on the sun's fiery energy. All our food, the minerals, and solid parts of our bodies come from the earth.

Whenever we begin a ritual, we call on the four elements because we know that everything depends on them. Each element goes with a different direction. Air is in the east, fire in the south, water in the west, and earth in the north. Where we live, on the west coast of California, the elements fit those directions very well, but your family may arrange them differently to fit your land and climate.

There is a fifth element, too, which is found in the center. We call that element spirit. You can't see it or touch it, but you can feel it inside, just as you can feel when somebody loves you.

Creation: A Story for Small Children[2]

by Diane Baker

Circle round, and listen how we came to be. . . .

The Goddess, alone in emptiness, felt the stirrings of love in her heart, love for a partner, love for a child, love for a friend. As love filled her heart, she became filled with swirling heat. She spun the heat into a great spiral, where it became the stars, including our own sun, making light. Delighted with her work, she laughed, and from this laughter formed the God, her partner and child. Now, knowing joy and life, she shared her gifts.

From our sun she blew great arms of fire that shot out into space, becoming swirling clouds that grew heavier and thicker, forming planets. The earth was one of these. Spinning around the sun, the earth grew denser, her surface covered with pale water and rock.

The Goddess, who holds within her the spark of all living things, found this planet mild enough for life, and scattered life's pieces across the earth in dense puddles.

She breathed upon these pieces. Tiny bits clumped together and made cells, each the tiniest quivering little piece of life, able to make itself again and again.

Life calls to life, and life comes from life. These bits

jumped, bumped, and collided. Some learned how to turn sun and water into food. Some ate each other. Others sucked up minerals, dissolving rocks into soil.

Bits of life fused together, joined by seed and pollen, by egg and sperm. Others just divided themselves in half. Some groups became animals, some became plants. Their breath sweetened the air and their bodies fed the new soil.

Life grew abundantly, always growing and dying, nourishing itself until the earth sang. Some creatures grew big, others stayed tiny. Water bloomed with plants and fish. Air filled with birds and insects. Floating seeds and pollen covered the land with plants, and roaming animals grazed and preyed. Some of them

thrived, some disappeared. Eventually, walking on two feet and flexing ten fingers, people came, carrying babies and making tools.

All life knew the Goddess, and people did, too. The first people fashioned her image from clay and stone. We drew her picture as we imagined her. We molded her image with clay. With words we wrote poems, with music we made songs, with our bodies we danced.

And now when we worship, when we journey toward the Goddess with our dance, our music, our songs, our drums, when we travel to our quiet places or our wild places, we feel her breath in our cells, that tingle of life we share.

Life comes from life, life calls to life, life goes on. ⟨𝕆⟩

The Goddess Dances the World Awake: A Creation Story[3]

retold by Starhawk

Long ago, before anything was, the Goddess awoke alone in the vast dark and emptiness. She had as yet no name and no form, but she felt an urge to move. She stretched, she rocked, she began to dance. Whirling and twirling, she wheeled and spiraled through space.

Her dance set in motion a great wind that followed her, playing catch, trying to caress her. The Goddess danced with the wind, and the wind took form, becoming the God in the shape of a great serpent, Ophion. Ophion wrapped his coils around the Goddess, trying to become one with her, loving her with all his being.

Suddenly the Goddess felt something stirring inside her, as if her dance had come alive. Something wanted to be born. She reached out, and her arms became wings. As a giant dove, she flew aloft while Ophion coiled himself into a nest for her. She settled onto his back and laid a huge, huge egg.

Ophion guarded the egg, sheltering it from below as the Goddess brooded it from above. At last the egg cracked open and the whole universe fell out—suns and stars and galaxies,

planets and moons and the green living earth, all spiraling and spinning, whirling and twirling through space in the Goddess's dance.

So that's how the world came to be. And the whole universe is still spiraling and spinning, whirling and twirling to this very day, in the dance of life! ⟊

Creation Song⁴

Words and music by Starhawk

I'm the voice that sings in you,   I cre-ate the world a-new.

I give birth and   I give shape,   I can dance the world a-wake.

CHAPTER TWO

Handing Down Our Traditions

Making Time

IN GODDESS TRADITION, no institution schedules time for us to focus on spirituality. We have to make that time ourselves.

Sharing holidays with other families decreases work and increases fun. Just as families divide up Christmas and Thanksgiving, we join others for different celebrations. Most families select one or two favorite holidays for going all out, and commemorate the others more simply.

Like other traditions' holidays, all our activities and celebrations don't have to be on the same day. After all, families don't trim a Yule tree, decorate the house, wrap the presents, bake the cookies, and send out cards all on the same day, at least not in most homes! My family (Diane's) starts making decorations and building an altar a week ahead of each holiday; we read stories, sing songs, and talk about the holiday's meaning as the week goes by. On the day itself, we usually have a relaxed short ritual and a treat. Casting a circle, doing an activity, singing a song, telling a story, and sharing food may take only half an hour.

Some celebrations are spontaneous, sparked by a special event such as harvesting the first tomato from the garden or losing the first tooth.

We also integrate our Goddess tradition values into ordinary family activities. I (Diane) want to instill respect and love for nature in my children. We spend about as much time doing this as other families spend attending church or temple. For example, we take weekly hikes. Our timing is flexible and our plans can be changed to fit in with other events.

There are many ways to gently open children's awareness to the values we treasure in Goddess tradition: the sacredness of life, our connection to the earth, our responsibilities to preserve her gifts. As we add each piece of Goddess tradition to our lives, we bring back her long-needed presence to our home, to our world.

When Kids Don't Want To

If your children decide they don't want to participate in your family traditions, the best tactic is to continue to offer rituals and celebrations on a regular basis. Just as parents who continue to serve vegetables eventually catch their kids in a vegetable mood, we can keep giving children the opportunity to participate in rituals. Their unwillingness may go on for years, but you will probably hit a time and place that attracts each child.

When children aren't interested in joining in a ritual, don't force them. You will only strengthen their resolve if you make their participation an issue.

There are helpful techniques to tempt children into participation. Keep your own devotions, but make them a little flashier. Try selecting a special site, like a beach or a wonderful trail. Prepare a favorite food. Make a ritual object that interests the children. Allow sharing without pressure to do more, whether it's helping to cook, or coming along without joining the celebration.

Let your children create something for the ritual even if they don't participate. Talk about how good it felt to have a piece of them there. Ask them for requests for any special blessings, or prayers they'd like you to say for them.

A Basic Structure for Ritual

What is a ritual? A ritual is simply an intentional process. Families create rituals all the time: the bedtime ritual, the getting-out-the-door-in-the-morning ritual, the how-to-get-the-child-to-eat ritual. Rituals are family customs, an accepted part of everyday life, and the vehicle by which family values and priorities are maintained.

A ritual with a spiritual focus has a purpose and is usually set apart from the ordinary flow of daily events. Such rituals follow a basic structure. We first purify and ground ourselves, then create sacred space by casting a circle and calling in the four directions. Once the circle is cast the ritual has begun, and we invoke the Goddess and the God to aid us in our work. Then we move into the body of the ritual, the central activity, which varies from ritual to ritual and season to season. Afterward, we offer food and drink to the Goddess and God, and share it among ourselves as well. We open the circle by thanking and saying goodbye to the powers we've called in, beginning with the God and Goddess and ending with the four directions.

When working with the shorter attention span and natural exuberance of children, we try to find lively ways to perform the basic elements of the ritual so that we can reserve their interest and energy for the heart of the ritual. We leave room for our children to experiment, have fun, and learn firsthand about their own power.

Purifying

Intent: To help us shed the cares, worries, and distractions of the outside world before creating sacred space.

☽ While running counterclockwise around the circle, children can beat pots and pans, or play drums, tambourines, or bells.

☽ Give the children sprigs of fresh herbs and a bowl of salt water. They can sprinkle people as they enter the room, or move around the circle once it is formed, sprinkling the circle as they walk.

Grounding

Intent: To bring all of our energy into our bodies, making sure we are not just "in our head" or "spaced out." Grounding strengthens our connection with the earth, which gives us more energy for our ritual. Do some sort of grounding or centering practice before attempting any magical work.

☽ The grounding we use most often is a Tree of Life meditation:

Now, for just a moment, we're going to turn ourselves into trees. That's right. Take a big, deep breath, and imagine your roots grow out of your toes and down into the ground. Can you feel them dig into the sand? [Or squish through the mud, crack the cement—whatever applies.]

Now take another big, deep breath, and imagine your trunk growing tall and straight. Stretch up as high as you can, and feel yourself grow taller.

Now take another big, deep breath, and shoot your branches out from the top of your head. Feel them reach the sky. Can you feel your leaves soaking up the sunlight? [Or moonlight, starlight, and so on.]

Now breathe in the light from the sun [moon, stars] and eat it up, just like a tree does! Breathe it all the way down into the earth.

☙ Sing a song, such as "My Roots Go Down."

☙ Crouch down near the ground, pretending to be a seed, and start a low sound: *eeeeeee*. Then begin to stand, still making an *eeeeeee* sound that gets gradually louder. Bring your arms up over your head and end with a big *oh!* sound. The seed has sprouted! Do this three times.

Casting the Circle

Intent: To inscribe a place "between the worlds," somewhat removed from the demands and structure of the waking world, which allows us to relax into deeper states of consciousness.

☙ Have children help by walking around, carrying wands, sprinkling water, or using some other special tool of their own to touch the walls at the four directions or draw pentacles in the air. Say: *By the earth that is her body, by the air that is her breath, by the fire of her bright spirit, and by the waters of her living womb, the circle is cast.*

☙ On the beach, draw a circle around you in the sand, with a stick or your foot.

☙ Hand-to-hand circle casting:

My Roots Go Down[1]

Words and music by Sarah Pirtle

Air I Am[2]

Words and music by Andras Corban Arthen

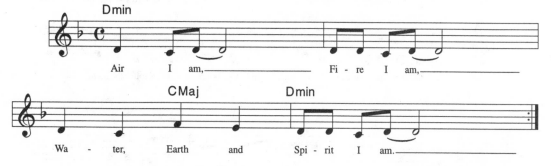

Everyone stands in a circle, and the first person takes the hand of the person to her left. Then that person takes hold of the hand of the next person, and around the circle clockwise the chain of hands is completed. This hand-to-hand casting of a circle can be silent, or you can say, *Hand to hand, the circle is cast.*

☙ Sing a circle-casting song, such as "Circle Round" or "We Welcome Air."

☙ See Casting a Circle with Hands, Feet, and Objects sidebar for other suggestions.

Calling the Directions

Intent: To call in the four elements and the elements of magic. Each element corresponds to a different direction: Air is east, fire is south, water is west, and earth is north. We face the appropriate direction to call in each element.

☙ Use a simple chant, such as "Air I Am" to bring each element into the circle.

☙ Let the kids call in an appropriate animal for each direction, imitating the animal's sound or movement.

☙ Give the children colored scarves to wave or dance with in the appropriate direction. This works well using a different drumbeat for each direction.

Casting a Circle with Hands, Feet, and Objects

With hands and feet:

For east and air: Gently flap arms and hands like a bird.

For south and fire: Hold hands up, shimmying boogie-woogie style.

For west and water: Swing arms in figure eights.

For north and earth: Stamp feet firmly on the ground.

With objects:

For east and air: Wave feathers or a fan.

For south and fire: Hold a lit candle. (A grown-up must supervise closely!)

For west and water: Hold a cup of water, dip a branch or some leaves in it, and sprinkle.

For north and earth: Hold a stuffed animal, a branch, a plant, a pentacle made from found twigs, or an egg.

Circle Round[3]

Verse

Words and music by Anne Hill

Cir- cle round the sun-rise, cir - cle round the breeze, Cir- cle round the flame in- side us dan - cing free, Cir - cle round the o - ceans, the wa - ters of our birth,

Chorus

Cir - cle round the stars at night and cir - cle round the earth. Oh, cir - cle round, cir - cle round, reach for the sky, stomp on the ground, cir - cle round, cir - cle round, reach for the sky, stomp on the ground, cir - cle round, cir - cle round, reach for the sky, stomp on the ground, cir - cle round, cir - cle round, reach for the sky, stomp on the ground.

We Welcome Air[4]

Words and music by Diane Baker

We wel-come air with e-very breath Our fie-ry heart beats in our chest Our

wa-ter's in our tears and sweat And earth's our bo-dy, dear. Our

cen-ter's in our spi-rit Our cen-ter's in our love And

all the guar-dian po-wers are be-low, a-round, a-bove.

☾ Light candles, one for each direction.

☾ Place an object in each of the four points to mark the circle. To call in each direction, touch each object in turn. See Outdoor Circle Scavenger Hunt sidebar for object-direction correspondences.

Invoking the Goddess and/or the God

Intent: To call in deities appropriate to the season or place, and to ask for their assistance, guidance, or consent for our ritual.

☾ Sing a song to the particular deity you are working with.

☾ Place an image of the Goddess on the altar or in the center of your circle at this time, saying: *We welcome you here to our circle. Please be with us now for this ceremony in your honor.*

Outdoor Circle Scavenger Hunt

Have the children hunt for objects that symbolize the four directions. (Don't destroy or mutilate to get these objects.) Some suggestions follow, but let the children make their own association and explain them to the circle.

Air: feathers, spiderwebs, airborne seeds

Fire: something dried, leaves for their light-converting capabilities

Water: water-worn stones, mud, shells, water-holding plant leaves (such as from succulents)

Earth: flowers, plants, stones, seeds

⊕ Older children can create their own invocations, especially if they have helped to plan the ritual. Invocations can also be thought up on the spot.

The Offering

Intent: To give thanks and offerings to the spirits that have helped us in a ritual, so they feel appreciated and will want to come back and help us again.

⊕ Let the kids spill a little milk onto the ground, or break off a piece of bread to throw in the fire, or pour some spring water onto a potted plant indoors. Say: *Goddess, God, air, fire, water, earth, spirit, ancestors, you have fed us. Now we feed you. As we eat, may you also be fed. Blessed be.*

Opening the Circle

Intent: As important as thanking the powers we have summoned is bidding them to depart. If we forget to say goodbye to an ancestor or deity we have invoked, we may find them bearing an undue influence on our lives after the ritual has ended! Opening the Circle also helps us reenter the flow of time in the waking world after being in sacred space.

⊕ If the kids have called in animals, let them briefly say goodbye. If you've used a chant, sing it through once. If you drummed in each direction, hit the drum one time in each direction and say:

By the earth that is her body, by the air that is her breath, by the fire of her bright spirit, and by the waters of her living womb, the circle is open, but un-

broken. May the peace of the Goddess go in our hearts, merry meet and merry part, and merry meet again. Blessed be.

Organizing Rituals with Children in Mind

Take into consideration your child's unique temperament and attention span. What works for one eight-year-old may not work for another, so be prepared to adjust your plans accordingly. Don't be afraid to experiment with both form and content.

Make the ritual as brief as possible while keeping the most important elements. Limiting rituals to include one central activity along with the circle casting and invocation structures seems to work for most age groups.

Keep it as hands-on as possible. Rituals in which we create something tangible, or use our bodies and voices to express our intent, keep us focused and help us participate on deeper levels than the spoken word alone can effect.

Avoid the impulse in ritual to Say What It All Means to your child. When we give pat answers to complex questions, we often squelch our children's innate capacity to create meaning from their own experience. Certainly some degree of explanation is called for, but while in sacred space don't be afraid to let the magic reign, without hindrance or worry.

If you really want to do a certain ritual for your children but they are adamantly opposed, don't take it personally. They just may not be ready. Pay attention to your child's signals and trust that the time will come.

Fitting In

Ten-year-old Daniel, of our children's circle Scarlet Cord, is disabled. He understands much more than he can say with his indistinct speech. Sometimes he rocks and flaps his hands. But he joins the ritual circle, holding up the object for the direction we're invoking and moving in time with the singing. His mom says he may not follow the stories that accompany each holiday, but he understands the hands-on work, the elements, the music. He knows circles are special. Scarlet Cord is a noisy group that includes children from toddlers to teens, and Daniel fits right in. The other children grasp his differences and accept him as one of them.

For circles to work for disabled children, it helps for parents to be very explicit about their needs. Some circles may not be willing to include a differently abled child. A child with severe allergies may not fit a circle that meets outdoors. But the Goddess has many forms and faces. For the most part families in Goddess Tradition embrace mainstreaming disabled children and adults and work out what needs to be done.

THE TOOL CHEST

In this section are basic instructions and explanations for the major components of all Goddess tradition celebrations: visualization and trance, altar building, song, rhythm, crafts projects, and baking.

Goddess tradition invites us to take a hands-on approach to sharing spirituality with our children. While it is unrealistic to expect every adult to excel at every skill we present here (just ask the three of us whether we make candles, bake, and lead elaborate visualizations at every occasion!), each person has some strength to share with children. With a working understanding of just a few of the practices presented in this section, you will be well prepared to adapt any of the ideas from this book into your own family traditions.

Altars

Altars are a fun and easy way to involve children in the seasonal observances that are at the center of Goddess tradition.

Central to many religious households is an altar, where an image of a protective deity, candles, and other devotional ob-

A few more ideas for altar placement: the windowsill over the kitchen sink, car dashboards, empty spaces at the ends of bookshelves, a mirror or window (decorate with see-through stickers and artwork fixed with tape), on top of the fridge, on the mantelpiece above the fireplace, a small shelf mounted by the front door, hanging shelves inside a closet door, a special rock or tree in the backyard, a set of hanging wire baskets in the kitchen. The list is limited only by your imagination.

jects reside, periodically joined by a fresh bouquet of flowers, a lighted stick of incense, or a small bowl of food offerings. A Goddess altar can be a shrine used for daily meditation and prayer, a special cupboard that houses the family's magical items, or a windowsill that is decorated for each season.

Try using the top of a bureau, a shelf just below eye level, or perhaps a windowsill as an altar. For small houses and apartments, use a tray that fits neatly into your altar spot. Then when you need your altar for a ritual, the tray is easily transported to any location. For small apartments with balconies, an outside shelf might be just the place to store crystals, statues, incense burners, and whatnot.

When I (Anne) was younger and on the move a lot, I had a wooden wine crate with a sliding lid that served as my traveling altar. All my special objects (well padded), as well as a small piece of colorful cloth, fit inside. When I wanted to do a ritual, I took out what was needed, set the cloth over the top, and arranged my things on what was now a modest table. The same idea can work well for children.

When your children are old enough, they may want an altar of their own. A low shelf, a wooden crate or cardboard box placed on its side, or a footstool covered with a simple cloth can serve quite well. Your children may demand total control of what goes on their altar, and if so, let them. Others may ask for suggestions. Gently encourage their own sense of expression, while providing basic guidelines. (For basic correspondences, see Casting a Circle with Hands, Feet, and Objects and Outdoor Circle Scavenger Hunt sidebars.)

In each seasonal section of this book, you will find suggestions for things to include on your altar, as well as craft projects to use as decorations. Have fun exploring your own home and finding just the right spot to set up your altar!

Visualization and Trance

What is trance? Our consciousness is a continuum, with our waking thoughts at one end and our deep unconscious at the other. Imagine the mind as a pond or pool. On the surface are our waking thoughts, and below lies our unconscious, where our mind works in images and associations rather than sentences and paragraphs. All the levels in between, where we still retain some waking awareness but move closer to our unconscious, are states of mind we call trance states.

Some trance states are familiar: daydreams, staring at a point but not really seeing it, drifting into dream just before sleep. Listening to music or even watching TV creates trance states.

In most magical work, we enter a light trance state. Light trance gives us enough of an anchor in waking awareness so that we can move and notice the things around us, while freeing our minds so that the powerful images and associations from our unconscious can surface more easily. We don't think it is necessary or advisable to go deeper than a light trance in working with children.

There are many ways to enter trance or to lead someone else in, but all it really takes is deep relaxation. I (Anne) might say, "Now, get into a comfortable position, feel your body completely relax, and take three deep breaths, letting all your tension and worry just fall away from you." If a child is very wound up, I might do a more detailed relaxation exercise, starting at their feet and going right up to their head: "Wiggle those toes, flex your feet, make your muscles as tight as you can possibly get them, till your feet are like rocks and no one would be able to bend your toes. Harder, still. Now, just let go and relax all the muscles in your feet and toes. Let them be completely loose and free, like leaves of kelp rocking on the ocean."

Storytelling can also induce a light trance. The listener easily becomes absorbed in the rhythms of language and the pace of the story, effortlessly creating mental images of the tale as it unfolds. This relaxed, focused attention is also called visualization, and it comes very easily to most children. Many of the activities in this book center on this kind of imagining, and in fact we parents use visualization all the time to teach our children. When we ask a child to imagine what will happen if she leaves her precious clay creation in the middle of the hallway, we are helping her to visualize—and not a moment too soon!

While we are all born with an ability to imagine, fantasize,

If your child wants to get better at opening to different information during a trance visualization, encourage her to simply pretend that she already can. Say, "If you could hear the music of the wind through the trees, what do you think it might sound like?" If she says she doesn't know, tell her to make something up! The very act of making it up will start exercising that part of her mind so that eventually information will come more naturally to her.

and dream, our minds and bodies do not all work in the same way. Some people "see" pictures and scenes easily, but others may naturally hear sounds, feel sensations in their bodies, experience sharpened emotions, or get other nonvisual information. All of these kinds of perception are normal, and we have tried to word most of our visualizations in an open-ended way, to include different strengths.

Song and Chant

Singing is an incredibly enjoyable and powerful tool for bringing Goddess tradition into your home life. Singing together creates a group energy that, once established, can accompany any work at hand. There are many ways to incorporate song and chant into family customs. Often chants start spontaneously at our house (Anne's) during craft or baking projects. Sometimes these are wildly irreverent spin-offs of standard tunes designed to make the children laugh, but often they are circle chants that come to mind because of their connection to our activities. Chants can be hummed as food is being cooked or as an altar is being prepared. Songs of protection can be sung at our children's comings and goings, and seasonal rounds or chants can bring harmony to otherwise chaotic moments.

During a ritual, songs can be used for virtually every aspect of worship (see A Basic Structure for Ritual for specific ideas). Humming a chant or simply starting a wordless tone to which all join in is a great way to focus and purify a group before the ritual begins. Chanting, especially in combination with drumming and move-

ment, is an excellent way to raise energy during the height of a ritual, and it is one of the things our children enjoy the most.

Above all, spiritual song is not about who has the better voice or a keener sense of rhythm. It is about raising our voices in praise of the Goddess and all her creation. Once you begin to make singing an important aspect of your home rituals, your children may take the lead in suggesting songs for each occasion.

Craft Cupboard

Throughout this book we provide craft activities to make holidays "hands-on." Not only do the crafts get children's attention and keep their interest, but each project in this book symbolically expresses what we're celebrating and reinforces the holiday's essential meaning with symbols that enter our deep consciousness.

Craft Supplies

We've tried to limit materials to those available in most households for the projects in this book. However, we do recommend you obtain a few special tools and supplies. Nothing is expensive or hard to find.

If you select only one tool, make it a glue gun. Miniature glue guns, which melt sticks of glue, sell for under ten dollars in craft and fabric stores and let you stick almost anything to anything else. They're not to be operated by small children; the tips and the glue get quite hot. But they're constructed for safety and the glue itself cools almost instantly.

Florist tape, florist wire, and wreath forms are wonderful for putting together wreaths or other natural assemblages. Any florist or craft store and most fabric stores carry these.

Pastry bags and tips are available in every kitchen department of discount stores or specialty shops. An assortment of tips lets you squeeze various batters and icings into all sorts of shapes, from stars to mushrooms to worms. We also recommend collecting whatever cookie cutters charm you.

We love papier-mâché and find that using undiluted liquid laundry starch gives the best results with no messy preparation. (Thanks to master preschool teacher Charlie Vincent for this hint.) The cleaning-supply section of grocery stores should carry at least one brand.

Pick up a disk of beeswax from the fabric store. Before stringing anything, from popcorn to beads, first pull the thread against the beeswax to prevent tangling and fraying. Quilting thread, which is thick, sturdy, and cheap, makes a durable base for wonderful necklaces and garlands. An assortment of tapestry needles, thick and blunt, is useful for small hands.

If you plan to work with fabric or paper, especially for the hat designs from paper plates, buy a rolling-blade cutter and a small cutting mat from a fabric store. Once you get proficient, you can whiz through stiff paper, but keep these razor-sharp tools away from children.

For making candles, craft stores stock wicks and little metal plates that hold them firmly at the bottom of a mold. If you're not using recycled candles, buy wax blocks. Although crayons suffice, special candle dyes make purer colors.

For small hands, hardware and discount stores carry little hammers and other tools that delight children and are easy for them to use.

Rhythm Instruments

We love rhythm in our circles. When we're clapping and moving, we feel the rhythm of the planet, of life, and of the Goddess herself. Keep a basket of rhythm instruments and devices handy for circles and ceremonies.

Safety

Most of the craft activities in *Circle Round* involve scissors, nails, needles, melting wax, small objects, and other potentially dangerous items. Please supervise your children every moment during crafting and clean-up, and keep all of the previously mentioned items well away from babies and toddlers.

Rhythm instruments are fun to make and decorate. I (Diane) keep a box of items to recycle into instruments: toilet paper rolls, big cans from nuts and coffee, wine corks, sturdy cardboard tubes, leftover plastic Easter-egg shells, bottle tops, old buttons, rubber bands, abandoned plastic boxes.

Don't forget: Overturned bowls and pans banged with wooden and metal spoons are in the kitchen waiting to make music.

The Simplest Drums

Brigit (Diane's daughter) discovered her favorite drum by beating the bottom of a peanut can with a cork. The drum has a wonderful hollow metal sound, which can be varied with the sharper sound of drumming fingertips or fingernails.

For more sounds, try chopping the tops off acorns and cleaning out the meat. Put your fingers in the caps—they turn fingertips into drumsticks!

Rattles

Recycle those pesky plastic Easter-egg shells by filling them with a few dry beans or buttons, then gluing them shut. You can do the same with hand-sized plastic boxes or bandage tins.

Yogurt containers and other plastic tub-style containers make nice rattles and don't even have to be glued. Toilet paper rolls filled with beans, a wine cork, or a little rice make a softer sound. Seal the ends with paper and tape. Decorate with stickers and markers.

Try these other fillers for rattles: acorns, pebbles, sand, eucalyptus buttons, pennies.

Ankle Dance Bells

You will need:

a length of 1-inch-wide elastic

6 1-inch spherical bells

sewing needle and thread

Measure the wearer's ankle and widest part of the foot. Cut the elastic to a length that will stretch over the foot and fit the ankle snugly but not tightly, plus two extra inches for seam allowance. Overlap the ends. One inch from the ends, sew the elastic into a circle. Attach three bells to one half of the circle. Place the unbelled side on the inside of the dancer's ankles so the bells won't scrape legs.

Finger Cymbals

Place a bottle cap, top side down, on the scrap wood and punch two holes button-style using the hammer and nail. Thread elastic through the holes and knot the elastic into a circle, leaving enough slack for a child to slip in a thumb or middle finger. Repeat with the other cap. Clapped together, they make a metallic, staccato sound. Big buttons also work, but they make a dryer, softer sound.

You will need:

2 metal bottle caps

elastic thread

a piece of scrap wood

hammer and a nail

Rain Sticks

Rain sticks make a soft, soothing sound for a wonderful accompaniment to a water invocation, or as a sound divider between parts of a ceremony.

Hammer the nails into the tube. Be careful not to crush the tube or to cluster the nails too closely together (the beans or rice have to sift through them). Seal one end of the tube with paper and tape. Pour in the beans or rice. Don't mix; each makes a different sound. Holding the open end shut with your hand, turn the stick over a few times to check the sound. Add or take out beans/rice until you find the sound you like. Seal the open end with paper and tape.

Decorating and hiding the nails: Dip newspaper strips in the liquid starch and lay over nail ends. Don't worry if the surface is still bumpy; all that's necessary is for there to be no chance of injury from the heads. To paint your rain stick, use thick, white paper for the final layer. Or finish with the colorful magazine scraps.

You will need:

a sturdy cardboard cylinder, 1 foot or longer

$1/3$ lb flat-headed nails (the length should be slightly smaller than the diameter of the cardboard cylinder)

hammer

sturdy tape

1 C dried beans or rice

strips of newspaper

liquid laundry starch

thick white paper, or colorful scraps of paper from magazines

We Are Instruments, Too

Hands clapping, feet stomping, fingers snapping, mouths popping—we're walking one-person bands. Try this car game sometime: Ask your children to make as many different sounds as they can clapping their hands. Then ask them to create rhythms using the variety they've discovered.

Salt Dough

You will need:

4 C plain flour

1 C table salt (plain or
iodized)

1½ C water

We like this dough best of all the "kitchen clays." Warm, pliable, soft, and smooth, it is also the most durable homemade clay after being dried in the oven. This is living clay, formed from the substances of the earth, made malleable by water, tempered and hardened by fire and air.

Mix the flour and salt together. Stir in the water half a cup at a time, mixing until the dough turns into unbeatable lumps. This takes muscle! Turn the dough onto a flat, clean surface and knead for ten minutes. For children, divide the dough into halves or quarters for them to knead.

Test if the dough is too wet or dry by rolling and flattening a small portion. If it won't hold together and the edges split, it's too dry. Wet your hands and continue working until the dough is smooth. Repeat cautiously, as the dough can quickly become too wet.

Dough that is too wet will stick to the kneading surface and melt when formed into shapes. Dust the kneading surface with a tablespoon of flour and knead it in, adding only one tablespoon of flour at a time.

Always cover the dough with plastic when you're not using it. For longer storage—up to about one week—keep the dough in a plastic bag or container in the refrigerator, bringing it to room temperature before using again.

Working with the Dough

Moisten your hands while you work with salt dough and let your fingers find the forms: animals with tiny pointy ears and twinkle noses, little fruits, a lumpy basket filled with eggs.

Be sure that the dough walls are never more than one inch thick. Thicker walls won't dry on the inside. For larger figures, make an *armature,* an internal structure covered with a thinner layer of dough. Aluminum foil makes a perfect armature.

Bake the forms on a cookie sheet in a 250° oven until the dough is rock hard. Drying time varies with the size of the item. Be sure to shift the figures about half an hour after start-

Experiment with tools to press designs into the dough. Combs, toothpicks, rings and other jewelry, scissors (to snip tiny points), and kitchen utensils all leave their impressions.

ing so they don't stick to the cookie sheet or get flat on one side, and turn figures over several times to ensure even drying.

Finish the figures with paint. If you want your figures to be permanent, coat with polyurethane.

For hanging your creations, before baking use a toothpick to make a small hole at least half an inch from the edge, or gently embed a loop of wire or a paper clip in the top center of the figure, leaving one end protruding as a loop.

Wreath Making

In Goddess tradition, the circle is a sacred shape, symbolizing the earth, the moon, and the sacred circle of death and rebirth. Making circles from nature's seasonal gifts transforms wreath making into a way of honoring the gate to the new time.

A wreath can be as simple or as elaborate as time and materials allow. Made in the right size, it may begin as a head circlet for a child, become the centerpiece for your holiday feast, and end on your door to welcome the turning of the season.

Be innovative with your materials. Use rosemary branches, wheat stalks, long pine needles lashed together with ribbons or jute, dried or fresh herbs, dark shiny leaves such as citrus or magnolia, blazing fall leaves, acorns, found feathers, shells, blown and dyed eggs, eucalyptus buttons, pinecones, eggs, or vivid berries. There are no limits beyond size and weight.

The Simplest Wreath

Cut a round hole out of the middle of the plate. If you're planning to wear this wreath first as a hat, make the hole the right size to fit the intended head. Be sure to leave enough of the rim to hold all the items you wish to use.

Arrange your selection of items around the rim in a way that pleases you. Fasten on the items, working in a circle so that the overlap hides the attached section. Punch holes in the rim to attach ribbons or hanging vines.

For more elaborate wreaths, there are many exciting books available in craft shops with instructions and inspiration.

You will need:

paper plate, 10 or 12 inches in diameter

scissors

flowers, leaves, ribbons, other decorative items

stapler, tape, glue, glue gun, or other ways to attach items

Shadow Boxes

One expressive, tactile way to capture a holiday's meaning is by making small clay figures and symbols for a shadow box that becomes a personal altar.[5]

A shadow box can be as simple as a shoe box lying on its side, painted or lined with pretty fabric to form a stage. A few holes in the roof of a box allows hanging of suns, moons, or other celestial items. Or forget the box and just build little scenes on children's altars.

This tiny theater makes a perfect place for the magical bits and pieces children collect. Incorporate special items such as stones, shells, and feathers as props, or embed them right into the figures.

No fingers are too small or too large for this work, and nobody can resist the fun.

Making Candles

In Goddess tradition, fire is a sacred element. Candles and rituals seem to go together naturally. Most religious traditions have treasured the ceremony of lighting candles and bring the element of fire into their worship this way.

Children enjoy making candles. For them, anything relating to fire, with its endless fascination, is high on their interest list. Candlemaking is not only a favorite pastime, but also an art that almost always has satisfying results.

Supplies

Use craft store supplies or wax recycled from candle ends. One cup will make about five or six small candles.

You may want to buy commercial wicks. They have a wire core and burn well, but cotton string will do. If you and your family love making candles, special equipment allows you to get more elaborate.

Wax and paraffin are hard to remove, so buy a used pan just for candlemaking. I (Diane) bought a little metal teapot that

Safety First

Candlemaking must always be supervised by a responsible adult. Melting wax, pouring, and making wicks must be done only by adults. Children can make the molds, insert the wicks, and unmold the candle.

Never melt wax or paraffin directly over a flame, but always in a double boiler: a container (a can or pot) over hot water. If you ever accidentally have a fire while making candles, don't pour water on the flame. Either use a dry chemical fire extinguisher, smother the fire with a pot or lid, or use baking soda. Be sure not to melt wax and pour candles in the same area.

I set into the hot water to melt wax. A can, label cleaned off and edge bent out to form a pouring lip, works well too, but remember your oven mitts when touching the can.

The Work Area

Cover your work area with newspaper, and have the molds ready before melting wax.

Melting Wax

Break the wax, old candles, or paraffin into ¹/₂-inch chunks and set into the pan, teapot, or can. Never fill it more than half full. Place this container into a larger pan one-quarter full of water and heat on the stove or hot plate. Add standard-size (³/₈-inch-thick) crayons for color: a 1¹/₂-inch piece of crayon will color one cup of wax.

Making Wicks

Cut the string into lengths a couple of inches longer than the height of the candle mold. When the wax is completely melted, dip the string in and lay it on newspaper. When it's cooled a bit, grasp with both hands and straighten. Be sure the wick is stiff. It may require another dipping.

Pouring Candles

Pour wax when it's slightly cooled but still quite liquid. Before removing the pan of melted wax from the water, have a dishcloth on a surface nearby. Set the pot onto this to dry the bottom of the pan after you pick it up. This keeps the hot water from hurting anyone while pouring the wax. You also want to keep water from dripping into the mold, where it will cause problems when the candle burns.

Carry the wax to the pouring area. Be sure your mold won't tip while pouring. Pour the wax carefully up to the brim of the mold and return the pot to the water.

Inserting Wicks

When the wax is firm but still pliable, plunge a toothpick, pipe cleaner, thin straw, or other straight, small stick into the

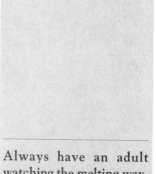

Always have an adult watching the melting wax. Never heat wax or paraffin directly over a flame.

Candle Safety

Many of the rituals in Goddess tradition involve lighting candles. We've discovered through hard experience that it is never safe to leave candles unattended or alone with children. **Be certain that a responsible adult is always in the room with a lighted candle.** Even candles floating in water and candles placed in sinks have caused fires, so always practice candle safety.

center of the candle, all the way to the bottom. Withdraw it and quickly insert the wick. Pour a little more hot wax into the hole to support the wick and to fill up the depression that forms as wax cools.

Removing the Molds

The candle projects in this book all have disposable molds. Simply crack off the mold to see the finished candles.

Candleholders

These projects, individually explained in each holiday section, are more permanent than candles and use largely recycled or homemade materials. Always be sure that the candle holders are stable, and placed on something fireproof.

Flavors of the Holidays

As we create new rituals, food creates memories and associations. Our senses are the building blocks of memory. The red food of Brigit, the sweet morsel of darkness in Winter Solstice cupcakes, or the exotic flavor of ancestral food on Samhain brings stories alive with scent, taste, and texture. By establishing holiday menus, with special foods reserved for these events, we develop the vocabulary of memory and root family traditions in our children's lives.

Symbolic food creates special memories, like the egg-shaped candies of Easter or the matzos of Passover. For children, food is a way to create anticipation and tempt involvement. The most self-absorbed adolescent will join in eating special holiday foods. Most children love to help cook. Making special foods for a holiday teaches skills children can use to join in the creation of our traditions.

While shopping for your holidays, remember to buy organic food. It's healthy, it tastes best, and organic farming promotes a caring relationship with the earth.

Salmonella Alert

Any uncooked mixture containing raw eggs carries a risk of salmonella. To be completely safe, first put the eggs (or yolks or whites) in a metal bowl and, holding it above a gas flame or electric burner, whisk the eggs quickly and constantly to keep them from scrambling. Raise the eggs' temperature to 160° (use a candy thermometer). Cool eggs to room temperature before using in recipe.

Sacred Baking

Making bread may sound difficult and time-consuming, but the new yeasts practically guarantee success, and with a little planning, baking fits smoothly into most days. The smell of baking bread blesses every corner of the home, and nothing tastes as good as fresh home-baked bread.

Bread and bread making are part of our most ancient rituals. In Athens, people baked round cakes, representing the moon, to honor Artemis. In ancient Assyria and Babylonia, special sacrificial cakes were offered to Ishtar. Bread pans in the shape of Astarte excavated in Israel are evidence that baking was part of ancient sacred ceremonies there as well.

Making bread brings us close to a common but profoundly transformational process. We work with the living loaf. We learn quiet secrets as the dough becomes supple under our hands, then grows larger with warmth and time, and is finally served to nourish and delight.

Baking bread also gives us the opportunity to create symbols that literally become part of us. We combine simple elements to make the loaf, shape it to reflect what is special about a moment of time, transform it with fire, sacralize it on our altar, bless it in our circle, and then share the bread, joining with the past and teaching those to come. The bread, consecrated on our altars and blessed by the circle, symbolizes the nourishing earth and sanctifies the simple act of sharing food.

Bread Making

If you've never made bread before, please go to the bookstore or library and obtain one of the many excellent books for a more thorough explanation. Basically, baking bread consists of several standard steps: starting the yeast, mixing the wet ingredients with the dry ones, kneading, a first rising, shaping loaves, a second rising, then baking.

Children can easily share the rhythms of baking bread. They can add ingredients, stir, and knead, especially if you divide up the dough. Punching the bread down is their favorite part, and shaping loaves is the most forgiving of all arts, since the second rising makes wonderful curving shapes out of every form.

Fitting Bread Making into Life

Timing is important. Mixing and kneading usually take about twenty minutes, the first rising between one and two hours, the second rising slightly shorter, and the baking between thirty minutes and an hour. Bread dough can be left in the refrigerator overnight for a first rising, punched down, shaped, and brought to room temperature for the second rising and baking the next day. Some bakers even take rising loaves along while riding in carpools; they punch down the mixture and form loaves, letting them rise in the trunk for baking on their arrival home.

The warmth of the kitchen, the tactile qualities of the process, and the transformation of ingredients into the cohesive, shapable dough, finished by fire, makes baking special and sacred.

PART TWO

CYCLES OF THE MOON AND SUN

Nature Cycles

The practice of Goddess tradition revolves around the natural cycles that surround us. Each month, the new moon appears, waxes to full, and then wanes to darkness. Each year, the days grow longer until midsummer, when the balance shifts to shorter days, which begin to grow longer after the Winter Solstice. Warm and cold, growth and hibernation come in their time.

These natural events are our mysteries. The Goddess reveals herself to us through the changes and transformations that happen around us. For children, seasonal rituals are often their first introduction to religious practice and spiritual teaching.

In this part, we include rituals, stories, and activities for the moon and sun cycles. Some are rituals we or others have done. Elsewhere we offer suggestions and directions for creating rituals of your own.

We have also included a wide variety of activities—holiday recipes for special foods and breads to bake, projects such as candle holders, suggestions for community service. Sometimes we have the time and energy and can enlist the interest of our children to create rich and beautiful ceremonies. Sometimes we settle for bunny-shaped quesadillas and call it a day. What is most important is to make these celebrations joyful, not stressful, for you and your children.

On Retelling Traditional Tales

Children love stories. Stories awaken the imagination and give young people a chance to envision a range of responses to the world. They teach values and shape expectations. They provide a way for even young children to enter into the complex transformational symbolism of our festivals and celebrations.

One of our goals in this book is to provide a rich source of stories connected to the passage of seasons and the passages in our children's lives. We want our children to grow up with knowledge of the myths and tales that can serve as the ground of a rich inner landscape.

But we are not a text-based tradition. The earliest Goddess cultures left no written records of their beliefs and rituals. The stories that have come down to us have been changed and altered with time. Much of the wisdom and values of the earliest Goddess traditions are still preserved in faery tales and folktales, but they are coated with the values and beliefs of the patriarchal cultures that followed. So to look at traditional tales requires us to decode them, to extract the symbols that are meaningful and transform the rest.

However, whenever we tamper with traditional stories, we run the risk of diminishing their power. If we simply eliminate the elements that seem counter to our politics or our philosophy, we may discard some of the encrypted information most vital to our inner being. For myths derive their transformative power from the very things that make us most uncomfortable—death, loss, jealousy, fear, sacrifice. If we try to pretty them up and make them nice, we end up with insipid, sugary tales that provide no real sustenance for the soul.

On the other hand, if we tell the tales unchanged from the versions popularized by the Brothers Grimm or by Disney, we risk perpetuating the stereotypes that we have found destructive in our own lives: the negative images of women, the association of light hair and skin with good and of dark with evil, the assumption that heterosexual marriage is the ultimate happiness ever after.

In Reclaiming's work of teaching ritual to adults, we often use faery tales and myths as a theme to take us on a transformative journey. We look for the symbols, colors, animals, and characters that we can recognize as carrying historical or ritual references to the ancient Goddess traditions. For instance, in the story of Vasalisa, we find significance in the red, white, and black that she and her doll wear, which are the colors of the Goddess. They tell us that this story has something to do with the passage from Maiden to Mother to Crone, and help us to interpret it as an initiation tale.

The inner work each story represents is revealed to us through the challenges the characters face. For example, Vasalisa's challenge is to bring fire from the house of death. When we consider that challenge with all its resonances, we find that the tale takes us into the heart of mystery,

where the life fire, the creative energy of the universe, can be found only by encountering death.

In choosing these tales, I (Starhawk) have looked for the stories that seem linked with the theme of each holiday or passage. I have searched for tales with strong, positive female characters. Almost all the tales in this book are stories I have worked with many times in trance and ritual, stories that continue to reveal to me new depths and insights. I have tried to retell them in forms that are at least partly decoded, where the symbols and challenges that seem to me the heart of the work are accessible enough so that children can take them in. I have tried to eliminate the worst stereotypes without losing the power of the uncomfortable elements of the stories. My versions will not please everybody, and no matter how careful I might be, I cannot guarantee that I haven't inadvertently changed some deeply valuable part of the story.

Many of the stories told here are initiation tales—that is, they record a character's passage through a set of challenges that leads to an encounter with the great forces of life and death. Initiation often takes place through an encounter with the Otherworld.

In Goddess tradition, the world of form and substance, of day and night, is seen as only the visible part of a vast realm of energies and forces that suffuse ordinary reality. The Otherworld, the spirit counterpart of this one, is just on the other side of the mirror, down the well, at the back of the north wind, and has a geography and ecology of its own. Its lands have many names: Faery, Avalon, Annwn, Tir n'a Nog, the land of the Sidhe, the land of the ancestors, the Land of Youth, the land of the dead, the realm of the unborn. Only when this world and the Otherworld infuse and inform each other can life thrive.

Many of the stories in this book are about those who journey to the Otherworld to face its dangers and receive its gifts. They are stories about gathering personal power—the power that allows us to use our best abilities, to express the gifts that only we can bring.

Gathering power requires certain personal qualities, the traits rewarded over and over again in faery tales, what we might call traditional Pagan values. The stories tell us to be generous, be courteous, be helpful, be brave, persist when difficulties arise, take help where it is offered. Again and again we are warned against jealousy, spite, and envy. In a highly competitive culture, we get ahead by being better, brighter, richer, or more successful than someone else. But traditional cultures value much more highly the harmony of the community as a whole, and that value is reflected in faery tales.

We have also included stories from cultures that range far beyond Europe and the Middle East. We are sensitive to issues of cultural appropriation, yet we do not believe that they should be resolved by limiting ourselves to European tales, thereby implying that Europe alone is the font of spiritual wisdom. Our community includes many different heritages and ancestries, and our children must live in a multicultural world of great diversity. Our young people need to know and respect many earth-based traditions. Somewhere between the pitfalls of ignorance and appropriation lies the path of cultural education.

In making our choices, we have looked for tales that illuminate the theme of each holiday, or that offer a perspective that expands the vision; for example, the Amaterasu story for Winter Solstice in which the sun is a Goddess. We have asked members of our extended community for stories that reflect their heritages. We strongly encourage families to delve deeper into the rich treasure of traditional myths and folktales from many lands.

We have not included Bible stories, as we feel they are already so strongly represented in literature and popular culture. However, Pagan parents may well wish to provide their children with some exposure to these myths so that they can be familiar with references they will hear around them throughout their lives.

These tales can be read aloud to younger children. Older children can read them for themselves. But faery tales are meant to be told. Read them over yourself until you become familiar with them. Then, around the dinner table or before you send your child to sleep on the eve of a Sabbat, tell the story in your own words. Lend the characters your voice, and hear what they have to say. The story may change in ways that surprise you, offering new insights and revelations. And so may these old tales come alive again.

CHAPTER THREE

Moon Cycle

EVERY MONTH, THE moon is born out of darkness to become a silver crescent. She grows to full, round radiance, lighting up the night, only to wane again to a crescent and then grow dark. She is our prime symbol of the circle of birth, growth, death, and rebirth. Her cycle moves the tides, so she rules the ocean and the element of water. Women's menstrual cycles, too, are linked to her timing. She brings fertility to human beings, plants, animals, and all the earth.

Our most important holiday is the full moon, which comes each month, painting the world with silvery light and bringing us energy and inner power. We meet to do rituals at the full moon because that is the time when magical energies are strongest.

Even animals sense the power of the moon: dogs, wolves, and coyotes howl!

What do you see in the face of the full moon? Some cultures see a man, some see a woman's face. Others see an eagle or a magic rabbit carrying an egg.

The Goddess

The moon as the Goddess has three aspects. The Maiden is the crescent moon. She is the power of beginning, and she loves all who are wild and free. She helps us have the courage to start new things. She protects children and helps mothers who are giving birth. Her colors are white and silver. There are hundreds of names for each aspect of the Moon Goddess, but in ancient Greece, she was called Artemis, the huntress. The crescent moon is her bow. She makes her home in the mountains, running through the forest with her wild dogs in pursuit of game; stags and bears are sacred to her. Young girls, especially, are under her care. Call on her to bring you freedom and protection.

The Mother is the full moon. She may be the mother of children or of projects, books, paintings, or gardens, for she represents the power to keep something going until it is complete. She sustains life, pouring out her light as a free gift to all living things. She is the power of love. Because the moon rules the tides, she is also connected with the ocean, where life began. Her color is red, and some of her names are Diana, Isis, Selene. We call on her to bring

us energy, life, abundance, and creativity, and to help us complete what we start.

The Crone is the waning or dark moon. She is the old woman, standing for the wisdom that comes with age and experience. She is the teacher, the healer, the guide, the grandmother. We picture her with a wrinkled face and a walking stick—but to us the signs of age are marks of beauty. In honor of the Crone, we are especially nice to older women. She understands death, and she knows that death leads to rebirth, so she is keeper of the mysteries. We call on her when we do divination—when we read Tarot cards or consult an oracle to find out what the future will bring. The Greeks called her Hecate and imagined her sitting on a three-legged stool, guarding the way to the land of the dead. Her color is black.

The God

Many cultures have seen the moon as the God and the sun as the Goddess. Japan, Arabia, and Scandinavia all had sun Goddesses and moon Gods. The God, like the Goddess, can be seen in three aspects.

The Blue God is the young, loving God, counterpart to the Maiden. He is pictured playing a flute, and he loves poetry, song, and lovemaking. He represents the power of imagination and the realms of spirit beings, dreams, and visions. We call on him for joy and inspiration.

The Green Man is the God of all plant life: flowers, grain, trees. Like the full moon, he sustains our lives by giving away his green things as a free gift. He is the seed sower, the father of life, plans, and projects; and he is compost, which sustains the soil. We call on him for abundance, for nurturing, and for food for both body and spirit—and especially we call him into our gardens!

The Horned God is the God of animal life. The waning crescent moon looks like horns, so the stag, the bull, the ram, and the goat are sacred moon-beasts. Like the Crone, the Horned God understands death, and gives his own life, allowing himself to be hunted and eaten so that other beings may live. He represents wisdom, and he is the guide to the Otherworld. He is the aspect of our God that Christians tried to turn into the devil, with horns and hooves and tail. But he is not evil—he is the power of love, knowledge of the mysteries, and unselfishness. We call on him for protection, for guidance, and for help when we need to do something very difficult.

The Altar

Here are some things you might want on your altar at the different phases of the moon.

Crescent moon: White or silver cloth; images of the crescent moon; a mirror; white or silvery plants or flowers, especially artemisia or mugwort; pine boughs or cones; white stones or pebbles; a bowl of water from some wild place

Full moon: Red cloth; images of the full moon; a round mirror; round fruits or vegetables, especially red ones such as apples or tomatoes; silver coins; crystals or red stones; scented plants; red roses; berries; seashells; a bowl of milk, seawater, or red juice

Waning moon: Black cloth; images of the stars; a mirror with its back painted black or a polished piece of obsidian; plants or flowers with dark leaves or petals—black irises, tulips, pansies, or hollyhocks; plums, eggplants, or other dark-skinned fruits or vegetables; dark stones; a crystal ball on a black velvet cloth; Tarot cards or other tools of divination

On the Land

When we are far away from the lights of the city, the moon and stars become much more important. We can watch the crescent moon rise over the hills, and notice how it grows from day to day. The full moon lights the trails and fields so the whole landscape seems almost as bright as day. When the moon is dark, the stars fill the sky, and the Milky Way is a brilliant stream of light.

In my (Starhawk's) garden, I have a birdbath I keep filled with water. When the moon is full, I go outside and catch its image in the water. Then I scry—I look into the water, let my eyes go into soft focus, and ask for visions.

Make a Moon Garden by devoting a portion of your garden to plants that will reflect the moonlight and look good at night. Make the bed a circle or a crescent, and outline it with white stones or shells. For a low-maintenance garden, plant herbs, bulbs, and perennials that require minimal care. Plant seeds or transplant small seedlings while the moon is waxing; prune and harvest when the moon is waning.

Here are some suggestions to get you started—but part of the fun of this project is searching out plants you like or finding white varieties of your favorites.

For a sunny area: Artemisia (Silver Mound is my favorite), lamb's ears, white roses, white lavender, silver sage, white iris, white cosmos, and many others

For a shady area: Mugwort, dead nettle (*Lamium*—White Nancy is a good variety), white anemones, white foxgloves, white primroses or species geraniums, white bleeding hearts

The Moon's Journey
by Starhawk

Circle round, close your eyes, and together we'll follow the circle the moon makes on her journey. . . .

Sailing, sailing out of Night's arms, a thin sliver of moon boat appears. We can see it: a silver crescent in the afternoon sky, glowing in the twilight with clouds for sails. Night gathers the moon boat in her arms, and the crescent becomes the cradle of Child Moon. All young, new, and growing things flourish under her light.

Moon grows. With joy in her strength and skill, she runs through the forests, dancing on the high canopy above the trees. All that is wild and free draws courage from her light. She takes the silver crescent as her bow and hunts the night sky. Loosing an arrow near the World Tree, she brings down a glowing silver apple.

Maiden Moon eats the apple and begins to change. She grows fat and round, pregnant with light. She glows in the night sky, and radiance streams from her hair, her breasts, her open arms. All that is fertile and fruitful grows strong and complete under her light. For now she becomes Mother Moon, queen of love and magic. When she rides the sky, Witches dance, wolves howl, and all of nature comes alive. Night becomes nearly as bright as day, and the stars are dimmed.

"What about us? What about us?" the
stars cry. "We shine, too! How long must
we hide our light? We have a right to be
seen and admired, too."

The clamoring stars
bother Moon so much
that she draws the
cloak of Night over
her face, for quiet.
Slowly, slowly, her
light dims. She is
tired now, and older,
and she sleeps late,
not rising until long af-
ter the sun has set. Her
secret dreams blanket
the earth under the
brilliant starlight. All
things of wisdom and deep
magic are nourished by Crone
Moon.

At last she grows so old that she
does not rise at all, but sleeps and sleeps
in Night's arms. The stars claim the
night sky, winking and dancing in their
triumph. Old Moon is gone.

But deep within the Moon's
belly, a seed of light remains.
And in Night's arms, all
weary things are renewed.
And so the time comes when
the seed puts forth a slim tendril
of light that grows and stretches into
a vessel to carry a reborn Moon.

Sailing, sailing out of Night's arms into
the dawn, a thin sliver of moon boat appears. We can see it: a silver crescent in
the afternoon sky, glowing in the twilight
with clouds for sails. . . . ❦❧

The Dead Moon

an old English folktale from the Lincolnshire area
retold by Diane Baker

Circle round, and I'll tell you a story. . . .

The area of Lincolnshire called the Cars in the old times had many treacherous bogs, often fatal to people who entered them on moonless nights.

Beyond the village, on the edge of the bogs, lived a few families. They kept on good terms with the townsfolk but were rarely seen. They were people of the old ways, who still held to the Goddess even though her people were bullied or hunted, their lands taken, their celebrations and rituals pushed into secrecy.

Meg, wise woman and storyteller, was the oldest of this small group. She shared her small house with a girl named Lyra, whose parents had died just after her birth. She called Meg Granny, as did everyone else in their circle. Lyra helped the old woman with the gardening, cooking, and household chores. At the end of each hard day they sat around their fireplace, often with their neighbors, listening to the old stories and keeping the Goddess's celebrations.

One night Meg and Lyra sat alone by the small fire. Lyra kept getting up to stir the pot of stew that bubbled over the flames. Finally she asked, "Why isn't anyone here tonight? We have plenty of food."

"Look outside, my dear. Tonight is the dark moon."

"But everyone knows the way between our homes. We don't need the moon's light to walk around outside."

"The Bogles, child," Meg replied, searching in her basket for a sock that needed mending.

Lyra shivered at the name. "Just who are the Bogles, Granny?" She took the needle from Meg's hands and threaded it for the old woman. Meg smiled her thanks and started to darn the sock.

"Legends around here blame every accident on the shadows of the bog. People call these the Bogles and frighten their children with stories about the Bogles if they don't obey. Those Bogles are not real, but people let themselves believe and grow fearful. And as happens so many times, what they imagine comes true. Greedy and lazy people began to set upon folks walking in the dark. Fear keeps the villagers from fighting back, so the Bogles have become real."

"But I like the dark, Granny. I hear better and smell better in the dark. Even without seeing, my feet seem to know where to go."

"That's because you have learned caution, not fear, dear Lyra. Fear dulls our senses. Yours are still keen. But," Meg sighed, "now we must not go out on moonless nights. All the Cars people would have to move together to banish the Bogles, and we have little influence in town. The Bogles feel safe in harming us because they know we cannot draw attention to ourselves with complaints."

Lyra stood up and stamped across the hearth to stir their stew again. "Why doesn't the Goddess help us, Granny?" she said, working to keep the tears from choking her voice. "We try so hard to keep her ways. Why doesn't she just wipe away all those people?"

Meg sighed again and put aside the sock. She held her hand out to Lyra, who let herself be pulled against the old woman. The skin on Meg's hand felt thin and dry, but the muscles beneath were strong. "She is sad about these hard times, but she won't stop them."

Sorrow as real as the cat purring on the hearth stood between the two.

They were not alone in their sorrow that night. The moon, who rests on her dark nights, often heard the people speak fearfully of her dark, and could not rest easily. She decided to go out onto the Cars to see for herself the dangers that threatened her people.

In her black robes, she climbed down the highest tree stealthily. She heard a young man's screams. Someone was being attacked by the Bogles. As she hurried, her hood got caught in a branch and fell back, revealing her light. Now, the Bogles never committed their crimes when there was light, because they were cowards. That night they had found a young man of the old ways named Bowen coming home late from finding a lost lamb. One Bogle seized the lamb and the others were beating Bowen.

At the bright flash of moonlight, the Bogles pulled back, covering their faces. Bowen took that instant to grab the lamb and run through the bog, where he knew the solid paths even in the dark.

The Bogles cursed their loss but realized what had happened. The youngest wondered, "Why would the moon shine out when she is supposed to rest?" Another said, "She must be here on land. If we can capture her, we'll have darkness every night!" They quickly forgot Bowen and hurried to where they'd seen the light.

The moon, hearing them come, tried to escape back to the sky, but they were too fast, and in a moment she found herself tied hand and foot by the foul Bogles. "Kill

her, kill her," chanted the youngest Bogle, but the oldest motioned him silent. "We cannot kill the moon. She can only die by being forgotten. We'll put her where no one will ever discover her again."

So the Bogles dragged the moon across the Cars to the place where the water was the deepest and darkest. Hurling her into the depths, they rolled a huge stone over her. They danced gleefully in the mud, then disappeared into the dark, dark night.

Night after night, the people of the old ways waited for the new moon to rise, but she never came. Fearfully they watched the sun go down each night and huddled in their separate houses. Then one night the Bogles came to the farthest house. They attacked, driving off the livestock and setting the house on fire. The family barely escaped with their lives. Still the moon did not rise.

The family fled to Meg's home. She wrapped them in blankets and brewed tea to warm their chilled hearts and bones. One by one, the others of the settlement slipped over carefully, carrying dark lanterns and stout sticks.

"Where is the moon?" they asked each other. "The Bogles have never dared to come to our homes before. When will this stop?" Meg took from under her bed a small dark bowl, which she carefully filled with water. Then she unwrapped a tiny twist of paper and sprinkled in a bit of salt. Breaking off a straw from her broom, she stirred the water, blowing upon it gently. When the water cleared, she peered long and hard into the dark, shimmering bowl, scrying. Her face was grave when she looked up.

"She is gone, and I cannot see where." The group sat in silence. After a long time, Bowen spoke up. "Do you remember the night I escaped the Bogles? I was so scared that I didn't remember before, but I was rescued by one bright flash of light. I'm certain that it was a moonbeam that saved me."

Meg looked into her bowl again. "Without her light, I cannot see her." She sat up straight. "But perhaps together, we can feel her. Come, let's try."

The small group stood holding hands. Even the youngest stood solemnly linked together without wiggling. Together they waited. Lyra spoke first. "I feel mud all over me, cool wet mud on my face, on my body, and a great pressing."

Dorothy, whose house had been burned, joined in. "It's deep, much water above. The last thing I saw was a high spreading tree by starlight. My hands and feet ache. They're tied."

Graham, from the next cottage, spoke softly. "Weak, so weak, so close to giving up, drifting away, joining the great dark."

Then silence. Meg snatched up her scrying bowl again. "There's a pool in the Cars, a deep and lonely pool, guarded by one great tree. She is there." Meg looked around her. "We must go and save her. She grows weaker. We must hurry."

"But the Bogles," cried Dorothy.

"We must go without light, and stealthily, so they won't stop us," said Meg.

"They'll see a group," Graham worried. "One person could slip away unnoticed."

"We only need one," Meg said. "One brave person."

Silence followed. Then Bowen spoke out. "I owe the moon my life," he said. "I offer it freely now. I know the Cars better than anyone else."

Meg nodded. "Brave Bowen, you are the one. She will die if you do not find her quickly."

Bowen swallowed hard. "The bogs are immense. How can I find the moon, and what can I do when I find her?"

Meg cautiously stepped outside, down to the pond. Singing a short prayer, she broke off a stout forked branch of the willow tree. Swiftly she stripped off the twigs and returned. "This will draw you to power."

From her pocket she drew a smooth round black stone the size of a baby's palm. "I've had this stone all my life." She gestured around the circle of grave and troubled faces. "Take this, and with it all our power."

Bowen held the stone. It felt warm. He opened the pouch that hung from his belt, trying not to show his fear.

"No," said Meg. "Hold it in your

mouth. You'll feel us better that way. From this moment on, speak no words, for now is the listening time." She raised her arms over him. "To hold the moon from her great journey is to interrupt the path from life to death and back again. Go, Bowen, and fasten the circle together once more."

❧

He stood alone under the huge arching sky, the stars shining like pinholes in black paper. No light came from any of the tiny dwellings.

The willow branch in his hand quivered. Carefully holding it in front of him, he turned a full circle. When the stick gently tugged, he started walking in that direction, following the high hassocks of grasses and ridges of mud that could support his weight.

Every few minutes he stopped and slowly waved the willow stick in a short arc, but its gentle tug always led in the same direction, so he tucked the branch in the front of his shirt and tried to move as fast as the spongy, treacherous ground allowed. After about a mile of difficult going that sometimes plunged him up to his chest in slimy water, he felt the stick vibrating against his skin. Climbing out, he turned another slow circle again, holding the willow stick at arm's length. This time, instead of a gentle tug, the stick dipped strongly toward the east. "Of course," he thought, "she would have come down from the east."

"Yes," he heard Meg's voice inside him, "the east."

Shocked, Bowen looked wildly around him, but the faint starlight showed only the bushy willows that gripped the earth beneath the marshes. "We're with you," whispered Meg's voice again. "All of us." The stone inside his mouth vibrated. In the dark Bowen nodded and went on.

Now the willow led him north. He knew what lay ahead, a deep pool where one huge oak tree spread. He often fished in its shadows. "Yes," whispered Meg. "Go."

The willow wand quivered against his wet chest the whole way. The pool looked different. The rock from which he'd fished was gone and in its place was a hole, filled with mud. "She is there," Meg's voice murmured.

He slipped off his sodden wet leather slippers and placed them against the huge trunk of the oak. Carefully he eased his way into the pool and swam into the middle. Taking a deep breath, he dove down, down, and down, turning upward only when he felt his lungs ready to burst. He dove again, and then a third time. Nothing. He had started to swim back to the edge of the pool when he sensed Meg's voice. "Again," she said.

Bowen felt like shouting back, "I'm trying!" but stopped his voice in his throat. His body screamed for rest. What more could he do? Who could defeat the Bogles? He felt like spitting the stone out, hurling it over the oak, and running away.

Then he heard a humming, which seemed to come from inside him. The circle was raising energy! He could hear all their voices separately, together, weaving the cone of power with their hearts and spirit, their love. Bowen felt his weariness slide away. His mind cleared. He felt strong and fit, revived. Again he plunged into the water, the hum filling him, filling the entire pond. This time he touched the top of a rock. He surfaced, breathed, and dove again. How could he move the rock? He surfaced again. "We'll move the rock, brave Bowen," he heard Meg's voice within. Again he dove. This time he slipped the stone from his mouth and pressed it against the rock. The stone trembled. Bowen pressed it harder, feeling his lungs begin to ache. The stone shook more and more. Bowen tried to keep it pressed against the rock. Now the rock was beginning to vibrate. He kept on fighting the pain inside. The huge stone began to roll back and forth. Finally he hit the stone hard against the rock, striking with the last of his strength. Then he swam desperately for the surface, a journey he feared he could not make. "Moon, I tried," was his last prayer.

But an upsurge propelled him to the top. He broke the surface at the same moment as a rain of stone burst from the black center of the pool. The waves pushed him to the side, pouring water over the pool's edge. Bowen's sore and aching hands clung to the roots of the oak. He hadn't the strength to pull himself out.

❧

And that is where the sunrise found Bowen, half in the water, his feet and legs waterlogged, his hands torn and bloodied. Rocks were strewn everywhere. He sat up, looked for his shoes, and in one of them found a round black stone the size of a baby's palm.

His shoes wouldn't fit over his swollen feet and his legs could hardly move, so he spent the rest of the day crawling weakly around the pool picking the few ripe berries the Cars animals and birds had missed. He drank from a fresh spring nearby and slept again. "Is she saved?" he kept asking himself. He turned his circles with the stick, but it did not twitch, except near the spring. He even put the stone back in his mouth but felt nothing. Finally, as the sun passed overhead, Bowen rubbed his feet and started back.

He met no one. As he walked he began to cry. "I've failed," he thought, tasting the bitterness of his tears. "I was too late." He sank to the wet ground and wept.

When he opened his eyes at last, it was night. All he could see was the quivering shadow of the marsh grasses in front of him. "Shadow?" he thought. "To have a shadow there must be light." Bowen sat up. Over the horizon, those many miles away, a gleaming silver white curve showed over the horizon. "Moon!" he cried. He tried to run toward home, but he fell. Lying on his back, Bowen watched the moon rising full and whole, the Cars coming alive in the silver glow. Never had the moon seemed so large or so close. And so it always is, for in gratitude, the moon always shines her brightest over the Cars in thanks for brave Bowen's rescue. ❧

New Moon House-Cleansing

At new moons, my children and I (Anne) sometimes do a ritual cleansing of our home. This is a type of housework that they love, since it does not involve picking up their rooms! In the evening before the ritual, we go outside and observe how dark it is with no moon in the sky. Back inside, and we begin our cleansing.

On your altar or a central tabletop, set a candle in each of the four directions. Find a special candle to use as a "moon candle," and place it in the center. Leave all the candles unlit.

Have the children help you open all the doors and windows in the house to let the old energy depart (this may not be practical during the winter). In a censer or ceramic dish, light herbs or incense. Or you can prepare a bowl of salt water instead.

Bless the herbs or salt water, saying some version of:

Dark Mother, you of the hidden doorway, Goddess of new beginnings, guardian of the mysteries of death and rebirth, we greet you in the hour of your greatest power, the time of the new moon. We honor you with this offering of sacred smoke [or salt water]. May our home be cleansed and purified, renewed as your light is renewed in the night sky. As we cleanse our house, we ask you to remove any obstacles that might be in the way of our health and happiness. So mote it be.

Pick up the censer or ceramic dish. Then, beginning at your front door, walk through all the rooms of your house clockwise, until your home is suffused with sweet-smelling smoke. If you're using salt water, the children can dip sprigs of rosemary or another herb and sprinkle the house. At each doorway, say: *May all who enter here come and go refreshed and in peace.* At each window, say: *May the light of the sun and the moon shine in our home; may we see clearly.*

When you are done, close the doors and windows again and snuff out the smoke. Then light your moon candle and say: *When the moon is gone from us, we light a candle to welcome the moon's return to the sky.* Sing "New Moon Song," lighting the directional candles in turn from the new moon candle. Remember to blow them out when you go to bed.

New Moon Song[1]

Words and music by Anne Hill

Moon, moon, fresh and new, come
Moon, moon, fresh and new, come

back to us we bid you.
back to us we bid you. We

look for you in the east - ern dawn, we look for you in the

south - ern lights, we look for you in the west - ern twi- light, we

look for you in the north's mid- night. And when we find you

we will say, the moon's come back to light our way.

Moon, moon, fresh and new, come
Moon, moon, fresh and new, come

back to us we bid you.
back to us we bid you.

Full Moon House-Blessing

This is a great ritual for full moons and it is a counterpoint to the New Moon House-Cleansing. Doing these two rituals over time will help you and your family align with the energies of the moon's waxing and waning.

On your altar or a central tabletop, arrange directional candles in a circle around your moon candle. Begin by saying:

Tonight we see the moon in all her fullness sailing across
the night sky
She shines in the farthest reaches of the east
[light the east candle]
She shines in the blazing glory of the south
[light the south candle]
She shines through the twilight in the west
[light the west candle]
She shines through the deep night of the north
[light the north candle]

Take the north candle (or a child can do this) and light the moon candle with it, saying:

Mother Mari, we have watched you emerge from the womb
of the night into your fullness. We greet you tonight and ask
for your good blessings on our health and happiness.

Carry the lit moon candle clockwise through the rooms of your house, bringing the blessings of the full moon into every corner of your home, filling the rooms with moonlight. You may like to sing "Full Moon Song" or another song throughout the procession.

After returning to the directional candles, if your children are still game, put the moon candle back in its place and do a blessing circle. This is a time when each person can step forward and ask for the moon's blessings of fullness and ripening on any project, any relationship or inner process they might be involved in. This is also an excellent time to ask for healing to be sent to someone you know, or perhaps your family has a special prayer that you all say together.

To close the ritual and snuff out the candles, some version of the following works for us:

Great Goddess of abundance, we have rejoiced with you in your fullness tonight! As you sail on through the night, we will follow you still, till you grow old in the sky and can be seen no more. Go if you must, but stay on with us if you will. Thank you for your blessings tonight, and may there be peace wherever your light shines on the earth!

Next, as you address each direction in the following devocation, snuff out each directional candle in turn:

By the earth that is her body, by the air that is her breath, by the fire of her bright spirit, by the living waters of her womb, the circle is open, but unbroken. May the peace of the Goddess go in our hearts; merry meet, and merry part, and merry meet again!

A simple feast of moon cookies and milk may follow, but whatever you eat on this night, be sure to save a portion and leave it outside afterward for the faeries!

Full Moon Song[2]

Words and music by Anne Hill

When the moon is full and the stars are out, there's a song we hear in the twilight, it's a song of hope for the grow-ing world, as we all dance round on the full moon night. So dance the world whole and spin the world round, o-pen like seeds be-neath the ground, we'll all flow to-ge-ther and we'll all flow a-part, as the moon-light de-scends in-to our hearts.

Banishing Ritual

One evening as I (Anne) entered the house, I saw my two daughters, ages eight and three, preparing for a ritual. They asked for some help lighting the candles and burning the slips of paper, and I'm glad I arrived when I did, because it would not have been safe for them to use fire in a ritual without adult supervision! This was their ritual:

On slips of paper, write down things you want to get rid of or let go of. Set up five candles, four for the directions and one for the center. Welcome each direction as you light the candle. Ask the Goddess in, to help take away the things you no longer want. Ask her for a good life.

Take the first slip of paper. Decide which candle to burn it in. Read it aloud, saying, "I want to have no more _____ in my life," or "I don't want _____ to happen anymore." Light the slip of paper in the candle flame, and put it on the candleholder (or in the fireplace) to finish burning. Do this with each slip of paper, until they are all burnt. Say your thanks to the Goddess for her help and attention, thank the directions, and snuff out the candles in reverse order, starting with the center. Take the ashes outside, and scatter them in the wind. Put away all the candles and clean up, and you are done.

My daughters did not know at the time, but that night was the first of the waning moon, a time when we do magic to remove obstacles and release those patterns in our lives that no longer serve us. Had the moon been in another phase, I may have suggested that they either alter the focus of the ritual or wait for a waning-moon night. The only other comment I had afterward was that when we ask to be rid of things, it should be things that are under our control, and should not involve trying to change the behavior of others. For example, to say "I want my brother to stop teasing me" will not be as effective as "I want not to be bothered by my brother's teasing" or "I want not to be afraid to stand up to my brother when he teases me."

Charging Objects
Under the Full Moon

As a teenager new to the craft, one of the first things that I (Anne) did was buy as much Goddess-related jewelry as I could afford. Wearing necklaces, especially, kept me mindful of my path and the power I was summoning within myself. I had not yet grown comfortable with the idea of rituals, but I wanted to do something with my necklaces that would build their power and, by association, my confidence.

The window of my college dorm room happened to catch the moonlight in the middle of the night, so I drove a nail into the outside molding near the window's opening and hung my necklaces out in the full moon's light each month. Objects can be hung from nails outside your door, on tree branches, placed on rocks or other garden surfaces that catch the moonlight, or simply placed on your altar around the moon candle. As you put your jewelry in place, ask the moon to cleanse them of any harmful influence and fill them with the radiance and strength of the Goddess.

Moon Water

By blessing this water in the full moon's light, we keep a source of her strength and blessings nearby.

Fill a ceramic or glass bowl with water, and take it out under the full moon. Holding the bowl to the moon, bless the water, saying,

Turner of the tides, you who are fullness, light which does not burn, bless these waters, bless our home.

Leave the bowl all night where it can catch the moon's reflection, or near a window. In the morning, dip your fingers in the water and sprinkle it as a blessing over everyone in your home, and a bit over whatever projects or endeavors need a boost. Leave the bowl on the family altar for everyone to dip into as needed.

Moon Spotting

Spotting the first pale curve of the crescent moon is as much fun as spying the first star of the night, with its rhyme, "Starlight, star bright."

We have our own rhymes for the moon cycle:

The Moon's a curve up in the sky
It's growing now and so am I!
I look inside myself to know
What I want to plant and grow.

The moon above is full and bright
We see clearly with her light.
What we're growing now bears fruit
Brilliant crown on solid roots.

Unlike the custom of wishing on a star, where only the first spotter gets a wish, everyone joins in and wishes together, silently or out loud, for the Goddess's blessings.

Sleepy Moon Candleholder

This was inspired by an imported wooden candleholder, a reclining crescent moon complete with a sleepy face and yawning mouth, which held a small taper. This simple salt clay sculpture has an internal armature made of aluminum foil.

Crumple and shape aluminum foil into a three-dimensional banana-shaped crescent, about half the length of an actual banana, and about the same width. Taper the ends, but don't make them into sharp points. About two thirds of the way along the inner curve of the crescent, press with your thumbs until you have a hole for the candle.

Roll out two-thirds of the salt dough into a sheet about half an inch thick and wrap it around the foil. Manipulate dough with your fingers to make the moon shape and pinch it into the hole for the candle. Roll out the remaining salt dough into another sheet and lay it over the inner curve between the hole and the far end of the crescent to form a thicker section. Smooth the join with water-moistened fingers.

You will need:

salt dough

aluminum foil

small tapered candle

Pinch out the moon's nose and brows from the thicker section. Using a tool—for example, a pencil or toothpick—press into the dough to make eyes, either awake or as sleeping semicircles. Fit the candle into the hole and adjust to make a good fit. Keeping the candle in the hole, roll a little cylinder of dough and fit it under the outside curve of crescent to make the moon stand with stability.

Remove the candle, and bake the holder following the directions in the Salt Dough section. The sheen of the flour and salt are a good match for the moon's white-silver color.

Moon Hat

You will need:

sheets of construction paper, white or pale gray

scissors

sticky tape

Try welcoming the moon with these hats, adapted from ancient images.

Cut two strips lengthwise from the construction paper about 1 inch wide. Cut one strip crosswise into two equal pieces. Tape one short piece onto each end of the long piece to form a longer strip. Measure the head of the hat wearer and tape the paper strip into a band that slips easily around the wearer's forehead.

Full moon: Cut a circle 3 inches in diameter. Tape an edge of the circle inside the brow band so that when the hat is worn, the circle is centered on the forehead.

New moon: Draw a crescent moon measuring about 5 inches between the horns, and tape the same way as the full moon, horns pointing up.

Moon Mobile

You will need:

cardboard

scissors

aluminum foil

white glue, thinned with an equal amount of water

hole punch

Make one or two moon mobiles to celebrate the phases: a crescent to mark the new moon, and a circle to reflect the full moon. Hang them where they catch moonlight.

Cut cardboard into either a crescent shape or a circle shape. Coat both sides of the cardboard with thinned glue and then cover with foil, which gives off a lovely silver gleam. Punch a hole in the moon, thread string or yarn through, and hang.

For a full moon with an embossed face, paint one cardboard surface with thinned glue. Lay string or yarn on the glue to make the face. Try gluing small buttons on for eyes. Paint the other side with thinned glue and cover with foil. Apply another piece of foil to the other side, smoothing and shaping it over the ridges formed by the string. Tuck in the edges to form a smooth finish.

You might want to make other shapes: stars, planets, rainbows, raindrops, or clouds.

string or yarn

buttons, sequins, glitter

Crescent Moon
Sweet Cream Biscuits

Serve these light and easy-to-make biscuits with butter and honey and eat them while contemplating the horns of the new moon.

Preheat the oven to 450°. In a small bowl mix all the dry ingredients together. Make a hole in the middle and add all the cream at once. Stir until the mixture is just moistened. Turn out the batter onto a lightly floured board and knead lightly until the batter just forms into a ball. Divide into two sections and roll into balls. Sprinkle a board and a rolling pin with flour.

Flatten one ball and roll out into a circle 12 inches in diameter. With a sharp knife, divide the dough pie-style into six pieces. Starting from the outside, roll each triangle toward the tip. Moisten the tip with a drop of water to seal the roll. Set the biscuit onto a lightly greased cookie sheet, with the tip of the triangle tucked under. Pull the arms into a crescent. Repeat with the other ball of dough.

Bake for about 12 to 15 minutes, until the biscuit is lightly browned. Serve while still warm. Makes 24 biscuits.

You will need:

2 C unbleached plain flour

1 T baking powder

1 t salt

2 t sugar

1 C heavy cream

Full Moon Circle Bread (Chapatis)

This East Indian flat pan-baked bread makes a perfect full-moon celebration treat. The rounds, cooked in a dry skillet, puff up to form darkly pitted circles with craters and paler valleys. If there's no time or inclination to roll out a batch on a full-moon evening, fix them ahead of time and freeze

You will need:

2 C whole wheat flour

1/2 t salt

2 T light vegetable oil, not olive

1/2 C water

2 t melted butter

the uncooked rounds, well wrapped, with a piece of wax paper between each round. Thaw and use later. They make a lovely accompaniment to a full-moon candle blessing, or for munching on while moon-gazing.

Mix the flour with the salt and make a well in the middle. Pour in the oil. Toss and rub with your fingers until the oil is evenly mixed in and the flour looks like rough meal. Add in water, stirring and kneading in the bowl, adding more water a teaspoon at a time until the dough just holds together. Knead until dough is flexible and smooth. Divide into 12 pieces. This is easily done by dividing the dough into four equal parts, rolling each piece into a thick cylinder, and then dividing each into three pieces. Cover these pieces with a cloth.

Press each piece into a circle, and with a rolling pin, roll from the center out until you have a circle about 6 to 7 inches in diameter. For perfect circles, place a bowl upside down over the dough, and cut around the rim.

Heat an ungreased skillet over medium heat. Cook the moon circles one at a time. They will puff up. When the heated side is puffy and browned, press the air out and flip it, browning the other side the same way. Remove, brush both sides with a light coating of melted butter, and place in a warmed oven. Finish the entire batch, then serve at once. Makes 12 chapatis.

Moon Soup

Use your favorite recipe to make black bean soup. Its dark color serves as the "night sky."

To make "moons" and "stars" float on the soup "sky," beat yogurt or sour cream (about a quarter cup per serving) until it's the consistency of heavy cream, thinning it with milk if necessary. Pouring carefully from a cup with a spout, dribble crescent moons near the sides of each bowl. Accent with tiny drops for stars.

For a full moon, pour the yogurt or sour cream into a spiral. With the back of a spoon, stroke the spiral gently until the white liquid has blended together to form a floating moon.

For a vegan moon soup, slice thin pieces of pale soy cheese, then with a cookie cutter or sharp knife cut out moon and star shapes and float them in the soup.

CHAPTER FOUR

Sun Cycle

THE GODDESS AND God have many aspects, many different personalities. Each one teaches us certain things. They change as the seasons change. The Wheel of the Year is the story of the birth, growth, death, and rebirth of the year, and the different ways we see the Goddess and the God at each season. The story teaches us not to be afraid of change. Winter will always be followed by spring, just as summer will give way to fall and winter.

The Wheel of the Year

- **Samhain** (SAH-win), October 31. The Goddess year begins.
- **Yule/Winter Solstice**; December 20, 21, or 22. The year is reborn.
- **Brigit**, February 2. The year is beginning to grow up.
- **Eostar** (A-yo-star)/**Spring Equinox**; March 20, 21, or 22. Day and night are balanced.
- **Beltane**, May 1. The earth is fully awake and everything is blossoming.
- **Summer Solstice**; June 20, 21, or 22. The sun reaches its peak and begins to decline.
- **Lughnasad** (LOO-na-sa)/**Lammas**, August 1. The days are growing shorter.
- **Mabon** (MAH-bon)/**Fall Equinox**; September 20, 21, or 22. Day and night are equal again.

Note on dates: Pagan holidays begin at sundown of the day before the given date. We have given the most traditional dates associated with each holiday, but in reality, Samhain is October 31 and November 1, Brigit is February 1 and 2, Beltane is April 30 and May 1, Lughnasad is July 31 and August 1. The dates of the solstices and equinoxes, true astronomical events, vary slightly from year to year. A good astrological calendar will give you the correct dates and times for the current year.

Gates of the Seasons:
Home Rituals to Share with Kids[1]

by Steven W. Posch

The Cross-Quarters, the holidays in between solstices and equinoxes, all have traditional door rituals associated with them. At Samhain, of course, the trick-or-treaters come to the door and we give them something to eat. At Beltane, the unnamed presences return to the door and leave May baskets full of flowers. So there's a balance struck: at Samhain a gifting-out; at Beltane, return gifting in the other direction.

I have another favorite door ritual for Samhain, an old Irish/Scottish tradition that kids love. Just at sunset on Halloween, we rush to the back door, throw it open, and send out the Old Year. We slam the door closed and lock it, "to lock in the luck." Then we rush to the front door, throw it open, and welcome in the New Year (usually scaring a few trick-or-treaters in the process). We grab horns and noise-makers and run through the whole house making a cacophonous racket to scare away the nasties. It's a fun, silly ritual the adults enjoy as much as the kids do.

Brigit has its doorway rituals, too. In Ireland, libations and oatcakes are offered to Brigit on the threshold. Usually you pour out milk and smush the oatcakes against the door-post. (Just the sort of thing kids like, right?) Here's another: Brigit comes to the door, knocks three times, and says, "Rise to your feet, open your eyes, and let the Black Brigit come in." Everyone inside, waiting in the darkness, replies: "Come in, come in, Black Brigit; welcome and a thousand times welcome." Then she knocks again and repeats the incantation, substituting "Red Brigit." The response is the same. Finally, the whole thing is repeated with "White Brigit," and then, indeed, she comes in, bringing the fires of Oimelc with her into the house.

Here's the Lughnasad/Lammas version. This is the time of year when the rowanberries ripen, so it's appropriate to invoke the powers of the red rowan: "Rowan tree and red thread, put the mischiefs to their speed." In Scotland, you go out secretly on Lammas Eve—or at latest, by noon on Lammas day—and cut several twigs of rowan, with its bright red berries. (If, like me, you are depending on rowan twigs from other people's yards, that's all the more reason to be secretive about it.) Then you tie the twigs into bunches with red thread and hang them over your doorways, front and back (preferably inside). The trick to this all, and the thing that makes it challenging and fun, especially for kids, is that you have to maintain total silence during the whole process: Seeking, cutting, tying, and hanging them all must be done without a single word, giggle, or snort, or else the charm is broken. Then at the moment of hanging, you say: "Peace be here and rowan tree." The enforced silence gives power to the words.

As usual, the tradition is telling us something important. Doorways have always been sacred and rather uncanny places: They're the place between two different states of being, which renders them both hazardous and holy. The Cross-Quarters are the doorways into the new seasons, new states of being, new possibilities, and the door rites we enact ease and enable our transition from one to another.

Symbolism aside, traditions like these are precisely what we need to give our kids if we want them to carry on the craft after us: holiday things that are fun to do, meaningful, and give them a sense of belonging to something ongoing and big. The price that we must each pay for learning the craft is to teach the craft to at least one other person. Where better to begin than at home?

CHAPTER FIVE

Samhain
OCTOBER 31

SAMHAIN (SAH-WIN) IS A holiday many of us know by another name: Halloween. Halloween is celebrated by Pagans and non-Pagans alike. Children of many different religions love to dress up in costume and collect candy. Adults often like to dress up, too! But there is more to Halloween than just fun.

In ancient times, Samhain was believed to be the time when the veil was thin between the world of the living and the world of the dead. Our ancestors could return to visit us, to give us help and advice. People set lights in hollowed-out turnips to guide the spirits of the dead, and put out food as an offering.

These customs live on today. The lights have become the jack-o'-lanterns we carve from pumpkins. The offerings of food became the trick-or-treat candy we give to children. And the spirits of the dead have become the ghosts and skeletons and scary monsters of our costumes and decorations.

Pagans are not afraid of the spirits of the dead. The dead are our friends and family, our ancestors, who gave us life. We call them our "beloved dead."

To Pagans, death is a natural part of life. If nobody died, there would be no room on the earth for new things to be born. There could be no change or growth. So death is one of the gifts of the Goddess.

Nobody really knows what happens when a person dies. But most Pagans believe that our spirits live on in some way while our bodies return to the elements and sustain other lives. There are many beautiful names for the place where our spirits go. It has been called Summerland, the place that is always summer and never winter. The Irish called it Tir n'a Nog, the Land of Youth, where spirits grow younger and younger until they are young enough to be reborn. Another name is Avalon, the Isle of Apples, where the dead wander in the orchards of the Goddess, whose trees bear fruit and flowers at the same time. However we imagine this place, we like to think it is a place of peace and rest where we stay for a time until we are ready to be reborn again, perhaps as another person, perhaps as an animal or a tree. In each life we learn new lessons, so our spirits are always growing wiser.

Samhain is also our New Year's Day. It may seem strange to have a new year begin in the fall, when the days are growing shorter and colder. But death and birth are two sides of the same thing. Because this is the time when we think most about death, it is also the time of new beginnings, when we think about hope and change and what the next year will bring.

The Goddess

At Samhain, we call the Goddess the Crone. The Crone is the Old One, the aspect of the Goddess that teaches us wisdom, that helps us let go when we need to change and grow. Growing up always means losing something as well as gaining something. Sometimes we're happy to let go of things, sometimes we're sad. The Crone teaches us that letting go is a natural part of life.

When we let go, we make space for something new. As we let the old year die we make room for the new year to be born. The time between Samhain and Winter Solstice is the waiting time, like when a baby is in the womb but not yet ready to come out. We don't yet know what the new year will be, but we can dream and imagine.

We can feel close to the Crone at this time by spending some time with an older person. Maybe you can visit your grandparents or an elderly neighbor, who can tell you stories about his or her life.

The God

At Samhain we invoke the Horned God, the stag whose antlers are fully developed. In earlier times, people depended on hunting for much of their food. The Horned God was the God of the hunt, and he represents the animal that gives away its life so other things can be fed.

Today, most of us buy our meat at the grocery store, and some of us are vegetarians and don't like to eat meat at all. But even the vegetables and grains we eat were once alive. The Horned God reminds us that our lives are gifts given to us by other living beings. Because all food is a gift of a life, it is sacred. We treat food with respect.

We can feel close to the Horned God

by stopping for a moment before eating, to thank the plants and animals that have given their lives to be our food. We can also say thanks for the work of all those who grew and harvested that food. And don't forget to thank the cook!

Maybe your family will have a chance to go for a hike in some natural area where deer can be seen. Dawn and dusk are the best times to look for them. Good luck!

The Altar

In my (Starhawk's) house, at Samhain we make a big family altar. On it we put symbols of the seasons, such as pumpkins, pomegranates, fallen leaves, and gourds. We also put there pictures of our beloved dead and things that remind us of them. I always bring out my Aunt Frieda's miniature blown-glass piano, and a long braid of my grandmother's hair that she kept when she bobbed it back in the 1920s.

Has anyone you loved died? Do you have pictures of them, or special things that belonged to them, for the altar?

In Mexico and Latin America, November 2 is celebrated as the Day of the Dead, El Dia de los Muertos. Special altars are created in memory of a loved person. Favorite foods and belongings are set out, along with beautiful cut-paper designs, marigolds, clay figures of skeletons, and bread shaped like people, called *pan de muertos*. Children are given sugar skulls to eat and wonderful candies shaped like skeletons.

In our San Francisco neighborhood, all these things are easy to find, so we have borrowed some of these beautiful customs.

On the Land

Late October is a beautiful time of year where we live. The big-leaf maples have golden leaves, but in the garden, tomatoes are still ripening and the squash plants are still producing. If we're lucky, the first rains have come, but the earth is still very dry, and fire is still a real danger. The days may be very warm, but the nights are often chilly. Luckily, the mosquitoes have mostly disappeared!

When Persephone lived in the underworld, she ate pomegranate, that many chambered, ruby-hearted fruit that appears in markets right around Samhain.

After eating this fruit, Persephone understood that the dark, far from being the place of death and endings, was instead rich with change and hope.

In our tradition we see our journey into the dark, into winter, as the time we restore ourselves, nursing the tender creativity that would perish with exposure to light.

So, just as Persephone embraced her sojourn in the dark, we share her embrace by peeling the pomegranates decorating our Samhain altars and sharing her fruit on Samhain eve.

This is a good time for planting, for soon the rains will water the earth and new shrubs can drink deep. We can set bulbs into the earth to flower next spring. If the rains come early, the hills will begin to turn green, and we will truly feel that Samhain ushers in a season of renewal.

Are the leaves turning where you live? Are you waiting for the first rain or the first snow? Have you planted bulbs to flower next spring?

A Journey to the Shining Isle
by Starhawk

Circle round, close your eyes, and imagine. . . .

It is late at night on Halloween, and you are very excited. All evening long you've been out, dressed up in costumes, collecting candy and apples and other treats from the houses in your neighborhood. Now you are quiet. It is time to go to sleep, but you can feel magic in the air.

"Do we have to go to sleep?" you say.

"Tonight is a night for magic dreams," say the old ones. "Set out an apple for Grandfather Deer, and maybe he will take you someplace." You choose your best apple and set it out on the windowsill for Grandfather Deer. Then you lie down and close your eyes.

Now the room is filled with an earthy, animal smell. Open your eyes, and before you stands the glowing spirit of Grandfather Deer, the oldest and wisest stag in the forest, with many-branching antlers he wears proudly on his head.

"Hop on my back, and I will take you someplace," he says.

You climb on his back, and hold tight to his antlers. He moves so swiftly and smoothly, you feel like you are flying, out of the house, over the tops of trees, out past the streets and the cars, out into the spirit world of swirling color.

At last you come to a sandy beach by the shore of a dark ocean. You are not afraid, even though you can't see much in the dark.

Get down off my back," Grandfather Deer says. "I cannot take you any farther. Now you must go on by boat."

You slide down off Grandfather Deer's back, and thank him. A boat glides across the water and you hear the crunch of sand under the keel as it reaches the beach.

"Do you wish to ride in my boat?" says a voice. You can't see anyone, but you know the voice is magic because it sounds different to everyone who hears it. Some hear a woman's voice, some hear a man's. Some hear a child or an animal or a bird. What do you hear?

"Do you wish to visit the Shining Isle across the Sunless Sea?" the voice says.

"Yes," you say.

"Then you must pay me something."

"But I don't have any money, I'm only a kid," you say. And you left all your candy at home.

"I like stories better than money or candy," says the voice. "Tell me a story about something you have done that was hard for you to do."

What story do you tell?

"Climb into the boat," the voice says.

You climb aboard, and the boat slips away from shore. It moves silently over the dark water.

In the distance, something shines. Slowly it grows bigger and brighter. You begin to smell something very sweet on the air, something that reminds you of fruit and flowers.

Now you can see the shining thing is an island in the distance, that grows bigger as you approach. On the shore are beautiful trees and flowers that shine with a light of their own.

"Who lives on that island?" you ask.

"The beloved dead, and the unborn," says the voice.

"Am I dead?" you ask.

"No. Tonight is Halloween, the only night of the year when the living can visit this island."

The boat reaches the shore, and the sand scrapes under its keel.

"Thank you, thank you!" you say, jumping off and wading through shallow water to the shore.

You step up onto the shore of a magic land that looks different to every person who comes here. You see the most beautiful place you can imagine, and just the sort of place you like best, whether it's a valley or mountains or a beautiful garden or a beach or a warm house. Someone is there to greet you, an ancestor, someone who loves you very much. Who is it? Is it someone you know and miss and remember, or someone you have never met before? Or is it someone you have met in a dream?

You play for a long time, and at last, when you get hungry and thirsty and tired, an old, old woman appears. She is so old her face is covered with wrinkles, but her eyes are so bright they glow like two big moons. At her feet is a big, round iron pot—a cauldron—and she is stirring something in it with a big wooden spoon, around and around and around.

You go close to the cauldron and look inside. At first it seems dark, but then you notice thousands of tiny, glowing lights, like little stars. Around and around and around they swirl, until you get a little dizzy from watching them.

"Those are the souls of the dead," the old woman says. "And they are also the souls of the unborn. In my cauldron, I brew them back into life. Would you like to taste my brew?"

She holds out her spoon and puts one drop of her brew on your tongue. It tastes like the best thing in the world you can imagine. Just one drop is enough to leave you perfectly satisfied. You look into her eyes again and realize she is the Goddess.

"Remember this taste," she tells you, "whenever you are afraid or have to do something hard. It will give you strength and courage. But now it is time to go."

Sadly you say goodbye to the Goddess, to your ancestor, to everyone you have met here on the Shining Isle. You walk slowly back to the shore. A whole year will pass before you can visit here again, but you will remember your ancestor, and maybe in your dreams you will meet again.

At the shore the boat waits for you. You step inside and feel the scraping of the keel on the sand as it pushes off across the dark, dark waters of the Sunless Sea.

On the opposite shore Grandfather Deer waits. You smell his warm, animal smell and the rich smell of moist earth. Now the boat reaches the shore again, and you thank the magic person who has guided the boat for you. You jump out, splashing through the shallow water, and hop onto Grandfather Deer's back.

Again you fly through the swirling colors of the spirit world, back over the treetops and the streets, to your own house again. You thank Grandfather Deer as you slide down from his back and feed him his special apple. Then you curl up to sleep, warm and safe in your own bed. ❧

Vasalisa[1]
retold by Starhawk

Circle round, and I'll tell you a scary story for Halloween. . . .

Once long ago, in a small village in Russia, there lived a merchant and his wife. They had one daughter, a young girl named Vasalisa, who was as beautiful as she was kind and generous. Vasalisa's mother loved her very much, and always dressed her in the colors of the Goddess: red, white, and black. She wore a white apron and a black skirt, but she was especially proud of her neat red boots.

They might have lived happily ever after, but one day Vasalisa's mother became very sick. None of the healers in the village could save her, and as she lay on her deathbed she called Vasalisa to come to her.

"My daughter," she said, "my greatest grief is that I must leave you like this, before you are grown, without a mother's protection. But here is my last gift for you. Take this little doll, who, like you, wears a white apron and a black skirt and little red boots—the colors of the Goddess. She is my blessing, and she will guide you and protect you. Keep her close to you, and keep her secret, and feed her whenever you can. Now kiss me for the last time."

Vasalisa kissed her, and her mother died. For a long time Vasalisa and her father grieved and mourned. But life goes on, even after a death, and Vasalisa grew until she was nearly old enough for her First Blood ceremony.

⌒⌒

Now in that time there was a custom that young girls who were on the verge of becoming women went away from their families, to stay with the wise woman of the forest. And so one day Vasalisa's father took her out into the woods, to the small cottage where the wise woman lived, and left her there.

"You must call me stepmother," the wise woman said, "for I will be like another mother to you." There were two other young women staying there in the house, a little older than Vasalisa, and the stepmother told her to call them stepsisters, "for they will be like sisters to you. You will work very hard here, but you will learn what you need to know to become a woman. But whether or not you will pass the test, who can say?"

Vasalisa did work very hard. The stepmother taught her all the arts practiced by the women of that time; spinning and weaving, healing, gathering of herbs, growing food, as well as teaching her the women's secrets that would help her to know her body and all of its mysteries. There was also the cooking and cleaning

and the usual housework to do. As Vasalisa was the youngest, much of the hardest work fell to her. She did it all cheerfully, without complaining, even though sometimes she was so tired she could hardly drag herself up to the little loft where she slept. But always, before she went to sleep at night, she fed her doll and whispered a little prayer to her mother's spirit.

Vasalisa loved learning all the women's skills and mysteries. Every day she felt herself growing in her abilities. Only one thing worried her. The stepsisters kept hinting at some terrible, frightening challenge she would have to meet.

"To be a woman means more than being able to spin and weave and gather herbs," the elder stepsister would say. "To be a real woman, you must have your own fire. And there's only one place you can get that fire. . . ."

"Where?" Vasalisa would ask anxiously. "Tell me where!"

"I can't tell you—it would scare you too much!" And she would run away, laughing.

"Where is the only place fire can be found?" Vasalisa asked the younger stepsister.

She smiled a secret, knowing, superior smile. "You'll find out soon enough," she said. "Remember, only a very brave woman has her own fire."

Vasalisa didn't think she was very brave. In fact, as the time of leaving grew closer and closer, she became more and more frightened, for she knew that the day of her challenge could not be long in coming. But she said nothing to the stepmother or the two stepsisters, because she didn't want them to think she was a coward. The only person she confided in was her doll, whom she talked to faithfully every night as she fed her the crumbs she'd saved from dinner.

"Don't be afraid, Vasalisa," the doll said. "When the time comes to face your challenge, I will help you."

❧

One night Vasalisa and the stepsisters were all sitting and working by candlelight. A low fire burned in the hearth.

Outside a cold wind was howling. The stepmother came in through the door, and a draft of wind snuck inside and blew out the candles. She closed the door, and the fire went out.

"Light and fire!" the stepmother exclaimed. "Fire and light! Who will go and get fire so that we can relight our candles? Who will go and get fire so that we can light our hearth?" For in those days, you see, matches had not yet been invented, and the only way to light a fire was to borrow a glowing coal from somebody else or to spend tedious hours trying to strike a spark from a flint and steel.

"My needle gives enough light for me to see by," said the oldest stepsister. "I have my own light and my own fire."

"My loom gives enough light for me to see by," said the younger stepsister. "I too have my own light and my own fire."

"Vasalisa," the stepmother said, "you must go and get fire. The time has come for you to face your challenge."

"Where must I go?" Vasalisa asked, trying not to show how frightened she felt.

"There is only one place to get fire," the stepmother said. "You must go to the house of the Baba Yaga (BAH-bah YAH-gah) in the heart of the forest, and ask her for fire."

"The Baba Yaga! Is that really the only place?" Vasalisa pleaded. She had heard stories of the Baba Yaga. The people in the village said she was an ugly and fearsome creature. She had only one eye, but that eye saw everything, and she had long yellow teeth eager to sink into the sweet flesh of little girls and boys. Nobody visited the Baba Yaga and came back alive.

Vasalisa was truly scared, but without saying a word, she went up to her loft, got her warm cloak, and fed her doll.

"Oh, doll, I am so scared," she said. "I'm not sure that I really want to be a woman. Maybe I should just stay a little girl for the rest of my life."

"Don't be afraid," the doll said. "Put me in your pocket, and I will help you."

So she did.

Vasalisa left the cottage and went out into the forest. The night was dark and the wind was blowing, and Vasalisa didn't know which way to go. But she began walking in the direction that seemed best to her, and she could feel her doll nodding in agreement. She walked on and on through the dark and scary woods, and each time she came to a branch in the path, she chose a direction and then asked her doll if her choice were right. Sometimes she was right, and sometimes she was wrong, but always her doll guided her. And so she walked all through the long night.

Just as she was beginning to tire, she

heard the noise of hoofbeats behind her, and a rider dressed in pearly white on a pure white horse dashed past her. Dawn came, and the sky grew light. Again she heard the sound of hooves, and a rider dressed in red on a blood red horse ran by. The sun rose. Vasalisa walked on and on, until she came to a clearing. In front of her was a high hedge made of human bones. Atop each post was a grinning skull. Hoofbeats rang out behind her, and a rider dressed in black on a midnight black horse rushed by and leaped over the hedge. Night fell, and all the skulls glowed with red fire.

Curiously enough, Vasalisa was no longer scared. She had been frightened for so long that now, when she was faced with what was truly the most terrifying sight she had ever imagined, she only felt a strange calm. "Well," she told herself, "this has to be the home of the Baba Yaga. I will live or die, but all I can do now is to walk the path that lies before me, and trust that my doll will help me."

Suddenly she heard a sound like the wailing of all the winds in the world, and the Baba Yaga herself appeared. She was truly a fearsome sight. She rode through the air in a huge mortar, steering herself with a pestle, which she used like an oar. Behind her trailed a broom, with which she swept away her tracks. Her clothes were black and her hair hung down in long, gray locks. Vasalisa looked hard at her face, expecting to see the horrible eye and the long, yellow teeth, but it seemed to her that the Baba Yaga's face kept changing, so that she couldn't have said if it was ugly or beautiful, old or young.

The Baba Yaga sniffed the air and wrinkled her nose. "What is that smell I smell?" she asked. "I smell Russian blood!"

"It is I, Grandmother," Vasalisa said, stepping forward. "I am Vasalisa, and I have come to ask you to give me fire."

The Baba Yaga examined her closely. "I know you," she said. "I know your people. Come into my house. There you will work for me. If you work well, I will give you fire, and if you do not work well, I will eat you up." She pointed her finger at the gate in the hedge. Vasalisa could see that the latches were made of human fingers, and the knocker was a clenched fist. "Open up, wide gate!" the Baba Yaga commanded, and the gate flew open. She entered, and Vasalisa followed.

Inside the hedge was the strangest house she had ever seen. It stood on tall chicken legs instead of posts, and the legs danced so that the house spun round and round.

"Be still, house," the Baba Yaga said, emerging from her mortar. The house stood firm on its legs. The door opened, and they went inside.

Immediately the Baba Yaga lay down on a low pallet on one side of the large room. Opposite the bed was an open hearth, with a brick oven built into the wall, and in the middle of the room was a table and chair.

"There is food in the oven," the Baba Yaga said. "Bring it to me."

Vasalisa opened the oven door, and there she found enough food to feed ten ordinary people, borscht and soup and roast chickens and potatoes and a whole side of beef. She served the food to the Baba Yaga, who ate it all with great enjoyment and no table manners whatsoever,

slurping the soup and cracking the bones between her teeth and leaving nothing for Vasalisa but a crust of bread and a few picked-over bones.

"I'm going out," the Baba Yaga said when she had finished. "I'll be back early in the morning. While I am gone, I want you to clean this house from top to bottom, scrubbing it so that not a speck of dirt remains. Cook my breakfast and my midday meal, and be sure to cook enough, for I eat as much as any ten ordinary people. Oh, yes—and behind the house, in my granary, is a pile of corn as big as a barn. Sort the mildewed corn from the good corn, and leave it in two neat piles. If you work well, I will be pleased with you, and if you do not, I will eat you for breakfast." And out she went.

Poor Vasalisa! Already she was so tired from walking all night. She knew she could never do all that the Baba Yaga had asked of her by morning. Why had she ever come? She would end up as one of the skulls on the Baba Yaga's gate! And she was so hungry! Nevertheless, she saved one corner of her small crust of bread and fed her doll.

"I might as well begin," she told herself, "even if I cannot finish." So she began to clean up the supper dishes, and to scrub the table and the floor, while tears dripped from her eyes.

"Vasalisa, why do you cry?" She heard the soft voice of her doll.

"Oh, doll, I will never finish all this work, and the Baba Yaga will eat me up."

"Don't be afraid," the doll said. "Didn't I tell you I would help you? Go to sleep, and get some rest. The morning is cleverer than the evening."

So Vasalisa took the advice of her doll, and lay down on the Baba Yaga's bed. Instantly she was asleep, and she didn't wake until the hooves of the white rider pounded past the window of the house. She awoke to the dawn. The house was clean, the food was cooked, the corn was sorted. While she slept, the doll had done it all.

The red rider thundered past the house, and the sun rose. With a sound like the wailing of a thousand winds, the Baba Yaga appeared, coming through the gate in the hedge in her mortar and pestle. She climbed out, and came back into the house.

"Breakfast, lunch, and dinner! Breakfast, lunch, and dinner!" she cried out. Vasalisa served her all the food the doll had cooked, enough for ten ordinary people. The Baba Yaga ate it all, leaving Vasalisa only a few spoonfuls of porridge.

"The house looks clean," the Baba Yaga said. "And the corn?"

"All sorted, Grandmother, every last grain."

"Hmpf, well I guess I won't eat you just yet," the Baba Yaga said. She clapped her hands, and out of the air three pairs of hands appeared, bringing the good corn in from the granary and grinding it into meal. Within a short time, every last grain was ground.

A clatter of hooves was heard outside, and the black rider dashed by. Night fell.

"I am going out," the Baba Yaga said.

"While I am gone, here is what you must do. Clean the house again, so that not a speck of dirt remains. Cook my breakfast, lunch, and dinner, and be sure to cook enough for ten ordinary people. And in the granary is a pile of poppy seeds as big as three barns together. Sort the seed from the dirt, and leave it in two neat piles. If you work well, I will be pleased, and if you do not, I will eat you for breakfast." She left.

Poor Vasalisa! She knew that she could never do all the work the Baba Yaga had left for her. Soon she would surely be one of the skulls on the hedge. Sighing, she fed her doll and then picked up a broom and began to sweep the floor. "I might as well begin," she told herself, "even if I can't finish."

"Vasalisa, why are you sighing?" her doll spoke up softly. "Didn't I tell you I would help you? Go to sleep and get some rest. Remember, the morning is cleverer than the evening."

So Vasalisa lay down, and in an instant she was asleep. She woke only when the white rider clattered past the window of the house, and dawn came. Again the doll had done all the work while she slept.

The red rider dashed by, and the sun rose. With a sound like the wailing of a thousand winds, the Baba Yaga rode in through the gate of the hedge in her mortar, climbed out, and came into the house.

"Breakfast, lunch, and dinner!" she cried. "Breakfast, lunch, and dinner!" And Vasalisa fed her all the food that the doll had cooked.

"The house looks clean," the Baba Yaga said. "And the poppy seeds?"

"All sorted, Grandmother, every last seed," Vasalisa said. The Baba Yaga clapped her hands, and the three pairs of hands appeared and ground the poppy seeds into oil.

"You have indeed worked well," the Baba Yaga said. "I am pleased with you, so pleased I will let you ask me some questions, because I'm sure you must have many. But remember that too many questions can make you old before your time."

The doll stirred in Vasalisa's pocket, and she thought to ask about the riders. "Who are the riders, the white, the red, and the black?"

"The white rider is my dawn, who brings the luck and willingness to begin. The red rider is my rising sun, my day, who brings the arrogance and confidence to try what seems beyond you. The black rider is my night, who carries the wisdom of letting go. For you know that I am the grandmother of time. Now, do you have any more questions?"

Vasalisa wanted to ask about the three pairs of hands, but she felt the doll jumping in her pocket, and so instead she said, "No, thank you, Grandmother. As you yourself said, too many questions can make a person old before her time."

"You are wise for one so young. Now I will ask you a question. Look into my face, and tell me how I look to you. Be honest, now. Am I very ugly?"

Vasalisa felt in her pocket, but the doll remained still. She looked into the Baba Yaga's face, but for all the world she couldn't have told her what she saw.

"Well, have you no answer?"

If I answer wrong, she will eat me, Vasalisa thought. *But I don't know what to say. So I had better tell the truth.* Outside, the hooves of the black horse clattered. The black rider went by, and night fell.

"Your face changes, Grandmother. I could not say whether you are ugly or beautiful, old or young."

"My one fearsome eye, my long yellow teeth—are they not horrible to you?"

"All my life that is how you were described to me, Grandmother, but in truth that is not what I see."

"Ah, child, come closer, and although you haven't asked, I will show you a mystery. You see, once I had a beautiful face. Once all people revered me and brought me offerings. They knew me as the grandmother of time itself, and when their time on earth was over, they came to my house of death as to a resting place. Here I helped them sort through their lives, separating what was sweet from what was spoiled. And when they were ready, I ground their souls up in my mortar, back to their original elements, and so they were reborn. That is why my house revolves and revolves. Enter the house of death, and turn round and come out through the door of life. Enter life through the door of birth, and round you come through the gate of death. Only when you know this mystery can you find your own fire."

"Why do people fear you?" Vasalisa asked.

"People forgot the mystery," the Baba Yaga said. "So death became a terrifying and ugly thing. They fear my teeth; they fear my eye! And since they no longer feed me their love and respect, I have become very very hungry, indeed!"

With those words, she seemed to change. Now when Vasalisa looked at her, she saw the fearsome eye, the yellow teeth.

"Tell me," the Baba Yaga said, "you have worked so well, you have shown such wisdom, knowing what to ask and what not to ask. How does one so young become so wise?"

"It is because of my mother's blessing," Vasalisa said.

"Blessing!" the Baba Yaga screeched. "We want no blessings here! Get out of here! Out! Now! Before I change my mind and eat you after all!" And she grabbed Vasalisa by the hand, dragged her out the door, shoved into her hands a glowing skull, and propelled her out the gate. "Here, take your fire and go. Now!"

Vasalisa turned to thank the Baba Yaga, but again she felt the doll jump in her pocket, and so she turned and fled as fast as she could into the forest. The doll guided her so that she took the right turn at every crossroads. The skull was glowing so fiercely and brightly that Vasalisa was afraid. She almost wanted to throw it away, but the doll warned her not to, and so at last she returned to the cottage in the forest.

The cottage was dark and shuttered. She opened the door, and found it empty. The stepmother and stepdaughters were gone.

"Your time of training is over," the doll whispered to her. "You are a woman now, with your own fire, your own hearth, your own knowledge of the mysteries. It is time to return to the village."

Vasalisa nodded. Yes, she would return to the village. She had her own fire now. She would live on her own, or perhaps with one of the lonely old women she knew who reminded her, she realized, just a little bit of the Baba Yaga. With her own light, she would be able to see to spin flax into the finest thread, to weave that thread into the finest cloth, to sew that cloth into fine shirts to house new souls. That is just what she would do, until it was time to do something else—fall in love, maybe, or travel to faraway lands, or do any of the many things a woman could do when she carried her own fire.

And so she did. ◈

Religion on Halloween

On the night of Samhain we honor our ancestors and visit our beloved dead. Often we hold a feast to "feed the ancestors" and connect to our shared history. But try telling children they are going to miss trick-or-treating, costumes, and hauling home sacks of candy, just to sit home and talk about the past. We'd hear the howls all the way to Hawaii!

Families have different solutions for Halloween. In my family (Diane's), there is a surge of energy that belongs to that special time and adds power and relevance to our worship. It's a wave we have to catch if we want to ride. The adults in our home never accept invitations to secular Halloween parties. Our family treats Samhain as a sacred day spent with our children. We have our ancestor feast on the following weekend but plan a significant celebration on Samhain itself. Before the big night, we spend several days making our family altar, creating salt dough figures: tiny pumpkins, owls, black cats, and people in tall hats. We carefully unwrap family treasures left to us by our beloved dead, which we place on the altar. We sort through old family pictures, telling stories as we place them on our holiday altar. We put out pomegranates, make apple chains, and light small jack-o'-lanterns. We hang up and study the roots of our ancestor tree.

When the children come home from school on Halloween, worn out from the excitement and parties, I have a snack waiting: their own roasted pumpkin seeds, a seedcake, and the bread of the dead we've made the night before. We light candles on the altar and read Samhain stories. Then we cast a circle and stand around our altar and pray together:

Beloved ancestors, we welcome you into our home this Samhain eve. We thank you for your gifts, our life, our family.

I then pray to individual ancestors, thanking them for different qualities and benefits we've inherited from them. "Grandma Ruth, we thank you for passing on your love of music. Grandpa Harry, we thank you for passing to us your inventiveness. Grandpa Lou, we thank you for taking the dangerous trip from Russia to America so that we were born free from fear." We ask their blessings for the new year, and ask them to watch over us. Then we sit quietly, waiting for any messages. Sometimes they come!

We close the circle and turn our attention to costuming for the evening's candy ramble.

After the children come back from their candy haul, they sort out their bags and eat a previously agreed amount of loot (or a little more). Before bedtime, we go back to the altar, place a few choice pieces of candy upon it as an offering, say good night to the ancestors, wish them well on their night out, read another Samhain story, put out an apple for Grandfather Deer, and finally, sleep.

Ancestor Feast

In my (Starhawk's) house, we celebrate Samhain with an Ancestor Feast.

On the day of the feast, each of us prepares some special food that our ancestors liked. My ancestors are Ukrainian Jews, so I often make a beet soup called borscht. Other people in the house have ancestors from England, Poland, West Africa, Germany, Holland, France, and many other places, so we have quite a variety of things to eat for dinner.

Before we eat, we take a little bit of food from each dish and put it on a plate. We put the plate on the altar, in front of the pictures of our beloved dead, and light the candles. We speak to them:

Ancestors, Beloved dead, You who gave us our lives, This food is for you. We give back to you. We remember you, And so you live on. Join us now. Feast with us. Visit us in our dreams. We love you. Blessed be.

After dinner, we sit back in comfortable chairs near the altar, and each person tells a story about ancestors. The story might be about someone in their family—or a traditional myth or folktale of their people. We pass around photos of our beloved dead and talk about them or play tapes of their voices.

Who were your ancestors? Where did they come from? Did you ever meet your grandparents or great-grandparents? Were you adopted? If so, you have two sets of ancestors, those of your birth family and those of your present family. This is a good time to ask questions and learn about the people you came from.

When it is time to go to bed, thank the ancestors. Blow out the candles, and put the food from the altar into the compost pile.

Visiting Ancestors

Visiting a cemetery around Samhain is a custom we (Diane's family) first began with our children's circle. We pick an especially beautiful fall day and an old cemetery, with leaning headstones, and statues. We spread a picnic lunch, including a large loaf of bread and fresh flowers, putting aside some choice fare for offerings. As we eat, we tell how Samhain is when the dead are nearest to us. Then we cut the bread into thick slices and use them as plates for food offerings. Holding flowers and our bread plates, we wander around the cemetery, each of us putting food and flowers on the grave that attracts us.

As we walk, we try to piece together stories from the family burial plots or mausoleums. We see the war dead, the women who died in childbirth, the tiny children's graves. We read on headstones celebrations of lives well lived. Some graves are tended and others neglected. Occasionally we'll weed a scraggly grave. We pick up any trash we find.

This yearly excursion makes a wonderful time to answer children's questions about death, ghosts, and other fears and mysteries. In the bright sunshine, we feel joy in life and respect for death.

Ancestor Tree

Our ancestor tree focuses on our roots, so we reverse the traditional drawing of the family tree by using roots to picture our origins.

Use posterboard, or sheets of paper pieced together to measure at least three feet square. Near the top draw the tree trunk. Write your children's names on this trunk.

Now draw two great roots coming from the trunk. Write

a parent's name on each root. If there are more than two parents, draw as many roots as needed. Branch out, writing in the ancestors' names as you go deeper into the earth. Add in important family friends, neighbors, and other people who are part of what you consider family.

When you lose track of individuals, start with general history: towns, regions, whatever else you know. Add in special traditions or affiliations: "They were farmers [or woodspeople, or scholars, or artists]"; "They adopted the religion of their country's regime, but kept these customs"; "Our family was famous for their cheese [or singing, or their ability to make/lose money]."

Go through the tree, telling your children stories. Invite other family members to share their stories. Don't forget history. For example, while my (Diane's) family emigrated to the United States to escape religious persecution, others were dragged here against their will. Some fled starvation, some came for adventure. You can't get too dramatic.

Remind our children that our heritage is what we live. For example, though my (Diane's) grandparents emigrated from Russia, their grandchildren, myself included, merged with this country's English origins. While visiting England, I found the roots of my own American culture. A visit to Mexico shows me roots of the culture that is so much a part of our lives in the West. The culture we live in, as well as the culture where our ancestors came from, becomes our heritage.

Ancestor Sticks

adapted from a Yoruba ritual taught to Starhawk by Luisah Teish

Cut long sticks or branches, one for each child. Provide strips of cloth, about one inch wide and eight to twelve inches long, of a variety of fabrics. Yarn, ribbons, and lace can also be used. Fabrics or clothing scraps that belonged to your beloved dead are especially appropriate.

Ask children to think about their ancestors, or to read the "Journey to the Shining Isle" story.

Blood of the Ancients[2]

Words and music by Ellen Klaver

It's the blood of the an-cients that runs through our veins, and the forms pass,_____ but the cir-cle of life re-mains._____

Then have the children sit quietly for a moment and imagine that they can ask their ancestors what colors, yarn, cloth, and so on they most like. Tell the children the dead will answer by making certain colors or fabrics most appealing. Tie the chosen strips onto the stick.

When the wands are complete, the children can pound the sticks as they say the names of their beloved dead or sing a song to the ancestors, or they can wave the wands, being careful not to hit or poke anyone.

Make a Doll

Make a doll to represent the blessings of the ancestors, to sit on your Samhain altar or to carry in your pocket when you face a difficult time or a separation from your family. A doll could also be useful, for example, for children who divide their time between separated parents, or who go away to summer camp or school, or stay overnight with friends for the first time.

There are infinite ways to make a doll, from tying two sticks together and wrapping them with a piece of cloth to designing your own porcelain molds. When my (Starhawk's) own mother died, she left me quantities of costume jewelry that were not my style. However, I could not bring myself to give them away. Eventually I incorporated a number of them into a small doll, which sits on my writing desk now.

Carving Pumpkins

On Samhain, as I (Diane) help the children carve pumpkins, we tell the history of pumpkin carving, how there were times when people tried to stop observers of Goddess tradition from keeping our holidays, and that these are the people who made Samhain scary. Circles of worshipers met deep in the woods far away from other people. We explain how the Pagans lit candles inside carved vegetables to scare away their persecutors.

We talk about how, no matter how risky it became, Samhain could never be demolished. Even though most people don't realize it, when they give candy to children on this day, they bless the birth of the new year and the sweetness of life.

Samhain Apple Chain

You will need:

several sheets of red, yellow, or green construction paper (or all of them)

scissors

tape

Make a chain of paper apples to symbolize the Isle of Apples on your altar.

Cut the construction paper in half lengthwise. Fold each half accordion-style into four sections.

Draw or trace an apple on the top folded section of one accordion piece, with the sides of the apple touching the folded edges of the paper. Cut this apple out through all the layers, being sure to leave an uncut section of fold on each side. Open the paper to see your apple chain. Repeat with the other accordion piece to make your next apple chain. Attach to the first with tape. You can make the chain as long as you wish.

Write the names of your beloved dead on each apple and hang across your altar. Imagine that on the Shining Isle they have eaten these apples and become new.

Sugar Skulls[3]

The recipe requires almond paste, which comes in a roll and is usually stocked in grocery stores' imported foods or baking section, also by gourmet and ethnic specialty stores. Some markets carry the paste only during the winter holidays, so buy extra; it stores well.

The dough requires at least eight hours of refrigeration time, preferably overnight, so plan accordingly.

On low, heat the marshmallow cream, corn syrup, salt, and vanilla together in a 3-quart pan. Add 2 cups of the sugar and stirring continuously, slowly heat the mixture to 110° (use a candy thermometer). Add the almond paste. Keep mashing it with a wooden spoon until it blends smoothly. Remove from heat.

Mound 2 cups of the sugar on a flat surface. Make a well in the middle and pour in the almond paste mixture. With your hands, move the sugar toward the paste, working the sugar in, kneading the mixture like bread. Knead until the dough is a smooth, cohesive ball, firm but not too hard to shape. Add more sugar if necessary.

Store the dough in a tightly sealed container in the refrigerator for at least eight hours. After refrigeration, divide the dough into eight golf-size balls and sculpt into skulls, using toothpicks and other sculpting tools to make the skull's features. Let the skulls harden on wax paper.

Mexican sugar skulls are elaborately decorated with frosting. Decorate with tinted Buttercream Icing, using a pastry tube with tips to make decorative effects. Makes 8 skulls.

Buttercream Icing

1 C sweet butter, room temperature
3 C confectioners' sugar
2 T water
1 t vanilla extract
pinch of salt
food coloring or icing dye

With an electric mixer, cream all ingredients together except for the coloring, until smooth and stiff. Divide into small bowls for tinting.

You will need:

1 C marshmallow cream

$1/3$ C light corn syrup

$1/8$ t salt

1 t vanilla extract

4–6 C sifted powdered sugar

7 oz almond paste

toothpicks and other sculpting tools

wax paper

Toasted Rice Treat Skulls

You will need:

3 T butter or margarine

10 oz marshmallows
(about 40 regular-sized or
4 C miniatures)

6 C toasted rice cereal

wax paper

The easiest way for children to make their own version of the Day of the Dead skulls is to use the ever-favorite toasted rice cereal treat recipe. This recipe makes 6 to 12 skulls, depending on their size.

In a pan, melt the marshmallows in the butter or margarine over low heat. Stir in the rice cereal and keep stirring until the cereal is evenly coated. Immediately turn out onto a sheet of wax paper and spread it to a thickness of about 1 inch to speed cooling. When the mixture is still warm but cool enough to handle, pass out ½-cup portions to each child. Let the children form the mixture into edible skulls. If the mixture is too sticky, use a little vegetable oil on their hands.

Fondant Skulls

You will need:

4 C confectioners' sugar
(1 lb)

1 egg white

2 T corn syrup

Try this simple fondant variation for shaping small sugar skulls.

Combine ingredients in a bowl and stir with a wooden spoon until ingredients are well mixed. Turn out on a wooden board and knead until mixture has the consistency of smooth clay. Divide into four pieces, shape into skulls, then let them harden overnight on wax paper. They may distort a bit as they harden, but that only adds to their charm. Decorate with Buttercream Icing (see Sugar Skulls recipe).

Roasted Seeds

On Samhain we love the smell of freshly roasted seeds, ready for nibbling. We save some of the seeds from our pumpkins each year for drying and roasting. Fresh sunflower or pumpkin seeds, walnuts, or pecans can be found at farmers' markets. Put the hulled seeds in a dry skillet on low to medium heat, or in a 300° oven. Turn frequently to avoid scorching, until they turn light brown and they become fragrant. At this point take them off the heat, as further roasting might burn the delicate seeds. They will become crisper and slightly darker as they cool.

To salt your seeds, dissolve 2 teaspoons of salt thoroughly in ¼ cup of water. Once off the heat, sprinkle nuts lightly with the salt water mixture. The water will evaporate, leaving a thin coating of salt on your freshly roasted seeds. Alternatively, try sprinkling the warm seeds with your favorite soy sauce.

Honeyed Seedcake

On Samhain we eat honey and seeds, honoring the sweetness of life and the promise of life renewed.

Preheat the oven to 375°.

Toast the sesame seeds in a dry pan over medium-high heat, stirring constantly until the seeds are golden. Listen for a slight crackling sound that indicates they're done.

Blend together the eggs, oil, honey, and sugar. Add the dry ingredients, then stir in the sesame seeds. Pour the mixture into a greased baking pan: 11-inch round, or 10-inch square. Bake.

While the cake bakes, make the topping by bringing the honey and butter to a boil.

After cake has baked about 15 minutes in a gas oven or about 12 minutes in an electric oven, pull cake out. It should be firm to the touch but leave a toothpick slightly coated. Pour topping over cake.

Return cake to the oven, for about 5 minutes for gas, about 3 minutes for electric, until the topping has been absorbed by the cake and toothpick tests clean.

This cake is very rich, so serve in small wedges.

You will need:

1½ C sesame seeds

2 eggs

⅔ C light vegetable oil, such as peanut, canola, or sunflower seed

¼ C honey

½ C brown sugar

1½ C unbleached white flour

½ t baking powder

TOPPING

⅓ C honey

3 T butter

Bread of the Dead[4]

You will need:

2 T dry yeast (2 packages)

1/2 C warm water

pinch of sugar

1/2 C milk

4 eggs, beaten

1/2 C sugar

1/2 C butter or margarine, softened

1 T aniseed

1 t salt (optional)

5–6 C white flour (unbleached is best)

TOPPING

1/2 C sugar

1/3 C orange juice

2 t grated orange peel

This traditional Mexican sweet and spiced bread is prepared to represent the souls of the departed. They are shaped in the forms of skulls or human figures and decorated with colored glazes or tinted sesame seeds, which represent happiness. The topping can be dripped on in patterns. The recipe makes two loaves. We usually make a skull and a human figure.

Sprinkle the yeast on the water, add the pinch of sugar, and let stand until foamy. Mix the milk, eggs, sugar, butter, seeds, and salt together, then add the foamy yeast mixture. Add the flour slowly, smoothing out lumps before adding more. When the mixture is too stiff to stir, turn out onto a floured surface and knead, adding flour carefully, just enough to keep it from becoming sticky. When the loaf is smooth and cohesive and begins to develop resistance to kneading, set in a buttered bowl. Turn it over, cover, and let rise in a warm spot until doubled.

Punch down the dough and divide into two. Form loaves on greased cookie sheets or a baking stone sprinkled with cornmeal.

To form a skull, make the dough into a flattish oval, about 10 inches long and 7 inches wide. With a sharp knife, cut slits for eyes, nose, and mouth. With your fingers, gently pull the dough back along these slits to form the skull-like hollows for the features. Cover and let rise till it is about 80 percent doubled. Use your fingers again to reestablish the holes and openings. Brush with an egg white beaten with a teaspoon of water.

To form a figure, break off a piece of the dough about the size of a Ping-Pong ball. Make the rest of the dough into a cylinder about 12 inches long. Cut one end of the cylinder in half lengthwise, separate into legs, and shape feet. Just above the legs, cut into the dough about an inch horizontally, then upward to within an inch of the top. Pull out to form arms, then smooth the sides of the torso. Add the reserved dough as the head. Let the loaf rise and brush with the egg white mixture.

Bake in a preheated 350° oven 35 to 40 minutes. Let the forms cool completely before glazing.

For the topping, boil the ingredients together for 2 minutes. Let it cool down until it's a thick liquid. Drip onto forms as decorations.

CHAPTER SIX

Yule/Winter Solstice
DECEMBER 20, 21, or 22

YULE IS THE ancient name for the Winter Solstice, the longest night and shortest day of the year. In northern climates, this is the darkest and coldest time of year. The sun seems to be weak, even dying, and we fear winter will last forever.

But just as soon as the Solstice passes, the days begin to grow longer again. The Solstice is a turning point in the wheel of the year, when the sun symbolically dies and is reborn from the womb of the Goddess.

In our tradition, darkness is not something bad or something to fear. Of course, we wouldn't want the world to be dark all of the time—that's why we're so happy when the sun begins to return after the long nights of winter. Light and dark must always be in balance. But we know that without the dark, nothing could live or grow. Without night, we would have no day, no chance to rest and sleep. We would have no dreams—and dreams are our gateway to the Otherworld. Babies develop in the darkness of their mothers' wombs. Seeds must be put into the dark earth in order to send out roots and push up new shoots.

Now, at Solstice, the balance has tipped as far toward the dark as it can go. We are ready for the light to come back, and we must do all we can to help it.

Yule is also one of the words Christians use for the Christmas season. This time of year was sacred long before the birth of Christ. Nobody really knows what time of year Jesus was born, but because people were so used to celebrating at this season, the early Church chose it for one of their most important holidays.

During this season, people of many different religions try to strengthen the light. Pagans and Christians bring an evergreen tree inside and decorate it with twinkling lights and shiny ornaments, to remind us that life goes on even in the depths of winter. Jewish people light candles for eight nights, adding one more each night to the Chanukah Menorah. And African-American people celebrate Kwanzaa, lighting candles for seven nights to symbolize the qualities of unity, self-determination, collective work and responsibility, cooperative economics, purpose, creativity, and faith.

On Solstice night, many Pagan grown-ups stay up all night to keep the Mother Goddess company as she labors to give birth to the sun, the new year, from her night-sky womb. We sing and chant and feast in our night-long ritual, hoping that the sun will be reborn. Children and grown-ups who can't stay awake ask for special dreams as they sleep in the womb of the Goddess.

In the very early morning, we like to climb up on a hill to watch for the dawn, to drum and dance and welcome the reborn child who brings back the light and the promise of summer. The sun rises, and we are reborn with the year. Within each one of us, whatever our age, the miracle child we were at birth emerges anew. The secret we learn from the Solstice is that just when everything looks darkest, the light is sure to be reborn.

The Goddess

At Winter Solstice time, the Goddess appears to us as the Mother, but in a very special way. She is the Dark Mother, Mother Night, Mother Winter. Because death is always followed by rebirth, the Crone Goddess of Samhain becomes the Mother who gives birth to the year.

The Dark Mother is the giver of gifts and the teacher of lessons. Her love for her children is without limit. Her greatest gifts are given to us freely. We don't have to earn them or deserve them; we simply receive them. We are worthy of her love simply because we are.

Life, of course, is the first gift that comes to each of us. Every child born is a miracle, as wondrous as the reborn sun. If we're lucky, in our lives we will also receive other gifts of the Mother—love, abundance, beauty, pleasure, learning, and fun. As we grow, we become capable of passing her gifts on to others. The Goddess teaches us to be helpful, kind, generous, and brave. Sometimes her lessons may seem hard, but she always gives us another chance to learn. No matter how many mistakes we make, she never gives up.

In Germany, Mother Winter was called Frau Holle, Holy Woman. Another of her names was Bertha; the name is related to the name of the birch tree, with its snow white bark. She is the goose-footed Goddess who migrates with the seasons, and who works the treadle of the spinning wheel with her big foot. As the Goddess of spinning and weaving, she spins our fate and weaves our lives. She also knows how to spin a tale—so she is the Goddess of storytelling as well.

With every new life comes new possibilities. In the realm of the Dark Mother, anything is possible. So if you want to change something in your life, or something about yourself, the Winter Solstice is a good time to work on it.

The God

The gifts of the Mother are like seeds that grow in the dark. They are born from her, but the God is the Bringer of Gifts, the one who carries them into the world and into our lives so they can be used and enjoyed. He is her messenger, dressed in her colors of red, black, and white. He may come knocking at your door in the middle of the longest night or swoop down your chimney looking like Santa Claus. Or he may awaken in our hearts the desire to give gifts to those we love, gifts that will warm the cold nights and help the sun to shine.

Old and tired by the longest night, the God goes to sleep in the arms of the Goddess and is reborn at dawn as the sun, the new year, the fresh possibilities reborn in us all. He brings all of our hopes and wishes and dreams for the new year with him. From him we learn to rest and be renewed when we are tired, and to trust, even when life seems hard, that change will come.

The Altar

The Winter Solstice altar is my (Starhawk's) favorite of the whole year. At our house, we find a figure of the Goddess and something to represent the sun. You might want to draw or paint a sun, or make one out of cardboard or clay. We put them in the center of the altar, as if the Goddess had just given birth to the sun and is now proud and happy. Then we gather all our stuffed animals, dolls, plastic dinosaurs, small figures, and whatever else catches our eye and arrange them so they are all looking at the center in joy and amazement at the birth of the year.

This is a tradition we adapted from our

Latin American neighbors. In Nicaragua and El Salvador, certain families in each village create a spectacular *nacimiento* or birth scene. It may include miniature horses, clay figures, toy animals—a whole scene that can take over several rooms of the house!

On the Land

In California, where we live, we rarely see snow except in the high mountains. Winter is the season of rain—if we're lucky—and the Solstice marks the time when we can expect heavy rains to begin. If the rains are too heavy, we might have floods. If the rains don't come, we won't have enough water in the reservoirs to get us through the dry summer.

This is also the coldest time of year, and we may get frost on the ground at night. The oaks, maples, and fruit trees have lost their leaves, but the redwoods, firs, pines, madrones, tan oaks, and live oaks are still green.

The hills turn green as new grasses push up with the rains. The coyote bush puts out white flowers. The toyon bushes are full of red berries. Native plants bloom now, so that their seeds will be formed and fall to the ground early enough in spring to take advantage of the rains.

Is anything blooming where you live? What is happening to the trees around your house? Do any still have leaves or needles? Do you get snow? Is this year a good one for snow? If so, you can make a snow woman and dress her as Mother Winter after you hear the stories in this section.

The Rebirth of the Sun
by Starhawk

Circle round, and I'll tell you a story about when the sun was born again. . . .

It was the middle of winter, and the sun had grown very old.

All year long the sun had worked very hard, rising and setting day after day. All year long the sun had fed everybody on earth, shining and shining, giving energy to the trees and the flowers and the grasses so they could grow and feed the animals and birds and insects and people.

All year the sun's gravity held tight to the spinning ball of the earth and the twirling ball of the moon and the eight other whirling planets as they traveled around and around and around, until the poor sun was dizzy watching it all.

Now the poor tired sun could barely make it up in the

morning, and after a very short time, needed to sleep again. So the days grew shorter, and the nights grew longer, until the day was so short it was hardly worth getting up for.

Night felt sorry for the sun.

"Come to my arms and rest, child," she said. "After all, I am your mother. You were born out of my darkness, billions of years ago, and you will return to me when all things end. Let me cradle you now, as I shelter every galaxy and star in the universe."

So Night wrapped her great arms around the sun, and the night was very long indeed.

"Why does the dark go on so long?" asked children all over the earth. "Won't the sun ever come back again?"

"The sun is very tired," the old ones said. "But maybe, if you children say thank you for all the things the sun does for us, the light may return in the morning."

The children sang songs to the sun. They thought about all the things the sun gave them.

"Thank you for growing the lettuces and the corn and the rice and the wheat," they said. "Thank you for growing the trees of the forests and the seaweed in the oceans and the krill that feeds the whales. Thank you for stirring the air and making winds that bring the rain."

Every time a child said thank you, the sun began to feel a little warmer, a little brighter. Wrapped safely in the arms of Night, the sun grew younger and younger.

At last the children had to go to bed. "We will stay up and wait for the sun to rise again," the old ones said.

"Can't we stay up, too?" the children asked.

"You can try, but you will get too sleepy," the old ones said. "But you can each light a candle, because all fire is a spark of the sun's fire. Put your candle in a very safe place, and let it keep vigil for you as you sleep and dream of sunrise."

So the children lit their candles and put them in very safe places, and each flame was a little spark of the sun's fire. And the sun peeped out from between the arms of Night, and saw all the little fires, and began to feel warmer and brighter and younger still.

Early in the morning, the old ones woke the children. Together they climbed a high hill and faced to the east, the direction of sunrise. They sang songs to the sun and ran around trying to keep warm. They waited and waited to see what dawn would bring.

The sky began to turn from black to indigo to blue. Slowly the sky grew light. A golden glow crept over the horizon. Night opened her great arms, and in a burst of brightness, the sun appeared, new and strong and shining.

For in the long night the sun had rested well and grown young from the songs and the thanks of the children, young as a brand-new baby, born out of Night once more.

Everybody cheered, and the children jumped up and down.

"The sun has returned! The sun is reborn!" the people cried. And they danced and sang to celebrate the birth of a new day, and then went home to breakfast. ❧

The Sun Is Born[1]

by Diane Baker

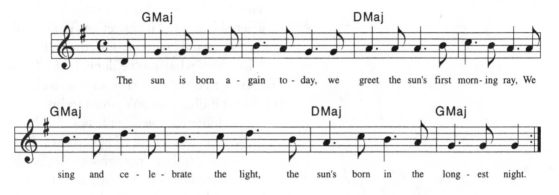

The sun is born a - gain to - day, we greet the sun's first morn- ing ray, We sing and ce - le - brate the light, the sun's born in the long - est night.

A Visit to Mother Winter[2]
retold by Starhawk

Circle round, and I'll tell you a story for a long winter's night. . . .

Once there were two sisters—we'll call them Johanna and Zelda, although they lived so long ago that no one remembers their true names. Zelda, the elder sister, was very beautiful to look at, but she wasn't kind. In fact, because she was so beautiful, she went through life expecting everyone to do favors for her and let her have her own way, and often enough they did.

Johanna, the younger sister, was different. She was kind to everyone she met, and helpful, especially to the older people in her village. She was always doing favors for them, and she tried to make sure they were comfortable and had enough to eat. Johanna was rather plain to look at—not ugly, but certainly no beauty. Only people who were wise enough to look beneath the surface of things would notice her beautiful spirit shining out through her eyes.

One day Johanna and Zelda were spinning beside the little well that supplied
their cottage with water. Johanna was
twirling her spindle to twist the thread
when she dropped it altogether. The spindle
went rolling and bouncing into the well.

"Now look what you've done!" said Zelda.
"You better go right down into that well and
get that spindle. We can't afford to lose it."

Johanna was afraid, but she knew
Zelda was right. They didn't have
money to buy another spindle. So she
lowered herself carefully into the well
and began to climb down the rough
stones.

She climbed, down and down and
down, until the circle of light from
the top of the well became a tiny star,
and then disappeared altogether. Still
she didn't find the bottom of the well.
But she had to go on—she had to get
that spindle! So on she went.

After a long, long time, she finally felt solid
ground beneath her feet. In surprise, she let go of the
stones. The well disappeared, and she was standing in the
middle of a broad field of silvery snow. She could see no sign
of either sun or moon, but the sky above her seemed to glow
with a silvery light, and in the distance she could see a grove
of trees with white bark that seemed to shine from within.

Johanna began walking toward the trees, and soon found
herself on a path that led beneath them. She walked on,
keeping a sharp eye out for her spindle. At last she came to
a clearing.

In the center of the clearing was a huge, old apple tree. Its
boughs were covered with silvery snow and weighed down by
apples with silver-red skin.

"Pick me, pick me!" the apple tree said. "My limbs are going to break under all this fruit. Harvest me! Help me!"

Johanna looked around and saw a big basket at her feet. "I'll help you," she said to the apple tree, and she got right to work. She picked all the apples she could reach, and then she climbed up high into the tree to get all the fruit that grew on the upper branches. As she picked, she began to feel strange and dreamy, to remember all sorts of things she thought she had forgotten, as if the apples were her own memories she was gathering. She grew very tired, but she didn't stop until she had picked the last one. Then she climbed down, thanked the tree for its fruit, shouldered the basket, and started off again.

❧

The path led back into the forest of silvery trees, where silver birds called high above her and silvery gray squirrels ran along the snow-clad branches. She was tired and the basket was heavy, but she continued on, still looking for her spindle. At last she came to another clearing.

In this clearing stood a big, old-fashioned brick oven. In front of the oven was a long wooden table, and on it were trays of unbaked loaves of bread, all nicely risen.

"Bake us! Bake us!" the bread cried out to her. "We will spoil if we aren't baked right away, and for just the right amount of time. Help us!"

"Of course I'll help you," Johanna said. "I know how to bake bread." She set down

her basket and put the trays of bread into the oven, and then sat and watched while they baked. Again she felt dreamy and sleepy, but this time she found herself thinking about all the things she wished for and planned to do with her life, as if the loaves of bread were her own hopes and dreams baking. Tired as she was, she didn't let herself fall asleep, but kept checking the bread until it was golden brown and crusty. Then she took it out of the oven, let it cool, and added it to the apples in her basket. She thanked the oven for its bread and started off again.

❧

She walked on through the forest, where silver foxes darted among the trees and white hares left tracks in the snow. At last she came to another clearing, and there she saw a house like none she'd ever seen before.

The house was made of every good thing to eat she had ever imagined. The walls were made of honey cake and gingerbread, the roof was shingled with white icing, the steps were blocks of hard candy, and the railings were candy canes. The eaves were studded with peppermints and gumdrops and chocolate kisses.

Johanna was very hungry, but she knew it was not polite to start chomping on somebody's house without asking permission, so she went up to the door, which was made of a big lemon cookie, and knocked.

The door opened, and Johanna saw a woman. At first the woman looked very,

Clean House

Everyone in the family can help clean house before Solstice. Be sure to sweep under the rugs and shake out any featherbeds you might have! When you empty the dustpan or throw out the vacuum cleaner bag, name some of the things you want to get rid of. Then steep some rosemary and bay leaves in hot water and add the scented water to the pail when you wash your floors, to bring protection for the new season.

What inner cleansing do you need at Solstice time? What is left over from the past year—what dust lurks in your corners? What would you like to get rid of or leave behind?

very old to her, but when Johanna looked again, she seemed quite young. Her face was as dark as old wood or the young night sky, but when Johanna blinked, the woman was white and pale and silvery as a full moon on a field of snow. One minute Johanna wanted to jump into the woman's arms and cuddle in her lap, but the next minute she found herself almost too afraid to speak to the bright, fierce eyes in the woman's face.

"I am Mother Winter," the woman said. "Who are you who comes knocking at my door?"

"If you please, Mother, I am Johanna," she answered. "I have come searching for my lost spindle, and I bring you a basket of apples I have harvested and bread I have baked."

"You've come to the right place," Mother Winter said. "All lost spindles come to me. And you have brought me good offerings. I will help you, but before I do, you must work for me. You must chop wood to keep me warm, and clean my house, and make my bed."

"Gladly, Mother," Johanna said, and she got right to work. Because she had always helped the people in her village, she knew how to split wood with an axe, sweep floors and clean the tables and wash the dishes. Mother Winter watched all that she did, and was pleased with her.

"Now all you have to do is go upstairs and make my bed," Mother Winter said. "Be sure to shake my featherbed out of the window, and shake it hard. For I am Mother Winter, and when you shake out my featherbed, you bring snow to the places in the world that get snow and rain to the places that get rain."

So Johanna went upstairs and shook out the featherbed as hard as she could, and sure enough, in the upper world, snow and rain fell on the earth.

"You must be tired and hungry," Mother Winter said. "Come have a drink of my soup, and eat some supper."

On the hearth, Mother Winter had a big cauldron full of steaming soup. She handed Johanna a dipper, and just for a moment Johanna caught a glimpse of what was inside. The brew in the cauldron was dark as the night sky, and studded with swirling stars and snowflakes.

"In my cauldron, you see all your dreams and possibilities," Mother Winter said. "Everything that has been and everything that has not yet come to be is all brewed together. Now have a drink."

Johanna drank, and the soup tasted better than all the candy and cookies in the world. It was nourishing and refreshing and exciting all at once, and yet that one sip satisfied all her hunger.

"Here is your spindle," Mother Winter said, and she handed it back to Johanna. When Johanna took the spindle in her hand, it felt heavy, and when she looked at it, she saw that it had turned to solid gold. Then she and Mother Winter feasted on bread and apples.

"You have done well," Mother Winter said when it was time for Johanna to leave. "You have brought me good offerings. You've fed my fire and cleaned my house, and you have shaken my featherbed good and hard! When you return to your world, you will find you bring gifts with you. For I am the Giver of Gifts and the Teacher of Lessons."

❧

So Johanna returned, all the long way through the silvery woods, past the big oven, past the apple tree, out to the open field where a dark circle hung in the sky like an open mouth. Johanna raised her golden spindle, and a thread of light beamed up into the darkness. Then, as if something above was reeling in the thread, she found herself rising and rising until she could feel the old stones of the well under her hands and feet. She climbed up and up, and at last she clambered out of the well.

Zelda was waiting for her impatiently. "Where have you been?" she asked. "What took you so long? And what has happened to you?"

For Johanna looked quite different from the girl who'd climbed into the well. Her features hadn't changed, but now her plain, kind face seemed to glow with a light of its own, and the goodness of her heart made her quite beautiful. She opened her mouth to tell her sister everything that had happened, and as she spoke, gold and silver and precious stones dropped out of her mouth and covered the ground.

"You've had quite a time, I can see!" Zelda said. She was very jealous. "Why should you get all the good things and me

Mother Winter's House

Consider building a gingerbread house as an offering, thinking of all the gifts of the Goddess you are grateful for and choosing candy and colors and decorations to represent them. The house then becomes a symbol of the abundant wonders we've received from the Mother—and the empty space inside can symbolize the unknown gifts we hope for in the future.

none? I'm going down that well for my-self!"

And she hopped over the edge and climbed down the well. Sure enough, she soon found herself in the silvery land, and walked across the snowy field and through the forest path under the silvery trees, until she came to the clearing with the big apple tree.

"Pick me, pick me!" the apple tree said. "My limbs are going to break under all this fruit. Harvest me! Help me!"

"Hah!" Zelda said scornfully. "Do I look like a gardener? Don't you think I have more important things to do than waste my time picking apples? Let them rot!" And she walked on.

Soon she came to the clearing with the old brick oven and the loaves of bread on trays ready to be baked.

"Bake us! Bake us!" the bread cried out to her. "We will spoil if we aren't baked right away, and for just the right amount of time. Help us!"

"Hah!" said Zelda scornfully. "Do I look like a baker? Do you think I have nothing better to do than sit around watching some dumb bread cook? Let it spoil, what do I care?" And she walked on.

❧❧❧

Finally she came to Mother Winter's house, made of all the most wonderful things she could imagine to eat. She was hungry, so she broke off a piece of the gingerbread wall and began to eat it.

The door of the house opened, and Mother Winter came out. "I am Mother Winter," she said. "Who are you, and why have you come here? Why are you eating my house without even asking permission?"

"Excuse me," Zelda said. "I was hungry. I've come because you gave such wonderful things to my sister and I think you should give me some gifts, too."

"Oh you do, do you?" Mother Winter said. "What offerings have you brought me?"

"Offerings?" Zelda said. "I didn't know I was supposed to bring offerings. I thought you were the Giver of Gifts."

"I am," Mother Winter said, "but gifts must be earned. You have nibbled at my house without asking permission, and you haven't brought me any offerings, but still I will give you a chance to earn my gifts. You must work for me. You must chop wood to feed my fire, and clean my house, and make my bed."

"Do I have to?" Zelda whined. "What do I look like, a housemaid?" But she didn't say it very loud. She went outside to chop wood, but because she had never bothered to help anyone with their chores before, she didn't know how to split a stump or use an axe, and after a few half-hearted tries, she gave up. She gathered a few loose sticks that were lying around and brought them in. Then she tried to sweep the floor, but all she succeeded in doing was stirring up the dust. She wiped the crumbs from the table onto the floor, making it even dirtier, and washed the dishes so badly that food was still sticking to the plates when she put them away.

"Now can I have my gifts?" Zelda asked.

"You have not done well," Mother Winter said. "You have nibbled at my house without asking permission, and you haven't brought me any offerings. You have not fed my fire or cleaned my house. Still, I will give you one more chance. Go upstairs and make my bed. Be sure to shake my featherbed out of the window, and shake it hard. For I am Mother Winter, and when you shake out my featherbed, you bring snow to the places in the world that get snow and rain to the places that get rain."

"Oh, all right." Zelda sighed. She went upstairs and tried to pick up the featherbed, but it seemed too heavy to her.

"She'll never know if I shake it or not," Zelda told herself, and so she just fluffed it a bit on the bed, and went back down. And so in the upper world, there was no snow or rain, and the ground stayed dry and brown and thirsty.

"Now can I have my gifts?" Zelda asked hopefully.

Mother Winter sighed. "You have not done well. You have nibbled at my house without asking permission, and you haven't brought me any offerings. You have not fed my fire or cleaned my house, and you didn't even shake out my featherbed. Still, I will offer you a taste of my soup."

"Soup!" Zelda cried indignantly. "I didn't come here for soup. I came for gold and jewels and beauty like my sister got."

"Very well," Mother Winter said. "I am the Giver of Gifts and the Teacher of Lessons. Return to your world, and you will find you have been given the gifts you deserve."

So Zelda went back, all the long way through the silvery forest, past the oven and the apple tree and and the field of snow, up the well, and at last she climbed out to find her sister Johanna waiting for her.

"Here I am! Here I am!" Zelda announced.

"But what has happened to you?" Johanna cried. For Zelda had changed. Although her features remained the same, they now seemed as pinched and narrow and twisted as her mean spirit. And when she spoke, clouds of mosquitoes and flies flew out of her mouth.

And so she remained until the end of her days—or at least until she learned a few lessons. Who knows? Maybe she'll go down the well again and do better this time. For Mother Winter is the Teacher of Lessons, who will always give us another chance.

The Story of Amaterasu
retold by Starhawk

Circle round, and I'll tell you a story from Japan about the time the sun disappeared. . . .

Amaterasu was the Goddess of the Sun. Golden and gleaming, she lived high in the heavens, giving warmth and light that gave life to all things on earth.

One day she heard a great noise approaching, a rumbling and crashing and banging. "Oh-oh," she said to herself. "That sounds like my brother, Susanowo, when he's had a bit too much to drink!" Susanowo was the God of the oceans and the storms that bring thunder and lightning. When he was in a good mood, he could be as kind as the gentle summer sea, but when he was in a bad mood, watch out! "I'd better protect myself," Amaterasu thought, and she armed herself with a golden bow and silver arrows in a quiver.

"Stand back," she warned her brother when he arrived in the sky world.

"My sister, why do you always suspect the worst of me?" he reproached her. "I mean you no harm. I've only come to say goodbye before I go on a long journey."

"I've heard that one before," Amaterasu grumbled.

"This time it's true!" Susanowo protested. "I'll tell you what. We are both Gods. To show my peaceful intentions, let us create something together. Let's use our divine power to make some children."

"All right," Amaterasu said. "Give me your sword." She broke the sword into three pieces, chewed them up, and blew a cloud of life-breath over them. They became three Goddesses.

"I can do better than that!" Susanowo said. "Give me your five necklaces of radiant jewels." He bit her necklaces, blew on them, and they became five Gods.

"Very good," Amaterasu said. "But since the Gods you made came from my jewels, they are my children too. Now go on your journey and leave me in peace." And she took the children and went to bed.

Susanowo was mad! All night long, while Amaterasu slept, he brooded, getting angrier and angrier. He stormed and thundered throughout the heavens and stomped over the earth, trampling the rice and breaking down the irrigation ditches. When he came to Amaterasu's temple, the sacred place where she wove the clothing of the Gods for the New Year festival, he knocked down walls and threw dung inside. By the time Amaterasu woke up, the roof was caving in. A spotted horse was rampaging through the sacred rooms, and her drunken brother was stumbling after it, running it through with his sword and defiling her temple with blood. Her weavers were so terrified that several of them pricked themselves with their own spindles and so died.

Furious, Amaterasu ran into her cave of night, locking the door after her. "I'm not coming out again!" she swore. "Who wants to shine in a world where a drunken madman like my brother can do so much harm!"

The world grew dark and cold. No sun shone to warm the earth, to coax the rice plants up out of the soil. Without the sun, all life began to die.

The Goddesses and Gods grew worried. "We must get Amaterasu back!" they cried. They found Susanowo and banished him from heaven. "Your brother is gone," they called to the Sun Goddess in her cave, but she refused to answer.

"Please come out," they cried. "The people are dying!"

But still Amaterasu sulked.

"What can we do? What can we do?" the Goddesses and Gods wondered. "How can we entice her out?" Finally they came up with a plan.

"Roosters crow to greet the dawn," one young Goddess suggested. "Let's bring some to the mouth of the cave."

"Let us bring the sacred eight-armed mirror to reflect her glory," an old, wise God suggested.

"I will dance," cried the beautiful Goddess Ama no Uzume. She dressed herself in leaves, set a tub upside down outside the mouth of the cave, and began to dance. Her feet pounded on the tub, making a great noise. Faster and faster she danced, becoming more and more wild with ecstasy, until in a frenzy she tore the leaves away and danced naked. The other Goddesses and Gods laughed in delight.

Amaterasu could hear the noise outside her cave: the roosters crowing, the tattoo of dancing feet, the laughter of the Goddesses and Gods. Curious, she peeked out of her cave. A sliver of light illumined the world.

"What's going on?" Amaterasu asked.

"The world has found a better Goddess than yourself," Ama no Uzume proclaimed as she continued to dance. "Me! If you don't believe me, come out and take a look!"

But Amaterasu had caught sight of her own reflection in the eight-sided mirror.

"What is that beautiful light?" she cried. "Whose is that beautiful face?"

"It is you who are the radiant one," the Goddesses and Gods all cried out. "Don't hide your light! Come out and let us admire your beauty!"

"Is that really me?" Amaterasu opened the door wider. The light grew even brighter. "How beautiful I am! Why should I hide such loveliness in a dark cave?"

Enchanted by her own reflection, she threw the door open wide and emerged. The sun rose, and the world turned warm and green again. And so all living things praise the warmth and beauty of the sun, for without the life-giving rays of Amaterasu, we could not live. ✺

Winter Solstice for Small Children

We (Diane's family) spend the afternoon making meringue cookies. Carefully we separate a dozen eggs, saying, "Eggs mean life. The yolks are the sun. Without the sun, we'd have no life. The white part is the moon, the sun's opposite, where we find rest and nourishment."

Then we bake dark chocolate pressed cookies and paint them with a rainbow of icing. "This is the dark," I say. "This is where dreams are born."

We make solstice suns and stars and hang them around the fireplace and on the children's bedroom doors.

Then for sunset we seek the high places, usually a friend's porch in the hills. The children huddle between my knees. "The sun sleeps longest tonight," I tell them, "and becomes fresh and new. Tomorrow at sunrise we'll celebrate the sun's birthday."

Before bed, we light red floating candles in a big crystal bowl of water, the spark of sun that will keep watch through the night while the children sleep and I keep vigil. We sing songs, read our solstice story, and talk about the life the sun grows with its warmth and light.

The children go to bed dressed in their clothes, nervous from the novelty and the promise of waking up in the dark. I make my own prayers and rituals, and then make custard.

Morning starts when I whisper in their ears that the time has come. They ride on my back one by one down to the car, and we go off in search of sunrise. The highest point in our neighborhood is well attended by other solstice-seekers this morning. We wait in the car, sipping hot cider and eating the dark cookies. Our world grows brighter. We leave the car and stamp around the parking lot, trying to get heated up, wondering if the clouds will clear. Then a thin line of blue shows in the gray just above the horizon. I start the song: "The sun is born again today." They join me slowly, then a little louder. I grab their hands and start to dance in a circle. We turn to the horizon and a blaze of yellow light spills through a cloud. "It's here," we shout. We cheer and shout some more, wish each other happy Sun's birthday, trade kisses and hugs, and go home to eat our custard.

Dream Incubation

There are some who say that we should stay up all night on the longest night, and others who say you should sleep all night and go fishing for dreams in the pools of Mother Night. If you are of the latter inclination, a wonderful family observance for the night of Solstice is a dream incubation ritual.

This ritual calls for a quiet, relaxed evening, so whatever will get your family in the mood—music, hot cider or warm milk, and plenty of fresh bread with honey seem to fit the bill at my (Anne's) house—should also be part of the setup. If you are able to fit all your family members (and friends, if you want to make it a party) in sleeping bags on the floor of one room, by all means do so. If everyone can sleep with heads facing toward the middle of the room, so much the better.

Central to this ritual is the altar, which should have on it a big bowl of water (ideally, Waters of the World; see Brigit Altar), dream and birth images, and a candle. In the interest of fire safety, the candle should be set in a glass container with sides reaching higher than the flame. Participants may come prepared with either a question to "put" into the water, or an object symbolizing something in their lives they would like dream help for. Nearby should be art supplies, paper, pens, dream journals, and small flashlights for those who wake up in the middle of the night with a dream to write down.

Once everyone is ready for bed, light the candle and say the following:

Winter Solstice is the celebration of the birth of the Sun, the divine child of the Goddess. In our own lives, this longest night can be a time of divination, of journeying deep into our inner dreamtime, to bring forth a dream that can help us in the year to come.

Speak over the bowl of water:

Sacred water, you who pass from the womb of the Mother into the rain and rivers and back again, you who nourish us and quench our thirst, you who can slip through cracks and erode even the strongest of obstacles, help us now to dive into the depths of the darkest night and ask for a dream. We ask for a dream of healing, a dream to show us where to go in the coming year, a dream to show us what we need to see. So mote it be.

Everyone in the circle takes a turn with the water, speaking their question into the water, dipping objects or body parts into the water, or doing whatever they feel moved to do in asking for a dream. After everyone has had a turn, put the lights out. You may want to talk quietly about dreams you remember from the past year, and what you learned from them, or perhaps tell stories of the Solstice, particularly if there are young children present.

In the morning, write or draw your dreams before getting up from the circle or speaking too much. Afterward you may all choose to tell each other your dreams, possibly offering comments or insights into the dreams of others. Let the person speak her dream uninterrupted first. A useful and respectful way to offer comments on someone else's dream is to use "I" statements: "If this were my dream, the cat on my dresser would be my desire to fit my artistic side into some compartment in my life," or "In my version of this dream, the tree is a ladder I can climb into the spirit world," and so on. (Thanks to Jeremy Taylor for this idea.)

Once this is done, give thanks to the water:

Blessed water, thank you for easing our journey into the night and back again. Thank you for our dreams and visions, thank you for the light that is born from the womb of darkness. As we send you on your way back to the Mother, we bid you hail, and farewell.

Pour the water into the nearest body of running water, to keep it cycling on its way. Pictures, poems, and other artifacts from Solstice dreams can be kept by the bed throughout the year. Kids: Remember to pitch in with washing the breakfast dishes and cleaning up the living room after this ritual!

Extra breakfast idea: If your family likes sourdough muffins, pancakes, or biscuits, set your sourdough starter out to rise that evening near the sleepers. The sourdough is a live culture and can pick up the dream energy in its own way, giving you a magical food for breakfast.

And We'll All Go Singing on the Mountain: A Game

One of our (Anne's family's) favorite observances is to rise before dawn on Solstice morning, go out to a high hill facing east, and sing up the sun.

"And We'll All Go Singing on the Mountain" is a game/song I (Anne) adapted from an older one played by New York City schoolchildren. I like it because it expresses how important the mountain is that we are standing on while we are all trying to get our first glimpse of the sun.

The rules for the game are simple. Everyone is in a circle holding hands and walking counterclockwise as the song begins, except one person who is outside the circle walking clockwise. At the words "One, two, three follow me," the outside person taps three people in the inside circle, and they join the person on the outside circle as the song and play continues. Pretty soon there are very few people in the

Singing on the Mountain[3]

Traditional, new words by Anne Hill

And we'll all go sing-ing on the moun-tain. The moun-tain is so high, it rea-ches to the sky, and it's one, two, three fol-low me.

inside, and lots more on the outside. The last one or two people in the center then become the "mountain" around which the others are singing, and the game ends with one final chorus. Then the last "insiders" become the first "outsiders," and the game begins again.

Yule Elves

At my (Starhawk's) house, we have a Solstice tradition of "elving" each other. About ten days before Solstice, we put all our names into a hat. We each draw a name—and keep it secret! Each of us then becomes the elf for the person whose name we've picked.

For the next ten days, we leave little gifts or secretly do nice things for our "mortal." We might leave a flower or a special piece of candy, or a lovely picture, or sneak in and make the bed or fold the laundry. We might have someone else call up and leave our "mortal" a message about how wonderful she is and how everyone loves her. And for those ten days, someone else is doing the same for us! The house has a wonderful feeling about it, with everyone tiptoeing around secretly doing good deeds. And we have a lot of fun trying to guess who our elf is.

On Solstice Day we have a special dinner. Each elf gives a present to her or his "mortal," and we reveal our identities. The spirit of Mother Winter fills the house for weeks.

Winter Solstice Suns

On Winter Solstice we decorate our doors with a two-sided image of the sun, one side light, the other dark. After sunset we hang these with the dark side out, and in the morning when we return from watching sunrise, we triumphantly turn them to their blazing yellow side. These suns can be whatever size you wish.

Glue together bright yellow construction paper and black construction paper. Draw on a picture of the sun and cut it out. Decorate with glue and glitter. Punch a hole about a half inch from the edge and insert string for hanging.

Snow Molds for Candles

Lighting snow mold candles symbolizes the light born in winter. If you have outside snow close to where you melt your wax, make your snow molds outdoors. If not, bring a large bowl full of snow into your work area; to delay melting, put it in the refrigerator or on the windowsill.

Gently pack the snow into the shape you want. Free-form shapes are fun here; try making bumps and other protrusions by poking fingers in the snow. Just fill in your mistakes. There will be some deformation from the hot wax melting the snow, so don't get too picky or detailed. And keep size in mind; it's easy to make them too big.

See the Tool Chest section for materials and instructions about making candles.

Tips for pouring the wax: If you're going outside, an adult should carefully bring the wax to the location. Pour the wax when it is still liquid but close to being cooled; if the wax is too hot, it will deform the mold.

Can Candles

Twinkling candleholders are easily crafted from tin cans with the tops cut off, and bring the long, starry nights to our homes and altars. Fill the cans with water and freeze solid. This can take up to two days, so plan ahead.

Cut a piece of paper to a size that fits around the can like a label. Draw the design you want to make and tape paper onto the can. Starting along one of the design's lines, use a nail and hammer to tap through the can and make a small hole. Move the nail a little farther along the line and make another hole. Continue working until the entire design is perforated.

Remove the paper and run the can under warm water until the chunk of ice falls out. Put a votive candle in the can, light it, turn off the lights, and enjoy your sparkling artwork.

Yule Tree Decorations

Chain of Memory Apples

Apples, sturdy enough to store, dry, and can, are practically the only fruit that follows us through all four seasons. Like Johanna in the "Mother Winter" story, we can capture our own memories by making a chain of apples as Winter Solstice decorations. Use the directions from the Samhain Apple Chain activity to cut the paper. Write a memory on each apple and stretch your memories across your altar, fireplace mantel, or Yule tree. If you don't want to share your memories, write them with your finger, so only you will know.

Trees are among our most powerful symbols. Deciduous trees enact the dramatic cycles of yearly death and rebirth. Evergreens display life's endurance even through times of killing cold. The Christmas tradition of bringing in an evergreen tree has been reclaimed by some Goddess tradition families to honor trees as the symbol of life renewed and everlasting.

Decorating the tree is great fun. My (Diane's) family's custom is to buy one special ornament each year. We make long strings of cranberries and popcorn, which we later drape outside for birds to eat. We also make ornaments from salt dough (see Tool Chest section for the recipe) and cut others from paper.

The favorite is the paper spiral. Cut a circle of colored construction paper between 3 and 4 inches across. Then cut it into a spiral, starting from the outside and making your way toward the center. Leave a section of at least $3/4$ inch intact in the center, so that the center looks like the head of a comma. Punch a small hole in this, run thread through, and hang so the spiral drapes nicely.

Children never tire of cutting paper snowflakes. Cut a circle of paper and fold it in half. Fold this semicircle into thirds, then fold again in half. Cut your snowflake along the edge with the multiple folds, making sure to leave some of the long single fold uncut. Pinking shears make a great effect. Unfold. Decorate with glue and glitter for extra sparkle and interest. Punch a hole about $1/2$ inch from the edge, insert string for hanging, and enjoy.

The Cinanimals recipe in the Fall Equinox section makes excellent fragrant ornaments that mingle with the scent of the tree and last longer than cookies. Smaller versions of Winter Solstice Suns (instructions in this chapter) also look lovely on the tree. We even hang up eggs we've saved from the spring holidays.

When the holiday has passed, our local zoo asks for donations of cleaned evergreen trees to give to the animals as toys. Remember to thank your tree for blessing your home before you take it out.

The Night and the Sun

This activity goes along with Starhawk's story "The Rebirth of the Sun." We create stand-up paper figures of Night cradling the Sun within the circle of her arms, and the Sun, refreshed and reborn for the coming year.

Sketch Night on black construction paper (see illustration 1). This figure is exaggerated in arm length, as they will be joined in a circle. Cut out and lay flat.

Draw Night's face with a white crayon: downcast eyes, the suggestion of a nose, and flowing hair. You might decorate the arms as sleeves, and add necklaces. Bring the arms together into an embracing circle, and fasten with tape on the back. We like to cut out a crown and tape it on.

Cut the Sun from a sheet of sun-colored paper, with a diameter of about four inches. Draw on a sleeping face. Tuck the Sun within Night's arms (see illustration 2).

ILLUSTRATION 2

ILLUSTRATION 1

Sun Crown

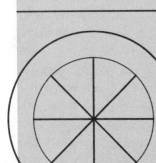

These crowns of light and color sparkle through the longest night.

Draw a circle inside the rim of a 10-inch paper plate, at least 1 inch from the edge. This will become the hat's brim. Draw lines dividing the inner circle into eight equal pie segments and cut along the eight dividing lines (see illustration). Push the pie segments up to form the sun rays with a crown effect. Color like a brilliant sun with yellow paint; scatter glitter while the paint's still wet.

Holly Wreath for Mother Winter

We invite Mother Winter to bless our home with her gifts of learning by making a wreath of one of her sacred plants, the holly. If you live in an area with holly bushes, respectfully ask permission from the bush (and its owner) to gather leaves. Each point of the leaf has a sharp spike, so this plant demands respect whether you offer it or not! Florists sell holly, as do many holiday tree lots.

See the Tool Chest section for materials and instructions about making wreaths.

If you're using the paper plate method, glue the leaves onto the plate. If you're using a form, tie on the leaves. Another option is to shape a form from supple, thin branches and accent them with the holly leaves. (Ancient traditions used the elder tree's branches.) Finish by trimming with red ribbon, for the sun and rebirth, or stick on red berries with toothpicks or glue.

Mother Winter's Wish Bread
(Monkey or Bubble Bread)

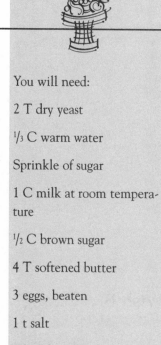

My (Starhawk's) circle's tradition is to bake bread on Solstice night as we keep our vigil. We try to time the process so that the children can help with the kneading while they are still awake. We each take a turn kneading the bread, putting in our hopes and dreams for the coming year, and we sing the "Wish Bread Song." When we rise at dawn to greet the sun, we have hot, fresh bread to eat. It's especially nice when we can eat it with fruit butter we bottled at the Summer Solstice!

This traditional recipe allows everyone to roll their wishes into a sweet, festive, and sticky loaf that pulls apart by hand. As the children make each ball of dough, encourage them to talk or think about what they wish for, their hopes and dreams, their seeds planted in the longest night to grow as they grow.

Mix the yeast in the water, sprinkle sugar, let set until foamy. Mix the milk, sugar, butter, eggs, and salt together in a large bowl. Add the foamy yeast. Stir in the flour, a cup at a time, until stiff. Turn out onto a lightly floured board and knead until the dough is smooth and pliant. Oil a bowl, put in the dough, turn it over, and cover the bowl with a moist tea towel. Let it rise until doubled.

Meanwhile, make the glaze by melting the butter and brown sugar together. Butter a Bundt or tube pan. Pour one $^1/_3$ of the glaze into the pan. If your children like nuts, sprinkle them over the glaze in the bottom of the pan.

Gather the children around a table. Tear or slice off pieces of dough the size of golf balls. Ask the children to think their wishes, their plans. They can share, but silence is fine. They can put a raisin or a bit of dried fruit inside each ball to represent their wishes. Urge them to finish with the condition, "If that's what is best for me."

Be sure they know they won't be able to keep track of their individual wish balls once they become part of the loaf. They just have to hope that everyone's wishes come true.

You will need:

2 T dry yeast

$^1/_3$ C warm water

Sprinkle of sugar

1 C milk at room temperature

$^1/_2$ C brown sugar

4 T softened butter

3 eggs, beaten

1 t salt

$4^1/_2$–$5^1/_2$ C flour

$^1/_2$ C raisins or other small pieces of dried fruit, optional

GLAZE

$^1/_4$ C butter

$^1/_4$ C packed brown sugar

$^1/_2$ C chopped walnuts or pecans, optional

Lay half of the balls evenly around the bottom of the pan, pour on another ⅓ of the glaze, then lay the remaining balls in the pan and pour on the last portion of glaze.

Cover the pan again with the cloth and let rise until the dough is about 80 percent doubled. Bake in a preheated 350° oven for 45 minutes. The sugar promotes rapid browning, so check the top after about half an hour, and if it's too brown, fold a piece of aluminum foil and place it across the top of the pan like a tent. You can poke a ball gently with a toothpick to test for doneness. The toothpick should be free of dough or crumbs, like a cake. When the bread is done, let it cool for a few minutes, turn it onto a rack, and serve warm. This is finger food, so provide napkins!

Wish Bread Song[4]

Words and music by Starhawk

All things from me are fed,—— Knead the dough and bake the bread.——

Mourn the dreams that now are— dead,—— but knead the dough and bake the bread.——

Meringue Cookies

Beat egg whites and cream of tartar at high speed in an electric mixer until the whites hold soft peaks. Continue beating and slowly add sugar. When combined, add the almond extract.

Cover a cookie sheet with parchment paper. Put the meringue into a pastry tube, and using a large tip (or by dropping spoonfuls of batter onto the sheet), shape the meringue into moons, stars, suns, or any other shapes. The cookies should stand about 1 inch tall, and not any larger than 6 inches across or they may be hard to remove without breaking.

Decorate if desired with raisins or chocolate chips.

Cook for two hours in a preheated 200° oven, or until the outside is dry and the mixture is set but not brown. Let them cool inside the oven. These store nicely if kept in an airtight container.

Meringue tips: Use superfine sugar, or pulse regular sugar in a food processor until it becomes fine. Don't beat the egg whites very much after you've added the sugar.[5]

You will need:

6 egg whites

1/2 t cream of tartar

1 1/2 C sugar

1 t almond extract, or other flavoring

raisins or chocolate chips (optional)

Chocolate Press Cookies

A cookie press, available from kitchen stores, is a cylinder with a plunger and plates that fit into one end. By pressing on the plunger, a shaped cookie is formed. Because the dough doesn't have to be chilled or rolled, making these cookies is satisfying for young children.

Melt and cool the chocolate. Cream the butter and sugar; beat in the egg and milk. Add the chocolate, and gradually blend in the flour and salt.

Fill cookie press and form cookies on lightly greased cookie sheets. Bake in a preheated 375° oven 8 to 10 minutes. Lift cookies off sheets as soon as they come out of the oven. Cool completely, then paint on icing with brushes.

Icing: Mix the first three ingredients together until smooth. Divide into small bowls and add drops of food coloring to each bowl.

You will need:

2 oz milk chocolate

1/2 C butter

1 C sugar

1 egg

2 t milk

2 C sifted flour

pinch of salt

ICING

1 C powdered sugar

1 egg white

1/2 t lemon juice

food coloring

Sun Custard

You will need:

¹/₂ C sugar

2 T water

²/₃ C sugar

6 egg yolks, beaten

2 C milk

2 egg whites, beaten stiff but not dry

1¹/₂ t flour

¹/₂ t vanilla extract

Caramelize the ¹/₂ cup of sugar: Mix with the water in pan, cover, and bring to a boil. Uncover. If crystals have formed on the sides of the pan, wash away with a wet pastry brush. Leave uncovered and boil some more. When syrup starts to turn a golden brown, swirl pan to distribute color. Pour into a quart-size glass or ceramic dish.

Combine egg yolks and remaining sugar, and beat until thick and pale yellow. Add the milk slowly, fold in the egg whites, flour, and vanilla. Pour into dish. Place dish inside a deep, oven-proof pan, then carefully fill the pan with hot water to the level of the custard in the dish. Bake in a pre-heated 325° oven for about 1¹/₂ hours. The custard is done when a knife inserted comes out clean, the custard is firm to the touch, and it has pulled slightly away from the sides.

Cool to room temperature, then chill in refrigerator. Before unmolding, run a knife around the sides.

Sun Cereal: Cream of Polenta

Cooked as a creamed cereal, this polenta has a golden color and summery taste that bring back the light for a dawn breakfast on Winter Solstice.

The proportions of this cereal are four parts milk to one part cornmeal. Allow 1 cup of milk per person. Bring the milk just to a simmer and add the cornmeal, stirring rapidly with a wire whisk to chase any lumps away. Add a pinch of salt and continue to simmer, stirring frequently, for 15 minutes. Pour out the steaming golden mixture into wide, flat bowls, thin with a little milk to your preference, pour on maple syrup, and taste the sun.

Snow Candy

Appreciate the kindness of trees. Besides exchanging our old breath for fresh new air, they clean the atmosphere, hold the ground together, and make maple syrup, too! High temperatures and hot liquids are involved, so closely supervise every stage. This makes a delightfully hard, chewy, taffy-style candy.

Combine 1 cup maple syrup (Grade B tastes better) and $1/2$ tablespoon butter together. Heat to 260°, or hard-ball stage. (A drop in cool water forms a hard ball upon contact.) Watch this carefully because at these temperatures, syrup scorches very easily. Remove from heat.

When the syrup has cooled but is still liquid, pour in a ribbon onto snow, lift, and eat. For non-snow areas, pour carefully onto a cookie sheet. Make any pattern you want.

Store the candy in a dry and tightly sealed container.

CHAPTER SEVEN

Brigit
FEBRUARY 2

BRIGIT IS THE holiday that marks the sun's growing strength. We begin to see the days grow longer, and in many places we observe the first signs of spring.

In ancient times in Ireland, Brigit was also called Imbolc or Oimelc, which means "ewe's milk," because at this time of year baby lambs were born and their mothers began to give milk. The Irish called this Spring's Beginning, and it was one of the major markings of the year. A Brigit doll would be made out of a sheaf of the last grain harvested the previous summer. Wheat or barley was bundled together so that the ears of grain made hair. The doll was dressed in white and carried in procession through the village and the fields, to protect the crops yet to be planted and bring fertility to the land.

Brigit is a time of initiation, which means beginning. We look forward to spring and summer, and start thinking about the work done in the warm time of year. We order seeds from catalogs, make plans for vacations, and make pledges for the coming year—our "new year's" resolutions.

Initiation is also the word we use to mean learning about the mysteries, the deepest insights of our tradition. An initiation is both a commitment and a test. It requires training, preparation, and the courage to face challenges. We have to leave the shelter of all that is comfortable and safe and take risks, but in the end we become more truly ourselves. Each of us comes into this world with unique gifts and special tasks to do. As we discover our gifts and do our work, we gather true power, wisdom, and understanding.

Brigit is also a time for weather magic and divination: reading Tarot cards, runes, using any of the techniques we know that can help give us a glimpse into the future. The sun is growing stronger, but in many places February is one of the coldest months. We know spring will come eventually, but we wonder how long it will take.

Weather divination survives in the tradition of Groundhog Day. If the groundhog can see its shadow when it comes out of its hole on Brigit, winter will last another six weeks. This story has its roots in ancient traditions. An old Irish custom at this time was to say this charm:

Early on Bride's morn
Shall the serpent come from the hole,
I will not harm the serpent,
Nor will the serpent harm me.[1]

There are no snakes in Ireland, but for many thousands of years, all over the world, snakes were sacred to the Goddess.

The Goddess

At this time of year, the Goddess is the teacher, the midwife, the foster mother. We know her as Brigit, the Irish Goddess of the holy well and the sacred flame. Her name can also be spelled Brigid, Bridgid, Brighde, or Bride. As the sun grows warmer, we turn our attention to those things that support life and growth.

All life depends on water. Water that comes up from the earth in springs and wells is special and precious. Since for us the Goddess is the living earth, wells and springs are her lifeblood. Because we drink from pure sources of water and feel refreshed, Brigit is also the Goddess of healing and inspiration.

Fire is energy, warmth, the spark of life itself. Fire helps us keep warm, cook our food, make the things we need to live. And when we feel inspired, we say we get all fired up.

Brigit, as a fire Goddess, was also in charge of inspiration—especially poetry. Poets were as important and respected in ancient Ireland as rock stars or football heroes are today. Both women and men were famous poets and also powerful workers of magic. A good poet could bless a field or a family. An angry poet might write a satire, which could raise blisters on an enemy's face or make someone sick!

Since fire is energy, Brigit is also known as the healer, because sickness was seen as unbalanced energy. And she is the Goddess of the forge, the place where metal is heated in fire until it is soft enough to be hammered and shaped into tools, horseshoes, and other useful things.

When the Christians took over Ireland, they found the people were so attached to Brigit that they couldn't get rid of her. So they simply called her a saint instead of a Goddess, and people went on tending her fire and worshiping at her sacred wells.

The cow was sacred to Brigit. For early people, the cow was a very magical animal, because it gives so much milk, to drink and to turn into cream and butter and cheese. The Celtic people measured their wealth in cattle, not money.

The serpent or snake was also sacred to Brigit. The snake is one of the oldest aspects of the Goddess. Snakes shed their skin and come out brand-new. They teach us about death and life. Death is like shedding a skin and becoming something new, and so is every initiation. The snake teaches us wisdom, and wisdom gives us inspiration.

The God

In Irish mythology, Brigit was the daughter of the Daghda (DYE-dah or DOW-dah), whose name means "The Good God." Although we often call the Goddess Mother Earth, we could just as well say Father Earth, for the Daghda is the God of abundance, food, and plenty. He is pictured as a giant, a big, big man who carries a big club, which stands for both life and death, for while it is shaped like the new shoots pushing out from the earth, or the rising penis that fertilizes new life, it can also hit you over the head and kill you! The Daghda reminds us that life and death are always linked.

In stories about the Daghda, he was known to eat an enormous amount. He was the keeper of the magic cauldron that was never empty. No matter how many people drank soup from it or ate what was cooked inside it, there was always more.

The Daghda is the powerful life of the earth itself that begins to reawaken under the rays of the growing sun. When the earth is respected, the land itself is like a

Way to the Well[2]

Words by Starhawk, melody: S. African trad.

We will ne-ver,— ne-ver lose our— way to the well— of her me-mo-ry,— and the po-wer— of her liv-ing— flame it will rise,— it will rise a-gain.—

magic cauldron, producing food and drink and everything we need in great abundance. But if we don't respect the earth— watch out! The giant figure of the Daghda reminds us that the earth is bigger and more powerful than we are.

As Brigit is the Goddess of poetry, the God at this time of year is also the poet whose words of power can bring healing or change the future, the guardian of secret knowledge. Fintan, who guarded the salmon swimming in the pool of wisdom, Merlin the wizard, and Taliesin the shapeshifter are some of his names.

On the Land

If you live in a cold place, don't get jealous when we tell you this, but in California, where we live, Brigit truly marks the beginning of spring. The fruit trees begin to blossom, starting with the early plums, and the bulbs begin to poke up out of the ground. Crocuses, then daffodils, narcissus, and hyacinths will soon be blooming. The heaviest of our rains usually come in January, but Brigit is still a wet time of year. By now, the ground has soaked up so much water that all the streams are flowing. Last year's dry grass is beaten down by the winter storms, and the land is green.

Brigit is the time to prune our fruit trees and plant new ones. Trees or shrubs planted now have a chance to get a good start before the dry summer.

What is the weather like where you live? Are any plants blossoming? Can you see buds swelling on the branches of the trees? Or is it still the deep cold of winter? Are you wondering how long winter will last?

The Altar

Our Brigit altar centers on a tradition we call Waters of the World. When we travel, we collect water from lakes, streams, springs, wells, oceans, and rivers. At Brigit, we make a holy well out of a big bowl and pour in all our different waters, naming where each came from and asking a blessing for the cleansing of all the waters of the world. We set this bowl on the altar, keeping aside some of the water to carry with us during the coming year, so that before we collect new water we can sprinkle a few drops as an offering. You might want to find a special bottle for your waters, but I (Starhawk) always end up using a small plastic squeeze bottle that fits easily in my pocket.

A bowl of the Waters of the World is a good centerpiece for the Brigit altar. You could add a Brigit doll, pictures or symbols of fire and water, and many candles. But be careful. Grown-ups should supervise the lighting of candles and all open flames. Never, ever leave the candles burning unless someone is watching them. (We can't emphasize this last point too strongly—we know of at least three homes that burned because of ritual candles. Not even the smallest votive candle in a glass holder is safe to leave burning unsupervised.)

Holy Water, Sacred Flame[3]

A round in four parts.

Words by Diane Baker, music by Anne Hill

Ho - ly wa - ter, sac - red flame, Bri - git we in - voke your name,

Bless my hands, my head, my heart, Source of heal - ing, song and art.

The Well and the Flame
by Starhawk

Circle round, and I'll tell you a story. . . .

Once there were two children, a sister and brother named Brigit and Alex, who lived in a land where winter brought deep snows and much cold. The children loved to play in the snow, to make huge snowmen and dig tunnels in the high banks and have snowball fights. But every year they waited eagerly for Brigit's holiday to come around, for they knew it meant that the days would be getting longer and that some-day spring would come again.

One year winter was especially harsh. Day after day, clouds filled the sky and the snow piled up on the streets. Night after night, a cold wind howled around the corners of the houses and blew smoke back down the chimneys.

Brigit and Alex grew very tired of staying in the house, for on many days the air was too cold to play outside for very long, even when they wore their warmest jackets with wool sweaters underneath and snowpants over their jeans and an extra pair of wool socks in their boots and all the hoods and scarves and mufflers they could put on. When they did go outside, they were so bundled up they could only waddle like penguins, and they were very tired of making snowmen and snow forts.

"How long will winter last?" they asked their mother.

"Only the Goddess knows," their mother said.

"Where can we find her to ask her?" Brigit asked.

Their mother smiled. "Light a candle on Brigit Eve, look into the flame with an open heart, and wait. Who knows, maybe she'll come to you. After all, you are named for her!"

So on Brigit Eve the two children lit a candle with their mother's help, placed it on the table, and looked deep into the flame. After a while, the flame seemed to grow and grow until it filled the whole room with a glorious light, and a beautiful woman appeared. Her hair was bright as living fire, her face dark as old wood, her cloak golden as a sunbeam.

"I am Brigit of the holy well and sacred flame," she said. "Why have you called me, my children?"

"Oh, Brigit, I am named after you," said the little girl. "We called you to ask a question."

"How long will winter last?" Alex asked.

"Winter will last until clean water rises in the sacred well and bright flame burns on every hearth," the Goddess said, and then she disappeared.

"What does she mean?" the two children asked. They went to their mother, but she could not say. They asked their father, but he only winked and said, "That's the trouble with the Goddess—it's hard to get a straight answer from her." So they went to bed unsatisfied.

❧

The next morning they woke up early and decided that they would go from house to house in their village and see whether or not a good, warm fire was burning on every hearth. And they would ask everyone if they knew of a sacred well.

So they did. They bundled up in their warmest jackets with wool sweaters underneath and snowpants over their jeans and an extra pair of wool socks in their boots and all the hoods and scarves and mufflers they could put on, and went outside, waddling like penguins. From house to house they went, all through their village. On every hearth, a warm fire burned, and while people were very kind to them and offered them good things to eat and warm things to drink, nobody knew about any sacred well.

At last they had visited every house in the village. The only one left was the cottage of Old Man Maddog, which lay across the frozen fields on the very edge of the forest. Nobody liked Old Man Maddog. He was crusty and mean and didn't appear to bathe very often. And he was a stranger who had come from far away. When children came near his cottage, he yelled at them and shook his big walking stick. And when all the other people in the village were working hard, Old Man Maddog simply sat on his porch, rocking in his old chair and smoking his pipe.

"Stay away from him," parents told their children. "He's a foreigner. He's lazy and dirty and probably dangerous." And the children stayed away.

But now, from the very edge of the village, Brigit and Alex could just see the roof of Old Man Maddog's house. There was no smoke coming out of his chimney.

"Surely the Goddess couldn't have meant that we were supposed to light a fire on his hearth," Alex said. "I'm afraid of him."

"He'll probably yell at us and shake his stick," Brigit agreed. "But still, I think we should go and see if he has a fire."

So they did, wading through the deep snow that covered the fields so thickly they seemed to be walking in a tunnel as high as their heads. At last they came to Old Man Maddog's house. The door was closed, and there was no smoke coming out of the chimney.

"Maybe he's not home," Brigit said. "Maybe we should just go away."

"Let's look in the window first," Alex suggested. They peered in the small glass window and saw Old Man Maddog lying on his bed. There was no fire on his hearth.

"Maybe he's sick," Brigit said. "We'd better go in and see."

The door was not locked, so they entered the room. It was cold as the cold air outside, and dirtier than any room Brigit

had ever seen. Old Man Maddog lay on his bed, moaning and shivering with fever.

"We've got to help him," Brigit said. She brought him a drink of water, while Alex took an old blanket and shook it outside and then covered the old man. They ran out into the forest and gathered fallen wood until they had a big pile. Then they lit a fire on the hearth, and soon the room began to grow warm. They found some potatoes and carrots and onions in a bag and cooked up a nice, hot soup. While it was simmering, they cleaned the house and swept the floor and washed the dishes.

Finally Old Man Maddog was warm enough to sit up and drink some soup.

"Pesky children," he said in a gruff voice. "I never did like children. Still, I suppose I ought to thank you."

"That would be polite," Brigit told him.

"But what we really want to know is whether you've ever heard of any holy well around here," Alex said.

"Holy well, jingle bell," Old Man Maddog said. "I don't hold with your holy wells. The only well I know of is that old fallen-in well in the woods, and it's all full of garbage."

Brigit and Alex looked at each other. Garbage! That didn't sound very holy. But still, it was the only well anyone had told them about all day.

"I guess we'd better go look for it," Alex said. "We'll bring in some more wood before we go, and when we get home, we'll send our mother and father to take care of you."

"Don't
do me any
favors," said
Old Man Maddog,
but they both felt he didn't
really mean it.

❧

Once again they bundled up in their warmest jackets with wool sweaters underneath and snowpants over their jeans and an extra pair of wool socks in their boots and all the hoods and scarves and mufflers they could put on, and went outside, waddling like penguins. They went deep into the forest, following the openings between the trees.

At last they came to a small clearing. In the center was a ring of stones, all tumbled down and scattered. They looked inside and saw nothing but a small puddle of frozen mud, all choked with stones and leaves and garbage.

"Could that be the holy well?" Brigit asked.

"It doesn't look much like it," Alex said. "But maybe if we clear it out a bit, we'll be able to see some water."

They began prying up the stones and pulling out big lumps of things, which turned out to be cans and bottles and old, rotting papers. Brigit took a big stick to clear away the fallen leaves. Alex took off his mittens and scooped out the mud. And soon clear water began to rise through the mud.

"We can't do much more," Alex said. "It's starting to get dark. We'll have to come back tomorrow, and bring a shovel."

"But at least we've begun," Brigit said.

"You've done well," a voice said from behind them. They turned and saw the beautiful woman with hair bright as flame and a face as dark as old wood. "You've begun the work—and that is all that anyone can do."

"Is this your holy well?" Brigit asked the Goddess.

"Yes, it is. A long time ago, the people of the village tended my well carefully, keeping it clean and dressing it with flowers in the spring. But now they have forgotten the way here, just as they have forgotten the law of kindness to strangers. Without the warmth of loving-kindness, how can the days grow warm again? And when my clear springs are choked with dirt, how can the rains of spring fall?"

"We'll remind them," Brigit promised. "We'll bring everyone out here to finish cleaning up the well."

"And we'll make sure to keep a warm fire burning on Old Man Maddog's hearth," Alex added. "Even if he isn't a very nice man."

The Goddess smiled. "Good. You have lit my fire and cleaned my well. And now I will tell you a secret. Inside the heart of every girl and boy is a holy well, full of the waters of love and joy and new ideas. That is the well you must keep clean, because it can easily be choked by hatred and greed and selfishness. And inside you also is a sacred flame, the flame of life. That is the fire you must tend and feed and keep burning, so that you grow to be strong and wise and brave. Will you do that?"

"We'll do our best," they promised.

"And now will spring come?" Brigit asked.

"Spring will come," the Goddess promised, and she winked at them. "Spring will come—as soon as winter is over."

And it did.

Let Me Find My Way to the Well[4]

Words and music by Diane Baker

Let me find my way to the well, let me find my way to the well. Let me quench my thirst with the wa-ters of the earth, Let me find my way to the well. Let me find my way to the fire, let me find my way to the fire. In Bri-git's sa-cred fire let me find my heart's de - sire, Let me find my way to the fire.

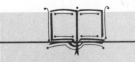

The Cauldron of Inspiration

retold by Starhawk

Brigit is not the only Goddess of poetry and inspiration. This story from Wales tells of the birth of Taliesin, who became the most respected poet of the ancient Welsh.

Circle round, and I'll tell you the story of Gwion and the cauldron of Cerridwen. . . .

The Goddess Cerridwen (KAR-id-wen) had two children, both very dear to her. Her daughter, Creirwy (cree-AIR-ree), was the most beautiful young woman in all the world. But her son, Avagddu (a-VAHG-thee), was the ugliest young man anyone had ever seen. Cerridwen worried over his future. She was afraid that nobody would like him or want to be his friend unless he had some special gift to make up for his looks. She decided to boil up a cauldron of inspiration and science for her son, so that everyone would admire him for his knowledge and brilliance and forget about his face.

The cauldron had to be kept boiling for a year and a day while she gathered the proper herbs and magical plants at the right seasons, bearing in mind the influence of the moon and the movements of the planets and the stars. So she set a blind man named Morda to tend the fire and a young boy named Gwion (GWEE-on) to stir the cauldron.

For a year they faithfully kept the cauldron boiling, day and night, whatever the weather or the changes of the moon. Morda kept the fire ablaze, and Gwion stirred, and Cerridwen gathered the magic herbs and plants. But one day, toward the very end of the year, three drops of the magic brew flew up out of the cauldron and landed on Gwion's finger. They burned his tender skin, and he put his finger in his mouth to cool it. But all the magic of the cauldron had gone into those three drops.

Suddenly the whole world changed for little Gwion. The birds were singing in the trees, and now he could understand their conversations as they gossiped. The branches of the trees whispered in the breeze, and he could understand the secrets they passed back and forth. All the world came alive and spoke to him, and all time swirled together and became one. Past and present and future were braided together like three twined strands of a rope, and he could see what was to come as clearly as he knew what had been. And one thing he knew for certain—he had better get out of there fast before Cerridwen came back, because she was going to be mad! For Cerridwen was mother of all inspiration and transformation—but she had a temper like a raging storm. Gwion turned and ran as fast as he could. Behind him, the cauldron burst into pieces, and all the remaining brew spilled into the stream.

❧

Cerridwen returned and saw the ruin of her whole year's work. She was so mad she flew into a rage and started to beat poor Morda on the head.

"Stop! Stop! It wasn't me!" he cried out. "It was little Gwion who robbed you."

"You speak truth," Cerridwen said, and ran after Gwion.

Gwion, running through the woods, saw Cerridwen chasing after him. Already he was getting tired and breathless. "What can I do? What can I do?" he cried to himself. "If only I could run like a hare, leaping and bounding along."

Instantly he was changed into a leaping hare. His weariness vanished, and he jumped and bounded so high he nearly seemed to fly. "She'll never catch me now," he exulted, but then he looked behind him. Cerridwen had changed herself into a greyhound, and she was running along the ground so fast, she would soon catch up with him.

"What can I do? What can I do?" he cried to himself. Ahead of him was a broad river. "If only I could hide beneath that water, she'd never find me there." He

leaped up into the air, and when he landed in the river, he became a fish. Quickly he swam away.

"I'm surely safe now," he told himself, but then he looked behind him. Cerridwen had changed herself into an otter, and she was swimming after him.

"What can I do? What can I do?" he cried again. "If only I had the wings of a bird, I could fly away from her." He made a mighty leap and hurled himself up on the riverbank. Instantly he became a swift bird and took wing.

Far and fast he flew, out over the sea. "At last I've escaped," he sighed, but then he looked behind him. There she was, changed into a soaring hawk. He wheeled and turned back toward the land, and she followed close behind.

"What can I do? What can I do? I'll never escape her!" For she was high above him now, and as he glanced up she folded her wings and began to drop like a stone, for the kill.

"I've got to find a place to hide!" he cried. Below him was a barn, and inside was a huge pile of wheat. Recklessly he zoomed into the barn as the hawk wheeled and dipped to follow him. He dove into the wheat pile and changed himself into a single grain of wheat.

"At last I'm safe," he thought. But Cerridwen changed herself into a big black hen. *Scratch, scratch, scratch* she went, turning over the wheat in the pile with her big black claws, testing each grain with her big red beak. At last she found the grain that was little Gwion, and she swallowed him up.

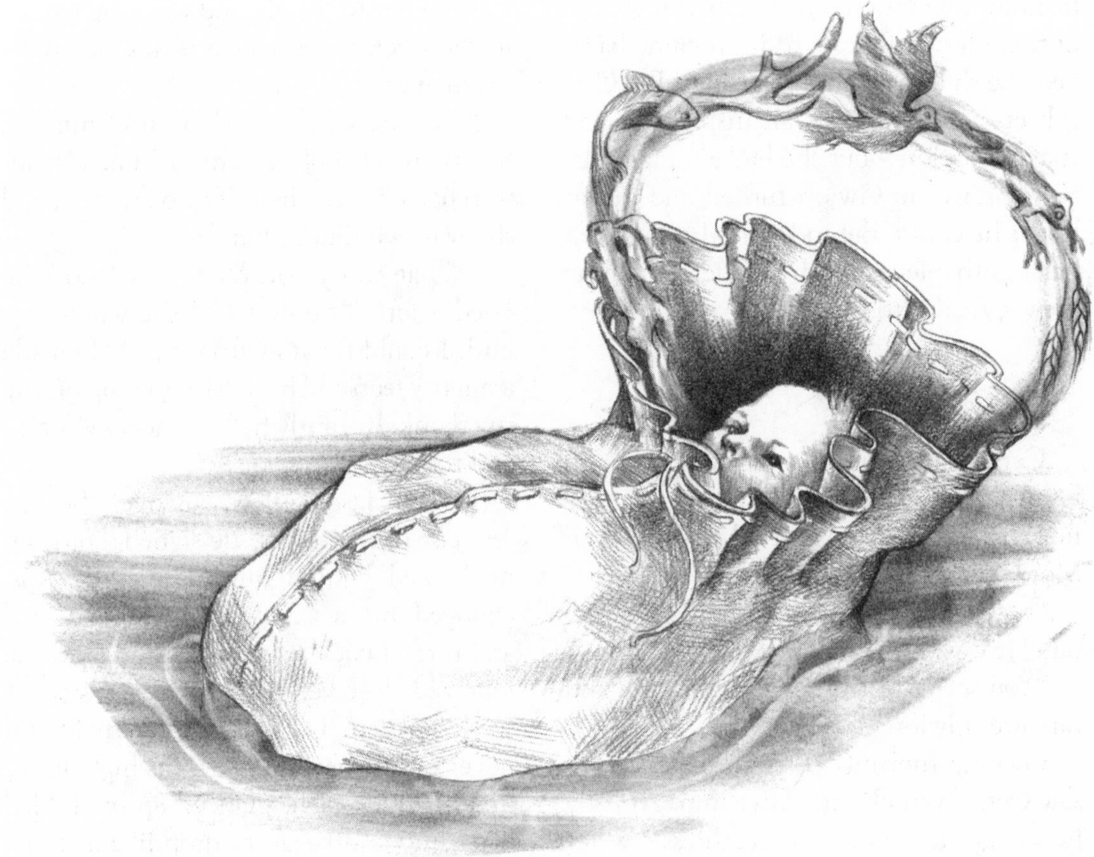

No
sooner did
she swallow little
Gwion than she felt life stirring inside her.
She changed back into the form of the
Goddess, and her womb began to swell.
Bigger and bigger and bigger she grew, until nine months later she gave birth to a
beautiful boy child with a shining brow.

Cerridwen was still angry, but now the
very person she was angry at had become
her own baby. And a beautiful baby he
was, too. She just didn't have the heart to
kill him. So she wrapped him in a leather
bag, took him down to the sea, and let the
waves
take him
away to meet his
destiny.

Now in those days there was a king in
that part of the country, named Gwyddno
(GWITH-no). He had a special fish
weir—a big fence of wicker set across the
river—that trapped the salmon as they
swam upstream. Every May Eve, many fish
were caught in that weir.

Gwyddno also had a son named Elphin.
Now, poor Elphin was the sort of person
that can never do anything quite right. If
he went out to hunt, he would trip over his
bowstring. If he went gathering berries, he

would fall into the brambles and come home all full of scratches, with an empty pail. If he went gathering mushrooms—well, those who valued their lives wouldn't dare eat the mushrooms that Elphin brought home!

Gwyddno decided to give Elphin a chance to improve his luck. He sent him down to the weir on May Eve to gather the fish that never failed to come, thinking that the sacred salmon would be a blessing for him.

But when Elphin came to the weir, there were no fish to be found. All that lay trapped in the weir was a strange, bulging leather bag.

"That's just my luck," Elphin sighed. "Every year since the beginning of time, this weir has been filled with fish, but now, because it's my turn to gather them, there's nothing there. Nothing good ever happens to me!"

He was feeling very sorry for himself as he drew the bag out and opened it up. A pearly, gleaming light shone from the bag, and he looked in and saw the forehead of a baby.

"What a radiant brow!" he exclaimed, and so the reborn Gwion was given a new name—Taliesin (TAH-lee-ehss-in), which means "shining brow." He drew the baby up and held it in his arms, and instantly felt comforted and strangely happy.

"Well, you are not a load of fish of great value, but you are something wonderful after all," Elphin said. He placed the child before him on his horse, and made her trot very gently back toward the castle. And the baby sat up and began to sing:

Dear Elphin, dry your tears,
Do not think you have no gain,
Put away your fears,
Let go of your pain.
Small as I may be,
Great gifts I bring
From the mountains, from the sea
From the rivers, I will sing.
My tongue will be your shield
My song will be the health
Of orchard, hearth, and field,
I am your luck, your wealth.

This was the first poem made by Taliesin. Elphin took the boy home to his father, and when Gwyddno asked who he was, whether human or spirit, and where he came from, he replied in another poem.

Cradled on the breast of the rolling sea,
Part of all being can I be,
I have been a frog, a chain, a crow,
A wolf, a cub, a fox, a roe.
A thrush, a martin, the antler of a deer,
A squirrel, a bull, a boar, a spear.
I have been a grain of pure white
    wheat,
I am anyone that you might meet.
Cradled on the breast of the rolling sea,
Part of all being can I be,
The seen and the unseen I can see,
All that lives can speak to me.

So Taliesin was reared in the court of Gwyddno, as the adopted son of Elphin. From that day on, Elphin's luck turned, until he was admired and respected by all. And Taliesin became the greatest poet of ancient Wales.

Health and Creativity Blessing

In her time, Brigit was treasured as the Goddess of healing and creativity. Brigit's day, which falls in February, our flu season, is a perfect time to pray for a healthy year.

Parents or other loved ones, holding candles, walk around the children in a circle, saying:

Great lady, healer, with this circle of fire bless the spark of life that burns within these children. Keep them safe and healthy in mind and body in the year ahead. Burn away any sickness that comes, let healing come quickly, all wounds heal smooth and whole. Shield them from all that could hurt, circle them with health. Blessed be.

Ask for Brigit's special attention if anyone needs it: "Lady, please help Ashley breathe freely and easily, may air's power bring her calm and vigor."

An adult holding a bowl of consecrated water, or Waters of the World, walks around the children again, sprinkling water on them lightly, saying:

Lady Brigit, Goddess of poetry, song and art, with this circle of water, bless these children's minds, let their imaginations draw from your well and flow with originality. Bless their hearts, may their compassion and love speak through their art. Bless their hands, may their craft be skillful and productive. May their work find those who treasure it. Blessed be.

Ask her to bless special creative projects: "May the girls' hard work in learning instruments make music they love."

Poetry Dinner

Here's a family tradition for Brigit Eve or some convenient night in her season. Have a poetry dinner in which each person brings a poem to read—either one she or he has written, or a particular favorite written by someone else. Let one poem lead to another.

Start with dinner. Make a big cauldron of Brigit soup (see recipe in this chapter), then let guests and family share their chosen poems. Serve Brigit's Serpents afterward (see recipe).

Brigit Fire

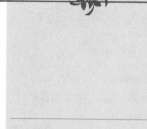

Whether we circle around a hearth, outdoor bonfire, or kindle a blaze in a cast-iron cauldron, in the season of Brigit we welcome the return of the light. Here are some suggestions for a safe and cheerful blaze.

Cauldron Fire

Any cast-iron pot can be made into a cauldron with a fire of Epsom salts and rubbing alcohol. This is a very safe blaze.

Once the cauldron is secured on a heat-proof surface, pour the Epsom salts in until the bottom is covered, approximately 1 inch deep. Pour rubbing alcohol over the salts until the alcohol is about an inch higher than salts. Hold a lighted match just above the alcohol. The liquid will light and produce a strong orange flame. The flame burns cool, unlike a wood fire, and it is difficult to burn things in.

When the flame gets low, cover to snuff out completely. Add more rubbing alcohol to the cauldron and relight carefully. The warmer the rubbing alcohol, the more quickly it ignites.

This fire recipe leaves a significant amount of sediment in the bottom of the cauldron. For this reason, it is best to dedicate a pot strictly for cauldron use.

Kindling a Fire

This holiday is a good time to teach your older children how to set a fire and kindle a blaze. Most children are eager to help lay a fire, but may be too scared to light one. Using long matches often eases their fear, and with supervision they can become quite proficient at lighting fires.

Children are great at gathering wood. A note of caution about burning found wood, however: Make sure you inspect the wood. Scrap plywood gives off toxic fumes, as does wood

You will need:

a cast-iron pot of any size

a lid that fits snugly, for putting out the fire

bricks, hot plate, or other heat-resistant material to set the cauldron on

Epsom salts

rubbing alcohol

To keep a blaze going for 45 minutes in a 5-quart cauldron, you need $1/2$ gallon of Epsom salts and approximately 4 to 6 pints of rubbing alcohol.

that has been painted or coated with urethane. Make sure the wood you are burning has not been coated with creosote. Creosote is a dark, often tarry preservative and is commonly found on wood washed up on the beach. Its fumes are toxic, and when burned, the treated wood creates a smoky, stinky blaze. Creosote is easy to identify by its smell, which resembles that of turpentine or paint thinner.

Egg Carton Fire Starters

Reuse all those old candle ends in this practical, convenient fire project.

Stuff each cardboard egg holder with sawdust or other flammable material. Melt the wax in a pot, over low to medium heat. When the wax is melted, carefully pour the wax into each depression in the egg cartons. Make sure the wax does not overflow. Let cool. After the wax has cooled down, use scissors to cut the fire starters apart from each other, leaving the hardened wax inside its cardboard shell.

To use, set one or two fire starters in your fireplace, surround with kindling and larger wood, and light. The fire starters will keep burning long enough to light even the most stubborn logs.

Fire Safety

Never leave candles lit and a blazing fire untended. It is a good idea to have a pail of water or a fire extinguisher close at hand when having a fire. If you often light fires at your home, try growing an aloe vera plant, or keep some of the pure gel on hand in the fridge, to use as first aid for burns.

Fires at the beach are popular in all seasons, and eliminate some of the risks of fires in the woods or in a meadow. Few people are aware of how to extinguish a beach fire safely, however. Covering up a beach fire with sand actually insulates the coals, keeping them burning through the night. Those hidden coals will still be red-hot in the morning, waiting for an unsuspecting person to step on them. Always douse a beach fire with water—seawater works as well as fresh water—until there are no more live coals. Wait for the steam to clear; then using a stick, turn over all the coals to make sure no smoldering coals remain.

You will need:

paraffin or beeswax (old candle stubs work great for this)

the bottom halves of cardboard egg cartons

sawdust, pine needles, scraps of cotton material, dry pinecones, or shredded paper

scissors

pot

Candle Hat

One holiday tradition in Scandinavian countries is for girls to wear garlands in their hair that hold a circle of lit candles and bless the light's return. We've adapted this candle custom to honor the returning light for Brigit. These paper hats are a simple and safe variation.

Draw an inner circle on a 9-inch paper plate, about an inch from the rim. Next draw very light lines dividing the circle into quarters. Draw four rectangular candle shapes, keeping the dividing lines as guides for the candles' centers (see illustration). The rectangles will meet in the center of the plate in a small square.

Cut out the candle shapes, preserving their connection to the ring at the rim. This connection serves as the base of the candle. Bend candles from their base to stand upright. Decorate candles with markers, crayons, and glitter. Use the discarded plate material to cut flame shapes. Color them bright flame colors, then glue or staple them to the top of the candles.

Brigit Doll

In old agricultural ceremonies a Brigit doll for the altar was made from the last harvested sheaf of grain, saved for this occasion. Wheat stalks are available from craft stores, but we prefer a simple doll that we make from the immense rosemary bushes that grow throughout northern California. Any long-needled evergreen branches, flexible and fresh, 8 to 12 inches long, work well.

Directions for branches:

Tie the cut ends of all but one branch tightly together, about $1\frac{1}{2}$ inches below the cut ends. This forms the neck, with the head above. About $2\frac{1}{2}$ inches below the first tie, tightly tie the branches together again, forming the waist. Cut the saved branch in half, and push each half in between the neck and waist, making two arms. Fluff out the spray of branches below the waist into a full skirt, or divide and tie for legs.

You will need:

10–13 branches of rosemary or evergreen, or twice as many bunches of long pine needles

twine or narrow ribbon

red holly berries, small cranberries, or small flowers

toothpicks

To crown the Brigit doll: Spear the berries or flowers with toothpicks, then insert the picks into the head. Arrange the crown to cover the branches' cut ends.

Brigit Candles

Honor Brigit with new special candles. These candles use molds made from coiled salt dough ropes so that each completely unique candle bears the spiral imprint of the coil.

Taper Candles

Make ropes by rolling salt dough clay between your hands. Each rope should be two or three feet long and ¼ to ½ inch in diameter. If younger children can't manage such lengths, have them make smaller segments that can be joined later with a little pressure and water. Dip your fingers into the bowl of water occasionally if the dough tends to crack.

Roll the paper into a 1-inch-wide cylinder and tape it shut. Around this cylinder, tape a piece of wax paper. Coat the wax paper with a thin layer of oil.

Lightly moisten a salt dough rope with water. Lay the paper cylinder on its side at one end of the rope. Roll it along the dough, wrapping the rope up the cylinder until it's six inches tall. Be sure the edges of the coiled rope always touch. To provide extra support, at intervals stick several toothpicks vertically through the coils.

Make a bottom for the mold by shaping another piece of salt dough into a ¾-inch-thick circle that's larger than the coiled tower in diameter. Moisten the bottom's surface, then carefully lift the coiled tower onto the bottom piece and press gently to make a seal.

Pull the paper cylinder out. This slides out easily, leaving the wax paper. Remove it by gently tugging on the wax paper with one hand while you support the clay coils with the other.

Inspect each part of the mold, looking for tiny cracks where melted wax could leak. Press these shut. If the coils start to sag, quickly fashion a paper cylinder around the outside of the coils and tape it closed. Trim it to the same height as the clay, so it won't get in the way when you're pouring wax. Set the mold in an empty bowl, in case wax leaks through. You are ready to pour, according to the candle-making instructions in the Tool Chest section.

Pouring the wax is thrilling. Go very slowly up each level to make sure no wax is leaking through. If a leak appears, carefully pinch it shut and pour again. Insert the wick.

The wax will harden within an hour, long before the clay dries. To unmold, just unwind the clay. If some sticks, soak the candle in cool water and then gently rinse off the clay. The candles have a wonderfully craggy spiral looping from bottom to top, and burn with a lovely strong flame.

Beehive Candles

You can also make beehive candles with great success by coiling ropes of salt dough in a small, deep bowl. A rice bowl is the perfect size. It's easiest to start with making a spiral, about 3 inches across, outside the bowl, then transferring this into the bottom of the bowl. Next, coil the rope inside the bowl until you reach the top.

The candle is burned with the dome side up, so the wick has to extend through the wax at the bottom of the bowl. When the wax is firm enough to insert the wick, use a slightly larger straw than usual, and push it firmly through the candle, into the dough beneath, straight to the bottom of the bowl.

The candle unmolds easily: Lift candle and mold from the bowl and uncoil the mold.

Brigit Candleholder

To echo the Goddess's symbol of the serpent, make this candleholder, which resembles a coiled snake. Follow directions for making a mold for taper candles, with the following differences:

1. Size your holder by wrapping a paper cylinder around whatever candle you intend to use. Remove candle before proceeding further.

2. Dough ropes should be about $1/2$ inch wide and a foot long. If candleholder is taller than 4 inches, use toothpicks for extra support.

3. Make the bottom by coiling a rope into a small circle.

4. After the paper cylinder has been removed, use your candle to gently test if the open end of the candleholder is large enough to accommodate the candle. If it's too small, delicately press the opening wider. If it's too large, fill in with bits of salt dough.

5. Bake the holder as directed in the Tool Chest section. Turn after the first hour to be sure it does not stick to the pan.

6. Cool completely after baking. Then paint with snaky patterns, finishing with eyes on the end of the top coil.

Braided Brigit Bread

The warm color and flavor of this bread come from the tomato paste and herbs.

Dissolve the yeast in warm water sprinkled with the pinch of sugar. Combine the milk, egg, sugar, oil, salt, garlic, and herbs in a large bowl. In a measuring cup, place the tomato paste and add water until it reaches the $\frac{1}{2}$-cup point. Pour into the milk mixture and stir well. Add the yeast mixture.

Begin adding flour, 1 cup at a time, until the dough can no longer be stirred. Turn out onto a floured board and knead, continuing to add flour to keep the dough barely dry. This is a loose and soft dough, so be careful how much flour you add. Don't let it get stiff. Place the dough in an oiled bowl and turn it over to coat both sides. Let it rise until doubled, about 45 minutes to an hour.

Punch down. Cut the dough in half, divide each half into thirds, then roll into thick coils. Braid three coils into a loaf and pinch the ends together. Set on a lightly oiled baking sheet. Repeat with the other three coils. When the loaves have doubled in size, paint all surfaces with the egg yolk and bake for 35 minutes in a preheated 375° oven, or until the internal temperature measures 200°.

You will need:

2 T yeast

$\frac{1}{2}$ C warm water

pinch of sugar

1 C milk

1 egg

$\frac{1}{4}$ C sugar

$\frac{1}{4}$ C vegetable oil

1 t salt

1 clove garlic, passed through garlic press

$\frac{1}{2}$ t each dried oregano, thyme, and basil

4 T tomato paste

water

5–6 C unbleached white flour

1 egg yolk, beaten

Brigit Soup

We use the color red to honor the returning light, and the promise of warmth to come. This unfussy pot of soup needs only a few minutes of chopping to prepare. All the ingredients are either red, orange, or yellow, for the colors of fire that warm our eyes, hearts, and stomachs.

   In a large pot, heat the oil and add the onion, garlic, carrot, and red pepper until they are soft. Add the rest of the ingredients, except the lemon juice, salt, and pepper. Bring to a boil, then reduce to a simmer, skimming any brown foam that may have formed. Cover and simmer for 1½ hours. Squeeze in the lemon juice and season to taste with the salt and pepper.

You will need:

1½ t olive oil

1 medium red onion, chopped fine

2 garlic cloves, minced

1 carrot, finely chopped or grated

½ to ¾ C finely chopped red pepper

6 C broth (beef or chicken, or vegetable for a meatless soup)

2 C (¾ lb) red lentils or yellow split peas

1 16-oz can of chopped tomatoes, juice included

½ t cumin

¼ t ground coriander

1 T fresh lemon juice

salt and freshly ground black pepper

Brigit's Serpent:
A Baking Meditation

You will need:

4 C flour

3 T sugar

1 t salt

1 T double-acting baking powder

4 T butter or margarine at room temperature

1½ C milk (or soy milk)

jam

dried fruit (cranberries, apricots, raisins, currants, or cherries)

Set aside six raisins or cranberries. Chop the remaining dried fruit until you have a cup and place it in a bowl. Cover it with water and let it soak.

Put the flour, sugar, salt, and baking powder into a sifter. As you sift them together, say thank you for the different kinds of grains and foods that grow out of the earth.

Cut the butter into small pieces, add to dry ingredients and mix, using your fingers. Say thank you for any of the extra good things in your life—the things that you don't need but that make life more fun or richer, like butter on bread. The butter should end up so well mixed in that you can hardly see it, the flour just looks a bit grainier than before.

Make a well in the center of the mixture. Think about the well you have inside you, and what you need right now to fill it up. Pour the milk into the well, remembering that the Goddess always does fill our well of love and joy and ideas, and thanking her. Mix everything together, kneading it with your hands just enough to make it stick together. Don't knead it too much or it will get tough.

Divide the dough into three parts. On a floured pastry board, roll and pull one section of the dough until it makes a long, thin cylinder. Then roll it lengthwise with a floured rolling pin until it is even longer and thinner. If you don't have room on the board, use the table. The dough should end up about ¼ inch thick or slightly less.

Spread jam on the dough, not quite to the edge. Make a line of the dried fruit all along the jam-covered dough. Think about what in your life you would like to see bear fruit, what poems you'd like to write, what pictures you'd like to paint, what creative things you'd like to do, and ask Brigit's blessing. Fold the dough up and over the fruit, so that you make a long tube. Pinch the seams shut.

Grease and oil a cookie sheet. Place the tube on the cookie sheet and form it into a loose, open spiral. Form one end into a triangular serpent's head and place raisins or cranberries for eyes.

Repeat with the other two sections of dough.

Bake at 450° for 20 to 25 minutes. Baking temperature is important. If your oven is not reliable, take special care.

Before serving, say: *Brigit, we offer you this serpent, made of grain and milk, with thanks for the food that feeds our bodies, the fire that feeds our spirit, and the waters of healing.*

Break off pieces and feed each other, saying: *May Brigit's serpent bring you inspiration.*

Bananas à la Brigit

Brigit, being a fire holiday, presents a fine opportunity to bring some drama to our celebration meal. This dish, known commonly as Bananas Foster, tempers the fireworks with vanilla ice cream. The flames burn away the alcohol.

Cut bananas in half crosswise, then again lengthwise. Melt the butter in a skillet, add the sugar, and let it bubble briefly. Add the bananas and cook over a low heat until lightly browned, about five minutes. Warm the liquor in a small pan, gently pour it over the bananas in the skillet, then light it with a match, being sure your arm is out of the way. The alcohol flares up dramatically.

Let the flame burn out, then spoon over scoops of ice cream. Serves 4.

You will need:

2 bananas

2 T butter

4 T brown sugar

1 oz rum or brandy

ice cream

Popcorn

On Brigit, we reflect on transformation, how the light has gradually grown until the mornings seem brighter, how we take ideas and turn them into music and art, how our body heals itself so neatly.

One of the easiest and most fun symbols of transformation is popcorn. For a quick Brigit snack, make popcorn the old-fashioned way, in a skillet with hot oil, and dance in the kitchen to the rhythm of the popping.

CHAPTER EIGHT

Eostar/Spring Equinox
MARCH 20, 21, or 22

EOSTAR, THE SPRING Equinox, takes its name from the Goddess Eostar, Eostre, or Ostara, a Germanic Goddess of fertility and spring. We celebrate this festival at the time when day and night are equal in length. The balance of the year has shifted—winter is on the wane and spring officially begins.

Eostar is a joyful holiday, centered around symbols of rebirth and growth: eggs, seeds, baby animals. But Eostar also has a deeper meaning. Because this is the time of balance between dark and light, it is also the time when we examine all kinds of balance in our lives—in particular, the balance between life and death. Birth is a time when the gates between the worlds are open. The seeds that were buried in the ground return as new shoots. Bulbs sprout and flower. And the dead return from the Otherworld as new beings.

Except in very cold climates, the Equinox begins the season of planting. We prepare the ground and sow the seeds—if only in pots on our windowsills to be planted outdoors when the ground warms up.

At the Winter Solstice, the sun is reborn; at Eostar, the earth is reborn. All life awakens as the days grow longer.

The Goddess

Eostar is the Goddess of dawn and new beginnings. Her name is similar to the word for the Christian Easter, because that holiday took its name from the ancient Pagan Goddess of Spring and rebirth. Another name in the same family is Ishtar, the Babylonian Goddess of the morning and evening stars. And let's not forget Esther, the Jewish queen whose story of courage is celebrated at the spring festival of Purim.

Eostar's sacred animal is the rabbit or hare. Rabbits have babies in the spring, so they have come to represent fertility and abundance. Hares, which are bigger and wilder than rabbits, have long been identified with magic, the spring, and the mysteries. Hares are associated with the moon—just take a good look the next time the moon is full, and you will see the rabbit in the moon. Even Christian tradition has not lost the symbolism of the magic hare and the spring—think of the

Easter bunny bringing us eggs decorated with all the colors of the flowers.

In some parts of Germany and Austria, the old Pagan traditions lingered on as Easter customs. A child dressed in a cape and rabbit ears would be sent out on Easter morning to visit her grandmother or another older woman. The child would carry a basket of colored eggs on her back. She would give the first egg to her grandmother. Then all the other children would chase her as she gave away the eggs, sometimes doling them out one at a time, sometimes dumping them in a big pile. When all the eggs were gone, everyone would eat a special breakfast of yet more eggs from a platter-shaped cake baked for the occasion.

The other Goddess we associate with the Spring Equinox is Kore or Persephone, daughter of Demeter, the Greek Goddess of grain and growing things. In the spring, Persephone comes back from the Underworld to be reunited with her mother. A part of the Goddess that has been sleeping all winter reawakens with the warming ground of spring. She who has been mother, midwife, and teacher throughout the winter now welcomes back her own daughter-self, the Maiden of Spring. At this time of balance, the Goddess is Mother and Daughter both.

The God

The God of Spring is the young God, playful and joyful, the trickster. He is the spirit of everything that is joyful, light, and changeable. Born at Winter Solstice, nurtured at

Brigit, now he's like a young and mischievous child, still wild and new. He is raw, creative energy that has not yet been harnessed, tamed, civilized. He sees with clear eyes and does not hesitate to announce that the emperor is naked. He deflates the pompous and laughs at self-importance.

The trickster is an important spirit power in many earth-based cultures. To many of the Native American tribes, he is Coyote. To the First Nations of the Northwest Coast, he is Raven, who creates the world. In parts of West Africa, he is Elegba, the small child-God who as a point of light constantly runs circles around the universe. To African-Americans, he is Brer Rabbit, who tricks his way out of trouble.

In European earth-based traditions, he is the Fool of the Tarot, who leaps blithely off a cliff as he follows a butterfly, yet always lands on his feet, because he takes himself lightly. He is spirit taking the plunge into matter, idea manifesting as form. And he is Robin Goodfellow, shapeshifter and wood sprite, child of the Faery King. He comes to us in the spring when all of nature is shifting and changing: seeds poking out sprouts, butterflies emerging from cocoons, tadpoles growing legs and turning into frogs.

We celebrate him on the Spring Equinox, but of course, his proper holiday comes shortly after, on April Fool's Day. In his honor, we play tricks on one another.

The Altar

The altar for spring includes—what else?—images of rabbits and birds, eggs of all sorts, nests, flowers, and living plants.

If you like to keep your altar up for a long time, blow your eggs after you've colored them. (See Activities section in this chapter.)

Take a small branch from a tree and hang blown eggs from it.

Start some seeds, to be planted out in the garden, and let your seed trays become the basis for your altar. Water them every day, talk to them, and watch them grow.

On the Land

Where we live, spring is fully here by the end of March. Wildflowers are beginning to bloom, and daffodils make bright splashes of color along the roadsides. The rains are beginning to taper off, but they still come often enough to keep the hills emerald green. The fruit trees are covered with blossoms, and the early rhododendrons are fragrant and colorful. Native irises bloom in shades of purple, blue, and white, and the wild lilacs are beginning to perfume the air. The weather is warm enough to plant peas, lettuce, and potatoes in the garden. It feels warm enough to plant anything. But sometimes we still get tricked by cold nights and even frost.

I think this is the most beautiful time of year for us, with the hills still green and fresh, the weather warm, and everything blossoming.

What is coming into bloom where you live? Has the snow melted yet? Have the first crocuses appeared? What is your favorite spring flower?

The Story of Demeter and Persephone[1]
retold by Starhawk

Circle round, and I'll tell you a very ancient story. . . .

On a beautiful day in spring, Kore (KOR-ray), daughter of Demeter, was gathering flowers with her maidens in a green meadow. The earth was green with new growth and lush with bright crocuses, sweet narcissus, and fragrant hyacinths. The young women sang as they picked the flowers and danced on the new grass.

In a far corner of the meadow, Kore noticed a golden gleam. She left her maidens and went to investigate. There grew a golden flower, more beautiful than any she had ever seen before. The flower's perfume made Kore feel joyful and carefree and just the tiniest bit afraid. She wanted to pick the flower and keep it for her very own. And even though she knew that you should never pick a flower that is the only one of its kind, she reached out her hand and plucked the blossom.

Instantly she heard a great roaring and cracking sound, and the earth shook under her. She fell to the ground. When the air grew still, she looked up and saw that a deep chasm had opened just in front of her, like a tunnel leading into the heart of the earth.

Kore was a very curious maiden. She had lived all her life on the surface of the beautiful earth, loved and protected by her mother, Demeter, who was the Goddess of all green and growing things. Her life was filled with pleasure and abundance.

But she had always secretly wondered what lay underneath the bright surface of the world. Where did the spring flowers come from when they pushed their way up from below? If they were so bright and lovely when they emerged, what wonders might lie in the place where they originated?

"Here's an opening that leads beneath the earth," she said to herself. "Now I can explore the realms below. Oh, maybe I shouldn't go down. I know my mother wouldn't like it. But it was as wide as a room, then it was as narrow as a hallway. Kore could not see very much, as the stone walls blocked most of the light from behind. But somehow the gloom made her even more curious.

"I should turn around," she said to herself. "My mother will be worried about me. But I think I'll go on, just a little bit farther."

So she went on, and the passage became narrower and narrower. Soon she had to stoop down and bend her head to avoid the low roof of the tunnel. Then she had to drop to her knees and crawl. All the light disappeared, and she had to feel her way through the dark.

"I should go back," she told herself. "This could be dangerous, and my mother will be so worried if I don't come home! But if I just go on a little farther, I might come upon something wonderful."

So she continued on, until she was lying on her belly, squirming along the ground. Suddenly she realized that the

I will, just a little way, just to see what's there."

She left her maidens and the bright flowers above and entered the cavern. At first the way was wide. Light came from the opening behind her, and she could see the beautiful colors and interesting shapes of the stone.

But the chasm began to narrow. At first

passage had become so narrow and tight that there was no room for her to turn around. She tried to push herself backward, but her hips stuck. For the first time she felt afraid.

"Oh, no!" she said to herself. "Now I've done it! How will I get out of here? My poor mother will be so worried! I can't go back, so I'll have to go forward and hope I come to a wider place where I can turn around!"

But the passage continued to narrow, until she was fighting to squeeze through the crack in the rocks.

"Stupid me!" Kore said to herself. "Why did I ever come here? Why did I leave the bright meadows and the beautiful flowers? Now I might never see my mother's face again, or dance on the new green grass."

At that moment the earth gave way beneath her, and she fell, tumbling and turning over and over, down and down until she felt like she was flying through the dark.

"I'll be smashed to pieces!" she cried. "Oh, Mother, why did I ever leave you?"

But she landed as softly as a feather floats to earth, in the heart of the Underworld.

❧

All day long, Demeter was waiting for the return of her daughter. While the bright sun was high in the sky, she didn't worry, but went happily about her tasks of helping the grain to grow and the trees to set fruit. But as the sun dipped into the west, she felt a chill in her heart. When evening fell, Kore's companions came running back from the field.

"Demeter, Demeter, Kore is lost!" they cried. "The earth shook and opened up, and when we looked back, Kore was gone. We can't find her anywhere!"

"Kore!" Demeter let out a heartrending cry. "My dear, only daughter! Kore, where are you?"

Nobody could tell her where Kore had gone.

"I'll search for her!" Demeter vowed. "I won't rest until I find my daughter!"

And so she began to search. Through the fields and the meadows, under the tall trees of the woodlands and along the rocky coasts of the sea, she wandered.

"Have you seen my daughter?" she asked every person she met. "Kore, the bright flower-maiden of spring, have you seen her?" But no one knew where Kore had gone.

Farther and farther Demeter wandered. From the hillsides of Greece she crossed the sea to the islands, climbing steep mountains and following the banks of streams. But no one in the islands knew where Kore had gone.

Demeter grew sadder and sadder. She couldn't eat or sleep, and she began to grow pale and haggard. She made her way to the mainland of Europe, following the great rivers through the dense forests and hidden valleys, but nobody could tell her where Kore had gone.

At last she wandered back to her homeland. She came to rest outside the gates of the town called Eleusis, in the middle of a broad plain that was the most fertile land in all of Greece. She sat beside the well, covered her head with her cloak, and mourned. She cried until she felt completely empty. Then she got mad.

"I am the Goddess Demeter!" she cried. "I shouldn't have to suffer like this! I am the one who makes all things grow, who gives the gifts of food and life. No more! Until Kore is returned to me, there will be no more growth! No food, no life; no seeds will sprout, no fruit will set, no grain will ripen, no young things will be born! Nothing, until the whole world is as dead and empty as I feel!"

And so the gardens died, the grapes withered on the vine, and the fields were parched and empty. The people went hungry, and there was no joy anywhere.

In the Underworld, all was shadowy and dim. Kore wandered and wandered through wide halls of stone. The spirits of the dead surrounded her like twittering ghosts.

"Help us, help us," they hissed and whispered. "We are so cold, so gray, so lonely. You are full of life and color and the memory of the bright sun."

"How can I help you?" Kore asked. "I am lost myself. Oh, why did I ever come down here? I want to go home, to the bright meadow and the flowers. I want to see my mother's face!"

"Stay with us, come close to us," the ghosts pleaded. They frightened Kore, and she ran from them, through the twisting passageways of the Underworld.

At last she came to the largest hall, a great underground cavern. In the center, on a huge, black throne, sat a God. He was dark and handsome, dressed all in black, and Kore knew instantly who he must be.

"Hades!" she greeted him. "Lord of the Underworld! I am your cousin Kore, the Maiden of Spring. Once this realm belonged to my grandmother Hecate. You took it from her, and now you must help me get back to the living world of sunlight and flowers."

"Kore," Hades greeted her. As soon as he said her name he fell in love with her. In that realm of gray shadows, she was like a golden gleam of spring sun, like a rare flower that scented the air. He wanted nothing more than to take her and keep her forever as his very own.

"My dear cousin," Hades said, "I am sorry to have to tell you that no one ever returns from this realm. You will have to remain here. But since you are a Goddess, I will happily make you my bride, and together we will rule the land of the dead."

"But I don't want to be your bride!" Kore protested. "I want to go home to my mother."

"Come sit here beside me," Hades said. She noticed a second dark throne next to his. "Rest from your wanderings, and have some food and drink. You'll feel better."

"I want to go home," Kore said, but she was very tired. So she sat on the throne next to Hades.

"Don't be sad," Hades said. "The Underworld is a place of great riches. All the gold and jewels and precious stones belong to us. We are wealthy."

"I don't care about gold and jewels,"

Kore said. "I want my mother! I want flowers and fruit and living, growing things." She was so sad, she couldn't eat or drink.

❧

Back on earth, the harvests had failed. Demeter still sat grieving beside the well. She was so shriveled and withered that no one recognized her as a Goddess. To the people of Eleusis, she appeared to be just an old beggar woman. Still, they took pity on her, and tried their best to cheer her up. They brought her a soothing drink of mint and barley water, but still she mourned. Baubo, the clown Goddess, came and told her jokes, but she did not smile. The Queen of Eleusis herself invited Demeter to her home. The Goddess was not comforted, but she did appreciate the kindness of the people of Eleusis. Their city became the site of her temple, and their fields were ever the most fertile in Greece. And so, if you ever meet an old beggar woman, be kind to her. Remember, she may be the Goddess in disguise!

Since there was no food to harvest, famine covered the land. Everywhere, people starved. At last even the Goddesses and Gods up on Mount Olympus began to feel hungry. No one was feeding them with sacrifices. No one was making offerings.

"This can't go on," Zeus the Thunder God said at last. "We must get Demeter back on the job. Can't anyone reason with her?"

"Until Kore is returned to her, she won't make fertility for the land or the people," said Hecate, the old Goddess who was Kore's grandmother. "Demeter can be very stubborn when she's angry. I think you'd better help her if you want to eat again."

"Well, where is Kore?" Zeus asked. "Didn't anyone see where she went? She can't just have disappeared."

"That's exactly what she did," said Helios, the Sun God. "I saw. I see everything. She went down to the Underworld, and now Hades wants to make her his queen."

"The Underworld! That's a serious matter," Zeus said. "No one returns from the land of the dead."

"Then the people will starve and the earth will die," said Hecate. "And even we, the Goddesses and Gods, will go hungry."

"Perhaps we could make an exception in this case," Zeus said. "As long as Kore hasn't eaten any food down there, we can let her come back."

❧

"Please, eat something," Hades begged Kore. She had grown sad and pale, yet to him she seemed even more beautiful, like a silver pearl gleaming in the dark.

"I'm not hungry," Kore said. "I want to go home."

Hades begged her to eat, and tried to cheer her by showing her all the beauties of the Underworld: the caverns of crystal and the glowing, jeweled halls, the underground rivers and vast lakes, the streams of molten golden lava. He was so kind, so attentive, so worried about her that she actually began to feel somewhat fond of him. Still, she wanted more than anything to go home.

"Please eat," Hades urged her. "You are growing so thin, it hurts me to watch you suffer."

He held out to her a handful of the seeds of a pomegranate. They were red as rubies, a brightness among the shadows. They appealed to her.

"After all, I can't go back home," she told herself. "I might as well enjoy what is here."

She reached out her hand and took the seeds. Popping them into her mouth, she sucked the sweet, tart juice.

Instantly everything changed. The shadows came alive. They were the ghost memories of all that had ever taken place above, but they were also the images of what had not yet been, rich with all the possibilities of change and growth. The dead and the unborn danced together like colors in a kaleidoscope, and from their movement new life would be born.

Suddenly Kore was filled with a joy and power she had never known before. She plucked two flaming torches from the wall of the cavern and began to dance. She whirled and spun and leaped, playing with fire, dancing the way from death to rebirth and back again. The dead followed her, and as they spiraled together, women in the upper world began to feel new life stirring in their wombs.

"This is where the seeds come from!" she proclaimed. "This is the wonderful place where flowers are born. And I am its Queen, Queen of fire. I am no longer just

little Kore, Demeter's daughter. I am myself, Persephone, Queen of the Dead."

❧

"She has tasted the food of the dead," Zeus said. "Now what do we do?"

"She has changed," Hecate said. "No longer is she the sweet young maiden Demeter grieves for. Now she is a Queen in her own realm. She can never again belong wholly to the upper world, but she cannot belong completely to the Underworld, either. She must be a bridge between them, showing the dead the way to rebirth and reminding the living of life's end so they remember to be fully alive."

"For every seed she has eaten, she must spend one month each year in the Underworld," Zeus agreed. "But in the spring, she can return to the upper world with the new shoots that rise from the bare ground, and bring life and hope and rejoicing to her mother."

"And so for part of each year the earth will be bare and brown and support no life," Hecate agreed. "But in the spring, when Persephone returns, all of nature will rejoice."

And so Persephone rose from the Underworld, and Demeter greeted her with great joy. They danced together on the new grass, and everywhere their feet touched, spring flowers bloomed. And so each year when Persephone returns, life blossoms everywhere. But when she descends, Demeter covers her head with her cloak. Leaves fall, the harvest is gathered in, and life rests until Kore returns once more. ❧

Persephone Song[2]

Words and music by Anne Hill

Per - se - pho - ne, Per - se - pho - ne,
De - me - ter,_____ De - me - ter,

Mai - den of the Spring - time. Now's the day, you
wait - ing all the Win - ter, cloaks the earth_____

know the way to climb back toward the sun - shine.
all in green, her daugh - ter's come to greet her.

Day and Night[3]

Words by Diane Baker, music by Aaron J. Feldman

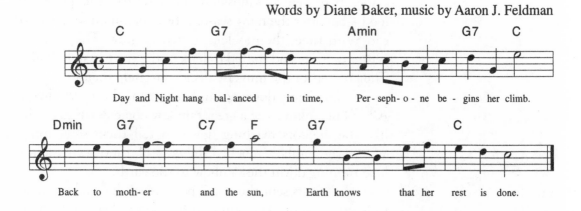

Day and Night hang bal- anced in time, Per - seph - o - ne be - gins her climb.

Back to moth- er and the sun, Earth knows that her rest is done.

The Rainbow and the Antelope[4]
by Charles Dabo as told to Starhawk

Lebon, they say—enter the circle of the story. . . .

Circle round, and I'll tell you a story from the Ashanti peo-ple of Africa. . . .

Two proud spirits, female and male, came together to cre-ate the universe. Nyama and Nyakpon were their names. When they had created the vast world, they took a visible form so they could be seen and praised. Nyama became the moon, Nyakpon the sun. Between them, they provided all that the world would need: dark and light, night and day, so that on earth all life could grow.

It is said that when Nyama and Nyakpon came together, rain fell, wet the earth, and from there, life started blooming. Humankind was created then, and started enjoying all the goodness found on earth.

As everything created started to grow and multiply, so did humankind. Human beings noticed that there were two sea-sons: a rainy season and a dry season. When the rainy season came, there were all kinds of fruits, water to drink, plenty of food—but after the rainy season, they couldn't find much to eat. With time, the problem started to grow. They got to-gether one day and started to look at the sky to call for help. The creators of the universe decided to help them.

The rain came down again, but it came down very light. All of humankind saw a great rainbow come down to earth, like the creators reaching down to tell them something. Where the rainbow touched the ground, they saw an ante-lope running down the rainbow to the earth.

The creators sent the antelope to teach humankind how to learn to plant. The antelope has pointy legs, and where the antelope runs, it makes holes. It ran all over the earth and showed human beings how to put the grain in the little holes. Then the antelope ran up to the sky and the rain came down and the plants started to grow. The plant that grew then was millet. The people understood that they must plant the grain in the ground in the rainy season and let it grow so

that they would have food during the dry season. The ante-lope taught us how to feed ourselves, and so all over Africa the antelope is honored and the life-giving rain is sacred.

Egg Hunt

We were getting ready for our Easter egg hunt one day, my son and daughter and I (Anne), dyeing eggs and chatting around our large kitchen counter. Feeling slightly guilty for holding our egg hunt on Easter rather than the Spring Equinox that year, I asked them whether they saw any ways that we could make our traditional "Easter" customs more Pagan.

My son's immediate response was, "Why bother?" Wasn't having an egg hunt during the height of spring celebration enough? And what was so Christian about dyeing eggs, hunt-ing for them in the tall grass, and eating the heads off choco-late bunnies?

I had to admit the whole thing was pretty Pagan, but that didn't stop my search for ways to bring Goddess tradition more clearly into our celebration. We know that rabbits were sacred to Eostar, and that the custom of dyeing eggs is wide-spread in European-based branches of Goddess tradition. Only a little imagination was needed to come up with a few additions to our family customs that would not thwart my son's desire to do something, for once, just for the heck of it. As to when to have your egg hunt, know that all the days be-tween Brigit and Beltane are the realm of Spring, and that celebrating is appropriate whenever you can fit it in.

Eostar Altar

My children would absolutely revolt if they did not find chocolate bunnies hidden somewhere in the garden on Easter/Equinox. But not leaving one for the Goddess doesn't seem fair. So I make an altar for Eostar in our garden.

Hide the eggs early in the morning (the dawn is sacred to Eostar) and find a special hiding place to hold all the choco-late bunnies. Next to this hiding place, create an altar, surround it with greenery, and place one chocolate bunny on the altar. This bunny, the Lucky Rabbit of Spring, is for the Goddess, and in exchange for taking one of the bunnies she gives them, the children leave one of their found eggs.

The Egg Hunt

If the weather (and neighborhood) permits, hide the eggs outside in an open space or public park, making it a potluck picnic for the children and families you know. To cast the circle for this ritual, first give each child a handful of wild-flower seeds or birdseed, then walk with your children around the perimeter of your egg-hunt site. As you all turn to the east, have them cast a portion of their seed to the winds while you say: *Welcome, powers of the east! Bright dawn of spring, we welcome you! Take our gifts of seed and grain, and give us clear sight for the celebration ahead! Blessed be the east!*

To the south, scatter more seed and say, *Welcome, powers of the south! Bright blaze of the sun at the sky's midpoint, take our gifts! We give thanks for your fire, and for the heat within us that helps us grow! Blessed be the south!*

To the west, again scatter seed, saying, *Welcome, powers of the west! Beauty of the twilight, mystery of the setting sun, we call you! Accept our gifts, help us greet each other in love and generosity on this day of abundance! Blessed be the west!*

And to the north, scattering the last of the seed, say, *Welcome, powers of the north! Strength of bone, power of muscle, we welcome you! Please take these seeds, help them find a place to grow or a hungry mouth to feed! Be with us as we search for the treasures of the earth! Blessed be the north!*

Call in the Lucky Rabbit of Spring: *Oh, Lucky Rabbit of Spring, your gifts are all around us. We catch glimpses of you through the waving grasses, we see you bounding through the meadows, always just out of reach. We ask you to reveal your blessings to us now, to help us on our search for spring's treasure in this garden. May we all get enough and not too much; may we share what we have with each other; may we remember the abundance and generosity of the Mother, in this season and all others. Blessed be.*

Begin the egg hunt, but if the children's eagerness permits, you may want to more formally call in Eostar as Goddess and the Fool or Trickster as God.

If you have set up a hidden altar to Eostar in the grasses, make sure you are close by when the first child discovers the secret stash of goodies. Let them know that they have come upon Eostar's special lair, and to take what the Goddess has for them, they must place one of their eggs on her altar as thanks. Any children who have not found eggs yet can return with one for the altar later. As they place their egg in the grass, they whisper one thing they would like to see brought to birth this year. The point is not only to have fun, but also to instill the practice of giving thanks for what we receive.

When all the hidden treasures have been found, and/or when the children run out of steam, it is time to close the circle. Thank the God and Goddess, and Eostar's lucky rabbit. Have the children raise their full baskets in each direction in turn, saying these simple parting words: *Powers of the east* [south/west/north], *thank you for your help, thank you for your gifts in abundance! Go if you must, but stay if you will. Hail and farewell!* Close the circle as it was opened, and have a cup of tea while the children enjoy their treats!

Eggs

Eggs are possibly our oldest symbol of birth and renewal, reminders of the incredible persistence and variety of life. Nature's elegantly packaged miracles, they never lose their symbolism of new beginnings.

Although coloring eggs is one of the great pleasures of childhood (and adulthood, too), what to do with all the eggs we color? Traditional hard-boiled eggs get tiresome showing up in lunch boxes and sandwiches for weeks. Besides, most children don't want their beautiful eggs unsentimentally cracked and eaten.

My (Diane's) solution is to dye uncooked eggs, then blow out the insides and save the shells. These are show eggs and very breakable, and not suited for hiding or piling in baskets for the egg hunt.

Dyeing Eggs

We like using natural dyes. They appeal to the recycling urges of children. We like their gentle colors and the game of kitchen chemistry. Natural dyes take some preparation beforehand, so plan ahead.

Chop up materials finely until you have about 1 cup of each material. Boil each separately with an equal amount of water for about 20 minutes. Strain and add two tablespoons of vinegar per cup of dye. Immerse the eggs in the dye until they turn the hue you like. A cup of hot water with food coloring plus two tablespoons of vinegar also makes a simple egg dye.

Hollowing Out Eggs

The old-fashioned way to hollow out eggs is to blow out the yolk and white. First pierce both ends with a small knife or pin. Make the hole very gently and slowly. Sometimes chipping lightly works best.

Hold the egg over a bowl, place your lips over one hole, and blow hard. Eventually the insides will be forced out the other end. The thick white often clogs the opening; blow harder or longer. If the blowing becomes truly difficult, enlarge the exit hole a bit.

After removing the yolk and white, rinse the insides. Pour a little water into the hole, shake it around, and then blow it out.

Some craft and toy stores sell cunning little pumps with handy egg hole punchers. The device can be operated by small children with supervision, and sells for about six dollars.

Egg Mobile

Find a place from which to suspend the mobile in progress, like a broomstick laid across the backs of two chairs.

Cut the pipe cleaners into 1-inch pieces. Tie a string tightly around the middle of one piece, leaving enough tail to use for hanging later. Slip the pipe cleaner into the egg, then gently pull on the string. The pipe cleaner will press against the hole, but won't come out.

You will need:

yellow onion skins for yellow

beets for pink

blueberries for pale blue

blackberries for pale violet

spinach, kale, parsley, red onion skins for pale green

You will need:

pipe cleaners

thread or light string

sticks, dowels, or branches, 1 foot in length

Tie a string around the middle of the longest stick or dowel and tie the other end of the string to the broom handle. Hang an egg on each end of the stick. Use loose knots so that you can shift eggs around until you're happy with the balance, and tighten them later.

Hang a stick on each end of the first stick, add eggs, and continue hanging and balancing until your mobile is the size you prefer (see illustration).

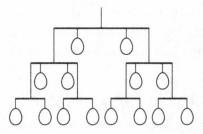

Using Eggs as Decorations

Try these other ways of displaying your colorful creations. Hang eggs from a branch and prop it up in a pot of sand as an egg tree or suspend it from a ceiling hook for an uncomplicated mobile. Hang eggs over windows, or over the children's beds. If you have an altar to Eostar outside, decorate the area around it with eggs. Once you get going, you may run out of eggs to hang up and have to dye another dozen!

Egg Cups

For displaying decorated eggs on tabletops, try these individual holders. Roll out salt dough (see Tool Chest) $1/2$ inch thick. Using a cookie cutter or a sharp knife, cut out star shapes, with the center at least 2 inches across and the arms at least 2 inches long. Drape the stars over large ends of empty eggshells and arrange the arms of the stars over the sides. Place in small cups and bake until stars are just firm.

Separate eggshells from stars. Make stands from the unused dough—a coil or three small balls for each egg cup—

and attach to bottom of cup. Return to the oven and continue to bake until dried.

Decorate with paint and finish with a coat of polyurethane.

Eggshell Vases

These small vases are another fresh reminder of life returning. Colored eggs as well as white and brown ones look lovely. Use eggshells with the tops broken off and the inside cleaned. Add a bit of water and fill the shells with fresh spring blossoms. Line them up in an egg carton, or stand them in sand, salt, or an egg cup. We often turn our casualties from blowing eggs into these vases.

Egg Candles

Use the bottom half of eggshells to hold mini tapers or other small candles. To anchor the candles in the shells, drop hot wax into the bottom of shell and press candle into wax. Set these candles in sand, salt, or gravel.

Here are two candle projects that celebrate spring, both requiring eggshells and candlemaking materials (see Tool Chest). Even though these candles don't burn for long, they are well worth the effort.

Eggshell Candles

Chip one inch of shell from the small end. Clean and gently rub away the inner membrane. Dry, then set in egg carton, open end up. Pour wax into each egg to about one inch from the top. Insert wicks.

When lit, the incandescently glowing eggshell is beautiful. Change the tilt of the egg so the flame burns cleanly in the middle and doesn't scorch the shell. You may have to empty out melted wax after the flame has burned awhile to keep the wick from being submerged.

Egg-shaped Candles

Chip about an inch of shell from the large end of an eggshell. Gently, with a sharp knife, poke a small hole in the small

Paper Egg Chain

Follow instructions for making Samhain Apple Chains but draw egg shapes instead. For smaller eggs, make smaller accordion folds.

end of the shell. Insert a stiffened piece of wick through the small hole and pull out the large end. Seal the small hole by pressing a piece of salt dough around the wick.

Place shell in egg carton, large side up. Wrap the wick around a toothpick or pencil so that it stands straight up. Suspend the toothpick or pencil across the shell. Fill the shell with wax. Check the small hole for leaking and press the dough more firmly around it if necessary.

When the wax is firm, break off the shell. Rub off whatever membrane sticks to candle. Remove the clay from the wick, rinsing if needed. Trim wick to $1/4$ inch.

Egg Rattles

Eggs have a special way of fitting smoothly into our hands, making them perfect for rattles. We offer two types, one loud and durable made from plastic Easter eggs, and one soft and temporary made from real eggshells.

Plastic Rattles

Fill a plastic egg with a few beans, close, and rattle experimentally. Add or take away beans until you're happy with the noise. Glue the halves together.

Eggshell Rattles

Fill a clean, blown egg with beans, rice, or birdseed, shaking to test the rattling sound. This will be a softer noise. Plug the hole with salt dough.

My (Diane's) children like to make these rattles with birdseed for our Spring Equinox ritual. Afterward, they delight in smashing them against trees.

Egg Hats

This "crown of eggs" is easy to make from a paper plate.

Draw a circle inside a 9-inch paper plate, about 1 inch from the rim. Inside this circle, draw egg shapes, small ends toward the center of the plate, large ends touching the drawn circle. Depending on the size you prefer, draw between 4 and 6 eggs.

Cut out the space between the eggs, leaving the eggs connected to the rim of the plate by at least an inch. Decorate with your wildest colors, then fold eggs up to form the crown.

Egg Wreath

Cut a paper plate or cardboard into a ring. The inner circle should be 7 inches in diameter. Lay 9 decorated, blown eggs around the ring, small ends facing in, sides just touching. Heat a glue gun and apply hot glue to the eggs, then stick them to the ring. Conceal any plate or cardboard that shows through by trimming with flowers or other decorations. Add string for hanging.

Spring Seeds

Using eggshells as containers to sprout seeds combines two powerful images of new life. With tops cut off and a small drainage hole pierced on the bottom, eggshells are well sized for starting vegetable and flower seeds. Fill with potting soil, add the seed, and keep moist until the sprout is ready to transplant.

Eggshells ready to sprout herbs or flowers make wonderful gifts. As part of our Spring Equinox celebration, we have cartons of shells filled with potting soil ready for visiting children to plant and take home with them. To transplant, just crack off the shell. Sprinkle the bits of eggshell into the plant's new hole to promote drainage around its roots.

Chocolate Worms

You will need:

1 C water

7 T butter, cut into pieces

3/4 t salt

1/4 C sugar

1 C flour

1 C eggs exactly (typically 4 large eggs), well beaten

4 oz semisweet chocolate (for topping)

Adapted from the pastry used in eclairs and other delicate desserts, this choux gets squeezed onto a cookie sheet in squiggly shapes to remind us about the good work of our little legless friends, who keep our earth soft and rich. Children love piping out worms with the pastry tube and dripping chocolate on afterward. Follow directions exactly; the results are well worth the effort.

Heat the water, butter, salt, and sugar to a boil in a heavy saucepan. Remove the saucepan from the heat and add the flour all at once. Using a sturdy wire whisk and a wooden spoon, stir the mixture in a back and forth motion until the batter forms a soft ball. Let it cool slightly. Add the eggs a little at a time until they are all incorporated, again using the whisk and spoon. The choux should be the consistency of a thick custard, smooth and shiny.

Spoon the choux into a pastry bag fitted with a 1/4-inch plain tip. Pipe the choux onto a greased cookie sheet in squiggly worm shapes, each no longer than 6 inches.

Bake in a preheated 425° oven about 12 minutes, until the edges are tinged with gold. After taking them out of the oven, pierce each worm gently with a small knife or toothpick to allow steam to escape. Cool completely.

Chocolate Topping

Break up the chocolate into small pieces and melt in a double boiler, or in the microwave at 50 percent power for 2 minutes. If it's not melted, stir and microwave again at 50 percent power in 1-minute increments. Chocolate burns quickly, so go slowly and watch carefully! Cool the chocolate to room temperature. Dip a small spoon in the chocolate and drizzle the topping onto the worms' backs, or spread with the back of the spoon. Leave the worms in a cool place for the chocolate to set.

Persephone Rising Spring Equinox Popovers

Basically just puffs of egg and hot air, this light treat helps use up some of the egg insides we've blown for our decorations. These are best served straight from the oven with a sliver of butter and fruit on the side.

Preheat the oven to 425°. Mix together all the ingredients except the flour. Then add the flour, using a whisk to avoid lumps. Butter a muffin tin or a popover pan generously (these tend to stick). Individual custard cups work well, too; you'll need 8 for this recipe. Fill the tins or cups 1/3 full. Bake for 15 minutes, then turn the oven down to 350° degrees and bake some more: 10 to 15 minutes for a muffin pan, 15 to 20 minutes for a popover pan or custard cups. The popovers should be golden brown and firm.

As soon as you take them from the oven, pierce the tops with a sharp knife to release the steam. Run a knife around the edges, pull out, and serve.

You will need:

3 eggs, well beaten

1 C milk

2 T melted butter

1 t sugar

1 t salt

1 C flour

Clafouti

This easy fresh-fruit custard dish sweetly brings together the two best symbols of spring, fresh fruit and eggs.

Preheat the oven to 350°.

Slowly combine the flour and milk, whisking constantly to avoid lumps. Add in the eggs, sugar, and vanilla, and beat until the mixture is foamy and thick. Spread the fruit in a well-greased 12-by-18-inch oblong or 12-inch round baking pan and pour egg/milk mixture over. Bake for 30 to 40 minutes until the custard is puffy and brown and a toothpick inserted comes out clean. The clafouti will fall somewhat while cooking. Sprinkle with powdered sugar and serve warm or cool, by itself or with ice cream.

You will need:

1/2 C flour

1 C milk

4 eggs

1/3 C brown sugar

1 t vanilla or almond extract

3 C fresh fruit, sliced and, if very juicy, drained

powdered sugar

butter or margarine to grease the pan

Easiest Egg Custard

You will need:

any quantity of whole eggs, up to 12

²/₃ C milk per egg

1 T sugar, brown or white, or honey per egg

¹/₄ t vanilla extract per egg

12-oz glass jars with tops

pots large enough to hold jars

This easiest egg custard, cooked in small glass jars, makes a great casual snack for groups of children. Overnight preparation is required, so plan ahead.

Combine all the ingredients, mixing until thick and frothy. Pour the mixture into the glass jars, evenly dividing the mix between the jars. Skim off the foam and screw on the tops firmly.

Boil water in pots. There should be enough water so that when the jars are in the pot, the water is level with the egg mixture. Turn off the heat. Gently place the jars into the pots and cover. Let rest undisturbed overnight, or for eight hours. The custard will be firm. Eat directly from the jars with a long spoon.

A Spring Equinox Meal for Fussy Eaters

Some days the only thing my (Anne's) children will eat is quesadillas. This was the case on Equinox one year, when I wanted to cook something special. They would have none of it, so I decided to dress up their quesadillas instead. From the quesadillas I cut out egg shapes and rabbit heads, as many as I could. With a little applesauce and some carrot sticks (for Eostar's rabbits, of course), this worked quite well as a Spring Equinox meal.

CHAPTER NINE

Beltane
MAY 1

BELTANE IS THE great spring holiday of the Goddess. Halfway around the year from Halloween, when we honor our beloved dead, Beltane is the festival that celebrates all of the living world: plants, animals, and human beings.

In most temperate climates, flowers are now in bloom, trees are in blossom or in full leaf, and gardens are beginning to grow. All of the hibernating animals are fully awake. The birds have nested and settled down to raise their brood. Here in

California, the daffodils and plum blossoms of early spring have been replaced by roses and wisteria.

Beltane is the holiday of fertility. For Pagans, one of the great gifts of the Goddess is the power of the earth to grow wonderful flowers and fruit and all the things we eat. We are thankful for the fertility of the earth, and our job is to keep the land and the soil healthy, to protect the animals and plants and trees so that fertility can continue. The earth is a living being, and all of her creatures are part of her body. Each has a place, a purpose, a special part in the great dance of life.

On Beltane, we also celebrate all the different kinds of human fertility and creativity. We give thanks for the power women and men have to make babies, to bring new people into the world. But people can create in other ways as well. When we paint pictures, make up songs, tell new stories, plant a garden, or cook a dinner, we take part in the fertility of the Goddess.

Beltane is also the time when we celebrate the joys of being alive. We give thanks for all the different kinds of pleasure our bodies give us, for without our bodies we couldn't see or hear or touch or taste or smell, run or jump or dance or sing or swim. Adults celebrate sexual pleasure at Beltane. For Pagans, the good, loving feelings that people can give each other with their bodies are special gifts of the Goddess. When we give each other love and pleasure, the whole earth is pleased. The flowers bloom brighter and the birds sing louder.

But sexual pleasure, like anything of power, must come at the right time and in the right way, when we have grown ready for it. It's a grown-up mystery. Children's bodies are constantly growing and changing, and you need time to get to know them and to enjoy the different things you are able to do as you get bigger. So Beltane is a good time to celebrate all the things you can do that you couldn't do before, and to run, jump, play games, climb trees, dance, turn somersaults and cartwheels, or do anything else that makes you glad you have a body.

Of course, bodies are different. People come in different shapes and sizes and colors. Not everyone can leap or dance, walk or see or hear. Beltane is also a time to admit that sometimes our bodies let us down. We get sick or hurt. Sometimes we feel very sad and angry about the things we cannot do.

Pagans believe that, just as the different plants and animals each have a special purpose in the web of life, so do the different kinds of people. That's why we never make fun of people because of how they look or what they can or cannot do. People who cannot walk or see or hear, or who have some other difference, have been given a special challenge in this life by the Goddess. Many things may be harder for them, but other things may be easier. And the harder the challenges we face, the more we can grow in our inner power.

In Lithuania, the spring festival called Jores (YOR-es) is celebrated near Beltane. One of their lovely customs is to set up a swing in the woods. People take turns swinging and pushing each other.

Because we celebrate life at Beltane, we honor those who have brought us into life: our mothers.

The Goddess

We have known the Goddess as Mother and as Daughter. At Beltane, She becomes the Lover of all living things. We could call her by some of the ancient names of the Love Goddess: Aphrodite, Astarte, Flora, Maia, Oshun. In our circles, we especially like to call her Queen Maeve, the Faery Queen, who comes riding forth from the Otherworld, the realm of dreams, imagination, spirits, and visions, to teach us how to move between the worlds.

In Irish mythology, Maeve was a fierce and beautiful Goddess, who honored her husband, Aillil, because he was generous, brave, and not jealous. She was associated with the sacred hare, which brings both magic and inspiration.

Like Samhain, Beltane is a time when the veil between the worlds is thin. At Samhain, we pass through to visit our beloved dead. At Beltane, the Fey, the Faeries, come forth to visit us.

To Witches, Faeries are not cute little Tinkerbell-like creatures, but powerful nature spirits that are the keepers of the magical energies that lie behind the physical world. In Ireland they were called the Sidhe (Shee), and their realm was called Tir n'a Nog, the Land of Youth, for they never grow old. In Wales, the magic realm was called Annwn (A-no-ven); in Britain, Avalon. In Scotland, the Faery Queen was known as the Queen of Elfland. The Faeries are called the Elder Children of the Goddess, the Fair Folk, or the Good People. We humans are the Younger Children.

Many myths speak of the separation of the magical realm from the physical world. When we lose our ability to communicate with plants, animals, rocks, and trees, when we believe that only what we can touch and count and measure is real, the realm of the Fair Folk recedes. The earth loses life and vitality and becomes a gray and polluted place.

But when we learn to love the living creatures of the earth, when we listen to the voices of the trees, the flowers, and the birds, when we recognize that all around us a great conversation is taking place, if we have ears to hear, then the world becomes again a place of magic. Plants and animals flourish, as do the arts of music, dance, and poetry, and we remember again how to live in harmony with nature.

The God

At Beltane the God is the Green Man, God of all growing things. He too is the lover of all that lives, the protector of the wild things and the guardian of the forest. Often he is depicted as a leafy face peering out from branches and foliage. He even appears in many old Christian churches, carved on pillars or decorating the altar screen.

One of the Green Man's ancient names was Robin Hood, the huntsman who lives under the Greenwood Tree. You may be familiar with the stories of Robin Hood, but did you know that he took his name from our ancient Pagan God? Robin Hood means "Rob in the hood"—the hood worn by the Good People, the Faeries. He dressed in green and lived in the wilderness with his companions, who protected the poor and taught some hard lessons to the selfish and greedy.

The Altar

The altar for Beltane can be a simple arrangement of the flowers in bloom at this time. May baskets can be made of paper strips (see Activities in this chapter) or created from existing baskets. Branches of hawthorne (the May tree) or oak leaves and branches (sacred to Robin Hood) can form a green background. You might also want to include pictures of the Fair Folk. And be sure to set out a bowl of milk or cream for them at night. Don't worry if the cat drinks it—she's probably a Faery in disguise!

On the Land

May is one of the most beautiful months in our part of the world. The apple trees are still blossoming, and the roses are in full bloom. The air is warm, but we can still hope for an occasional shower of rain. The hills remain green, but as the month goes on, they often begin to turn a pale, delicate gold. Poppies and lupines are blossoming, and the meadows are full of wildflowers. If we start our gardens early, we might already have lettuces, greens, snow peas, and radishes to eat.

The newts have been awake and active for many weeks, but now the snakes are beginning to wake up. One year we found two rattlesnakes sleeping just a few feet from where we were setting up our Maypole. We shoveled them into a box, drove them up the road, and released them far away from any houses. We love the Snake Goddess, but that was a little too close for comfort.

What is blooming where you live? What animals are coming out of hibernation?

Thomas the Rhymer[1]

a retelling by Starhawk of a thirteenth-century Scottish ballad

Circle round, and I'll tell you a story about the Faeries. . . .

On a bright day in early May, when the warmth of the sun had finally burned away the chill mists of the Scottish winter, Thomas of Ercildoune (ERLS-ton) laid himself down on a grassy bank in the shade of a hawthorne tree. The sweet flowers of the May tree—for so the hawthorne is called— perfumed the air, and bees buzzed around his head. The peacefulness of the day lulled him into sleep.

The sound of bells woke him. Opening his eyes, he looked out over the green moors dotted with heather and ferny bracken and saw riding toward him the most beautiful woman he could ever imagine. She wore a grass-green skirt and a velvet mantle, and she held her head high and proud. Her horse's mane was twined with silver bells, so that as she passed the air rang with a high, sweet sound.

Thomas jumped to his feet, took off his hat, and swept a low bow as she rode up and halted before him. "Lady, Goddess, Queen of Heaven, I hail and greet you—for never before on earth have I seen anyone like you," he said.

The woman laughed, tossing back her hair, which was as bright as silver. "Oh, no, Thomas," she said. "I am no Goddess. I am the Queen of Fair Elfland, who has come to visit with you. And now you must come with me, and serve me for seven years, for good or for ill."

With those words, the milk-white horse she rode turned, and Thomas found himself jumping up onto the horse's back, clasping his arms around the Queen's waist. The horse began to run, faster and faster, until it seemed to Thomas that they were riding faster than the very wind itself. They rode on for days and days, through rivers of red blood up to their knees, as if they were riding through the tides and currents of all the life that flowed in the veins of every living human being. The sun and the moon disappeared, and Thomas lost all

sense
of   day
and   night.
The air was bright
with the silvery glow
of twilight, and his ears
were filled with the roar of the
sea.

On and on they rode.

❧

At last, when Thomas had begun to believe they would never come to the end of
their journey, the landscape around them
began to change. The tides of blood receded, and Thomas began to smell sweet
flowers and to see around him green grass
and graceful trees. The horse slowed her
gallop to a trot, then to a walk, and at last
she stopped in front of a huge old apple
tree that was heavy with ripe fruit.

"Lady, let me pick some of that fruit for

you,"
Thomas
offered. The
truth was, he
was terribly hungry
and thirsty himself, but
he wanted to be polite.

"Oh, no, Thomas," the
Queen said. "Do not eat the fruit of that
tree—for what grows here in my country
contains all the great powers of life and
death in their pure forms. This food is too
strong for mortal human beings. To you, it
would be poison. Instead, let us get down
from this horse and rest, and I will give you
sweet wine to drink and good bread to eat."

So they dismounted and lay together in
the shade of the tree. Thomas ate the bread
of Elfland, and never had anything tasted so
good to him before. A few bites were all he
needed to satisfy all his hunger and revive
all his strength. He sipped the sweet wine
the Queen offered him, and it tasted like all
the joy of a fresh, summer day.

When he could eat and drink no more, the Queen told him to lie down and rest, with his head pillowed on her lap. "I will show you three wonders," she told him.

As she spoke, his inner eyes opened, and suddenly he could see to the farthest horizons and beyond, to the great stone gates that divided the land of the living from the realms of the dead. The whole of the Otherworld lay spread out before him, shining with its own light. Vast forests of silvery-leafed trees tossed their branches in the breeze, and beyond, white horses rode the backs of the rolling breakers of the sea. The woods were crisscrossed with roads and paths, like silver threads winding through the canopy of palest moonlight green.

"Do you see that broad, broad road?" the Queen asked. Instantly a wide, smooth road appeared in Thomas's vision. Crowds of shadowy figures danced along its pavement. On its sides were booths where good food and ale and every pleasure and luxury imaginable were displayed.

"That road is the easy way, the way that most people take," the Queen said. "Some call it the road to paradise—but look, look closely." Thomas looked, and saw the figures on the road pushing and shoving each other aside to reach the enticing food and the gorgeous clothing and jewels displayed on the roadside. He saw some people stuffing themselves with meat and fruit and cakes, only to run and push and shove until they could reach the next booth and begin again, as if no matter how much they ate, they were still hungry. Others were dressing themselves in fine robes, but

no sooner did they have one thing on than they were reaching for the next thing, until they were layered so thick in shirts and capes and mantles that they couldn't move. And some were loading their necks with so many chains of gold that their heads were bowed down to the ground and they could no longer rise.

"And now look," the Queen said. "Do you see that narrow, narrow road?" Thomas looked, and saw a path barely wide enough for one person to walk on. It was lined with briars and thorn bushes that grew so closely together that the few stalwart souls who walked on the road had to push between them, getting scratched and bloodied as they went.

"That is the hard road," the Queen said. "Some call it the road of righteousness, but look—look closely." Thomas looked, and he saw the pale figures who moved along the road growing thinner and thinner, as if they were starved of life. The farther along the road they went, the thinner they became, until many of them were no more than walking skeletons, disappearing into the far distance to fade away.

"And now look," the Queen said a third time. "Do you see that bonny, bonny road that winds along the green hills?" Thomas looked, and saw the third road, which dipped under trees and emerged to climb high, open moors. The third road was neither broad nor narrow, and along it moved figures who seemed to shimmer with color. Apple trees and fragrant hedges of roses and ripe berries lined its shoulders. Those who traveled the Third Road reached out their hands from time to time to pluck the

Truth Day

Notice how many small lies we tell all the time. When asked "How are you?" we answer "Fine," when we're really feeling sad or angry. When asked, "How did you like my song?" we answer "Oh, great," when really we hated it. When told "Please stay for dinner," we say "Oh, I can't, I have to be somewhere," when really we just don't want to. In honor of True Thomas, pick a day in which you will tell only the truth. What happens if you actually tell the truth?

fruit. With each fruit they tasted, they seemed to glow with deeper-toned hues, to walk with more joy and purpose in each step, and they sang as they traveled, so that the sweet tones of their voices drifted upward on the wind to where Thomas lay.

"That is the road to fair Elfland, where you and I must go," the Queen said. "You will serve me for seven years and see many wonders. But in all that time, whatever you see or hear, you must not speak a single word, for if you do, you will never get back to your own country, but will belong to Elfland forever. But if you keep silence and serve me well, I will return you to life with many gifts. You will have the tongue that cannot lie, to sing of the wonders of Elfland and keep our memory alive in the world of sun and moon."

And so it happened. True Thomas served the Queen for seven years, as true companion, helpmate, and lover. In all that time he spoke not a single word, but he kept his eyes open and remembered all the wonders of Elfland.

What were the wonders that he saw? Elfland lies on the borders of the land of the dead, in a place outside of time. There the sun and the moon, the markers of day and night, never shine, and all is twilight gray. In Elfland, nothing fades and dies, for all things exist there only in their unchanging true forms. The flower you pluck in Elfland is not a rose of earth that droops and fades, but the essence of roseness itself, that which makes a rose a rose and not a cabbage or a daisy. But nothing of the green earth is truly alive there, either, for life is change. No creature of the living earth can stay too long in Elfland, for we must constantly change or cease to be.

And so when the seven years had passed, Thomas lay down one summer afternoon to doze, with his head in the Elf Queen's lap. And he awoke alone, under a hawthorne tree on a sunny bank near Ercildoune. He was dressed in a fine green coat, and shoes of Elfish green, and ever after he could tell no lies, but only the honest truth. His words carried great power, and he became an honored poet, making many songs in memory of the Elf Queen, preserving the memory of

Elfland in the human world at a time when the green earth was growing ever farther away from the realms of twilight.

If you ever tire of the good green earth, if you ever need to dip into the well of magic and drink deep, if you ever need the healing that can only come from beyond time, remember the instructions of True Thomas. Pass by the broad road and the narrow road. Look for the third road, follow it with a generous heart, and you too may come to fair Elfland. ❧

The Goddess Blesses All Forms of Love
by Starhawk

Circle round, and I'll tell you a story about how the Maypole came to be. . . .

Once upon a time, a long time ago—or maybe in a time not yet come—there came a springtime when no flowers bloomed.

The plum trees and cherry trees showed no white or pink or red blossoms. No daffodils pushed up from the cold ground; no buds formed on the roses. No lilacs perfumed the air, and no poppies opened their bright petals to the wind. And the worst thing of all was that nobody seemed to notice.

Except for one young girl, named Vivian.

"Where are the flowers?" Vivian asked everyone she met, and everyone looked at her strangely.

"Flowers? What flowers?" asked the woman who delivered their mail. "I don't have time to worry about flowers—I've got a route to cover."

"Maybe she means flour," said the man who ran the corner shop. "Maybe she wants to bake a cake."

"I've heard of flowers," said the woman at the library. "I know I've seen a reference to them somewhere."

"I've got a great computer game with flowers," said her brother. "Who needs to dig in the dirt when you can grow your own virtual garden?"

"Maybe she needs to go to bed early," said her mother.

"Perhaps she's coming down with something."

"Doesn't anyone miss the flowers?" Vivian cried.

"She's confused," said her teacher. "We must be kind to her."

"She's ill," said the doctor. "We must cure her."

"She's loony!" said the other boys and girls, and they made fun of her until Vivian got so mad she ran out of her schoolyard into the deep woods.

She ran and ran until she couldn't run any more. She flung herself down in a patch of grass and began to cry.

"Nobody loves me!" she cried. "Nobody cares about the flowers! Nobody cares about me!"

"That's exactly how I feel," said a small voice by her ear. Vivian lifted her head and saw a tiny, scruffy, shabby little dandelion. Its petals were tattered, its stem was bent, and it looked like it might collapse at any moment. But it was the only flower she had seen all spring, and she was thrilled down to her toes.

"Oh, dandelion!" she cried. "I'm so happy to see you. You are so beautiful!"

"Not really," the dandelion said modestly, but it perked up.

"Why aren't there any flowers this spring? Why doesn't anybody miss them?" Vivian asked.

"Exactly," the dandelion said. "Nobody misses the flowers, so why should we bloom? Some kind of love has gone out of the world, and so the earth spirits are sick and the flowers have disappeared. But with the right kind of love, you can call them back again."

"What kind of love?" Vivian asked.

But the dandelion only said, "Do you really think I'm beautiful? After all, I'm the most common of flowers."

"I think you're gorgeous!" Vivian said.

The dandelion sighed. "Then I can die happy!" It collapsed on the ground, and one by one its petals shriveled and faded.

"Poor flower!" Vivian mourned. "You really were beautiful!" But she sat up and dried her tears. For now she knew that if she could only find the right kind of love, she could bring the flowers back.

❧

Vivian dried her eyes and went home.

"Oh, Vivian! I was so worried about you!" cried her mother.

"I was looking for you everywhere!" said her father.

"I was surfing the Web, trying to locate you," said her brother.

"Do you love me?" Vivian asked.

"Of course," said her parents.

"I guess," said her brother.

"Then help me bring the flowers back! Help me find the right kind of love."

Her parents shrugged and raised their eyebrows, but they followed Vivian down into the town. Her brother rolled his eyes, but he came, too.

❧

"Vivian! Where did you go?" cried all the girls and boys.

"I went to find the flowers. And now I know that if we can find the right kind of love, we can bring them back!"

"Flowers, always flowers!" said one of the girls. "You've got flowers on the brain!"

"She's distressed," said the teacher. "We must be patient with her."

"She's disturbed," said the doctor. "We must humor her."

And so they let Vivian form them all into a circle in the center of town. They held hands and closed their eyes, but nothing happened.

"The circle isn't big enough," Vivian cried. "We need more kinds of love!"

"I'll go get my Uncle Donald and Uncle Rick!" cried one of the girls. "They love each other."

"Do you think their kind of love can bring the flowers back?" hooted one of the boys.

"We need all kinds of love," Vivian said. "We don't know what kind of love is the right kind of love."

"I'll go get my boyfriend!" cried the older sister of one of Vivian's friends.

"I'll get my mothers," said one of the boys. "They love each other, and they love me, too."

"I love my job," said the woman who carried the mail, stepping into the circle. "I love bringing letters to people."

"I love my neighborhood," said the grocer, taking her hand.

"I love the trees," said an old woman who lived in the woods.

"I love to read," said the librarian.

"I love my garden," said a tall man carrying a spade.

"I love my dog!" said a very small boy.

"Your dog!" All the children laughed. "You think your dog will bring back the flowers?"

"My dog loves me better than any of

you!" the boy said, and he ran to get him.

The circle grew larger and larger.

"It's still not big enough!" Vivian cried.

"No circle of love can ever be big enough to hold all forms of love," she heard a voice say. Holding her hand was a beautiful woman, her hair crowned with all the flowers of spring, her eyes deep as wells and dancing with light like the sparkling surface of a laughing stream. Her face was old and young at the same time, and it seemed to change before Vivian's eyes. One moment she was dark as a velvet pansy, in the next she was pale as a white lily. She was young and fresh and smooth as a newly opened rose, and then ancient and wrinkled as a walnut.

"Who are you?" Vivian asked.

"I am the Goddess," the woman said. "The Queen of the May. You have called me back from the Otherworld with your circle of love."

"Then we did find the right kind of love after all!" Vivian cried joyfully.

The May Queen smiled. "There is no right kind of love," she said. "The Goddess blesses all forms of love. Whenever you join together in a circle with love and trust, you call me."

"Then how do we bring the flowers back?" Vivian asked.

"Here's what you must do," the May Queen said. She pointed to the center of the circle, where a tall pole stood. "My tree of life has become a dead stick—but you can bring it to life again. Make a circle of your arms, as if you were trying to hug the air." Vivian did, and found herself hugging a big silver ring. "That is my circle of re-

birth—tie it to the top of the tree and set the pole in the ground." She tossed her head, and from her hair shining ribbons of a hundred colors fell to the ground. "And here are the ribbons of love. Tie each one to the ring of life—for each ribbon stands for a different kind of love, and without all of them, my circle is not whole.

"Here is the love parents have for their children . . .

"And here is the love you have for your best friend . . .

"And here is the passionate love two women can have for each other . . .

"And here is the love you have for your grandparents . . .

"And here is the love you have for a pet . . .

"And here is the love and passion a woman and a man may have between them . . .

"And here is the love you have for a friend that you fought with and then made up with . . .

"And here is wild, devoted love between men . . .

"And here is the love you have for a really great teacher . . .

"And here is the love you have for your sisters and brothers . . .

"And here is the love you have for your sisters and brothers when they're driving you crazy . . .

"And here is the love you have for your aunties and uncles . . .

"And here is love for music and for art . . .

"And here is the love that generates children and calls new souls . . .

"And here is the love people have for each other when they work hard together . . .

"And here is the love that generates new ideas . . .

"Take hold of my ribbons, dance around my tree, wrap the tree of life in love, and the flowers will bloom again."

❧

And so the people built a maypole and danced the maypole dance all through the day. And as they danced, white and pink blossoms popped out on the plum trees and cherry trees. Daffodils pushed up from the ground, and buds formed on the roses. Lilacs perfumed the air, and poppies opened their bright petals to the wind.

When the dance was over, the May Queen gathered all the children close to her. "I must leave you now," she said, "but the flowers will remain in all their different shapes and scents and colors, to remind you to honor all forms of love. And because it was a child whose love brought me back, I will give you children three gifts: that many kinds of love will come to you, each in the right time; that you will be able to say yes to the love that is right for you; that you will be free to say no to the love that is not right for you. For while all love is blessed, only you can know what kinds of love are right for you. And now I must leave, but every year, when you dance the Maypole, I will be with you, whether you can see me or not. For in that way, I am just like love." And at that she disappeared.

But the flowers remained through the whole summer. And ever after, when the spring came, the people danced the Maypole with bright ribbons in honor of the flowers and all the colors of love. ❧

The Battle of Summer and Winter[2]
retold by Carol Lee Sanchez

Circle round, and I'll tell you a story of the Pueblo people of the Southwest. . . .

A long time ago, when the earth was still very young, the people lived in a village in the north called Whitetown. The leader of this small village was named Broken Hand. Now Broken Hand had several daughters, but his oldest, named First Born Daughter, decided to marry Spirit of Winter. This man had a bad temper, which he expressed as a swirl of snow and sleet or blasts of freezing cold air wherever he appeared. After he married First Born Daughter, he was in and out of Whitetown a lot and so the village began to experience freezing cold weather most of the time, and it seemed to be snowing or sleeting quite often as well. As this continued, the people found that their crops couldn't ripen properly, and so they had to live on cactus ears and other wild desert plants that managed to survive under such extreme conditions.

One time, while searching for cactus for her family's meals, First Born Daughter wandered a long way from home. She had gathered quite a bundle of cactus ears, and as she was singeing off their thorns to prepare them for her journey home, she was startled by a presence nearby. When she looked up from her work, she saw the face of a handsome and bold young man staring down at her. She noticed the clothes he was wearing seemed strangely different. His yellow shirt was woven from corn silks and his belt was made from the broad leaves of the corn plant. On his head he wore a tall pointed hat, also made from leaves, with a golden corn tassel waving from the top of it. His leggings were woven from the green stringy moss that covers springs and ponds, and his moccasins were embroidered with flowers and butterflies. He carried a perfect ear of green corn in his left hand. In a most pleasant tone of voice, he asked First Born Daughter what she was doing. She explained that she was gathering cactus ears for food. The young man immediately handed her an ear of green corn, saying: "Here, eat this while I go and bring more for you to take back home with you."

He left and went toward the south, returning in a short time with a huge load of green corn. First Born Daughter was surprised to see it.

"Does this corn grow nearby?" she asked.

"No," he replied, "this corn grows in the south, far away from here, and the flowers bloom all year round there, too. Would you like to go back to my country with me?" First Born Daughter said she could not go away with him because she was married to Spirit of Winter, but admitted she would like to see his beautiful country. Pretty soon she was telling the stranger how cold and disagreeable her husband was and that she really didn't care for him anymore. He urged her to go with him to the warm south lands, insisting he was not afraid of Spirit of Winter. First Born Daughter remained firm and did not give in. Finally the young man told her to return to her village with the corn he had given her and cautioned her not to throw any of the corn husks out of doors. As he was leaving he said, "You must meet me at this place tomorrow, and I will have more corn for you."

First Born Daughter had not been traveling too long when she met her sisters on the road. They had come in search of her since she had been gone a long time. They were quite surprised to see her carrying an armload of green corn instead of cactus and began asking all sorts of questions. First Born Daughter explained what had happened, and they helped her carry the corn the rest of the way home. When they got there she had to tell her story to her father and mother. As soon as she described the young man and his strange clothes and how she was to meet him again on the following day to receive more corn, her father, Broken Hand, cried: "It is Summer's Spirit!"

"It *is* Summer's Spirit," said her mother. "You must bring him home with you tomorrow."

First Born returned to the meeting place the next day, and Summer's Spirit was already there waiting for her with another huge bundle of corn. She told him of her parents' invitation to him, and he agreed to accompany her home to Whitetown with the bundle of corn. When they arrived, they distributed it among the people, and there was more than enough to feed them all. There was a great thanksgiving and celebration to welcome Summer's Spirit to the village and to Broken Hand's home.

That evening, as was his custom, Spirit of Winter returned to his home. He came in a blinding storm of hail, snow, and sleet because he was in a boisterous mood. As he neared the village, his very bones told him that Summer's Spirit was in the vicinity, so he called out in a very loud voice: "Summer's Spirit, are you around here?"

Summer's Spirit came out and faced him.

"Hah! Summer's Spirit, I will destroy you!"

"Hah! Spirit of Winter, I will destroy you!" replied Summer's Spirit, still advancing. Spirit of Winter paused. He was covered with frost from head to foot. Icicles draped around him, and the fierce cold wind emanated from his nostrils.

As Summer's Spirit drew nearer, the wintry wind changed to a warm, gentle breeze. The frost and icicles melted and showed the dry, bleached bullrushes that clothed Spirit of Winter. Seeing that he would be defeated, Spirit of Winter cried out: "I will not fight you now, for we cannot try our powers. We will prepare ourselves, and in four days from this day, we will meet here again and fight to see who is the supreme winner. The victor may claim First Born Daughter for his wife, if she chooses." Saying this, Spirit of Winter withdrew in a rage, and the wind roared and shook all the houses. But the people inside were warm indeed, because Summer's Spirit was with them.

❧

The next day, Summer's Spirit left Whitetown for his home in the south. Once there, he began making preparations to meet Spirit of Winter in battle. First he sent an eagle messenger to his friend Shale Rock (which becomes very hot in fire), asking him to come and help in the battle against Spirit of Winter. Then he called together the birds and four-legged animals that live in the sunny climates. For his advance guard and shield, he chose the bat, as its tough skin could resist the sleet and hail Spirit of Winter would hurl at him.

Spirit of Winter had gone to his home in the north at the same time to prepare himself for battle. He called all the winter birds and four-legged animals to his aid, and for his advance guard he chose the magpie. When these impressive forces had been selected by the opponents, they returned to Whitetown, Summer's Spirit from the south and Spirit of Winter from the north, both in splendid battle array. Shale Rock kindled his fires and piled great heaps of resinous fuel upon them until huge clouds of steam and smoke rose and hurried forward toward Whitetown and the battleground. Upon these clouds rode Summer's Spirit with his army. All the animals in his army touched by the smoke from Shale Rock's fires were colored by it, and from that day have been black or brown in color.

Spirit of Winter and his army came out from the north in a howling blizzard and came forward on black storm clouds driven by a freezing wintry wind. As he came on, the lakes and rivers he passed over were frozen and the air was filled with blinding sleet.

When the combatants drew near to the village, they advanced rapidly and their arrival upon the battlefield was explosive. Flashes of lightning darted from the clouds of Summer's Spirit. When Spirit of Winter's animals were struck, their hairs were singed and whitened, so that from that day the animals of the north have a covering of white or have white markings on them.

From the south, black clouds continued to roll upward and the thunder spoke again and again. Clouds of smoke and vapor rushed forward, melting the snow and ice weapons of Spirit of Winter. Finally he was compelled to leave the battlefield. Summer's Spirit, certain he was winning, chased him. To save himself from total defeat and destruction, Spirit of Winter called for a truce.

❧

And so a truce was granted by Summer's Spirit, and the rivals met at Whitetown to arrange the terms of the treaty between them. Spirit of Winter announced his defeat and consented to give up First Born Daughter to Summer's Spirit. It was then agreed between the opposing forces that for all time from then on, Summer's Spirit was to live at Whitetown for half a year, Spirit of Winter would live there the other half, and they would not disturb each other during each other's residency period.

The people of Whitetown rejoiced when they heard the terms of the agreement and congratulated the spirit forces and each other. Then they set about to celebrate their good fortune and the return of balance to their daily lives. ❧

Maypole Dance

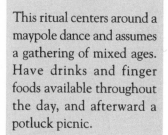

As the celebrants gather, have a project on hand that people can get started on. Make head wreaths with fresh flowers, vines, and floral tape. Younger children will need lots of help, or you can have them make hats or paper chains. You may also want to try making percussion instruments, so those who don't want to dance can keep the beat for the dancers. The point is for everyone to have something festive to wear or to hold, so all can participate.

When it is time to begin, have a procession to the dancing grounds. Those with percussion instruments can start out, and all sing the processional song. Parades can be so much fun: You may want to walk around the whole area a couple of times, picking up stragglers as you go, until everyone is gathered around the maypole. If you like, lead the procession once all the way around the maypole circle, envisioning the circle being cast with singing, drumming, and color. This activity can be enough to ground and center people, especially children, but you may prefer a more standard grounding and circle casting after the procession.

If your circle is filled with children of all ages, there is not much time for lengthy invocations. For a brief but effective way to call in the quarters, have someone take a tambourine or other noisemaker, and lead a call-and-response circle cast-

This ritual centers around a maypole dance and assumes a gathering of mixed ages. Have drinks and finger foods available throughout the day, and afterward a potluck picnic.

Beltane Processional[3]

Words and music by Anne Hill

ing. Starting in the east, set that percussion to work making noise, and say loudly, "All welcome the east!" Everyone repeats, "All welcome the east!" Continue around the circle, stopping at each direction to lead the call and response. Finish in the center, the maypole, and say, "All welcome the center!" The circle is now cast, and the ritual has begun.

One thing we like to do before invoking the Goddess and God is to pour a bowl of fresh cream around the base of the maypole, as an offering to the Faeries, and some Waters of the World, as an offering to the spirits of the land. This can be done silently, or with some version of the following words.

While holding and then pouring the Waters of the World, say:

> Spirits of this land, you whose bones we walk upon, you who knew the names of the plants and the ways of the animals before our ancestors arrived on this continent, we call you. Please accept this offering of sacred waters as a sign that we wish for peace between our peoples. We ask your permission to celebrate our ancient seasonal festivals here and, with your blessings, to learn to live in balance with all that nature provides. Blessed be the land.

While holding and then pouring the cream, say:

> Faeries, you who have traveled from the land of the standing stones, ancestors, teachers of the old ways, we welcome you here today. Be welcome in this circle, come into our lives and our hearts, help us to remember who we are and where we came from. Blessed be.

Invoke the Goddess and God as you see fit, perhaps honoring the Goddess as Flora, the Goddess of Spring, or Maeve, Queen of the Faeries, and the God as Robin Hood or the Green Man. Before everyone gets a ribbon to hold, you may want to go over the basic dance step.

For music during the dancing, you can use the processional song, adding and improvising new lyrics. It can also be sung as a round. If the children are familiar with "The Goddess Blesses All Forms of Love" story, you may want to weave in verses suggestive of the story. Because Beltane is a festival of creativity and increase, ask people to sing in those qualities they wish to bring into their lives: Happiness is a-coming in; a new job is a-coming in; vegetables are a-coming in, and so on.

As the dancers get comfortable with the steps, as smiles spread on everyone's faces and the lovely ribbons weave themselves down the pole, feel how the magic weaves around and through the crowd, joining our lives, creating a tapestry of joy and friendship in this one spot on the earth. When the ribbons are all woven and everyone is clustered around the pole, change the song into a wordless hum, touching the pole and raising a cone of power to bring all you've wished for into being. As the hum drops down into silence, wait a few moments and say, "So mote it be."

Say goodbye to the Goddess and God, thank the Faeries and the spirits of the land, open up the circle, and feast!

Maypole Dance Step

While standing in a circle around the pole, have everyone pair off and face a partner. The first step will be to pass to the left of their partner, and then face their next partner. The second step will be to pass to the right of this partner and so on, alternating between passing left and passing right. With ribbons in hand, this becomes a weaving motion, with each participant alternately passing under her partner's ribbon and raising her own ribbon for her next partner to pass under.

Blessing for Mothers

Because Beltane is a celebration of fertility, and also because it is so close to the secular Mother's Day holiday, you may want to have as part of your celebration a blessing of all the mothers. For without our mothers' fertile wombs, and without the daily acts of cooking, bathing, caring, and loving, where would any of us be?

We call these acts of mothering, though we know that men are equally capable and often strongly called to these acts of service and devotion. This prayer is not intended to exclude men as caregivers, nor is it meant to codify the stereotype of woman as mother and nurturer. It is meant to acknowledge and sanctify the work of mothers. When mothering is truly valued as the most priceless gift we can give to a child, and when women are truly honored and supported for all the work they do in raising children, we may see a great shifting of priorities in the world.

We include as mothers all those who do the work of mothering: adoptive mothers, stepmothers, and foster mothers, as well as biological mothers.

Imagine if everyone was parented well enough. Imagine if mothers didn't have to worry about whether they would be able to afford what their children need. Imagine if children were brought up with no deficit of love or caring. Imagining these things, we offer this prayer:

Mother of All, hear our prayer this day for the protection and blessing of all the mothers! You who hold the seed in warmth and darkness till it knows to seek the sunlight; You whose winds carry the rain across the vast, arching sky, spilling it down on the thirsting soil;

You in whose arms we rest at the end of the day, in comfort and peace; we call you!

Hear our words of praise for the mothers of the world!

We call your blessings down to the women in our circle who are raising children. Speak through their hearts and hands as they guide the growth of their children. Help them feel your love, help them replenish their stores from your endless well of strength and energy. Help remind them, even when they don't think they need it, that we are all grateful for their work in raising the next generation.

For all of these children are our children, and they bring great joy into the world. We know that what happens to the smallest of us also affects the largest. What befalls one child soon befalls the nation. And so, Mother of Creation, while we bless the mothers here, let us also bless ourselves with open hearts and open hands so that no child in this circle shall go wanting. By our love and by our efforts, may we be known as a people who honor mothers; as a people who give their children what they need to thrive; as a people thrice blessed by happy children, healthy families, and the boundless outpouring of your love into our lives. Mother of the World, with your blessing may we all grow in our capacity to love unconditionally, to nurture where there is

*need, and to tend well the fruits of our creation. Blessed be
the mothers! So mote it be.*

Maypole Construction

Putting up the Pole

We (Anne's family) are very fortunate to have a yard large
enough so that our maypole can stay up all year, bedecked
with its Beltane ribbons, until the next year, when we clean
off the old ribbons and attach the new. Our maypole was a
young redwood some years ago, cut down so that the many
other trees crowding it could grow more fully. Thinning forest growth is an old practice, and if done wisely, it can actually aid the health and fertility of a stand of trees. If you are
in search of a maypole, check with people who are stewards
of forested land and find out if they will be doing any thinning that might yield a suitable maypole. It may be necessary
to peel the outer bark before using the pole.

Another tried-and-true method is to use a two-by-four
piece of lumber. We have used a sixteen-foot length successfully, but for a small dancing area, use a shorter pole. Before
the dance, lay the pole on the ground and provide paints and
brushes. Adults and children alike enjoy decorating the pole.
To set this pole in the ground, you must first dig a hole (post-
hole diggers are your best bet) and keep the excess dirt in a
pile right beside it. When you are ready to dance, plant the
pole in the ground and pack it in firmly with dirt.

Your maypole can also be a long piece of wooden dowel
or metal pipe, two inches in diameter. To set this up on a
lawn or meadow, you need a short piece of pipe (about eighteen to twenty-four inches long) with a slightly larger diameter than your pole. The pole should be able to slide easily
into the short piece of pipe. Taking a sledgehammer, pound
the short pipe into the ground until approximately one foot
is left above ground, then slide in the pole. The short pipe
will pull out of the ground afterward with a minimum of dis-
ruption to the surrounding sod.

Making the Ribbons

We have used spools of ¼-inch-wide present-wrapping ribbon, discount spools of satin ribbon, and skeins of colorful yarn for maypole ribbons. Because of their narrow width, these are difficult for people to keep hold of during the dance, but for small gatherings or when you have no prep time, they work well enough.

The best and cheapest, though most time-consuming, solution we have found for ribbons is to use old sheets and other long pieces of fabric, torn into 1-inch-wide strips. Once you have had your way with a few sheets, it is time to sew. The quickest technique is to sew all the pieces together one by one, until you have one giant ribbon of many different colors.

Next you need to find out how long the ribbons must be. Measure (or estimate) how tall your maypole is, and what the radius of your circle is. The radius in this case is the distance from the pole to the edge of the circle. Remember Pythagoras and his equation $A^2 + B^2 = C^2$? Use the height of the pole for A and the radius for B. Square both numbers, and add the two together. Then take the square root of the sum and you have your ideal ribbon length, C. For example, let's say your maypole is ten feet tall and the radius is twelve feet. That makes $10^2 + 12^2 = C^2$, or $100 + 144 = 244$. The square root of 244 is between 15 and 16, so your ribbons should be around fifteen or sixteen feet long.

Attaching the Ribbons

Here is the perfect opportunity to put that old, worn-out straw hat or lampshade to good use. Woven branches or even a circle of strong twine will do for a hoop, with a twine crosspiece. Nail, staple, or tie the middle of the crosspiece to the top of the pole. With the pole on its side, tie one end of each ribbon to your hoop.

Raising the Pole

If you want to have the pole and ribbons set up before people arrive, gather the ribbons into one or two bunches and hold on to them as the pole is set into its hole. Taking care not to tangle the ribbons, extract one at a time from the bunches and stake securely around the perimeter of the circle with nails, or small rocks if it is not too windy. (Nails pose an obvious safety issue with children, so they must be collected immediately after each child has selected a ribbon.) Or the flowing ribbons can be tied loosely with twine to the pole about four feet from the ground. When the dancers arrive, the twine can be easily removed and the ribbons claimed.

We like to erect the pole as part of our ritual, so we leave the ribbons and pole on the ground until we are ready to dance. Everyone comes up to select a ribbon and checks to make sure it isn't tangled with someone else's. After the ribbons have been claimed and everyone has fanned out to the side, two or three people hoist the pole into the waiting hole in the earth and pack it in firmly with dirt. Very few moments in ritual are as grand as this, with the pole gradually turning into a tree with colorful ribbon branches held firmly all around, catching the breeze and the light of the sun.

After the Dance

At my (Anne's) home, used maypole ribbons find their way into a bonfire. They work well for tying garden plants to their stakes and wrapping presents. Shredded into even smaller pieces, old ribbons make fire-starter tinder (see Brigit Fire activities).

Feeding the Faeries

Beltane is a particularly good time to honor the Fair Folk, however you imagine them. Faeries are one of the things children instinctively believe in, one of their natural links to the Otherworld that we can encourage with our attention and good examples.

It is an ancient custom to go out on Beltane morning before the sun has fully risen and wash your face in the morning dew. The dew is said to hold the Faeries' blessings and will make anyone who washes with it as beautiful on the outside as they are on the inside. Remind your children that true beauty lies within, and the gift of the Faeries is to let our inner light shine forth through our features, regardless of how beautiful we seem to others.

Another custom associated with Faeries on Beltane is to leave out offerings for them in the form of their favorite foods on Beltane Eve, also known as Walpurgis Night. Again, this is a practice that immediately commands children's attention, even if they are dubious adolescents. What can't be seen can't be proven, but neither can it be disproven. A chance to appease the spirits and to bring a bit of luck our way is often considered a worthwhile ritual, even among those children who scoff at most things Pagan.

Leaving offerings for the Faeries can be problematic in some locations. You may not want the food to attract the raccoons, neighborhood cats, and other unwanted visitors—even if they are Faeries in disguise! One solution is to pick a tree, shrub, large stone, or other natural marker farther away from your house on which to leave food, and then keep using that particular spot for all your family's offerings. Your offering place can be close enough to walk to easily, but far enough to discourage local animal life from coming to your back door. Food can be set in a crook of tree branches, by the roots of a large bush, in a cleft of rock; if this place is in a public park, just make sure that your offerings are not too conspicuous to passersby or mistaken for trash by your neighbors or the park rangers.

Once you have chosen a likely spot, ask the place to receive your offerings for the Faeries, and thank it for providing a safer haven than was possible at your home. As you and your children leave food for the Faeries, remember to thank them each time for all their help and blessings.

Body Song

This song, inspired by the Hokey Pokey, celebrates our wonderful bodies. We gather in a circle and start from the top with our heads (or at the bottom, with our feet), changing the words with each round. As we sing "Shake it out," we shake that body part. After the shout, we call out what we do with that body part. For

Body Song[4]

Words and music by Diane Baker

I got my hands, shake it out, I got my hands, shake it out, I got my

hands, shake it out, And hear me shout, HANDS!

example, for hands: "Write, build things, feed ourselves, draw pictures!" Then we move to the next part.

May Day Fruit Baskets

Combine two symbols of Beltane, fruit and flowers, by carving citrus fruit into little flower baskets to decorate your altar.

Cut the fruit into a basket shape. The top half makes the handle, the bottom half makes the container part (see illustration). If you want to get even fancier, make scallops or zigzags around the edges. Using a grapefruit knife, carefully remove the fruit and pulp. Rinse the basket, then sliver a little bit of peel off the bottom to make a flat bottom without creating a hole. Pour a little water in the bottom and fill with small fresh flowers.

Keep in the refrigerator in a closed container if you're making them the day before.

May Baskets

Recycle strawberry baskets, ribbons and wrapping paper to make a pretty nest for love tokens.

Cut the wrapping paper into strips 6 inches long and 1/4 inch wide. Weave them in and out of the strawberry basket's plastic mesh. Use ribbons the same way. Use more ribbons to form a handle and trim with a bow. Fill with flowers and cookies.

Rainbow Hats

On the day we celebrate love, we honor all forms of love with the rainbow colors of our maypole, and by wearing rainbows.

Trim off about 2½ inches from one side of the plate, cutting straight across. Starting from the straight edge, cut out the center of the plate, leaving a 2-inch-wide rim. This forms an upright headband. If the band is too tight, carefully trim the inner edge.

Color the headband in rainbow stripes. Punch a hole at each end of the colored stripe, about ½ inch from the edge of the plate. Add ribbon streamers. Curl the streamers with scissors or let them hang straight (see illustration).

Daisy Chain

This simple flower chain can be made with any kind of flowers, but to make it last, pick the sturdier varieties. Help keep them fresh by misting them with water every few hours. Careful children who can hold on to a straight pin can manage this craft by the time they're about five years old.

Use a straight pin to make a lengthwise slit in the stem about an inch from the flower. Poke the stem of another flower into this slit and pull it through until the flower's head is next to the stem. Slit that flower's stem, insert the next flower, and continue. You may want to twist several flower chains together for a garland. Use florist's tape to fasten it into a circle.

You will need:

9-inch paper plate for each hat

scissors

markers, crayons, paints

hole punch

narrow ribbons of rainbow colors, about ¼ inch wide and at least 24 inches long

Flower Wreath

Beltane is the time to make a fresh flower wreath. Look in the Tool Chest section for instructions for making wreaths. Insert fresh flowers and be sure to mist them often to keep them fresh.

Paper Hearts

Make chains of hearts by following instructions for creating Samhain Apple Chains. Write on each heart what you love, be it a person, pet, sport, book, or favorite place. Decorate your altar or your room with the chain.

Faery Circle Meringue Mushrooms

These are easy enough for children to make and loads of fun. Mushrooms come in all sizes and shapes, so while making these, don't worry if your caps and stems come out all different ways.

Preheat the oven to 200°.

Whip the egg whites and cream of tartar with an electric mixer until the whites hold their shape. Slowly add the sugar, beating until it's all blended. (For meringue tips, see Winter Solstice Meringue Cookies.)

Load the meringue into a pastry bag fitted with a writing tip, about 1/2 inch. Using a bit of meringue, stick the parchment paper to cookie sheets.

To make the stems, start with the bag perpendicular to the parchment paper, about 1/2 inch above the sheet. As you pipe, pull up until the stem has an elongated shape. Stop the pressure and pull away. You'll trim off the little pointed top later.

To make the caps, again start with the pastry bag perpendicular to the parchment, but instead of pulling up, let the meringue form a soft hemisphere to your desired size. As you stop piping, pull away with a gentle swirling motion to keep the shape smooth. Make an equal number of tops and stems.

Bake for 2 hours, and let the meringues cool in the oven. Before removing them from the parchment paper, dust them with the cocoa powder, using a sieve to create a nice mushroom mottle. Fan the mushroom pieces vigorously for a moment with a sheet of paper to make the cocoa scatter and make pleasing woodland tones. (Thanks to Alice Medrich for this creative technique.[5])

To assemble the mushrooms, melt the chocolate in a double boiler or in the microwave at 50 percent power for 2 minutes. Cut the pointy tips from the stems at an angle. With a flat knife, scoop a bit of the melted chocolate and spread it on the flat side of the mushroom caps. Stick the angled end of the stem on. The mushrooms will last several days when stored in an airtight container.

You will need:

4 egg whites

1/3 t cream of tartar

1 C sugar, superfine or pulsed in a food processor until finely textured

parchment paper

2 t cocoa powder

2 oz semisweet chocolate

Sweetheart Cookies

You will need:

1 C (two sticks) butter

1²/₃ C sugar

2 eggs

2 t vanilla extract

3¹/₄ C flour

2 t baking powder

pinch salt

decorative red sugar (found ready-made in stores)

Fill your May basket with sugar cookies to share with everyone you love. Before making the dough, have all ingredients at room temperature. The dough must chill for about two hours before being rolled out, so figure that into your schedule. The dough can be kept in the refrigerator overnight.

Cream together the butter and sugar until it's light and fluffy. Add the eggs one at a time, beating thoroughly after each. Add vanilla. Mix all the dry ingredients except the red sugar together and add to wet mixture. Stir together until well blended.

Divide the dough into thirds. Roll each third into a ball and flatten into a disk. Wrap well and refrigerate for at least 2 hours.

Preheat the oven to 350°. Place the dough disk on a lightly floured surface and roll out to ¹/₄ inch thick. Cut into hearts. Reroll the scraps. Try tracing children's hands, then cut a heart into the cookie palms. Use a spatula to lift the cookies carefully onto a lightly greased cookie sheet. Sprinkle them with red sugar. Bake for about ten minutes, rotating the cookie sheets halfway through. Remove the cookies from the sheet when they've cooled.

Beltane Spiral Goddess

This silky, lightly orange-flavored bread celebrates the Goddess's love.

Combine the yeast and water, sprinkle with the pinch of sugar, and let it set until foamy. Cream together the butter and sugar, then add the eggs, milk, orange peel, yeast mixture, and salt. Mix in the first 3 cups of flour 1 cup at a time, first with a whisk, then with a wooden spoon. Add flour ¹/₂ cup at a time until the mixture is too stiff to beat. Turn out onto a flat surface dusted with flour and knead, adding flour until the dough is silky and barely dry. Continue kneading for a few minutes.

Put dough in a lightly oiled bowl, turn the dough over, and cover with a damp cloth. Let rise in a warm place until 80 percent doubled in size. Punch down and divide the loaf into two parts, one about 60 percent of the dough, the other about 40 percent.

Roll the larger part into a long coil about 2 inches in diameter. On a lightly oiled cookie sheet, wind the long coil into a spiral. From the second piece of dough, pinch off a piece about as big as a Ping-Pong ball and set aside. Roll the rest out in a coil the same width as the first piece and form the rest of the Goddess (see illustration). Use the remaining piece as her head. Cover with a clean cloth and set in a warm place. Let rise until almost doubled; this bread has egg in it and will rise even more in the oven.

Bake for about 45 minutes in a preheated 350° oven or until it tests done. When the loaf is still warm, spread the glaze over it and sprinkle with nuts.

Move this loaf carefully; the sections may separate, so try sliding it onto its serving piece.

Glaze: Whip ingredients together until blended.

You will need:

1 T dry yeast (one packet)

¹/₄ C warm water

pinch sugar

8 T butter, softened

²/₃ C brown sugar

3 eggs

1 C milk, at room temperature

1 T orange zest, minced or grated

pinch salt

4¹/₂–5¹/₂ C flour

chopped almonds or walnuts

GLAZE

2 T melted butter

¹/₂ C powdered sugar

2 T honey

1 egg white

Strawberries and Cream

You will need:

2 pints of strawberries

1 C whipping cream

1/4 C sugar

1 t vanilla extract

What better way to celebrate love than with those two best of all flavors, fresh sweet strawberries and real whipped cream? Honor the sweetness of love with the extra step of dipping the berries in brown sugar!

Cream whips best when everything is chilled: the cream, the bowl, the beaters. Pour the cream into a dry mixing bowl, and beat at the highest speed until the cream forms peaks when you lift the beaters. Add the sugar and vanilla and continue to beat until they are incorporated. Don't overbeat or else you'll have fresh butter!

More luxurious strawberry ideas:

Set out bowls of melted semisweet or milk chocolate, or bowls of powdered sugar, for dipping.

Slice strawberries and cover with heavy cream.

Make strawberry shortcake by slicing homemade or bakery-bought pound cake. Cover with sliced strawberries and top with whipped cream.

CHAPTER TEN

Summer Solstice
JUNE 20, 21, or 22

THE SUMMER SOLSTICE is the longest day and shortest night of the year. The sun has grown to its full strength, and summer begins. Even as we enjoy swimming and picnicking, we know that the days will begin to get shorter again as soon as Solstice passes.

The Summer Solstice reminds us that nothing lasts forever. We do not live in the unchanging twilight realm of Faery, but in the living, dying, fading, and growing realm of earth. Whenever something is completed, we must let it go.

Because the things we love don't last forever, we love them all the more while they are here.

But letting go of things and people we love is never easy. The Summer Solstice is a time to practice giving things away, letting go of what is completed and done—whether it's our old toys, a flower, or a part of our life, like being a baby or a little kid.

Letting go of something doesn't mean just getting rid of it. When we let go, we allow someone to change and grow and become different. A mother lets go of a grown child so that the child can become independent. Mom can be happy her child has grown up well and strong, but she still might be sad that her baby is gone forever.

At the Summer Solstice, we remember that those times of feeling happy and sad are very special and sacred to the Goddess because they are times when we are changing, as the Goddess is always changing.

The Solstice is a fire festival. For thousands of years, people all over Europe celebrated the Solstice by lighting huge bonfires. The bonfire reminds us of the heat of the summer sun. In Norway, many people stay up all night with the fire. They are so far north that the sun barely sets at all, so why sleep? In Wales, a huge wheel was set afire and rolled down the mountainside. If it stayed burning all the way down, the harvest would be a good one.

Here in California, our main ritual takes place at the beach. We make a big "wicker" God out of scrap lumber and driftwood and decorate him with flowers and herbs that stand for things we want to let go of, for offerings we want to make, and for our hopes, our joys, and our sadness. When we are done, the God looks very beautiful, all dressed in green leaves and covered with flowers. Then we burn the God image and the flowers in the fire, so that we feel happy and sad at the same moment. All the beautiful things we have put into the image be-

Daylight Follows Night[1]

Words and music by Diane Baker

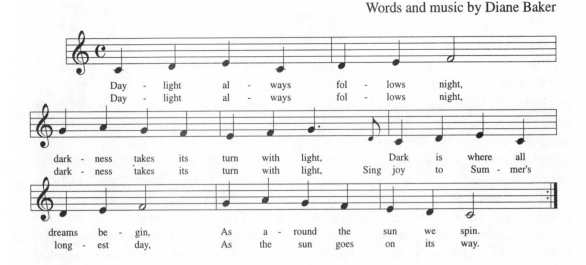

come gifts to the spirits, messages sent to the Goddess and God. In return, we will have fresh new ideas—and room on our walls for new changes.

Just as we honored our mothers on Beltane, we honor fathers at the Summer Solstice, for fathers plant the seed of life and give nurturing, love, and protection to their children.

The Goddess

At the Summer Solstice, the Goddess is the Generous Mother, Freya, Flora, Habondia, she who gives life and fruitfulness to all her children. Everything in nature is generous—otherwise we could not live. The apple tree makes hundreds of apples every year, when only one seed in one apple would be enough to reproduce the tree. Bees make honey so that the hive can survive the winter, but they keep on working all summer long, storing enough to share. Life could exist without climbing roses, striped butterflies, songbirds, raspberries, or wildflowers, but the Goddess keeps making new forms of beauty for us to enjoy.

The Goddess at Summer Solstice gives us not just what we need, but extra. We can feel close to her by being generous, giving more than we're asked to give, doing more than our fair share. That way we make abundance for all.

The rose is the Goddess's symbol at this time of year. Roses bloom abundantly in June, and we can take joy in their sweet scent and the lovely colors of their petals. But roses also have thorns. They remind us, again, that whenever we're most happy, we feel a little sting of sadness that nothing in the world lasts forever.

The God

All through the first half of the year, since his birth at the Winter Solstice, the God has been growing into this life in the visible, tangible world. Now, at the Summer Solstice, he transforms. The daylight is longest and strongest at this time, but now the power of night must begin to grow again. Everything and everyone who fulfills their purpose must change. The God dies in this world in order to be born into the Otherworld. Before, he was awake in this world and asleep in the Dreamworld. Now he becomes the Dreamer, asleep in this world but awake in the world of dreams and visions, the seeds of what will come to be in this world. He becomes the Messenger, carrying our hopes and prayers to the spirit realms.

The God is also the partner of the Goddess, bringing abundance to all of nature. He is Lugh, the Sun God, and he is the ancient power of life who was known simply as the Good God, Keeper of the Crops, provider for his people.

The Altar

At the Summer Solstice, the family altar can be covered with flowers, especially roses. On or around the altar, you might also place things you have completed and let go of, or are trying to let go of—your baby blanket, last year's textbooks, outgrown shoes, or a bad report card.

Add any first fruits of the season and, of course, images of the sun, sunflowers, and other symbols of the holiday.

You might have a special section on the altar for things to give away. Take one thing off your own altar and bring it to the family altar, or find something special to contribute. Let the things stay during the holiday season to soak up blessings, then give them away before Lughnasad rolls around!

On the Land

Around the Summer Solstice the hills here are turning from green to gold. Our gardens are in full bloom. Although the height of wildflower season has passed,

golden poppies still dot the hills. In a good year for fruit, the plum tree in my (Starhawk's) backyard in San Francisco will be covered with ripe plums and we can make jam for our Winter Solstice bread.

Some of the streams are still flowing. The deep pools in the bottoms of the streams are still full, but the land is beginning to look dry and the smallest, seasonal streams are empty now. The birds are nesting and the mosquitoes are out. During the day, the weather is often quite hot, but the nights stay cool. And the days are long; it doesn't get dark until 9:00 or 9:30 at night.

How late does the sun set where you are? The farther you are from the Equator, the longer will be the longest day. And if you're up above the Arctic Circle, the sun won't set at all!

Summer Sunset[2]

Words and music by Anne Hill

Sum-mer sun, sum-mer sun we watch as you set, Send-ing your long arms of light from the west,

Sum-mer sun, sum-mer sun, you shine so bright, As you be-gin your re-turn to the night.

The Twelve Wild Swans[3]
retold by Starhawk

Circle round, and I'll tell you a story for the solstice. . . .

Once there lived a queen who had twelve fine, strong sons, but no daughters. One day as she sat spinning in her chamber, she happened to look out the window, and there below on the fresh snow, she saw a hunter killing a deer. The deer's red blood dropped down onto the white snow, and black ravens gathered around, hoping for a feast.

"Oh," the queen said to herself, "if only I had a daughter with skin as white as that snow, hair as black as the raven's wings, and lips as red as those ruby drops of blood, I'd give all my twelve fine sons for her."

Instantly an old woman appeared. "That was an ill wish that you wished," she said, "but it shall be granted. You will have a daughter, with skin as white as snow, hair as black as the raven's wing, and lips as red as ruby drops of blood. But at the moment she is born, you will lose your twelve fine sons."

"Wait," the queen cried. "I didn't mean it!"

But the old woman was gone.

In great distress, the queen went to her husband, the king, and told him all that had happened. "Don't worry, my dear," the king said. "We will make a plan together. But now you must rest and take good care of yourself."

For the queen was indeed pregnant. Nine months passed, and when the time drew near for her to give birth, the king called all his twelve sons together and shut them up in the deepest dungeon of his castle, where nothing could get at them or harm them. Twelve staunch guards stood at the door. The princes had plenty of good food and warm blankets to comfort them, and one tiny, high window to let in light and air.

The queen gave birth to a beautiful baby daughter, with pale, pale skin and black, black hair and ruby red lips. But at the very moment when the child's first cry was heard, her twelve brothers changed into twelve wild swans. With a rush of wings, they flew out of the tiny window and disappeared from the kingdom.

As joyful as the queen and king were at the birth of their daughter, they were even more grieved by the loss of their twelve fine sons. They made a vow that they would never tell their daughter about her brothers. Rose, as they named the child, would be raised in happiness and joy, not burdened by regrets and grief.

❧

Rose grew to be a lovely young maiden. She was not only beautiful, but kind and good-tempered, so that everyone who knew her loved her. She had all the toys and lessons and beautiful clothes and good things to eat that any princess could want. And yet, deep in her heart, Rose always felt a strange sadness, as if she was missing someone or something she couldn't name. Sometimes when she went to play with the children of the village, she would hear them whispering behind her back, or catch them falling suddenly silent when she appeared.

One of the village children was a very bad-tempered little girl whom everyone called Nasty Nancy. One day Rose and Nasty Nancy had a race to see who could run down the village street and back the fastest, and Rose won. Nasty Nancy was so mad that she stuck out her tongue at Rose and said, "Nah, nah, nah—you think you're so great, well, all your brothers are swans! And it's all your fault!" Then she ran away, before Rose could ask her any questions, and so did the other children, for they were afraid they'd get into trouble.

They had been warned never to say anything to Rose about her brothers.

Crying, Rose ran to the queen. "Tell me about my brothers!" she insisted. "Where are they? Why didn't you tell me before?"

Sighing, the queen told her the whole story. "We wanted to protect you," she said. "We didn't want you to grow up sad, missing brothers you never knew."

"I understand," Rose said. "But now that I know, it seems to me that I must go and find my brothers. Since it was because of me they were changed into swans, I should be the one to save them."

The queen and king begged her not to go. "You are all we have left," they sobbed. "If you are lost, we will have no child at all to comfort us in our old age."

But Rose knew she had to go.

❧

Late that night, she slipped out of the back gate of the castle, taking only a small loaf of bread with her. She headed into the deep woods and began to walk.

She walked and walked and walked. She didn't know where she was going or where to look for her brothers. "I'll just have to begin where I am," she told herself. "If I don't know where to go, I'll go where my feet take me."

She walked through most of the night, until she began to get very tired. "I'll sit and rest for a moment," she thought, "and eat a bit of my bread." Beside the path was a big stone, and she sat down on it and prepared to eat her meager meal. At that very moment, an old woman appeared.

"I'm so hungry, dearie," the old woman said. "Won't you give me a bit of your bread?"

"This bread is all I have," Rose said, "but I will gladly share it with you." She stood up, spread her shawl to make the old woman a comfortable seat, and tore off a generous half of her loaf.

"Thank you, dearie," the old woman said. "You've done a good turn for me, and maybe I can do one for you."

"I don't think so," Rose said. "Not unless you know where I can find my brothers. I have twelve brothers, but they've fallen under an enchantment that has turned them into twelve wild swans."

"Swans!" the old woman said. "Now that you mention it, I believe I've heard of some swans being seen far, far away from here, down by the shore of the sea."

"Really!" Rose cried, all her weariness forgotten. "How can I find the sea, Grandmother?"

"Follow the river to its end," the old woman said.

"Thank you, thank you, Grandmother!" Rose cried.

⚬⚬⚬

She headed off, following a small stream until it joined a great river. She walked and walked and walked, day after day, night after night, following the banks of the river, clambering over big boulders and pushing through scratchy bramble bushes. At last the river spilled itself out into a wide, sandy shoreline and emptied into the great ocean. Ex-

hausted, Rose stood on the shore, watching as the sun began to sink beneath the waves. Suddenly, out of the pink-streaked sky, twelve wild swans came flying, circling the shore and then landing on the sand. As the last ray of sun disappeared, they changed into twelve fine young men.

"My brothers!" Rose cried out in joy. "My brothers! I am your little sister, Rose, and I have come to break the spell and free you, if I can!"

The twelve young men looked at Rose and began to rush forward in delight to meet her. Suddenly they stopped, and looks of horror appeared on their faces.

"What's wrong?" Rose asked. "My brothers, won't you greet me?"

"Oh, evil luck, to meet like this!" said the oldest brother. "Our poor, dear sister! If only we had known! For we have sworn a vow. Since it was because of a woman that we were changed into swans, we vowed to kill the first woman we met. And that is you."

Rose stood frozen, too shocked to speak or move. At that moment an old woman appeared. She looked at the twelve brothers and shook her head sadly.

"Break your wicked vow that never should have been made," she told them. "This is your sister, Rose. You must cherish her, for only through her can you be freed." Then she disappeared.

The twelve brothers rushed forward happily and embraced Rose. "How lucky we are," the oldest brother said, "that you came to this shoreline today. All year long we live in an enchanted land far, far over the sea. We are swans by day and men by night, and only once a year, at the time of the Summer Solstice, can we return to the land of our birth. The way is so long that we need all the hours of the longest days of the year to make the journey. For if night were to catch us on the way, we would be changed back to men and fall into the sea and drown."

"If only I could come with you to that land!" Rose said. "I know that there, in the land of magic, I could find the way to free you."

"We will take you there," her brothers promised. They gathered reeds from the riverside and wove a giant basket from them, with ropes woven of cattails tied on the rim. Then they all slept through the short hours of darkness.

❦

In the morning, just as the pearly dawn was lit by the first rays of the sun, the twelve brothers changed into twelve wild swans. Rose climbed into the basket, and each brother took one of the ropes in his beak and flew off, carrying her along with them. The youngest brother flew above to shade her from the sun.

They flew and they flew and they flew, all through the longest day of the year, and just as the golden sun was sinking in red fire beneath the waves, they came to an is- land. With a rush of wings they landed, setting Rose gently down in her basket, and not a moment too soon. For just as their feet touched the rock of the island, the sun disappeared and the twelve wild

swans changed back into twelve fine young men.

The island was very small, just a few black rocks rising out of the sea. They had barely enough room to stand on it, even all huddled together as close as they could, but there was no room to lie down. So they slept standing up, while all through the short hours of darkness the seas stormed and crashed around them.

When dawn came, the twelve brothers changed back into twelve wild swans. Again Rose climbed into the basket, and her brothers picked up the ropes in their beaks and flew off.

Again they flew and flew, all through the longest day. As the sun began to dip toward the far horizon, Rose could see a golden gleam among the billowing clouds. As they drew closer, she could make out the shape of a tall palace, with pillars of gold and windows of crystal.

"What is that beautiful palace?" she asked.

"That is the home of the Dark Faery, the Fata Morgana," answered the youngest brother. "She is an enchantress of great power and wisdom. But no human being can enter her castle."

"Perhaps I can find a way in," Rose said. "I feel sure that she could help me find the way to free you."

At last they landed on the shore of the magical land across the sea, just as the last rays of sunlight disappeared. The twelve wild swans transformed into Rose's twelve brothers, and together they climbed up the path from the shore to the cave, where they lived on the side of the mountains.

They were all very tired, and after a simple supper of berries and nuts, they slept.

❦

Rose slept deeply, and as she slept she dreamed that she was standing on a silver shore at the foot of the golden palace of the Fata Morgana. In her dream, she climbed up a narrow path and found a high golden door that stood open for her to enter. Gathering her courage, she entered the high hall of the Fata Morgana. The walls gleamed with gold, lit by the cool rays of sun that penetrated through windows of crystal and precious stones.

She walked slowly into the palace, her heart beating. At the far end of the hallway, she could see the form of a woman, waiting for her. Rose walked on until she could see that the woman was dressed in swirling dark robes, rich with colors of indigo and purple and the velvety black of the night sky. Her eyes were dark and gleaming, and her face was neither old nor young, neither dark nor light, but somehow seemed to be all things at once.

"Who are you?" asked the Fata Morgana—for it was she. "Why have you come to my palace, where no human can enter except in dreams?"

"I am Rose, if you please, ma'am," she said. "And I have come to ask for help. I want to free my brothers, who are under an enchantment since my birth. They are swans by day and men by night. Because of me they were changed into swans. Somehow I must free them."

The Fata Morgana looked at Rose for a long, long time. Rose forced herself to stand still and breathe deeply, even though she felt that the Dark Faery could see straight through her and knew all of her secrets and faults. At last the Fata Morgana spoke.

"I know your story," she said to Rose. "And I know the fate of your brothers. It is not because of you that they were changed into swans, but because of your mother's careless words. Nevertheless, you can free them—if you have the courage, for the task will not be easy. Are you willing?"

"Yes, I am," Rose said. "I will do anything to free my brothers."

"Around the cave where your brothers sleep, stinging nettles grow," said the Dark Faery. "You must pluck the nettles with your bare hands, and crush them with your bare feet, and spin them into thread. If you use up the nettles by the cave, then you must gather nettles that grow in a graveyard. From the thread you must weave cloth, and from the cloth you must cut and sew twelve shirts, one for each of your brothers. And the whole time that you do this work, even though it will take you years and years, you must not speak or laugh or cry out loud. Now, do you still want to free your brothers?"

"I do," Rose said. "I will."

Suddenly she found herself back in the cave, waking up with the first light of morning. Without speaking a word to her brothers, she left the cave and began plucking nettles with her bare hands. The nettles stung, and her eyes filled with tears, but she spoke not a word. When she had gathered a big pile, she took off her shoes and began to crush them with her feet, and by the time they were all reduced to fiber and pulp, her poor feet were red and smarting. But she sat down and began to spin the fiber into thread.

Days and weeks passed. Every day Rose picked nettles and crushed them and spun, and when she had gathered enough thread, she began to weave. She spoke not a word, and her brothers understood that she was engaged in a task of magic. They fed her and sheltered her and treated her kindly, and in spite of the pain she suffered in plucking and crushing the nettles, Rose was very happy to be in their company. But she never laughed nor cried.

Months passed, and years passed, and Rose grew into a beautiful young woman. One day as she was sitting outside the cave, spinning and weaving, a handsome young man on a black horse rode by, pursuing a deer. He stopped when he saw Rose, and bowed politely to her. She smiled at him, and he spoke kindly to her, but she did not answer, only pointed to her mouth and shook her head to show that she could not speak.

"I am the king of this land," the young man said. "Every day I am surrounded by people who want this and that from me, who badger me with questions and petitions and ask for judgments. I find your silence very peaceful. May I simply sit with you and be in your presence as you work?"

Rose nodded, and after that the king came every day to sit with her. He found so much pleasure in her company that after a time he asked her to marry him. Rose had grown to love him very dearly, and so she nodded yes. The king helped her gather her nettles and weaving and the shirts she had finished so far, and they rode off together with twelve wild swans following behind.

They were married in his castle, and he built a special room for her, with the walls all painted nettle green, where she could continue her work of weaving and sewing the shirts. He felt very peaceful in her company, and somehow when he talked over a problem with her, although she spoke not a word, he could read her thoughts in her face, and often came by himself to a wise decision. So he gave fair judgments and governed his kingdom well, and everyone was happy, except for the king's younger brother and his wife.

For the king's brother feared that if Rose and the king had a child, he would no longer hold power in the kingdom. And the king's sister-in-law had always hoped that her own children would inherit the kingdom eventually. So they conspired together to get rid of Rose, but in the meantime they pretended to befriend her.

After a time, Rose ran out of nettles. She remembered the words of the Fata Morgana, so that night she slipped out of the castle and across the road, and entered the graveyard. The night was dark, and she was very frightened, for the graveyard was full of lamia, who had the heads of women and the bodies of snakes. She could hear them hissing all around her, and as she bent down to pick the nettles she could feel their dry, scaly bodies slither beside her. But she took a deep breath and thought about her brothers, and gathered a huge supply of the nettles, which she brought back to her special room.

Rose didn't know it, but all the while her sister-in-law was spying on her. She watched Rose go out the gate and peered into the graveyard. The next morning she ran to the king.

"Brother dear," she said, "I grieve to tell you this, but that woman you married is an evil Witch! At night she goes into the graveyard and consorts with lamia. I've seen her myself!"

"I don't believe you," said the king. "My wife is a good woman, and I love her dearly. Even if she did go into a graveyard, I know she must have a good reason. Perhaps she was bringing an offering to the dead. Don't bother me anymore with nasty gossip."

So the sister-in-law was thwarted, but she and her husband bided their time.

❧

A year passed, and Rose gave birth to a beautiful baby girl. All through the pangs of her labor she never once cried aloud, and though she was thrilled with joy to see her baby daughter, she did not laugh. When the child was sleeping, she continued to work on the shirts.

That night, the sister-in-law came to the room where Rose and the baby were sleeping, watched by all the women of the court.

"Let us celebrate this joyful occasion with wine," she said, and they did. But she had put a sleeping potion into the wine, and all the women of the court fell sound asleep. Then the sister-in-law took the baby from Rose's side and threw her out the window. A wolf, passing below, grabbed the baby in her jaws and carried her out to the woods. The sister-in-law killed a litter of newborn puppies, and smeared the blood around Rose's mouth and on her hands.

When morning came, the watching women awoke in horror to find that they had slept and the baby was gone. "What shall we do? What shall we do?" they cried. "The king will never forgive us!" So they concocted a tale, and when the king came to see his daughter, they cried out tearfully that Rose had gone mad and devoured her child, although they had fought with all their strength to stop her.

"You see," the sister-in-law said, "she is evil, just as I told you. You must get rid of her."

But the king shook his head. "She is my wife, and I love her dearly," he said. "I do not believe your story. Something else must have happened, although I do not know what. But my wife is a good woman, and I cannot believe she would harm her child."

Rose was terribly sad at the loss of her baby. Still, she did not cry out loud, but continued to work on her shirts. The king consoled her, and she consoled him.

Another year passed, and again Rose gave birth, this time to a beautiful baby boy. Once again the sister-in-law gave a sleeping potion to the ladies of the court, took the baby from Rose's side, and threw it out the window. Again the wolf caught the child in her jaws and carried it out to the woods, while the sister-in-law smeared Rose's face and hands with puppies' blood. But this time the king could not defend his wife. Try as he would to convince his court and his advisors that she was a good person, his own brother led the people in condemning her.

They took Rose and threw her into the deepest dungeon below the castle, and they took all her shirts and thread and weaving and threw them in after her. "Here, Witch!" they cried. "Take your filthy spells!"

All the while, Rose still did not speak to save herself. By this time she was almost finished with her task. She was working on the twelfth shirt. Deep in the dungeon, she continued to spin and weave and sew. When morning came and the guards arrived to take her away to her execution, she was still busily working. They bound her into a cart, but her hands were free, and as they wheeled her through the streets she hardly noticed the jeering crowds of people, because she was still working so hard on the last shirt. Even when they took her from the cart and bound her to the stake, she spared no thought for fear, but continued her work.

The king was weeping and could not bear to light the pyre, but his brother took the torch and walked toward Rose. At last she looked up from her work, to see the torch thrust into the wood at her feet. The wood caught fire, and the flames began to rise around her.

Suddenly, from the sky, twelve white swans appeared, wheeling in a great circle around the stake where Rose was bound. She took the shirts and tossed them, one by one, onto the backs of her brothers, and as they landed, the twelve wild swans transformed into twelve fine, strong men.

"I am innocent," Rose cried, and dropped dead. The flames around her changed into roses.

The king cried out and ran to her, cutting her down from the stake and holding her in his arms. Her eyelids fluttered, and she took a deep breath. She wasn't dead after all—she had only fainted!

A great roar burst from the crowd. Suddenly an old woman appeared, holding a newborn child in her arms. A year-old girl toddled by her side.

"Here are your lost children," she said to Rose. "Guard them and cherish them well, for now they are restored to you."

With great joy, the king and Rose embraced their children. The crowd cheered, and everyone was happy, except for the king's brother and his wife, who were so mad that they burst and were never heard from again.

Then Rose's brothers walked up and greeted her with great happiness. "You have freed us," they said. "With your courage and perseverance, you have broken the spell that bound us. Now we can all be together."

One by one she kissed them. But Rose had not quite finished the very last sleeve of the last shirt. And so when her youngest brother came forward to embrace her, he reached for her with one human arm and one swan's wing.

The Nahua Creation of the Sun and the Moon[4]

retold by Rafael Jesús González

At the beginning of this world, when darkness was yet everywhere, all the Gods met at Teotihuacán (teh-oh-teh-wak-AHN), Place Where the Gods Are Born. They said, "It is not good that darkness should prevail. It is not good that there is no light. How shall the corn grow? How will humankind live?"

And they all agreed. "A sun is needed; we must make a sun." So said Quetzalcóatl (keht-zahl-cóh-AH-t'l), Feathered Serpent, God of the Wind; and Chicomecóatl (chi-coh-meh-cóh-AH-t'l), Seven Serpents, Goddess of the Corn; and all of the other Gods and Goddesses too many to name.

So they said, "One of us must agree to be the sun. One of us must leap into the holy fire to become the sun." They brought oak and cedar and mesquite and many other precious woods, and built a huge fire that sputtered and hissed and sent a storm of sparks into the dark.

And they said, "Who shall it be? Who shall leap into the fire and become the new sun?" They all looked at one another, and they were all afraid.

From their midst stepped forth Tecuciztécatl (teh-coo-sis-téh-CAH-t'l), God of the Conch Shell, The Beautiful God, and he said, "I will become the new sun." As he walked through the crowd of gods, he was very beautiful to look at. He wore a loincloth and embroidered cape of the finest cotton, soft as the tassel of new corn. On his head he wore a crown of the finest plumes: quetzal, macaw, hummingbird, parrot. Jade and turquoise adorned his throat.

He was a proud god and rich. His tools of sacrifice were of the finest. He carried not thorns but sharp slivers of coral with which to prick himself for blood to offer to the Earth, Coatlicue (co-aht-leé-COO-eh), She of the Serpent Skirt, Tonantzin (tohn-ÁHNT-sin), Mother of all the Gods and of us all. To offer perfumed smoke, he carried only the finest of white copal.

And so he made sacrifice; four full days he sacrificed. He drew blood with his slivers of coral and caught it in his balls of quetzal feathers and offered it to Mother Earth. He took his precious white copal and placed it on a live coal and sent the perfumed white smoke into the skies.

Then he closed his eyes, took a deep breath, and ran toward the roaring, sputtering, fuming fire.

But the fire was too hot, too intense, too fierce. And he stopped short.

Again the Beautiful God closed his eyes, took a deep breath, and ran toward the blaze.

Again the pyre proved too hot, too fierce. And the God stopped short.

One more time, Beautiful God closed his eyes, breathed deeply, ran.

And stopped short.

And one more time the Beautiful God tried. And again, could not.

The Gods murmured among themselves and the Beautiful God was ashamed, for his heart had not been strong enough and he could not leap into the fire to become the new Sun. And the Gods again asked themselves who among them would agree to become the new sun.

And from far back, from the edge of the crowd of Gods came forth the least of them, Nanahuatzin (nahn-ah-WÁHT-sin), the Ugly God, his skin mottled with sores. And poor he was. His loincloth and cape were of coarse maguey (mah-gay) weave. His headdress was of amate (ah-MÁ-teh) paper. His tools of sacrifice were only black maguey spines. Too poor to afford even common copal, he had only chips of the bark. The Gods murmured among themselves.

But he said, "I will go into the fire." For four full days he said his prayers to the Earth, pierced himself with his thorns, caught the blood in his balls of grass, and offered them to the Holy Mother. He took his chips of copal bark and placed them on a hot coal, and the feebly perfumed smoke rose to the skies.

Then he came to the fire. He closed his eyes. He took a deep breath. He ran.

And,

    with his heart in his throat,

      he leaped into the fire.

The flames rose higher. They sputtered. They roared. They leaped. They sparked and they fumed. Sparks swirled up into the sky. Embers and coals shot out from the blaze. The fire threatened to break its bounds, to lick its red and gold tongues into the grasses and shrubs of the land.

Seeing this, the eagle swooped down from the sky and with its wings swept the burning embers back into the fire. But the live coals tumbled onto the grass and, seeing this, the jaguar scraped them back with his paws and rolled upon them to put out their flame. From that moment forth, the tips of the eagle's wings are charred black and the skin of the jaguar is marked where he was burned by the embers.

The fire still rose, higher and higher. And for many days the Gods watched and prayed until the sky reddened in the east and from the center of the flames rose the heart of the least of the Gods, all ablaze and brilliant and flaming.

It rose higher and higher and stood high and still in the middle of the sky.

The Gods stood silent and amazed, and they called him Tonatiuh (tohn-ah-TEÉ-oo), the Sun. And he burned fiercely and bright, and his light was blinding and it became exceedingly hot.

The Beautiful God all this time watched from where he stood among the other Gods. A deep shame overcame him. Taking heart, he closed his eyes, breathed a deep breath, ran toward the fire—and leaped.

The fire blazed and it rose and it fumed and it sputtered and sparked. And from its blaze rose the heart of the Beautiful God, became a second sun, and stood close by Tonatiuh, the new sun.

And the Gods said, "This is not good. If there are two suns and both stand burning so fiercely in one spot, all upon the earth will be scorched and burned. The corn cannot grow and none of the animals, including humankind, will be able to live."

Quetzalcóatl, Lord of the Wind, said, "This is so." And he put on his Wind Mask and took a deep breath and blew a hard wind that set the two suns moving across the sky.

And the Gods were amazed and they said, "This is not good. It cannot be, for if we have two suns equally bright following so closely one upon the other, all will scorch and burn, wither and die."

And Quetzalcóatl said, "It is so." And seeing a hare hop among the grasses and the nopales nearby, he ran after it, chased it down, caught it by the ears, and, with all his might, swung it over his head and threw it at the second sun, hitting him round on the face.

Immediately the light of the second sun was dimmed and his flight slowed so that he followed a goodly pace behind Tonatiuh, the new sun. And the Gods said, "This is good. The second sun will be the Moon. The new sun will rule the day, and the Moon will follow a goodly pace behind and light up the darkness of the night." And it was so.

And because he was ashamed, the Moon had to make penance and atone for his pride and his lack of courage. So he fasts, and when he does, he is seen to become, from his plump and beautiful self, thinner and thinner, until he is a mere sliver, a shadow of himself. And then he breaks his fast and again grows plump and beautiful until he fasts again.

But even when he is plump and beautiful, one can still see the mark left by the rabbit where it struck his face long ago in Teotihuacán, where the Gods are born.

❧

Wicker Man

For this ritual, we make and then burn a wicker man. When we are on the beach, he is a life-size structure of boards and branches. If we are out camping, he can be a foot or two tall, made of dead branches tied together with cotton twine in the crude shape of a man. Whichever spot you choose, try to be where you can watch the sun set and build a campfire.

The wicker man is Lugh, the Sun God, the Shining One, who dies today as the sun sets. Lugh is the messenger to the Otherworld, the one who carries our gifts over to the other side. Tied to his body are our gifts: old artwork and spells that need to be released so that we can open to new creative urges, wishes written on slips of paper and bound to Lugh with bits of string, things from our altars that we wish to transform, to let go of, to ask for help with.

Before leaving for your trip, make sure everyone has time to collect things to give over to the wicker man. On the day of the ritual, set aside a few hours in the afternoon for everyone to observe sacred silence. In the quiet, all can help build the wicker man with foraged materials and have time to purify themselves, in whatever manner they choose, to prepare for the ceremony. In the silence, each act becomes a meditation, sharpening focus and awareness. If there is a stream or other body of water nearby, purifying can entail a ritual bath. Lay a fire and set the wicker man on top of it, so that when the time comes he can be lit easily.

Holy Shining Sunlight[5]

Words and music by Sparky T. Rabbit

Ho- ly Shin- ing Sun- light, Ra di- ance! Ra - di- ance! Broth- er, come to us.

Shortly before sunset, gather together to start the ritual. Ground, cast a circle, and call in the directions. In the spirit of stretching their abilities, encourage adolescents and older children to try leading a part of the ritual. With some coaching beforehand, they can call in a direction, cast the circle, or lead the grounding meditation. After creating sacred space, call in the Goddess and Lugh with the song "Holy Shining Sunlight." Say a Father's Blessing, calling the power of the God into the men present.

Take some time now to attach all the objects to the wicker man. As people come forward, keep singing or humming "Holy Shining Sunlight" softly. When everyone is finished hanging things on the wicker man, light the fire beneath him. Stand up and begin singing "Dance the Gift of the Summer's Sun."

Circle the fire, clapping and drumming as you dance and sing the wicker man on his way to the Otherworld. Imagine that the sparks and flames ascending are your messages, making their way through the veil to where they need to go. Let the singing and dancing peak, and with the energy you raise, visualize Lugh sailing off from this world into the next.

When the song has died away and the dancing has stopped, ground the energy to the earth, for Her healing. Say,

Lugh of the Long Arm, Shining One, Fierce One, we have sent you on your way. Go well and safely now, as you journey into the arms of night to be reborn. Though we mourn your passing, we will remember you shining in strength and brilliance on this longest day. And until we meet again, hail and farewell.

Say goodbye to the Goddess in similar fashion, open the circle. End with all saying in unison,

The circle is open but unbroken. May the peace of the Goddess go in our hearts. Merry meet, merry part, and merry meet again!

Share food and drink, and enjoy the dying embers of the longest day.

Gift of the Summer's Sun[6]

Words and music by T. Thorn Coyle

Blessing for Fathers

In poring over the thealogy for the Wheel of the Year, we realized that just as mothers have special recognition at Beltane, we need a place in our seasonal festivals to honor fathers. We include adoptive fathers, stepfathers, and foster fathers, as well as biological fathers. Fathering is not an easy job today. Shifting cultural standards that demand more participation by fathers in the home, combined with economic pressures that demand greater performance and sacrifice to hold down a job, put fathers in a very difficult situation. Men are challenged to come into equal partnership with women, to pay more attention to their children than their fathers did, and on top of it all, often to be the main wage-earner for their families.

At the same time the need for positive male role models in the lives of boys and girls has never been greater, and many men are rising to the challenge. To honor these men and the strength of their commitment to children, here is a Blessing for Fathers, similar to the Mother's Blessing presented at Beltane.

Father of Life, Horned One, Green One, Seed Sower, we call you! You who are the Comforter, the Consoler, who steadies us to face our fears, who challenges us to overcome obstacles, we call you! Protector of the young, Initiator, you who guide our boys to manhood, we call you and welcome you into our circle today!

Father of Life, you whose voice is the rumble of thunder and the shifting of the earth beneath our feet, you bring change to the lives of us all! We ask you today to embrace the men here who are raising children, help them walk with sure footing. You who dazzle us with light from the distant stars arching across the vast bowl of the heavens, help these men see the beauty of their ways and the great good they are doing for their children and all future generations. Great One, we give thanks for the power of slow and lasting change that is your blessing!

Seed Sower, you who rise with the grain in the spring, we thank you for sustaining our bodies and feeding our souls. May your blessings take root and grow to abundance in the lives of the fathers here, so that all the children in our circle will be nurtured and cared for as they grow. Speaker of the unspoken truths, Challenger at the gates, you who listen to the greatest and the least among us in equal measure, with your help may we teach our children to listen, to be compassionate, to fight for what is just, to love with passion and live without fear.

Father, we ask you today to dwell in the hearts of these men, these fathers. Give them strength every day. Let them know love and praise, and let them love and praise themselves as well. Stand with them today and every day, lighten their hearts and ease their burdens, help them open to the love that is all around them, especially the love from their children, who are so blessed to have them in their lives! Blessed be the fathers!

Turning the Wheel Dance

This is a wonderful dance to celebrate the turning of the wheel of the seasons if you have a dozen or more people. The basic formation requires four people to be the center spokes in the wheel, each with their right arm stretched toward the center and grasping the hand of the person directly across from them (see illustration 1). The second set of four dancers takes the left hand of each of the center spokes. The third set of four takes the left hand of the second set, and so on, depending on how many dancers you have (see illustration 2). Be sure that each spoke has about the same number of people in it.

Singing together whatever song you have chosen, begin walking around in a circle. Care must be taken that the center spokes not walk too fast; otherwise the people at the end of the lines will be running to keep up.

Once the human wheel has made one complete rotation,

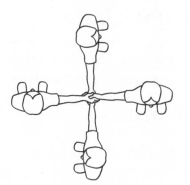

ILLUSTRATION 1

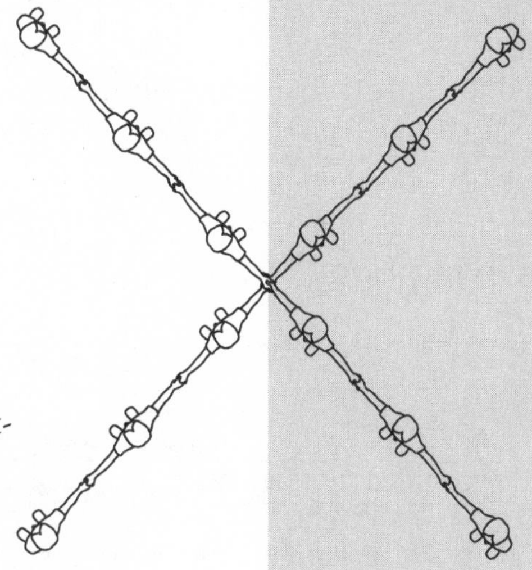

the center spokes let go of both their partners' hands, and walk out to the edge of
the wheel to become the last person in
their line (see illustration 3). The second set of four dancers must draw close to
form the new center spokes. Repeat until everyone has had
a chance to be a center spoke and help turn the wheel of the
seasons.

ILLUSTRATION 2

This is an exhilarating dance, with a steady feeling of
building energy. It works best if there are plenty of adults
along with the children, to make sure the circle always has a
center. Having others outside the wheel to drum and sing
helps, too, as it can be hard with a big group to dance and
sing at the same time.

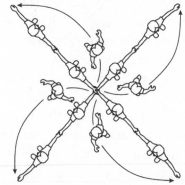

ILLUSTRATION 3

The Giving Game

Each child brings something to give away. After all the gifts are placed on a cloth, everyone holds hands, forming a circle around the gifts. Then everyone dances (like Ring Around the Rosy) while singing "The Giving Song."

When the song ends, all the dancers drop hands and take the gift that calls to them. Sing the song again, and dance in a circle with the gifts.

The Giving Song[7]

Words and music by Pandora Minerva O'Mallory

Help us take what we have been giv-en, Help us take what we have been giv-en,

Help us take what we have been giv-en, Help us take it and give it a-way.

Time Capsules

On Summer Solstice we (Diane's family) mark our children's growth against the wall. But we also honor the other ways in which we've grown by making time capsules of writings and drawings.

My preparation begins a few days before Solstice. I look over the vast amount of home and school projects my children collect through the year, select my favorites for my own archives, and choose some for the children to consider putting into their time capsule. We start our celebration by opening last year's time capsules to remember what we were like then, what we were thinking, what we wanted. After we've looked at last year's time capsules, we make new ones. I spread out art supplies, paper, and writing materials for the children to use. I begin by suggesting that the children write a letter to themselves to read a year from now. They might write down what they accomplished this year: learning to blow a bubble-gum bubble, riding a two-wheeler, making a first dive. The adults act as scribes for the youngest children.

Then the children decide which projects to include. Everything goes into large envelopes, prelabeled with the children's names, and they're saved for our next Summer Solstice.

> We learn many lessons from our time capsules: how something we can't even remember seemed very important, how a new accomplishment that seemed too hard is now quite simple.

Growing Up and Out

Many families include a giveaway of items that children have outgrown, such as toys, clothes, books, and music, as part of their Summer Solstice celebration. The children can choose special things as gifts for their younger siblings or specific friends. Be sure to label these. Place the rest of the giveaways in baskets in front of the altar; after the ceremony, offer them to others.

If there aren't any appropriate recipients for what's been outgrown, take the items to charities or resale shops.

Faery Money

In ordinary life, often our giving and taking are conducted with money. Children rarely have a lot of money to give away, so why not make Faery Money? Ask them to draw their own currency on white paper, but instead of having them represent dollars, the kids might try writing good-luck notes on them, or blessings, or inspirations, à la fortune cookies. Photocopy the designs and cut them into notes. During this season, you and your children can carry the notes in your pockets and give them to people for the things you value— a smile, a hug, a favor. Enjoy feeling rich!

Shadow Play with City Kids

Because the holidays of Goddess tradition track seasonal cycles, we try to strengthen our connection to nature, even in the most urban environments. Children can learn the paths of the great cycles by turning the city into a big sun clock, especially at the solstices and equinoxes.

Create your own solar calendar by marking where shadows fall on the solstices and equinoxes. Pick out a building that has an unobstructed shadow. Visit this spot at the same time of day on holidays, noting the shadow's progress on the ground. This reminds us that no matter how or where we live, we're still part of the big circle.

Sun Piñata

You will need:

balloon, at least 16 inches across and spherical when blown up

liquid laundry starch

newspaper

2 wide, shallow kitchen bowls

cone-shaped coffee filters, size 0 or 00

scissors

hole punch

sun-colored poster paint

glitter

string

Although a little messy to make, the finished piñata is delightfully festive. Depending on the weather, plan to include up to two days' drying time. In a hot, dry climate, the piñata can dry in three hours, the paint in another hour.

Take 12 single sheets of newspaper, tear them into 1- to 1½-inch-wide strips, then in half for shorter strips. Spread more newspaper sheets over work area. Pour laundry starch into one bowl, and place blown-up balloon in the other bowl, keeping the balloon's knotted neck down.

Drag a paper strip through the laundry starch, then through 2 fingers, held scissors style, to remove excess starch. Cover the balloon with the strips. Leave a small section around the knot uncovered; this is where the piñata stuffing will go in. Repeat for a second layer. Be gentle so you don't break the balloon.

The coffee filter cones make the sun-ray spikes. Turn them inside out so the seam is inside, then stuff them with crumpled newspaper. Place a spike on the sun. If it's too big and out of proportion to the sun, cut off a little at the bottom. To attach the spike to the sun, use small newspaper strips soaked in laundry starch. Lay a strip lengthwise along the sun and up the stuffed cone, smoothing the paper at the join. Use as many strips as needed to firmly attach spike. (My [Diane's] family doesn't mind small gaps at the join, but you can be as meticulous as you want.) Repeat with other spikes, attaching them at regular intervals for a nice effect.

Let the sun dry, rotating it in the bowl for even drying and to keep it from sticking to the bowl. If you're drying it outside, don't forget to bring it in at night, since it will wilt in the dew. The balloon will lose air as the piñata dries. If not, undo the knot and let the air out slowly or prick the balloon—but only after making sure the piñata is thoroughly dry and stiff.

Paint the piñata bright yellow and sprinkle glitter onto the wet paint. Let dry. With the hole punch, make three holes well below the opening and attach string. Fill with stuffing. If you want, you can close the opening with more papier-mâché.

Piñata Stuffing

We favor gold chocolate coins with their shiny outsides and dark chocolate insides, a wonderful Solstice symbol. We've also put in small mirrors, candied fruit, and yellow flower petals. One year my neighbor Rachel made dream pillows from sun-patterned blue cloth and filled with yarrow and rosemary, which we still treasure.

Dream Pillows

When filled with herbs and slipped under pillows, these small pillows promote good dreaming. This method makes a whole batch of pillows quickly.

Fold the fabric in half lengthwise, wrong side out, to form a long, narrow strip. Make a seam down the side, 1/2 inch from the cut edge.

Now, mark off each pillow on the fabric. Starting at one end, make a line that's perpendicular to the seam and is 1/2 inch from the open edge. The second line is 4 inches from the first line. The third line is 1 inch from the second line.

Substitution for Liquid Laundry Starch

Use a flour mixture of 2 parts water to 1 part flour, starting with 2 cups water and 1 cup flour, blended until smooth. Make more as needed.

You will need:

1/4 yard of 45-inch-wide fabric

thread, same color as fabric

dried herbs

Keep alternating between the 4-inch and 1-inch measurements until you reach the end. You should have nine 4-inch squares; these are your pillows.

Sew along the lines, leaving 2 inches of one seam open on each pillow. When all the seams are formed, cut exactly halfway between the seams that are 1 inch apart. Turn the pillows inside out, stuff with herbs, and stitch the openings shut.

Floating Sun Candles

You will need:

2 foil cupcake baking cups for each candle

$^1/_3$ to $^1/_2$ C wax per candle

wicking

Children can have their own candles to which they can whisper their wishes for the coming season.

See Tool Chest for instructions on melting and pouring wax and inserting wicks.

Remove the paper inserts from two foil cups and put one cup in the other. (Two layers give the mold enough stability to hold the wax.) Using your thumbs and index fingers, pull and push the foil to form sun rays. Be sure that the sides are level with each other. If they're not, when you pour the wax, it will spill out.

Pour the wax and insert the wick when the wax has just firmed. After the candle has cooled, remove the layers of foil. Float in water bowls and light.

Sunflower Hat

You will need:

1 sheet of construction paper

2 9-inch paper plates

Use the construction paper to make 12 to 14 flower petals, 2 inches wide by 4$^1/_2$ inches long. On the paper plates, draw a circle 2 inches from the edge. Cut out the circle and discard, leaving the brims to form the headband, which should fit most children's heads snugly. If headbands are too tight, carefully trim the inner edge.

Glue the petals evenly around one headband, then glue the other headband over this. Decorate the hat with glitter or markers.

Sun-Baked Tangerines

This recipe is inspired by the childhood picnics I (Diane) packed for my many solitary woodland rambles and by the lovely *Bunny Planet* series by Rosemary Wells.

Peel several tangerines and place the separated sections on a surface where they will be exposed to the sun. Let the sun bake the tangerines until the outside is firm but still pliable, about an hour. Eat while still sun-hot.

We like to put out the sections before we start our ritual. They're ready by the time we break the piñata.

Summer Fruits

The fruits of summer are surely one of the Goddess's best gifts. Many areas have pick-it-yourself farms. A visit makes a wonderful prelude to a Solstice ceremony.

Slice the fruits into bite-sized pieces and spread in luscious patterns across a platter or tray. Leave some uncut for a basket offering on the altar. Tuck fresh edible flowers or tender leaves of lettuce around the outside rim of the platter. At the ritual, bring the platter into the circle, and provide plenty of napkins for fruit-sticky faces and fingers.

Summer Solstice Cupcakes

You will need:

½ C butter (one stick), softened in the summer sun

1 C sugar

2 eggs

1 t vanilla extract

2 C flour, sifted first and then measured

pinch of salt

2 t baking powder

1 C milk

1 C chocolate chips

Just as Winter Solstice gives birth to the light, Summer Solstice, with its day that never seems to end, holds the seeds of darkness. We discover darkness in the bits of chocolate concealed inside this sunny cupcake. Use a cake mix or try this favorite yellow cupcake recipe.

Cream together the butter and sugar until light and fluffy. Beat in the eggs one at a time. Add vanilla. Mix together the flour, salt, and baking powder. Add half of the dry ingredients to the wet mixture and stir in. Follow with ½ cup milk, then the other half of the flour mixture and the rest of the milk. Stir in the chocolate chips.

Use paper liners or grease and flour cupcake tins. Bake for 25 minutes in a preheated 375° oven.

Makes 20 to 24 cupcakes.

CHAPTER ELEVEN

Lughnasad/Lammas
AUGUST 1

LUGHNASAD, OR LAMMAS, is the holiday that celebrates the beginning of the harvest season. Summer is at its height, but already the days are growing shorter and we know that autumn is on its way. Some things in the garden are ripe; others are still not ready. The grain is standing in the fields but not yet harvested.

Lammas is a time to think about our hopes and fears. We hope that we'll be able to pick and eat all the things we worked hard to grow—but a lot could still happen.

We could have bad storms or scorching sun or high winds. Here in California, Lammas is the beginning of the most dangerous part of the year for fire. Because we don't usually have rain in the summertime, the trees and grass and brush are dry, dry, dry!

To harvest, we must cut down the plants we've tended so carefully. To people who live close to the earth and growing things, this almost feels like killing a person. We mourn and grieve for the spirit of the grain and the green things. We honor them because they give us life by letting us eat them. We feel sad that summer must end for us to reap the harvest. But we feel happy, too, thinking about all the good things we'll have to eat! Just as the Summer Solstice taught us that we can feel happy and sad at the same time, Lammas teaches us to feel sad and happy.

Because Lammas comes at the season when the grain and many fruits first begin to ripen, it was always a time for special offerings. The first fruits to ripen and the first grain that was ready to reap were considered to be especially sacred, as if they carried within them the spirit of the Goddess herself. The bees are very active now, and their sweet, golden honey is a symbol of this sunny time.

At the Summer Solstice we learned to be generous, to sow many seeds. Now, at Lammas, we must learn to be protectors and nurturers of what we've planted. We become full partners with the Goddess and God.

In ancient Ireland and throughout the British Isles, Lammas was a time for great fairs and markets. It marked a time of sacred peace. As the fruits ripened, people brought their crops to market. For country people who rarely saw anyone from outside their village, this must have been one of the most exciting days of the year, when they could meet friends from far away, see new faces, learn new customs. No one was allowed to disturb the holiday peace by fighting, thieving, or making war.

Are you fighting with anyone? Have you quarrelled with a friend, or with your brothers or sisters? Now is a good time to make peace by doing something fun together.

The Goddess

At this season, the Goddess becomes the Mother of the Harvest. Picture her strong, with her face dark from the sun and wind, carrying a scythe and a basket of fruits, vegetables, and ears of corn. She knows that in order to eat bread we must cut the grain— that, in fact, if we didn't cut it, it would die anyway, for that is the only way next year's grain can grow.

We can call on the Harvest Mother when we have to do hard things or make difficult choices. We must face our fears of failing, of losing the harvest, of making mistakes. She gives us the strength to do what needs to be done, to tell the truth even when we are afraid, to say no to things that are not right for us. She helps us clean house and get rid of what we don't need, and she helps us finish what we start. She loves her children, and the gifts she gives us are food, abundance, and plenty—everything we need to live and grow.

She is hope as well as fear, so if there is something special you are hoping for, you can ask for her help. But remember, she expects you to work for what you want.

In ancient times, the storehouse was seen as a magical and powerful place. Dark and cool, filled with grain, oil, foods, and treasures, it reminded people of the Otherworld. In Sumeria, Inanna was both the Goddess of the storehouse and the morning and evening star, the Goddess of love. At this time of year, as the harvest begins, we tell the story of how she went down to the land of the dead to visit her sister, Ereshkigal.

We honor the Harvest Mother whenever we don't take the easy way out, when we do what is right, when we face a fear and go ahead anyway, when we work hard at something and wait patiently for rewards.

The God

The God at this season is Lugh (Loo), called Samildanach—the Many-Skilled, the God of all the arts and skills of human culture—by the Irish. At this season, when we can feel the sun begin to wane and the days grow shorter even in the heat of summer, we say the God is already halfway into the Otherworld. He is in that realm where ideas are born, where the dreams and inspiration that come from the spirit can be brought into the world of day and night by our work, our skill, and our art. In his honor, sacred games in which champions could test their skills and strength were held in ancient Ireland.

One story about Lugh is that he came to the Hall of the Gods asking to be admitted. He said he was a poet, a warrior, a carpenter, a musician, and a healer, and went on to name all the other arts and skills. But the Gods already had someone who was master of each craft he named. "But do you have anyone who is master of them all?" Lugh asked. That they did not, and so Lugh became leader of the Gods.

Lugh is also a sun God. He is called Lugh of the Long Hand or Long Arm—the long rays of the sun as it sinks lower in the sky at this time of year. He is always reaching out to us with warmth and comfort. We can feel close to the God at this season by practicing our skills, making art, playing music.

Lammas is also the time to honor our teachers, all those people who help us learn.

Sunlight pays no attention to locks and bars and chains. With his spear of light, Lugh fights against all forms of slavery and injustice. We can call on Lugh to help us whenever we struggle to make the world fairer and freer for everyone.

The Altar

The altar should have on it some of the first fruits, grains, and vegetables that are now ripening. You can also add things that represent your skills: a baseball glove, a computer diskette, a book, a drawing, or a hammer.

One section of the altar can represent your hopes. Look for pictures in magazines and make a hope card (see Activities).

Another section of the altar can be for your fears. Draw pictures of them, fold them up, and when Lammas is over, let a grown-up help you burn the pictures and release your fears.

What struggles for justice have your family and ancestors been part of? What struggles going on in the world right now do you think could use some help from Lugh's spear? Put something on the altar to represent those struggles.

On the Land

Lammas is the beginning of the most dangerous time of the year where we live.

Everything is very hot and dry. Fires can start easily. Until the rains come, we'll be very careful with any open flames. Even a glass jar full of water can start a fire on a sunny day—it acts as a magnifying glass, and can set dry grass on fire.

The garden is full of good things to eat. The wildflowers are mostly gone, but the flowers we planted and tended are dancing with color and fragrance. Wild blackberries are ripe, and we can make jam and pies. And it's lovely just to relax on a hot afternoon, to go swimming or lie in a hammock in the shade of the big redwoods, which keep us cool all year long.

Do you have a garden? What is ripe now where you live? Can you pick wild berries or fresh corn? What is your favorite thing to do in the summertime?

The Queen Bee
A Brothers Grimm Tale
retold by Starhawk

Once there were three brothers, the sons of a king. The two eldest princes were handsome, dapper young men who thought a great deal of themselves. They went out into the world to seek their fortune, but soon fell into lazy ways, preferring to drink and gamble and enjoy themselves rather than work or seek adventure. The youngest brother was a plain and simple fellow who did not talk very much. The family didn't think much of him, and neither did anyone else. They called him the Fool.

When the two elder brothers did not return home one day, the Fool went out to look for them. Eventually he found them in a poor tavern by the crossroads. He was overjoyed to see his brothers again, but they laughed at him for thinking that he could make his way in the world when they, who were so much cleverer, had failed.

But the Fool roused his brothers to continue seeking their fortune. They set out together. After they had traveled for a while, they came across a large ant hill.

"Let's smash it!" said the oldest brother. "It'd be fun to watch the ants run around and try to save their pitiful ant eggs. We could put a good scare into them!"

But the Fool stopped them. "Leave the little creatures alone," he said. "Let them be in peace. I won't let you harm them."

They continued on their way, and eventually they came to a lake where ducks were swimming.

"Let's catch a few and roast them," said the second brother. "We could make ourselves a good meal!"

"I won't let you kill them," said the Fool. "Leave them in peace."

They continued on their way, and at last they came to a beehive in a tall tree dripping with honey that ran down the trunk.

"Let's light a big fire," said the two older brothers together. "We can smoke out the bees and kill them and take their honey."

"I won't let you burn them out," the Fool said. "Leave them in peace."

On their way they went, and at last they came to a great stone castle. No one came out to greet them. There were no courtiers in the courtyard, and in the stables there were only horses of stone. No living creature seemed to be around.

The three brothers were afraid, but they had come so far, they were reluctant to go home without exploring the castle itself. They entered its empty halls and wandered through dusty rooms, seeing no signs of life.

At last they came to a high tower. At the very top was a door with three locks on it and a small hole in the center. They looked through the peephole and saw a gray dwarf sitting at a table. They knocked loudly and called out to him, but he did not hear them. Again they knocked and called, and still he did not answer. But when they knocked and called a third time, he got up and unlocked the door.

He spoke not a word to them, but led them to a table that was spread with all sorts of good things to eat and drink. When they were finished, he led each one to his own bedroom.

In the morning, the dwarf went into the room of the eldest brother and brought him to a room deep in the heart of the castle, where a stone tablet stood. On the stone was an inscription that told how the castle could be rescued from its enchantment. Three tasks had to be performed.

The first task was to gather the thousand pearls of the king's daughter that were scattered among the moss of the forest, all before nightfall. If so much as one single pearl was missing, the brother would be turned to stone.

The eldest brother went to the moss and

searched all day long. For once he worked as hard as he could, without a trace of laziness! But at the end of the day, he had found only a hundred pearls. As the sun set he turned to stone.

The next day the dwarf took the second brother to the stone tablet. He too read the inscription, went to the moss, and searched and searched. He looked so hard that his eyes crossed and sweat dripped down his nose, but at the end of the day he had found only two hundred pearls. As the sun set he too turned to stone.

The third day, the dwarf took the Fool to read the inscription on the stone tablet. He went out to the moss and began to gather pearls, but soon he began to feel that the task was impossible. He sat down on a rock and wept.

While he was sitting and weeping, the Queen of the Ants, whose life he had saved, came to his aid with five thousand ants. They searched the moss and gathered the pearls, and before the sun had even dipped toward the horizon, all the pearls were gathered and neatly stacked in a pile.

The second task was to find the key to the bedroom of the king's daughter. The key had fallen into the lake. When the Fool went down to the shore and saw the depths of the cold, blue waters, he almost wept again, for he was sure he could never swim to the bottom and return alive. But just then, the ducks he had saved came swimming up, and they happily dove down to the bottom and brought him the key.

With the key, he could perform the third task. He entered the bedroom of the princess, and there three beautiful young women lay asleep. His task was to recognize the youngest daughter, but all three looked exactly alike! The only difference between them was what they had eaten before falling asleep. The eldest had eaten a spoonful of sugar, the second daughter had eaten sweet syrup, and the youngest had tasted a spoonful of honey.

Just as he was about to give up, the Queen Bee the Fool had protected from the fire flew in and buzzed around the lips of the three princesses. She stayed on the mouth of the princess who had tasted the honey.

"She is the youngest princess," the Fool cried, and the spell was broken. Everyone awoke, and all who had been turned into stone were restored to life. The princess gave the Fool a handsome reward. And the Fool's brothers never made fun of him again! ∾◉◞

Inanna Goes to the Underworld
retold by Starhawk

Circle round, and I'll tell you a story about Inanna (ee-NAH-nah). . . .

Inanna was a powerful Goddess, the Queen of Heaven. She reigned in ancient Sumeria, the land that today we call Iraq. She was the morning star and the evening star, the daughter of the rain, the life of the land.

One day as she was walking out on the green fields, she heard a call from the land below, the land of the dead. Inanna was a curious Goddess, and she made up her mind to explore that land, where her sister, Ereshkigal (eh-resh-KEE-gal), ruled.

She called her best friend and helper, Ninshubur (neen-SHOO-bur). "I am going to explore the land below," she said to Ninshubur. "It's dangerous, I know. Watch for me, and if I don't return, send help." Ninshubur promised that she would watch for Inanna.

Gathering all her courage, Inanna set out on the dark road that led to the land below, the land of the dead. She walked and walked and walked. Down and down she went.

She came to the gate to the land of the dead. The Guardian of the Gate spoke to her.

"What do you want?" he asked.

"I want to visit the land of the dead," she said.

"You can't come in here."

"But I am very powerful! I am the Queen of Heaven, and I can do whatever I want!"

"Not down here you can't," the Guardian said. "But if you really want to enter this land, you must remove your crown."

Inanna took off her crown and entered through the gate. She walked and walked and walked. Down and down she went.

She came to a second gate. The Guardian of the Gate spoke to her.

"What do you want?" she asked.

"I want to visit the land of the dead."

"You can't come in here!"

"But I am very powerful! I am the Queen of Heaven, and I can do whatever I want."

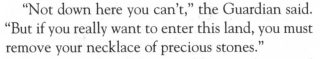

"Not down here you can't," the Guardian said. "But if you really want to enter this land, you must remove your necklace of precious stones."

Inanna took off her necklace and entered through the gate. She walked and walked and walked. Down and down she went. She came to another gate, and another, and another, until she passed through seven gates in all. At each one she took off some of her jewels or clothing, until she wore nothing at all and passed through the last gate naked.

Beyond the seventh gate lay the heart of the land of the dead. The great Queen Ereshkigal, Inanna's sister, sat on her throne, and all the spirits of those who died passed before her.

Inanna greeted her sister.

"Why have you come here, my sister?" Ereshkigal asked. "Now you can never return to the land above."

"But I am a very powerful Goddess," Inanna said. "I can go where I want and do what I want."

"Not here you can't," Ereshkigal said. "I am more powerful than you. I am death, and everyone must come to me in the end. Now you must stay here."

And Inanna felt her power leaving her. She felt weaker and weaker, as if her very blood was draining from her veins. She heard a roaring in her ears, and then she could see and hear nothing at all. Her muscles would no longer hold her up, and her life-force leaked away until she was nothing but an old rag of skin and bones. The servants of Ereshkigal hung her on the gate, and there she stayed.

In the lands above, people noticed that Inanna was no longer with them. They cried and mourned for her, and they began to feel afraid. Without her life-giving power, the crops died, and new seeds would not grow. Animals stopped having babies, and the people went hungry.

Inanna's friend, Ninshubur, had watched and waited for her faithfully. When she did not return, Ninshubur became very worried. She went to Inanna's father, Enki (EHN-kee), the God of water.

"You must send help to your daughter," Ninshubur said. "She has gone to explore the land below, to visit her sister Ereshkigal, the Queen of the Dead. I'm afraid something terrible has happened to her."

"Why did she do that?" Enki said. "Doesn't she know that nobody returns from that land?"

"She is a very powerful Goddess."

"But her sister is more powerful," Enki said. "Still, I will send help to her if I can find creatures who will travel to that land with the food of life and the water of life."

He sent two flies to find the land below, to carry the food of life and the water of life. Buzzing away, they entered the great hall where Ereshkigal sat on her throne. She had a terrible pain in her belly, and was moaning.

"Oh, oh, my stomach hurts so bad!" she cried.

"Oh, oh, your poor belly!" the flies cried. "We feel so sorry for you."

Ereshkigal looked up in surprise. Not many people felt sympathy for the Queen of the Dead.

"Oh, oh, I hurt inside!" she cried.

"Oh, oh, your poor insides!" they buzzed back.

"Oh, oh, I hurt outside!" she cried.

"Oh, oh, your poor outside!" the flies cried with her.

Ereshkigal was not used to anyone caring about her. Most beings were simply afraid of her. She looked at the flies with tears of gratitude in her eyes.

"Little flies, you are so kind," she said. "Nobody else cares about me like you do. Name what you want. Anything in my realm is yours."

Ereshkigal ruled all the things that come from below the earth, precious stones and metals and many hidden treasures, so she was making quite a generous offer.

"No, no, we couldn't take anything of yours," the flies protested.

"Please, go ahead, I want you to."

"Oh, no, really, you're too kind."

"Choose something. Do."

"Well, if you insist," the flies said. "We'll just take that old rag hanging on your gate."

"That old thing?" Ereshkigal asked in surprise. "I offer you all my treasures, and that is all you ask for?"

"It's the thought that counts," the flies said, and they flew to the rag that was all that was left of Inanna, and put a few crumbs of the food of life in her mouth, and a few drops of the water of life on her tongue. Inanna came back to life, and without wasting any time, they all ran back to the world above as fast as they could go. Inanna stopped only to retrieve her jewels and clothes and crown.

❧❧❧

Ereshkigal was furious when she found that she'd been tricked. She sent the demons of the land below chasing after them. Faster and faster they ran, but Inanna and the flies were just a bit faster. Breathless, they reached the surface of the green earth. They could hear Ereshkigal's voice thundering behind them.

"You have cheated me!" she raged. "But you can't cheat me forever! Unless you want to die again, you must send a substitute for your life down to me in the land below."

Inanna's friend Ninshubur came to greet her, and they hugged and kissed and laughed. Ninshubur told Inanna how she had gone to Enki to plead for the Goddess's life. Inanna could see how worried Ninshubur had been. She was thin from not eating, and her clothes were in rags.

"I can't send my faithful friend down below," Inanna said to herself. "She saved my life."

Inanna wandered through her land, and all over she saw how the people had mourned her. Great kings and queens, merchants and pottery makers and gold-smiths and farmers—all were dressed in rags, thin from fasting, their faces streaked with tears.

"I can't send my faithful subjects down below," Inanna murmured.

She walked on until she came to her own home. There was her husband, Dumuzi (DOO-moo-zee). Was he crying for her? Was he wearing rags and mourning?

No. He was dressed in his finest clothes, feasting and sitting on Inanna's own throne.

She was furious. "Take him!" she said to the demons of the underworld, and they rushed toward Dumuzi. He ran away as fast as he could go.

He ran to his friend in the city. "Hide me!" he pleaded, but his friend was too scared. So Dumuzi ran on, to the country-side, where his mother and his sister hid him in the reeds that grew by the river.

But the demons of the underworld were not easily fooled. They could smell like bloodhounds, and they sniffed Dumuzi out. His sister, Geshtinanna (gesh-tee-NAH-nah), ran and held him.

"Don't take him," she begged. "Take me instead!"

She cried so hard that the demons felt sorry for her. They were impressed by her courage and unselfishness.

"We will allow you to share the life below with him," they said. "Half the year you will live in the land below, and he will stay above on the green earth. And half the year he will dwell in the land of the dead, and you will return to the living."

And so they did. For Dumuzi is the spirit of the grain, which lives under the ground as a seed half the year and then sprouts and grows in the open air. And Geshtinanna is the spirit of the grape, which grows in the open air and then is pressed into wine and sent down to the cool storehouse under the earth. And so life and growth were restored to the earth again. ❧

Let the Games Begin

The God Lugh was uncommonly skilled at many things. We celebrate Lammas with games. They can be traditional summer games, such as relay races, sack races, water balloon tosses, and egg tosses. Nothing could be more evocative of the golden disc of the sun sailing across the sky than a Frisbee flying through the air. Ultimate Frisbee, with two teams working together to send the disc through their goalposts, is a terrific team sport. Younger kids get a real thrill out of learning how to throw a Frisbee. For shade-seekers, or in case of bad weather, the gaming need not be limited to the outdoors. Chess, dominoes, checkers, or any board game works. Directions for other games are included later in this section.

Make sure that there will be enough food to feed a large and hungry mob. Have a lot of drinks on hand throughout the games, and some snack food for the little ones who can't wait to eat.

To begin the festivities, cast a circle and call in the Goddess of the ripening harvest. Have everyone stand in a circle with the teachers in the center and, raising a cup of beverage, say,

Lugh! Shining One, Lugh of the Long Arms, Lugh the Many-Skilled, hear us! We stand here to pay tribute to you, as you sail across the sunless sea to the dawn of the new year. This is the day of your wake, and we mourn your departure from this world. Lugh, you were the best of us, the best we ever had. On Summer Solstice we sent our hopes and fears with you, riding into the night sky. And here we are today, friends, neighbors, children, and kin, to honor your name, to remember what you taught us, and to celebrate our skills and teamwork. Join us now in celebrating our abilities and taking pride in our strength! Be welcome here! Blessed be.

Say a Teacher's Blessing; pass the cup around the circle, and have each person take a sip. What is left over in the cup can be poured on the ground as an offering. Then let the games begin.

Lammas is a holiday that honors teachers, coaches, tutors, and friends—all those who give of their time, sharing their skills and love with children. Plan on honoring them in some way: with a blessing, by giving them an identifying sprig of greenery to wear, or putting them in charge of some of the games.

As is true for most parties and other gatherings, one of the most important things for a host or hostess to do is delegate responsibility. Ask people beforehand to be in charge of different games and contests, and make sure you are not the only one who knows where the napkins, food, utensils, and extra drinks are. This will make your job less stressful, and will give others a chance to feel fully involved in what is, after all, a community gathering.

Once the games and contests have been completed, gather in a circle again, this time with the children in the center, and say,

Lugh, Great One, teacher of us all, see how we shine! Our children are growing straight and tall, Lugh, and each one among them is blessed with strength and skill. [Name individuals here if you want, and if possible, say something about each child. Don't leave any out.] We thank you for the keen eyes and sharp minds of these children, and ask that you watch over them, protect them from harm as they grow, and help them know the joys of challenge and mastery in whatever they choose to do in life. Now leave if you must, but stay and feast with us if you will. Hail and farewell! [All repeat:] Hail and farewell!

Say goodbye to the Goddess, open the circle as it was made, and feast. Enjoy the last true holiday of the summer, and the company of good friends!

Oh Tell Me Why

Words and music by Raven Moonshadow

Oh tell me why, oh tell me why, Tell me
why must the clouds come to dark-en the sky. dark-en the sky.
This is the wake of Lugh the Sun King, He lost his life on the
Sol-stice day; This is the wake of Lugh the Sun King, He
steps in-to the dark and guides the way.

Teacher's Blessing

Say this blessing at Lammas, as an acknowledgment of all
that we give to each other.

*Gather the children in the center, with all adults around the
edge. Say: We are all teachers of one another. We all have
gifts to give the children. Now we honor those who would
take our children under their wing and teach them. Look to
the left and to the right around our circle, and remember*

what you have learned from those around you. After a few moments of silence, say: Goddess of the Harvest, you who winnow and thresh, you who know what is of true value, Keeper of the Storehouse, Guardian of the memories and lessons of childhood, we call you to help honor those among us whom we call teachers. As our community grows and changes, help us remember to keep our children in the center of our circle, for they are our most precious harvest, the greatest treasures we have.

Be with us as we express our gratitude to those who mentor, befriend, help, advise, and apprentice our children. We know you have a thousand faces and a thousand names. Our children will also learn from a thousand different faces and names as they grow. May we remember that those faces are all part of you. We pray that all of the teachers our children have in their lives are as wise, respectful, and loving as those gathered here today. Blessed be the Teachers!

The Sacred Knot

An even number of people stand in a circle. Each person reaches out and clasps the hand of a person across the circle. Then each person reaches out with their other hand and clasps hands with a second person. The circle has now become a living knot. Without dropping hands, participants attempt to untangle the knot into a single ring of people holding hands.

Hug Tag

One person is It. All the others are safe as long as they are hugging, in pairs or groups. The person who is It counts to five, and then everyone must break apart from whomever they're hugging and run and hug someone else. Whoever is caught becomes It. This game is often hilarious.

Musk Oxen in Peril

One person is the saber-tooth tiger. The rest are oxen—safe as long as their butts are together, in pairs or groups, and their horns (fingers held pointing out from the brow) are pointing out. The tiger counts to five, and each ox must find another ox or group of oxen to join.

When the tiger catches an ox, the ox becomes a tiger. Now there are two tigers. Soon there are more and more—until the entire group becomes tigers and there are no more oxen left to eat. The tigers starve, and the game is over.

This is even more hilarious than regular hug tag, and possibly teaches something about predator-prey relations.

Cougars and Joggers

One person is the cougar, the others are joggers. Joggers are safe as long as they are hugging in pairs or groups. The cougar counts to five, and each jogger finds another jogger or group of joggers to hug.

When the cougar catches a jogger, they both yell, "Freeze!" Then the jogger has one minute to introduce herself to the cougar and persuade the cougar not to eat her.

If the jogger is persuasive enough, the cougar can let her go, and the game resumes. If the cougar eats the jogger, the jogger becomes a cougar. The game continues until there are no joggers left, as above.

This is a good game for a new group to play, as it will help the players get to know each other. And it teaches an important survival lesson—when you encounter a cougar, don't run! Otherwise they'll think you are prey.

Sun Ball

A golden or yellow ball (volleyball-sized) is tossed into the air. The group attempts to keep it from touching the ground. The longer it stays up, the longer summer will last.

For a fun variation, or for playing indoors, use a yellow balloon.

The Bee Dance

All the children gather together in a tight group. With their arms pressed to their sides, they spin in tight circles, making a buzzing noise and gently bumping up against each other. When this dance gets going, it develops a momentum of its own. Dancers on the outside are sucked into the center; dancers in the center are spun out to the edge.

Be careful to set some clear boundaries at the beginning: no pushing, no shoving, and no hard bumping, or the dance can easily get out of hand.

First Fruits Wreath

You will need:

3–4 firm-fleshed apples

9-inch paper plate

glue gun

Welcome the first fruits of the harvest by creating this wreath from apples dried in the late summer sun.

Cut the apples crosswise into $1/4$-inch slices. Set slices on screens or wax paper in the strong sun to dry. Turn them every hour until they're dehydrated but still slightly flexible. They'll be wrinkled and browned in the center. Sun drying takes about four to six hours. If you don't have sun space, dry the apples in the oven set at the lowest temperature. Turn the slices every hour. Oven drying may take longer than sun drying.

Cut the center from the paper plate, leaving a 2- or 3-inch rim. Apply glue to the apples and press them onto the plate. Either overlap the apple slices or apply them in staggered layers.

If any cardboard shows after you've finished, conceal it by tucking in pretty leaves or flowers.

Tips: Thick-skinned oranges are beautiful dried, too. Cut them into $1/4$-inch slices, dry, and apply the same way as apples. Small, colorful dried fruits, like strawberries and cranberries, make wonderful accents.

Corn Husk Chain

Festoon your altar with this chain of circles made of corn husks. Fresh corn husks can be used immediately. Dried husks should be soaked in warm water for five minutes and patted dry.

Tear the husks lengthwise into strips about one inch wide. Form the first one into a circle and staple shut. Put the next strip through the first loop and form that into a circle and staple. Continue until your chain is the desired length. If you're using fresh husks, they will dry and shrink, but still make a nice decoration.

Hopes and Fears

On Lammas we bring our hopes and fears to the Goddess for her blessings and her help. Often this delicate and frightening process is best expressed through our hands rather than language. For this, we provide our children with clay to model what's in their hearts. Bring the figures into the circle, bless them, and then hide them outside, where they'll be received by the earth as they melt in winter storms and snow.

If your children don't want to show their work to others in the circle, provide handkerchiefs as a cover. If they absolutely cannot create a shape to express their feelings, suggest they make a little Goddess or God and whisper their hopes and fears to the figure.

After the blessing, everyone in the circle takes turns naming hopes. Then let each child hide his or her figure outside. No peeking is allowed.

Blessing

Lady and Lord, now the fruit hangs on the trees, the grapes tremble on their vines, the grasses bend with their seeds. We watch and wait with our hopes for a harvest of plenty. We fear they will be destroyed by storms, frost, or pests. Bless those who work with the earth to feed us, and bless their harvests.

Lammas Candleholders

For your altar, turn the reddest apples into holiday candleholders. See Harvest Candleholders in Mabon Activities for instructions.

We who are not farmers also have our hopes for a harvest of plenty. We each have worked hard to create what we want. We pray that we can reap what we have tended. We fear failure, obstacles, losing what we treasure. In our hands we hold our hopes and fears. We are in your hands. Help us hold on to our hopes during the hard times, the storms we face in our lives. Let our hopes stay whole. Bless our efforts, let them come to full fruit.

Clay

Mix all the ingredients together except the food coloring and cook over medium heat until it thickens. Turn out into a bowl and let it cool. Knead until it becomes a cohesive, smooth ball. Divide into several portions and knead in food coloring.

Store unused portions in a covered container in the refrigerator.

Cornstarch Clay

This clay allows for finer modeling but dries out quickly.

Mix the dry ingredients, add water, and cook over medium heat, stirring constantly. The liquid will become quite thick and then form into a ball. Turn out, let cool, and knead. Use right away. Store unused portions in a tightly covered container in the refrigerator.

Hope Cards

Ask the children to think about what they hope to harvest, literally or symbolically, and help them make cards that represent those hopes. They can draw on construction paper or any scrap paper, or create collages from magazines, greeting cards, and old calendars.

All the cards are put into a basket and shuffled. Then each child draws a card. The card each child receives be-

You will need:

1 C plain flour

1 C water

1 T cream of tartar

1 T vegetable oil

food coloring

You will need:

½ C cornstarch

1 C baking soda

½ C plus 2 T water

comes a symbol of luck and blessing for the harvest. And by giving away our hopes, we are asking the Goddess to help them be fulfilled.

Orange Candles

Pumpkins aren't the only fruits that can be transformed into lanterns and candleholders. Hollowed-out oranges glow on altars, scenting the air with their zest.

Cut the top third of the orange off. Scoop out the pulp using the grapefruit knife, then scraping with the spoon.

Put a votive candle into the orange, light, and enjoy.

If you're making your own candle, follow Tool Chest instructions for melting and pouring wax. Pour wax into the orange. When the wax is firm but still pliable, plunge a straw or toothpick down the middle, being careful not to pierce the bottom of the orange, and place the wick. The candle is ready to use when the wax has firmed completely.

You will need:

1 thick-skinned orange (navels work well)

grapefruit knife or other sharp, small knife

teaspoon

votive candle or candle-making supplies (see Tool Chest)

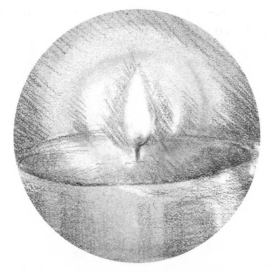

Spiral Cookies

You will need:

$\frac{1}{2}$ C butter (one stick)

$\frac{3}{4}$ C sugar

1 egg

$\frac{1}{2}$ t vanilla

1$\frac{3}{4}$ C flour

$\frac{1}{2}$ t baking soda

dash of salt

1 oz semisweet baking chocolate

On Lammas, the most important thought to hold is that life is a spiral. We move around the circle, but we never come back to the same place. We're reminded of the ever-changing spiral dance when we eat these simple cookies.

Cream together the butter and sugar. Add the egg and vanilla. Blend the dry ingredients together and mix in slowly. Set aside one cup of the batter. Melt the chocolate and add it to the remaining batter, blending until the color is uniform.

Work the light-colored batter quickly with your hands until it's smooth. Place between two pieces of wax paper, flatten, and roll out into a 14-by-9-inch sheet. Set aside and do the same with the dark-colored batter. Gently peel off one of the pieces of wax paper on each dough layer. Pick up one layer and invert it as you place it exactly on top of the other layer. Do this carefully; once the layers meet, you won't be able to shift them around. Remove the wax paper on top, and use the wax paper at the bottom to help you roll the sheets into a long cylinder. As you roll, press gently to re-move any air pockets. Put the cylinder in the freezer a few minutes to harden.

Preheat oven to 350°. With a sharp knife, cut the cylinder into slices $\frac{1}{4}$ inch thick and place on a lightly greased cookie sheet. Bake for 12 to 15 minutes. This recipe yields about 50 spiral cookies.

Spiral Almond Orange Buns

Warm the orange juice and blend with the yeast. Combine the butter, sugar, egg, salt, and almond extract. When the yeast mixture is foamy, add to the butter mixture, then add the flour. Stir until well mixed. Turn the dough out onto a floured board and knead until the dough is smooth and elastic. Let rise until doubled. Punch down and let rest for 10 minutes.

Roll out the dough into a rectangle, 8 by 24 inches. Brush with melted butter, and sprinkle with brown sugar and almonds. Roll up into a cylinder from the short end. With a sharp knife, cut 8 slices, 1 inch thick. Lay slices on a lightly floured cookie sheet and let rise until doubled. Bake in a preheated 350° oven for 25 to 30 minutes. Makes 8 buns.

Toasting Almonds

Place slivered almonds in a dry skillet over *low* heat. Stir constantly until almonds are fragrant and lightly browned.

You will need:

1/2 C orange juice

1 T yeast

2 T melted butter

1/2 C brown sugar

1 egg

1/2 t salt

1 T almond extract

2 1/2 to 3 C flour

FILLING

2 T butter

1/3 C brown sugar

1/2 C slivered almonds, toasted

Lammas Bread Blessing[1]

Words by Diane Baker, music by Anne Hill

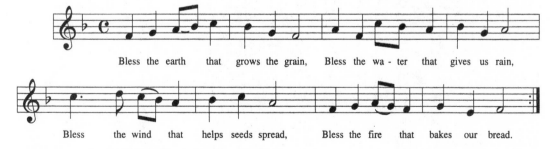

Bless the earth that grows the grain, Bless the wa-ter that gives us rain,

Bless the wind that helps seeds spread, Bless the fire that bakes our bread.

Long-Arm Lugh Shish Kabob

Favorite Children's Meat Marinade: Combine ½ C orange juice, 1 t soy sauce, and 1 t honey.

Dessert Fruit Kabobs: Cut up all kinds of seasonal fruits and set out on plates with miniature marshmallows. Use bamboo skewers.

Shish kabobs make a perfect dinner in honor of Lugh. The skewers remind us of his spear, and children help themselves by making their own kabobs, with a little adult supervision.

You can make shish kabobs with just about everything. Here are a few suggestions: cherry tomatoes, green and red peppers, summer squash, mushrooms, pineapple chunks, pearl onions, corn on the cob, tofu and/or meat.

Cut up your kabob ingredients into even-sized pieces, no larger than 2 inches in diameter. Cube and marinate tofu and meat in Favorite Children's Meat Marinade (see sidebar) or another marinade you like. Barbecue or broil in the oven.

Be sure children wash their hands after handling uncooked meat.

CHAPTER TWELVE

Mabon/Fall Equinox
SEPTEMBER 20, 21, or 22

THE FALL EQUINOX is our harvest celebration. Twin to the Spring Equinox, it's a time, again, of balance between dark and light. But now we are moving from light into darkness, from warmth into cold. We gather in the harvest of summer and prepare for the winter ahead.

Everything in nature is constantly giving to and receiving from everything else. The oxygen we breathe in is exhaled by the trees, and they take in the carbon dioxide we breathe out. Bees sip nectar from the flowers and in return carry their pollen to other blossoms so that the plants can make seeds. Nothing exists separately from the whole.

When we receive a gift, we give thanks. Sooner or later, we try to give something back to the person who gave it to us—or perhaps to pass the gift on to someone else. That's part of keeping the balance. At this time of year, when we are gathering in the gifts of the Goddess, the fruit, nuts, grain, and vegetables that are ripe, we also try to give something back, to make offerings and express our thanks. The Fall Equinox is our Thanksgiving. In fact, the Thanksgiving we celebrate in the United States came from the old European Harvest Home, the special customs and rituals done when the last sheaf of grain was gathered in.

In ancient Greece, the Fall Equinox was the time when the mysteries of Demeter and Persephone were celebrated. (Demeter is the Goddess of grain and agriculture; Persephone is her daughter, who becomes queen of the Underworld. Although we tell their story at Eostar, we could tell it again now!) The mysteries were celebrated for nine days. Those who wanted to be initiated made a procession from Athens to Eleusis, nine miles away, where Demeter's temple stood. They bathed in the sea, washed and sacrificed a pig, and took part in an all-night ritual that was so secret that nobody in all of ancient Greece ever told what happened. All we know is that initiates learned the secrets of death and rebirth. For this is the time of the death of the year, but in a dry climate like that of the Mediterranean, it is also a time of rebirth, when the rains come and renew the plants just when the days are getting shorter and darker.

The Goddess

At Mabon, the Mother of the Harvest becomes the Old One, the wise grandmother who teaches us to rest after our labors. At last we are done with cutting the grain, culling the vegetables and the herds, picking the fruit. Now we can enjoy what we've worked so hard to grow. When all is gathered into the storehouse, we can relax. We no longer need to fear disaster: the harvest is in!

In ancient Greece, the Goddess of this season was both Demeter, who can be generous with her gifts of grain or hold them back when she mourns for her daughter, and Persephone, who goes into the underworld and learns to return again.

In the British Isles, the ancient name for the Goddess of this time was Modron, which simply means "mother." Sometimes she was pictured as a trio of women, each seated on a throne. Together they were called the Mothers. They were responsible for abundance, for sustaining the life of the people. In the Celtic myths, it is Modron's son who is stolen away into the Underworld.

Whenever we feed the hungry, we honor the Mothers.

The God

This holiday takes its name from the God Mabon. He was called "Mabon, son of Modron," which means "Son, son of the Mother." He is such an ancient God that most of the stories about him have disappeared. All we know is that he was stolen away from his mother when he was only three nights old, and imprisoned until he was rescued by King Arthur's companions.

Like Persephone, he is hidden away from the world of light. Like Inanna, he must be rescued by someone else. For he is the spirit of the grain taken into the storehouse, grain that must be "rescued" before it can be eaten and give life to the people. He is the magical child, who, like Persephone, is a bridge between this world and the Otherworld, a link between the living and the dead.

Because Mabon knows what it is like to be imprisoned, he is also the God of freedom. He frees the animals from their cages and loosens the bonds of all those unjustly imprisoned. He protects all things that are wild and free.

His totem animals are the owl, the blackbird, the stag, the eagle, and the salmon. Owls are awake at night and see in the dark. The blackbird is itself the color of night. The stags are growing their antlers at this time of year; now is when they come into their full power, fighting and mating. The eagle flies high, wide, and free. The salmon is always associated with wisdom; in many parts of the world, this is the time when the salmon return, swimming upstream to the place of their birth to spawn.

We honor Mabon when we protect the wild things, the animals, and when we work for freedom for all people.

The Altar

The Fall Equinox altar is simple. We just make an arrangement of some of the things we've harvested that will keep for a few weeks: winter squash, dried corn, herbs, pumpkins. If you haven't harvested anything yourself, this is a good time to go to a farmers' market or a pick-your-own farm and choose what you want on the altar. You might add autumn leaves, a bouquet of late-blooming flowers, or pictures of animals.

Do you know any stories of people who have been imprisoned for their beliefs, their religion, or their race? You can put their pictures on the altar. Teenagers might wish to contact Amnesty International, and put letters on behalf of prisoners on the altar before they are sent.

On the Land

Where we live, the Fall Equinox marks the beginning of the rainy season. It doesn't always rain this early, but now at least we can start hoping. The land is very dry, and we look forward to seeing it turn green again.

We might still have some very hot days ahead of us, but already we can feel a chill in the air at night. The leaves of the big-leaf maples are turning yellow and beginning to fall. The poison oak is turning a brilliant, beautiful red.

This is a good time to start planting some things that need the winter rains or the winter's cold to grow; for example, bulbs, many native shrubs, and wildflow-ers. And one great thing about this time of year—the mosquitoes are almost all gone!

What's happening to the land where you live? Are you waiting for the first rain, or the first snow? Do you have to put your garden to bed, with mulch? Are the leaves turning colors? What time does the sun set?

The Story of Mabon, Son of Modron[1]

retold by Starhawk

Circle round, and I'll tell you the story of the oldest of animals. . . .

This is the story of Mabon, son of Modron (MAH-dron), one of the elder Gods, whose name means "Son, son of the Mother." He is such an ancient God that even in the time of King Arthur hardly anyone remembered his name or knew his fate. All anyone knew was that he was taken from his mother's side as she slept, when he was only three nights old, and had been imprisoned ever since.

Long ago, in the time of King Arthur, a young knight by the name of Kyllwch (KESH-lookh) fell in love with a giant's daughter. He was not the first young man to fall for Olwen's kind eyes and beautiful face, but nothing much was left of the others. For Olwen's father, the giant Yspadaden (iss-pa-THAW-then), was under a geis (jess), a doom, so that when Olwen married he would lose his own life. So whenever a brave and gallant knight came to call, Yspadaden sent him off to perform an impossible task. None had ever returned.

Olwen and Kyllwch met one day by the riverside, and they spent the day wandering the green banks beside the flowing water, talking, laughing, and falling in love. At the end of the day, when the time came for Olwen to go back home and prepare the giant's dinner, Kyllwch took her hand.

"I love you," he said. "I want to marry you."

Tears came into Olwen's eyes. "I love you, too," she said. "And for that reason, I beg you to forget me. For my father will never let any man live who seeks my hand. And I would rather be separated from you, and know that you live, than to have you die trying to wed me."

"I'd rather die than live without you," Kyllwch said. He was young, and Olwen was his first love. Also, he was a stubborn young man.Olwen left, and Kyllwch went home, dressed in his finest clothes, and made his way to the castle of the giant.Yspadaden was enjoying his dinner when Kyllwch arrived—and when a giant enjoys a meal, bones go flying, grease spatters the walls, and anything loose in the vicinity of the table is likely to get gobbled up. Kyllwch stood up before the giant boldly—nevertheless well out of spitting range—and spoke.

"Yspadaden, I want to marry your daughter, Olwen."

"What!" the giant roared. "Not another one! How many of you miserable little worms do I have to send to your deaths before you learn?"

"I'm not afraid," Kyllwch said. "I love Olwen."

"Oh, you do?" the giant thundered. "Well then, you can have her, provided you prove yourself worthy by performing a few trivial tasks." Whereupon he proceeded to list so many heroic tasks and dangerous quests that it would take an army of heroes a hundred years to perform them, a separate volume to record them, and a course in Old Welsh merely to pronounce them.

Only the last task, however, concerns us in this story. "Should you accomplish all these challenges," the giant concluded, "you must know one thing. Olwen can only be married if my hair is brushed and combed and I am shaved with the brush, comb, and razor that lie between the ears of the great boar, Tyrch Trwth (terkh trooth). And they can only be got by hunting and killing the boar, and that can only be done with the help of Mabon, son of Modron, who was taken from his mother's side when he was only three nights old, and no one has heard of him since."

"Well then, that is what I will do," Kyllwch said confidently, not wanting the giant to know that deep inside he felt a sinking sensation underneath his ribs. "And I guess I'd better get on with it. Good evening to you." And he left the giant's hall.

Outside and alone, our hero passed a few bad moments wondering just how much he did love Olwen after all, and what he'd gotten himself into. However, he was indeed a stubborn young man, and once he began something, he never quit until he finished.

"I need help," he thought. "This quest is too much for one young knight to do alone. I must go to the court of King Arthur, my cousin, and ask him to send some of his champions with me. And maybe someone there will know where to look for Mabon."

❧

So Kyllwch made his way to King Arthur's court, and announced himself to the doorkeeper and the assembly of knights. King Arthur greeted him warmly. Kyllwch told the king of his quest, and Arthur was touched by the young knight's courage. King Arthur always liked a good love story.

"I will send three of my most trusted knights to help you find Mabon and rescue him," Arthur promised. He chose Cei (kay), Arthur's foster brother; Eidoel (AY-dol), who was called Mabon's kinsman; and Gwrhyr (GOOR-hear), Interpreter of Tongues, who could speak all the languages of all the peoples and animals in the world. So they set off into the wilderness, searching everywhere for someone who remembered Mabon and knew where he might be.

They wandered and wandered, and at last they came to the home of the ancient bird known as the Ouzel (Blackbird) of Cilgwri (kil-GOOR-ee).

"Ouzel of Cilgwri," Gwrhyr said to her, "we are Arthur's messengers, come to ask you in the name of all that is sacred if you have news of Mabon, son of Modron, who was taken from his mother's side when he was only three nights old."

"I have been here a long time," the Ouzel replied. "When I first came here, there was a smith's anvil, and I was a young bird. No work was done on that anvil except for when my beak lay upon it in the evening, and today there is not so much as a nut of it that has not been worn away. But in all that time, I have not heard anything of Mabon, son of Modron. But since you come from Arthur, I will guide you to a place where there is an animal older than me."

❧

The Ouzel guided them through the forest until they came to the home of the Stag of Rhedenfre (reh-DEN-vray). The stag was very ancient. His antlers had so many points they looked like a forest of many-branched trees growing out of his head.

"Stag of Rhedenfre," Gwrhyr said, "we are Arthur's messengers, come to ask you in the name of all that is sacred if you have news of Mabon, son of Modron, who was taken from his mother's side when he was only three nights old."

"I have been here a long time," the Stag

said. "When I first came here, there was only one small antler point on either side of my head, and there were no trees here except for a single oak sapling. That grew into an oak of a hundred branches, and the oak fell and wore away and today there is nothing left of it but a red stump, and in all that time, I have heard nothing of Mabon, son of Modron. But since you come from Arthur, I will be your guide to a place where there is an animal even older than me."

❦

The Stag guided them through the forest until at last they came to a deep woods, where the Owl of Cwm Cawlwyd (coom COWL-id) lived.

"Owl of Cwm Cawlwyd," Gwrhyr said, "we are Arthur's messengers, come to ask you in the name of all that is sacred if you have news of Mabon, son of Modron, who was taken from his mother's side when he was only three nights old."

"I have been here a long time," the Owl said. "When I first came here, I was a young bird, and this whole valley was an ancient forest. People came and cut down all the trees. In time, a new forest grew up, and new people came and cut it down, and this now is the third wood. And look at me! My wings are worn away to mere stumps, I am so old. And in all that time, I have not heard word of Mabon, son of Modron. But since you are Arthur's messengers, I will be your guide to a place where the eldest of us all lives."

❦

The Owl guided them through the forest and up to a high mountain, where the Eagle of Gwernabwy (gwer-NAH-bwee) lived.

"Eagle of Gwernabwy," Gwrhyr said, "we are Arthur's messengers, come to ask you in the name of all that is sacred if you have news of Mabon, son of Modron, who was taken from his mother's side when he was only three nights old."

"I have been here a long time," the Eagle said. "When I first came here, I had a stone so tall and high that from its top I could peck at the stars, and now it is worn away so small that your hand would cover it, and in all that time I have heard nothing of Mabon, son of Modron."

At that, Cei, Gwrhyr, and Eidoel became very discouraged. The Eagle was their last hope. If they couldn't find anyone who knew of Mabon, they would have to return to Arthur with their quest a failure. And Mabon, wherever he was, would remain imprisoned forever. But then the Eagle spoke again.

"There's just one thing," he said. "Once I flew as far as Llyn Llyw (shlin shloo) seeking something to eat. I saw a huge silver salmon swimming in the lake, and I sank my claws into him, thinking he would make a great feast for me for many days. But he was so strong, he pulled me under the water, and I barely escaped with my life. I gathered all my kin and we went after him to destroy him. But he sent messengers to me and asked to make peace. He came to me and asked my help, for his back was covered with tridents that had been thrown at him to try to catch him. I pulled fifty out with my talons, and so we were friends. If he doesn't know something of the man you seek, nobody does! I will be your guide, and take you to where he lives."

The Eagle guided them down the mountain, through the valleys, and along the river until they came to the shores of Llyn Llyw. There they saw the great Salmon swimming in the clear water.

"Salmon of Llyn Llyw," the Eagle said, "I have come with Arthur's messengers, seeking news of Mabon, son of Modron, who was taken from his mother when he was only three nights old. In the name of all that is sacred, tell us what you know."

"This is what I know," the Salmon said. "On every high tide, I go up the river until I come to the bend by the wall of Caer Loyw (care loy), and there I hear the sounds of such suffering that never in my life have I met such distress before. Two of you come on my back, and I will take you there."

Gwrhyr and Cei hopped on the Salmon's shoulders, and he swam upstream until they came to the high stone wall of a castle, grim and frightening. From the other side of the wall, they could hear the sound of crying and wailing.

"Who is that wailing and crying in this house of stone?" Gwrhyr called.

"It is I, Mabon, son of Modron," they heard in reply, "and I have reason to cry, for no one was ever so miserable as I am, imprisoned here."

"How can you be freed? Can you be ransomed for gold or silver or worldly wealth, or must you be freed by fighting?"

"No gold or silver or worldly wealth can free me," came the answer. "I can only be freed by fighting and battle."

"Don't despair. We will go and get the help of Arthur, and surely we will free you!"

Gwrhyr and Cei returned with the Salmon to where Eidoel waited. They thanked the Salmon and made their way back to Arthur's court, where they told their story.

"I will summon all my warriors," Arthur said, and so he did. They all journeyed to Caer Loyw, and besieged the castle where Mabon, son of Modron, was held prisoner. Cei and Gwrhyr again journeyed upriver on the shoulders of the Salmon. While Arthur and his warriors attacked the front gate, Cei broke through the wall and took Mabon upon his back. He carried him out of the castle, and so Mabon, son of Modron, was freed at last.

"How can I ever thank you?" Mabon, son of Modron, said when the battle was over and he stood at last outside the walls of his prison.

"Help me with my quest," Kyllwch said. "Only you can succeed in hunting the Great Boar Tyrch Trwth and winning from him the comb, brush, and razor that lie between his ears."

So they set off into the deepest forest any of them had ever seen. Day and night they traveled, and always Mabon, son of

Modron, led the way, guided by his instinct. At last, at sunset on the third day, they heard a great snuffling and bellowing and stamping in the woods. Quickly they took their places on either side of the path. Then, with a roar like a hundred lions, the giant boar came rushing out of the forest. He was big as an elephant, with tusks as long as a small tree and sharp as a knife, and between his ears was a comb, a brush, and a razor.

Mabon, son of Modron, stood tall and unafraid, and thrust his spear deep into the Boar's heart. With a bellow that shook leaves from the trees five leagues around, the Great Boar died. Kyllwch took the comb, the brush, and the razor from between the boar's ears, and he and his companions went back to the castle of the giant. They carried Tyrch Trwth in a sling among the five of them, to be roasted for the wedding feast.

Yspadaden turned pale when he saw that Kyllwch had returned successfully. Sighing, with tears running from his eyes, he allowed the companions to brush and comb his hair and shave his beard with the comb, the brush, and the razor from between the ears of the Great Boar. Then Kyllwch and Olwen were married, and a great feast of roast pork was held. And when all the feasting and rejoicing was done, they cut off the giant's head.

And that's the end of the story. ∾

Amiyao and the Magic Gongs[2]
retold by Tala Divinia

Circle round, and I'll tell you a story from the Philippines. . . .

Amiyao was a Tinguian youth who lived with his widowed mother, whom he helped with the work in their small rice field and camote (sweet potato) and vegetable garden.

The village where Amiyao lived was a poor one. The people did not grow enough rice to last until the next harvest, so they had to eat camote and vegetables. Amiyao and the rest of the villagers worked very hard from dawn to dusk. They enjoyed no rest. Each day was the same—monotonous and ordinary. In their lives, there were no high points or beautiful memories of the past. There was no celebration of the harvest.

When the rice fields were idle, in the months after harvest, Amiyao went hunting. One day he espied a deer. He watched the deer eating and prancing through the forest, and quietly followed. Just as he was about to catch the deer, the wind shifted and melodious ringing sounds caught Amiyao's attention. He followed the source, and soon came upon a village laughing and chanting and having a feast. People dressed in rich and colorful clothing were dancing happily to the magical sounds of curricular bells.

Bong, bong, bong, bong! sang a large gong.

Dong-a-long, dong-a-long, dong-a-long! answered another.

Ding-tup-tup-tup! Ding-tup-tup-tup! a smaller gong shouted.

And an even smaller one, with its high-pitched voice, rang above the bigger gongs: *Ting-tung-tung! Ting-tung-tung! Ting-tung-tung!*

Amiyao listened, fascinated, but was soon drawn to dance. He stomped his feet, turned, and flapped his arms like the wings of a bird in flight, in perfect time to the rhythms.

Amiyao flushed with pleasure, immensely enjoying the dance. With much reluctance and sadness he left his new friends, but he was eager to share this wonderful experience with his people. Now he understood why his village never danced nor held feasts. There were no magic gongs!

Amiyao returned to his village, but he could not forget the music of the gongs. He courageously asked the village elders where he could get the magic gongs, but some of them just shook their heads sadly because they couldn't remember ever hearing of these instruments. Others said they vaguely remembered that the gongs came from far away, across the seas and skies.

Finally, a wise old shaman, a *mumbaki*, told Amiyao that the gongs belonged to Kabunian and Bugan, the benevolent Skyworld God and Goddess who created the world.

"Long, long ago," the *mumbaki* said, "our village had these

Gongs of the mountain peoples that dwell in northern Luzon in the Philippines are owned only by the rich and are a symbol of wealth. Many mountain peoples attribute divine origin to their gongs. The story of Amiyao is woven around that belief.

magical gongs. They were used for our religious rites and healing and thanksgiving ceremonies. There were many days of feasting and dancing. But one day, Kabunian and Bugan were displeased when people forgot to offer them sacrifices. In anger, they took back the gongs and hid them in the heart of the mountain."

The *mumbaki* looked intently at the youth and continued, "They are still there, imprisoned, until some brave young man brings them back to our impoverished village."

For a long time, Amiyao thought about the words of the *mumbaki*. Deep in his heart, he knew the old priest was challenging him to search for the magic gongs. He soon forgot the words of the *mumbaki*, however, as he had to work in the rice fields and tend the sweet potato and vegetable garden.

Harvest came and went without a murmur. As usual, Amiyao went hunting, and this time he went in pursuit of what he thought was an animal in the bushes. He thought the others had followed him, but they had not, and now he realized he was lost. He noticed with dismay that the sun was setting quickly below the horizon. He hurried back to try to find his way before darkness covered the safe mountain trails.

Suddenly, in the dimming light, he saw a wild boar, luminously aglow. It was a rare, milky-skinned albino. He remembered a village legend and heard the voice of the *mumbaki*: "Whoever sights a white boar will be very lucky, because the Gods will rain down abundant blessings on him thereafter."

Amiyao instantly gave chase. He re-fused to let the animal out of his sight, but every time he thought he had caught up with the boar, he would suddenly find it out of his reach again. Then he saw the boar disappear into a mountain wall.

As Amiyao felt his way closer to the wall, he found the opening of a cave. Amiyao stepped into the darkness and slowly made his way through the cave, forgetting about any danger. All he wanted was to catch the boar to ensure the blessings of the Gods on his village and himself.

Finally he saw a light and, going toward it, found a very large, tall tree that stood in the heart of the cave, whose branches were beckoning to him. It was the ancient Tree of Life, laden with gold, silver, bronze, and copper jewelry; sugar cane juice; golden rice; and gongs—all symbols of the sources of life: earth, water, fire, and air. Unafraid, Amiyao slowly reached for a bronze *anting-anting*, or amulet. He placed it around his neck, and it seemed to belong there. Then he put on some gold earrings, silver armlets, copper leglets, and lo! He looked like a handsome young chief. Then he played the gongs, each bigger than the next.

Meanwhile, his friends had tracked down Amiyao and followed him inside the cave. They were amazed to see all the wondrous treasures. They all gathered as much as they could carry. And especially they did not forget to bring home the magic gongs.

All throughout their journey back to their village, they sounded the gongs. Their melodious notes filled the mountainside and reverberated through all the villages along the way. The people of

Amiyao's village wondered at the sounds getting louder and louder. They saw it was Amiyao, and ran to welcome him. Amiyao excitedly told them about his great adventure and showed them the gongs.

The whole village now knew how to celebrate, and celebrate they did, with feasting, chanting, and dancing that lasted for many, many days.

They decided to make Amiyao their chief, because of his bravery and courage. From that time on, their village grew prosperous, for Amiyao was kind and wise.

The magic gongs stayed with Amiyao and his people, for they never forgot to thank and honor Kabunian and Bugan, and the other Gods and Goddesses of the Skyworld, for blessing them with gifts of abundance and magic gongs! ❧

Animal Celebration

On this holiday we honor the Goddess for her blessing of the harvest. We also honor Mabon, the God who protects that which is wild and free—our human spirits and the animals of the earth. Although these two aspects of the holiday can be combined in ritual, children have such strong caring for and identification with animals that they love an entire ritual devoted to them.

We prepare the circle with our altar laden with animal symbols, including edibles such as animal crackers. Call in the powers of the directions by invoking the animals we associate with each direction and making their sounds. (See sidebar on page 265.)

Invoke the Goddess and the God. You may want to call upon the Goddess as the Lady of Beasts, protector of animals, and the God as Mabon, the Horned One of full power who protects all that is wild and free.

We call in the animal spirits that we care for and wish to bless and protect using the phrase "I care about . . ." Start with the animals that are closest and best-known to your family: your personal pets, your neighborhood pets, horses at the local pony ride, the classroom mascot: "I care about my pet rats, Michele and Rainbow, and call them in. I care about Lupine, the dog whom I love to play with, and call him in. I care about Popcorn, my favorite horse, and call her in."

Move out to the next circle, those animals that are wild and close to us. "I care about the raccoons and call them in, even though they upset our garbage cans. I care about and call in the deer that eat our garden and make Mom and Dad mad, because they are beautiful and I love looking at them."

Move out into the next circle, the wild animals who live on our continent. "I care about mountain lions and call them in. I care about wolves and call them in, and I hope they can continue to return to live in the wild."

Continue out into the world: "I call in the whales and sea lions, and ask the Goddess and God to protect them and their habitat. I call in the elephants and bless those people who are trying to save them. I call in the butterflies, and ask that we can save their rain forest home."

When the circle has filled with the spirits you've called in, raise a cone of power by making animal sounds and movements. The energy from the yipping and howling, roaring and barking, protects and saves the animals. When the energy reaches its peak, ground everyone with a quiet blessing: "May the earth and all her wild creatures, may all the people who work to save the earth, absorb our blessings and be strengthened with our power. Blessed be."

Bless the food and drink, and pass them around to share. While it's quiet, help the children think of ways they can help adults save animals. It is important to link action to intention. Make schedules and commitments, sing the animal song together, then open the circle.

Pet Blessing

Gather any pets you have in your home to join your circle. Young children may want to bring beloved stuffed animals, or you may ask for the spirits of animals you love and which live with other people to join you. Sprinkle the animals and symbols with the Waters of the World (see Brigit Altar) or the blessed water you have on the altar, saying: *We thank you*

For east and air: birds, with their mastery of air, their unparalleled vision, the maneuverability of the hummingbird, the speed of the raptor.

For south and fire: the spirited animals, especially lions, with their sun-gold color, their courage, their sun-heated habitats; other large cats; and the small, quick animals that hunt and fight for their survival.

For west and water: the water animals, whales, dolphins, and seals; fish, with their incredible variety of colors, shapes, and sizes.

For north and earth: the large animals, bears, elephants; the grazing animals, elk and moose; the animals that live in the great northern cold, wolves and foxes; those that live underground, rabbits, gophers, ferrets.

for sharing your lives with us, and ask the Goddess and God to bless you with health and safety. You give up your wildness to remind us of ours. You teach us how to talk without words, to sing without tunes. You show us love without questions. From you we learn how love grows from kindness alone.

Share a treat with your animal friend.

Animal Blessing[3]

Words by Diane Baker, music by Aaron J. Feldman

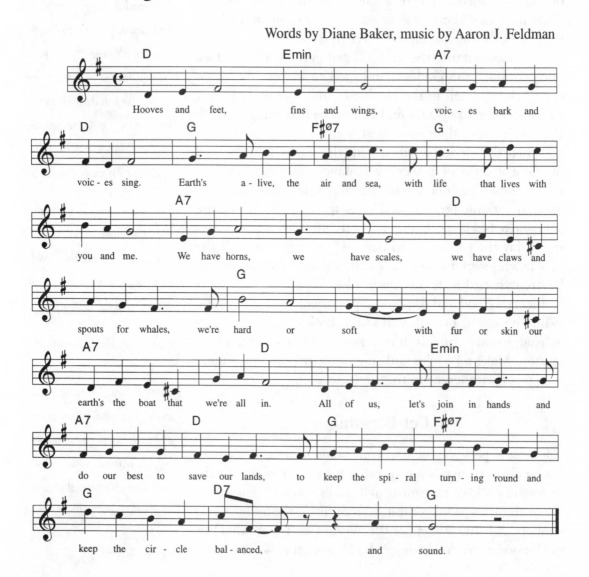

Hooves and feet, fins and wings, voic - es bark and voic - es sing. Earth's a - live, the air and sea, with life that lives with you and me. We have horns, we have scales, we have claws and spouts for whales, we're hard or soft with fur or skin our earth's the boat that we're all in. All of us, let's join in hands and do our best to save our lands, to keep the spi - ral turn - ing 'round and keep the cir - cle bal - anced, and sound.

Family Thanksgiving Feast

Because we don't have to replicate the secular Thanksgiving (one is enough!), this is our chance to create a unique family tradition. For example, you could have each person in the family choose their favorite dish, and sit down to a table with only those dishes.

In my (Diane's) family, we set the table with candles, one for each person. Each candle is held by a fruit, vegetable, or gourd serving as a candlestick. Then we go around the table, talking about what we're grateful for. This is not the time to ask for more, but to feel gratitude for what we have. We talk about our teachers, a best friend, each other, our work and hobbies. After each person speaks, we all thank the Goddess and God together and say, "Blessed be!" with enthusiasm. We respect silence for what is too personal or tender for speaking aloud. After each one's turn we light one of the candles on the table. As the sky darkens outside, the room grows brighter with each added candle.

Restoring the Balance

As day and night are in equal proportion, so are the forces of creation and destruction that we all possess. The Autumn Equinox can be a time when we work in some way to restore the balance in nature. There are many sacred acts, large and small, we can do with children to counter some of the social and environmental destruction that exist around us.

One year, my (Anne's) family took part in a weekend camp-out to restore the salmon run in a local creek. This annual event was the perfect way for us to work with others at an enjoyable pace on reversing the habitat destruction evident in all our waterways. It was satisfying for our children to know that being Pagan and caring for the earth is not only about words, but about action as well. The project your family chooses to participate in need not be environmental, but can reflect your own sense of priorities. Here are some ideas:

⚬ Take a walk around your neighborhood and attend to something that needs doing. Pick up trash, fix something that is broken, talk to someone you haven't spoken to in a while.

⚬ Go to an event put on by a group that does not share your views or ancestry. Listen to their words, dance to their music, extend your understanding and acceptance of diversity.

⚬ Bake something delicious and take it to a nursing home with your children. Present your gift with a spirit of gratitude for all the wisdom and experience our elders have to teach us. Eat and talk with the residents.

⚬ Serve a meal at a soup kitchen. Serving others is a classic way to instill values of compassion and respect in children.

⚬ As a family, adopt a local nonprofit group whose work you support. Find a way that everyone in your family can help them.

⚬ For a day, use only transportation that does not require gasoline.

The Earth Is Our Home

On Mabon, we (Diane's family) explore someplace where we've never been, and we are overt about making this a trip for a sacred purpose. For people who don't have new destinations within a reasonable distance, try another theme: your family's favorite place, your childhood haunts, an area that needs a litter patrol, somewhere you haven't been in a while.

From this place we gather something to take home to use for our altar, mobile, or wreaths. We gather dried flowers, pretty grass seed heads, special rocks, pinecones, and whatever else the children find interesting. The rules are that we do not pick anything that's living and we do not take away everything: for example, every pinecone that's fallen. If the children want more than we can use, build an on-site altar of whatever they fancy. If we bring along string and scissors, we make a mobile to hang from branches.

When we leave, we thank the earth for Her gifts and for showing us how big, beautiful, and varied she is. At home, we add what we've found to our altar, and start making wreaths from our found treasures.

Mabon Mobile

On Mabon, we focus on balance by creating a mobile of autumn leaves and other objects.

Select your longest twig and loop thread around it. Move the thread around until you find the twig's balance point. Knot the thread and hang the twig where you can comfortably work on it. Hanging it from a broom handle suspended across two chairs works well.

Select the next two largest twigs and use more string to suspend them from either end of the first stick, finding their balance points.

Now the fun begins. Pick out four objects of approximately the same weight, and tie short lengths of string onto them. Hang them from the sticks, making sure to maintain the sticks' balance.

Continue this way, building down and out, adding sticks and natural objects until you've created a balanced, multi-level mobile. Carefully hang it up, either over your Mabon altar, or somewhere where people won't crash into it.

You will need:

pretty colored leaves

other natural found objects that are small and light, such as seed pods, thistle heads, small pinecones

8–12 supple twigs, 6 to 18 inches long, about 1/4 inch to 3/4 inch in diameter

sturdy thread or light string; a dark color looks best

Harvest Necklaces

Recycle your decorative corn by making harvest necklaces from the kernels. Sometimes called Indian corn, these multicolored dried ears have the botanical name *Zea mays*. Kept dry, these necklaces should last several seasons.

Children age five and up can easily pop the kernels off the cobs using a fork or a dime.

When you've reaped enough kernels, place them in a

You will need:

decorative corn

small fork

shallow pan, like a roasting pan

bowl

water

sturdy sewing needle

quilting thread

beeswax disk

bowl, cover them with boiling water to kill any critters, and let them soak. They can be pierced after four hours but will be more workable with longer soaking, preferably overnight.

Take the kernels out of the water and dry on top of a towel. Thread the needle (#10 tapestry sharp works well) and make a good knot. Run thread over the beeswax disk for strengthening and to prevent tangles. The kernels will still be hard on top, but the bottom should be easy to pierce. You can make a simple single-stranded necklace, or use extra strands for fancier bead work. Embellish with shells and feathers, or other found objects.

Try making patterns with colors or twisting strands of different-colored kernels together. Another variation is the "four quarters" necklace. Make one strand each of yellow corn for the east, red corn for the south, blue corn for the west, and variegated corn for the north.

Adding Feathers

Pick feathers that have a quill, the hollow tip of the feather's shaft, large enough to let a needle pass through. Snip off the end. Thread a thin needle and make a small knot. Holding the needle at a downward angle, stick the needle into the shaft about an inch from the end. Carefully push the needle through the quill's hollow core and out the open end. Loop the thread a couple of times around the place in the necklace where you want the feather, and tie off.

More Ideas

Glue guns allow us to attach just about anything to a stout thread, such as small pebbles, bits of wood, and other objects that our children find.

Drape long strands of corn on altars, wind them around wreath armatures, intertwine with other materials for garlands or door decorations.

Tips

If you have leftover kernels that you plan to use later, don't let them dry out again. Cover them with water and store in the refrigerator. They will keep another day or two.

Don't make the strands too long. Pulling the kernels over the thread frays and weakens the thread.

Don't push the kernels too closely together. Tightly packed kernels make a less flexible strand.

For a child who's too young or uncoordinated to pierce the kernels, have an adult make a strand using a large needle and doubled thread. Pull the kernels off the strand and let the child restring them using a smaller needle.

Cinanimals

Animals get ready for winter by fattening up for hibernation, growing heavy, shaggy coats of fur, storing nuts and seeds, fixing burrows, or flying to warmer climates. As we enter the long darkness, we honor animals and make fragrant animal shapes for our altars.

Combine the applesauce with one cup of the cinnamon. Stir until well mixed. The cinnamon is very dusty, so stir slowly to prevent little cinnamon clouds from forming. Now add more cinnamon, a teaspoon at a time, until the mixture has a firm consistency, easy to roll out but not dry. With different applesauces and varying levels of humidity, the amount of extra cinnamon needed varies.

Work on wax paper dusted with cinnamon. Roll kiwi-size balls out to about $1/4$ inch thick. Use cookie cutters to cut out shapes. As you work, bless each animal and give thanks for its particular gift: the cow for milk, the giraffe for its long-necked beauty, and so on.

Gently transfer the shapes to wax paper or a cookie sheet. If you plan to hang these cinanimals, use the toothpick to carefully form a hole, making sure the hole is at least $1/4$ inch from the edge. Let the cinanimals dry in the sun or, if the weather is damp, in the oven set at the lowest temperature for about two hours.

These cinanimal figures are a bit stronger than a cookie. If handled with care and kept dry, they and their spicy scent will last indefinitely.

You will need:

1 C applesauce, smooth variety

$1^1/_2$ C cinnamon (spice stores sell it in bulk, and warehouse stores sell it in restaurant-size tins)

rolling pin

wax paper or parchment paper

cookie sheet

toothpick

assortment of cookie cutters shaped like animals (miniature ones work best)

Harvest Candleholders

You will need:

fruits and vegetables, like apples, acorn squash, small pumpkins, or any kind of medium-size gourds

sharp small knife—grapefruit knives or pointed peelers work well

candle tapers

Try using fruits and vegetables as candleholders to decorate your altar and in your ceremonies. Group five or six different fruits and vegetables together for an effect of abundance and variety.

Polish the fruits and vegetables with a soft cloth until they shine. Stand one on a flat surface and find the point where it rests most solidly. Press your finger along the top to find the best place to cut and still keep the fruit or vegetable's stability.

With the knife, dig a neat hole, the same diameter as the candle taper, about two inches deep. Secure the taper in the hole with a little dripped wax.

Tip

Apple holes should be rinsed with lemon juice to slow the browning process.

Mabon Wreaths

Mabon lends itself to handsome, full wreaths, bristling with reminders of the richness of the season. You will need the usual wreath-making supplies: a wreath form, florist's wire, tape, toothpicks, and a glue gun. But let imagination be your guide as you select what to cover the wreath form with and what to use for embellishments.

Try green leaves, vines, pine needles—anything that creates a luxuriant effect. Embellish with seed pods, berries, bright fall leaves, and/or dried chili peppers for jazzy color, feathers you've been collecting, pinecones, eucalyptus buttons, dried flowers, and fruits. Try something completely nontraditional, like shed snakeskin or ticket stubs to a winning game.

Begin by firmly taping your background material onto the form. Next, add larger items like pinecones or eucalyptus buttons. Generously squirt the items with hot glue, then press them onto the wreath and hold in place until fixed. Smaller, lighter items like feathers or dried flowers can be wedged in or fixed in place using florist's wire. Fix berries on toothpicks and stick them in dense areas.

Hang the wreath with the charms or blessings you've made over the year. Take all the ribbons you've been saving, fashion them into one huge bow, and attach.

While the family works on the wreath, envision your creation as the embodiment of your gratitude for the richness and diversity of your lives together, how each family member brings their surprises, talents, and special qualities to form the unique circle that is your family's alone.

Leaf Chain

Gather armfuls of brightly colored leaves with stems that are at least 3 inches long. Use the pin to make a slit in the stem about two inches down from the leaf; the slit should be $1/2$ inch long. Poke the stem of another leaf into this slit and pull it through until that leaf is flush to the slit. Slit that leaf's stem, insert the next leaf, and so on until you have a chain of your desired length.

To make a crown or a wreath, use a bit of florist's tape to fasten the chain into a circle. Lay one across your mantelpiece, your altar, or around the candlesticks on your table for a thanksgiving feast centerpiece.

Harvest Rainbow

Add a rainbow made from fruits and vegetables to Autumn Equinox celebrations. Start with turning a trip to your garden or produce market into a treasure hunt for rainbow colors. Prepare the produce as finger foods. Arrange on a large platter in the curving stripes of a rainbow, and place on the altar until you're ready to eat.

Many vegetables and all fruits are great raw. For those who don't like raw broccoli, green beans, squash, and so on, steam them until they're bright and still crunchy, then run the vegetables under cold water right away to stop the cooking. (This is called blanching.)

Roasted vegetables are easy and delicious. Preheat oven to 350°. For nonroot vegetables and potatoes: Cut veggies such as potatoes, eggplants, and squash into wedges. Lay them on a lightly oiled cooking sheet and brush the vegetables with oil. Bake for 25 or 30 minutes, turning after 10 minutes and checking each piece for tenderness after 20 minutes.

For root vegetables such as beets, carrots, and turnips, preheat the oven to 400°. Cut long vegetables into 2-inch lengths, and cut the wider sections into halves. Cut round vegetables into quarters or eighths, about 2 inches long. Put the vegetables into the roasting pan, and pour about 2 tablespoons of olive oil or vegetable oil over the vegetables. Shake and toss the vegetables until the oil is evenly distributed. Cover and roast for about 45 minutes, shaking them thoroughly every 15 minutes and checking for tenderness. Rub the skin off the beets and other vegetables that need skinning when they're cool enough to handle.

A Rainbow of Fruits and Vegetables

◐ Red: Peppers, strawberries, red apples, raspberries, watermelon, beets

◐ Orange: Oranges, cantaloupes, some peaches and nectarines

◐ Yellow: Squash, corn, yellow apples, banana, some peaches and nectarines

◐ Green: Green beans, green apples, zucchini, peas, green grapes, honeydews, apples, kiwis

◐ Blue: Blueberries, blackberries, blue potatoes, blue corn or corn chips

◐ Indigo/Violet: Grapes, plums, eggplants, purple cabbage, purple-topped turnips

Mabon Bread

This golden bread combines pumpkin and corn. It's still sweet enough for children to love, but not too sweet for adults to enjoy. The richness comes from condensed yogurt.

Preheat the oven to 350°. Mix together the eggs and sugar. Add the pumpkin, condensed yogurt, and orange juice.

Sift the cinnamon, baking soda, baking powder, salt, and flour together. Add the cornmeal. Incorporate this slowly into the wet mixture.

Oil two loaf pans. Divide the batter between the pans and smooth the top. Bake for 1 hour. Test for doneness by inserting a knife or skewer into the center. It should come out clean and dry. Let the loaves cool for 5 minutes, then remove from pans and let cool completely.

This batter also bakes well as muffins, with the baking time about 40 minutes.

Condensed Yogurt

Place 2 cups of plain yogurt in a colander lined with cheesecloth or a sturdy paper towel. Let yogurt drain for six hours or overnight. You'll be left with 1 cup of condensed yogurt.

You will need:

4 eggs

1 C brown sugar

1½ C cooked and pureed pumpkin (or one 15-oz can pumpkin), drained

1 C condensed plain yogurt (nonfat or lowfat is fine)

2 T frozen orange juice

1 t cinnamon

¼ t baking soda

4 t baking powder

½ t salt

1½ C flour

1 C cornmeal

Sugar Pretzels

You will need:

1 T yeast (one package)

¼ C warm water

pinch of sugar

3 C flour

½ t salt

½ C chilled butter (one stick)

½ C sugar

3 beaten egg yolks

1 C whipping cream

TOPPING

1 beaten egg white

½ C brown sugar

½ C shredded coconut or rainbow sprinkles

Being grateful is part of our harvest festival of Mabon. Twisting pretzels into sacred shapes may sound comical, but it's sure fun. Asking children to put a shape to what they are grateful for helps them to connect with their appreciation. The dough must have at least two hours' rising time or may rise overnight in the refrigerator, so plan accordingly.

Sprinkle the yeast in the warm water, add sugar, and set aside. Mix together the flour and salt. Cut butter into eight pieces and incorporate into flour with a pastry cutter or by rubbing butter and flour together with your fingers. The flour should look like coarse meal.

Add foamy yeast, sugar, egg yolks, and cream, stirring until the mixture is thoroughly moist. Turn out onto a floured board and knead lightly until the dough just forms into a ball. Let dough rise for 2 hours, or cover it and let rise overnight in the refrigerator.

Preheat oven to 375°.

Place the risen dough onto a floured board and roll out into a 16-inch square. Fold the dough twice and roll out into a 10-by-20-inch sheet. Using a sharp knife or pizza cutter, cut the dough into strips 10 inches by ½ inch. On a lightly greased cookie sheet, form the strips into the shapes of whatever you are grateful for. Don't forget to make regular pretzel shapes, too; these are sacred to the triple aspect of Maiden, Mother, and Crone.

Space them about 2 inches apart. Brush with egg white and sprinkle with brown sugar and, if your children like them, coconut or rainbow sprinkles. Bake for 20 minutes until pretzels are puffed and golden brown. Makes 30–40 pretzels.

Mabon Apples

Apples are the fruit that carries us through winter. These simple baked apples can be embellished with your family's favorite fillings.

Preheat the oven to 350°. Using a grapefruit knife, an apple corer, or a melon baller, core the apples, leaving the bottoms intact. Peel the skin off the top inch of the cored apple.

Place the apples in a pan that just holds them. Put 1 teaspoon of sugar into each apple hole, plus a pinch of cinnamon. Pour apple cider into the pan until it reaches the depth of $1/2$ inch. Bake for 50 minutes to 1 hour, basting the apples with the juice from the pan every 15 minutes. Serve while still warm, with cream or a scoop of vanilla ice cream.

Filling the Apples

Try filling the apple cavities with honey or maple syrup, granola, or raisins and nuts, sweetened with honey or maple syrup.

You will need:

4 large apples (Golden Delicious bake best)

4 t brown sugar

$1/2$ t cinnamon

$1/2$ to 1 C apple cider or juice

Optional: cream, whipped or plain; vanilla ice cream

Starhawk's Easy Applesauce

Loosely chop and core the apples, and place in a covered saucepan with half the liquid. Bring to a boil, then simmer until apples are soft, adding more liquid as needed and being careful not to burn the apples. You can adjust the amount of liquid to taste—more makes a softer applesauce, less a chunkier mixture. When the apples are soft, mash them with a potato masher. Add the sugar, adjusting the amount to your taste. If the applesauce is too sweet or too bland, add the lemon juice. Simmer until the mixture thickens.

Refinements

⑥ Substitute lesser amounts of honey or maple syrup for sugar.

⑥ Peel the apples before cooking.

You will need:

5 apples

$1/2$ to 1 C apple juice, apple cider, or water

$1/2$ to 1 C white sugar

1 t lemon juice (optional)

⑥ Run the finished sauce through a blender or food processor for a fine, even texture.

⑥ Add cinnamon, nutmeg, cloves, or other spices to taste.

⑥ Reduce liquid and cook in a crockpot.

Applesauce Cream

You will need:

1 C applesauce

2–4 T heavy cream

Place applesauce in a bowl and stir in the heavy cream. Experiment with amounts to get the texture and taste you like best. This treat can be eaten straight as an ice cream substitute or stirred into oatmeal. Thick applesauce cream can be spooned onto biscuits or scones. You can also slather a biscuit with applesauce cream and top with whipped cream to make applesauce shortcake.

Maple Popcorn

You will need:

¼ C popcorn

1 C maple syrup

1½ t butter

This reaches back to the foods first tasted on this continent: maple and corn.

Pop the popcorn. Boil together the maple syrup and butter until it reaches 234°, or the soft ball stage. Pour over the popcorn and mix well. This treat is irresistible, so be prepared to make more.

Fall Equinox Disaster Meal

I (Anne) had a great Fall Equinox ritual planned for my kids. Since we live in apple country, I was going to bake apple cobbler from our own apples, and set up a feast under our prolific apple tree. We were going to hold hands and sing around the tree, pour a little drink around its roots, feed it, and generally make the tree feel thanked and appreciated.

Harvest Chant[4]

Words and music by T. Thorn Coyle

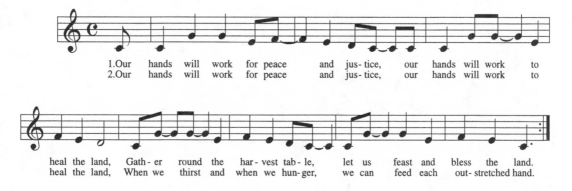

1. Our hands will work for peace and jus-tice, our hands will work to
2. Our hands will work for peace and jus-tice, our hands will work to

heal the land, Gath-er round the har-vest tab-le, let us feast and bless the land.
heal the land, When we thirst and when we hun-ger, we can feed each out-stretched hand.

But the kids hated the cobbler I made (so much for culinary improvisation). Then a cold wind came up, several unrelated crises occurred, and the beans I had been cooking for dinner burned badly. I realized that I'd better scale down my expectations or the evening would be a total disaster. So I made drop biscuits for us to slather honey on, and cut fresh apples into slices and spread them with peanut butter. With some baby carrots I happened to have from the farmers' market, this made a fine indoor feast.

Before we ate, we lit a candle and sang "Harvest Chant." We talked about where our food came from, acknowledging all of those who had helped it get to our table.

The kids appreciated that I was able to jettison my plans, which they had been balking against from the beginning, in favor of something that was simple and pleasurable for all of us. And I came away feeling that the core of the harvest celebration—giving thanks and appreciating the food we have—had been amply observed in our house.

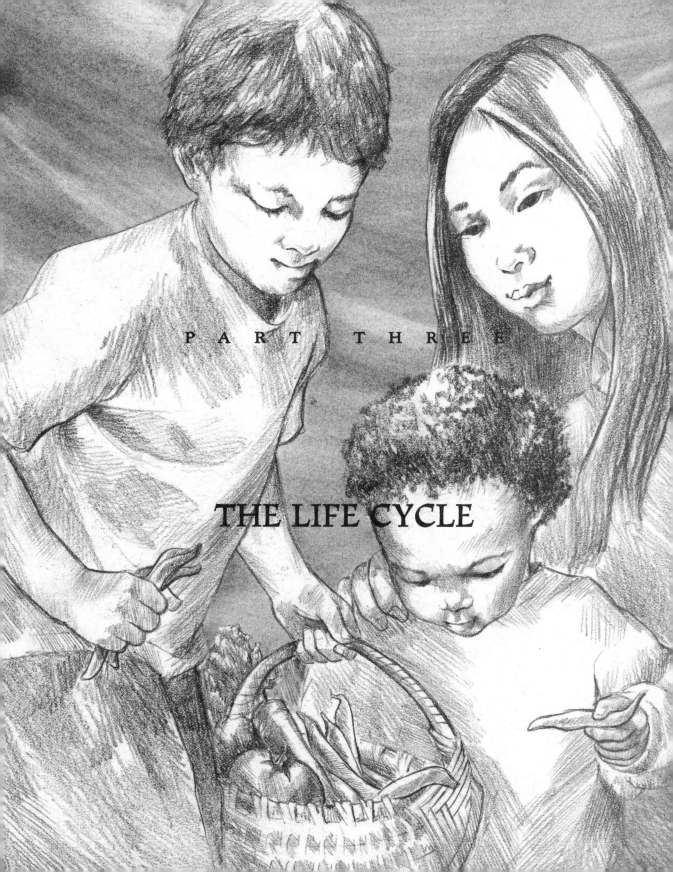

PART THREE

THE LIFE CYCLE

Moving from One Stage of Life to the Next

When my friend Margann and I (Anne) were housemates, just out of our teens, we used to fantasize about being old women together. There we'd be, on our front porch in the Appalachians, sipping lemonade, rocking, and passing out judgment, advice, opinions, and stories to all passersby.

It was a glorious future, one that gave us both the comfortable vision of a simpler life to come. Becoming a Crone, we thought, was uncomplicated—and even if it was complicated, at least by then we would have earned the right to be whoever we were, with no apologies to anyone. Becoming a Mother, a full-grown woman, on the other hand, was so challenging that we didn't know quite where to begin, or where to turn to find a map, or even a clue.

In the absence of rites to mark our passage from one stage of life to the next, we remain spiritually, physically, and emotionally ill at ease with ourselves and unsure of our basic self-worth.

In the absence of rites of passage, children and teenagers will either create their own set of risks and challenges in order to pass across the threshold themselves, or sometimes they will turn against themselves, into drug addiction and self-destructive behavior, even suicide.

This is a great human tragedy in both personal and cultural terms. Children are our greatest natural resource and deserve to be treated as such. Because Pagan communities are generally small and far-flung, support and congregation has been minimal. Our children get what they can from our adult-centered celebrations and rituals, and handing down our traditions to them is assumed to be the particular responsibility of parents. But as more of us have children, and especially as children almost dominate the population at many Pagan events, it is time to reorder our priorities as though we actually were a clan, a tradition, and a cohesive culture, if that's what we think we are or would like to be. That means putting children in the center of our circle, and carefully supporting their passage from one stage of life to the next.

One of the great advantages of Goddess traditions is the value placed on celebrating all stages of life. With the Maiden, Mother, and Crone, Wise Woman, Healer, and Lover all celebrated as beautiful and sacred, we have positive images to pass on to our daughters as they grow. And with the Green Man, the Horned One, the God in his aspects as the Wild One, Lover, Consort, Father, Teacher, we can pass on the riches of manhood in all its forms to our sons.

Coming-of-age rituals for adolescents are perhaps the most familiar rites of passage. But each passage into a new phase of life is an opportunity for celebration. Magically, the point of transition between stages is a moment of crisis, carrying both danger and opportunity. Our old rules and habits no longer work. We are on the threshold of new powers and possibilities but do not yet have the skills or knowledge to use them well. We need support from others; we need entreaties to the Goddesses and Gods; we need those who have already passed through to help us and guide us with their songs and stories.

In this section, we celebrate the cycles of life from birth and childhood through adolescence, with rituals, blessings, activities, songs, and prayers. The Beginnings section celebrates all different kinds of beginnings: conception, pregnancy and birth, and adoption. The Growth section contains rituals and anecdotes for the rapid growth and change of the middle phase of childhood, before adolescence. Most of *Circle Round* is geared toward this age group, so we invite you to adapt the activities and ideas contained in other sections to inspire your rituals for the middle years.

Coming of Age is divided into two sections: Adolescence and Rites of Passage. In Adolescence, we have included meditations, activities, and information to support the physical, emotional, and spiritual changes taking place during the teenage years. In the Rites of Passage section are several accounts of coming-of-age rituals, as well as ideas for quietly marking this passage when a big celebration is not appropriate.

We also cover transitions that occur in family life but that are not issues particular to any one phase of life: moving, separation and divorce, changes in and loss of family members.

Extending the Family

Children need the attention and encouragement of many adults, not just their parents. Adults who may not have children of their own still need to feel connected to the next generation. As a veteran Auntie/Goddessmother/Stepmother/Stepgrandmother myself, I'd (Starhawk) like to offer some guidelines for maintaining extended family relations:

For Aunties and Uncles

(I use the terms *Auntie* and *Uncle* as they are used in Hawaii, to mean someone who has a close relationship with a child, who is part of a larger extended community.)

Being close to someone else's child is never the same as having your own. Your relationship is almost always dependent upon your relationship with the child's parents. So:

⚬ Be reliable and responsible. If parents are entrusting you with their children, be worthy of their trust. Be on time, make sure the parents know how to reach you and vice versa, know what to do with the child in case of emergencies.

⚬ Set your own standards of behavior for your own space and time, even if they differ from the child's home. Children need exposure to differences. Perhaps you are a vegetarian, and the child comes from a meat-eating home. Listening to you talk about your reasons for not eating meat, seeing how your commitment to your principles is carried out in your daily life, can be one of the most meaningful moral teachings a child encounters. Or maybe the difference is one of boundaries. Maybe four-year-old Lisa is used to wandering all over the house with her plate of spaghetti. You might need to say, "Lisa, in this house we eat at the table. We don't grind our pasta into the expensive Oriental rugs."

⑥ As much as possible, work out your conflicts with the child directly, not through the parents. "Lisa, I'm sorry but I need to take that spaghetti away from you until you're ready to sit at the table" is highly preferable to "Lisa, if you don't behave I'm going to tell your mother on you!"

⑥ Be tactful with advice, but honest about your perceptions. You, as someone who stands one step outside the tangle of family dynamics, often see what a child needs with a fresh, clear vision. You may be the first to recognize problems or to note emerging talents and interests.

⑥ Don't get in the middle of a fight between parents and children, or between battling parents, for that matter. If at all possible, try to remain a somewhat neutral, objective ally of both. Older children and teenagers especially often need an older person to go to who can give them some perspective on their power struggles with their parents. But to play this role, you must keep your objectivity and not use the child as a sounding board for your own conflicts.

For Parents

⑥ Be secure enough to let your child go. Young children may often cry at separation, but children are resilient. Your bond will not be severed by an absence of a few hours.

⑥ Recognize that standards may differ from your own, and that's okay. Children are adaptable. Of course, you should never countenance abusive behavior: physical violence, name-calling, or humiliation. But short of abuse, your friends will still have different boundaries and standards than you do, and children benefit by exposure to that diversity.

⑥ Some boundaries, some manners, make your children much more likable and auntie-prone. For example, if your child is used to a set bedtime and a bedtime routine, she or he will be a much more attractive babysitting proposition than a child who is notorious for keeping everyone up all night. A child who learns early to say please and thank you, to offer help with any work being done, and to respect other people's possessions and privacy will attract many more adult friends than a child who is whining, demanding, and intrusive. Of course, every child is all of the above occasionally, more often with her or his own parents than with other adults. Train your children in even minimal politeness, and you will often be amazed at how well they behave with others.

☽ Don't complain about the oppression of motherhood to your childless friends who wish they had children of their own. This is like complaining about the trials of great wealth to your friends who are lining up for welfare. It's not that the problems aren't real—but find more appropriate places to get support.

☽ Invite your child's Aunties and Uncles to offer their perspectives and suggestions. Don't discount their advice because they are not parents themselves.

☽ Allow your friends to remain neutral in conflicts; don't try to force them to take sides. Don't draw them into the middle of custody battles.

☽ Recognize that an adult who spends time with your child is offering a gift of themselves and is in a very vulnerable position. You will always be connected to your child; Aunties and Uncles know very well that their connection, however important it may feel to them, is dependent on their relationship with you and on the whims of your child's development.

CHAPTER THIRTEEN

Beginnings

Rituals for Birthing

BIRTHS NEED NO ritual to make them sacred. The energy of birthing casts its own circle, purifies all who are within its sphere, and gives itself as offering to the Great Goddess. With each breath of labor, women invoke their ancestresses. The babe's umbilical cord is but a segment of the cord of life, which hums and throbs back in time to the far reaches of ancestral memory and extends from us unbroken, beyond the veil that hides the future from our knowing.

That being said, it is also true that birth is a time to make special magic. Our devotion to the Goddess is made acute when our unborn child calls to us, and our desire for protection, reassurance, and blessing is strong throughout pregnancy and birth.

Birth is an initiation into the blood mysteries. During pregnancy, we may feel the beautiful abundance and pleasure of the Goddess, but in labor it can be the battle raven who seizes our bodies and calls us into our warrior aspect. Our greatest spiritual challenge is to let each birth be what it is, and to let ourselves move with the energy of the Goddess flowing through us.

Too often, a woman's greatest physical challenge is to find capable, affordable birthing assistance, whether it be from a doctor, midwife, or nurse-midwife, at home, hospital, or birthing center. Though a discussion of birthing options is beyond the scope of this book, it is worth bearing in mind that regardless of where you intend to give birth, you may find yourself giving birth somewhere else. The more portable your magical items, the more likely it is that you will have them near you when the baby comes.

Visualization and Prayer for Pregnancy and Birth

Our inner knowing is our best ally during pregnancy and birth. Yet the stresses and challenges of the birth process often overpower the small voice of intuition. Meditations that center and ground us can help, as can guided visualization. Following is an adaptation of the visualization I (Anne) used periodically through my last pregnancy. I used this journey when I wanted to check in with myself on how the pregnancy was going, when I was faced with a decision to make about the birth, and when I needed to tap into the current of power and strength flowing through me. This visualization starts in your place of power, a real or imaginary spot where you feel completely safe, strong, and free. (See Spirit chapter for a full Place of Power meditation.) Each time I did this visualization, I found myself a little farther downstream. Finally, in the days just before the birth, I could hear the sound of the ocean.

Find a place to relax, where you can be as comfortable as possible. Cast a circle, or call in whatever protections feel right to you before the journey. When you are ready, take several cleansing breaths, and imagine yourself in your own place of power. Allow the power of this place to enter you through the ground below your feet, sliding up past your ankles and knees, into your thighs, hips, and belly. Feel how the strength of the earth cradles and nourishes the child within you, supporting and sustaining each of you through the umbilicus of your grounding cord. Let the earth's rich energy flow through the rest of your body, your breasts, arms, neck, and head, until you feel rejuvenated. Feel the sun's warmth on your skin, and know that your body is open to nourishment from above as well as below.

Soon you hear the sound of a flowing

stream nearby. When you're ready, move toward it. Which way do you go to get to the stream? In what direction does it flow? Notice how the land here makes a cradle for the water, as the water in turn shapes the earth. The stream looks so inviting; the water fairly beckons you to enter. You look around; do you see a vessel to ride in, or do you want to just plunge in and take a dip? Maybe you just want to sit or walk alongside the stream for now. How fast is the water moving? What size is the stream?

Whatever you feel like doing here at this sacred stream, let yourself do it. Notice how your body feels. Is there anyone or anything here for you as guide or companion? What else do you notice about this place? Know that you can come here anytime to immerse yourself in the river's ever-changing journey. For this is the water that will lead you to the ocean, the life-giving source at the mouth of every river where, by the sea's pulsing waves, your baby will come into the world.

When you feel done with your exploration of the river, say thanks and goodbye and move back to your place of power. Then, when you are ready, move back into the room and into your body, until you are fully present. Thank the powers that you have invoked, open your circle, and take a well-deserved nap.

Prayers for a safe childbirth can be said throughout pregnancy, usually more so toward the baby's due date. If you have massage oil on hand, use it to anoint your body while saying the following:

Maiden Huntress, Warrior Woman, help me meet labor wholeheartedly. May I know all the strength of my powerful body, may my thoughts remain clear and focused, and may my spirit join effortlessly with the power of birth. Mother Goddess, nurturer and sustainer of life, grant my child safe passage into the world. May he be born strong, healthy, and alert, and may his spirit meet ours in love and recognition once he is born. Help my arms to support him, my breasts to nourish him, and my body to warm him on the day of his birth and beyond. Ancient Crone, Queen of Wisdom, Goddess of Endings, once my baby is born safely may you guide the one who cuts the cord, and may you help my womb to close fully and quickly after the birth is done. With your blessings may our days of waiting and preparing end with a rebirth of joy for me, my baby, and my family. Blessed be.

Altars and Charms

Baby showers today are a secularized version of what in many cultures must have been a ritual welcoming the woman into motherhood and a rite of preparation before she entered the ordeal of childbirth. With gifts bestowed on the mother-to-be, and advice and stories flowing freely throughout the room, baby showers still retain some of their sacred origins, yet there is much we can add to this modern ritual to restore its original power and meaning. The following ideas can be incorporated into a traditional baby shower, or used alone or in combination to create a unique rite of passage for mother and child.

⚭ Create a birth altar. If you are having a baby shower or ritual, ask each person to bring a special object to be placed on your birth altar. Let each person have an opportunity to give the object to you, along with the story of why they chose it. Candles, Goddess statues, and special objects can all add to the experience of childbirth and provide a visual focus during labor. Birth altars can include mandalas, photographs, gifts for the baby, bundles of herbs and grasses, and pieces of your favorite jewelry. If you are in the habit of taking long walks during your pregnancy, keep your eyes and heart open for objects of meaning that might be taken and added to your altar. Children often find the best rocks, shells, feathers, and sticks for altars.

⚭ Some women keep an altar in their living room or other common area, to be maintained by friends or family members during labor. This sort of altar can be a focal point from which others send you their prayers and blessings, regardless of where you are giving birth.

⚭ Invite friends over for a candle-blessing ceremony. For this ceremony you will need a quantity of unused candles, and some oils to anoint them with if you like. Lavender and rose oils are good for anointing. Long tapers work well, as do the large candles in jars that burn for a long time. You might also want to have a penknife on hand in case people want to carve protective runes or pictures onto their candles. Sitting in a circle, ask your assembled friends to take a moment to think of the blessing or protective wish that they most strongly want to send to you and your baby. Ask them to concentrate that desire into their candle as they decorate it. You might suggest that they hold their thought or image clearly in mind while breathing slowly on their candle three times.

Once all the candles are completed, ask everyone to go around and share their wishes with the group. After that, the candles are charged by raising and focusing the group energy, typically by chanting a tone or singing a song. Each person will bring her candle home with her, to be lit as soon as your labor begins or whenever else they feel the need to send you energy.

⚭ Another idea is to bring together women who have had children or are beyond the Maiden phase to have a Sacred Stories ritual. Ask the women beforehand to think of an important event in the Mother phase of their lives, and the wisdom they learned from it. All women, whether or not we bear or raise children, pass through the Mother phase of life. In requesting that your guests come with a story, you honor the many ways we find wisdom during this time of our lives.

In sacred space, give each woman time to tell her story. Have special beads on hand, with a length of string. As your guests impart the lessons gained from their experience, they can each add a bead to the string, and their wisdom will be passed on to you in the form of a colorful necklace. (Weaving flowers into a head wreath also works very well, as does dropping stones or crystals into a pouch.) When the stories have been told, the necklace can be presented to you ceremonially, marking your initiation into the Mother realm and your readiness for childbirth.

☙ In preparation for labor, have an attendant (or two) loosen and brush your hair, and untie any knots in your clothing. This is a very old custom for making sure that there are no physical or energy obstructions to a smooth delivery. Once your baby has arrived, have the same person retie those bows and knots, to reinforce the closing of the birth portal and the return of your normal energy flow.

☙ Make a birthing pouch for yourself. The pouch can be small enough to wear around your neck or hold in your hand during childbirth. Because this is an intensely personal talisman, only you can know what to put in it, though you may want to consult books, oracles, or wise friends for ideas. You may decide to visit your place of power in meditation (see Spirit chapter) to receive guidance on what to put in your pouch, or you may find yourself in an herb garden being pulled to specific plants to pick a sprig for your pouch. You may even want some small mementos from close friends included in your pouch.

The purpose of making a birth pouch is to gather and hold benevolent energies that can support you and your baby during childbirth. Having a birth pouch with you during labor can remind you of your connection to the Goddess, and may make it easier for you to let go and trust the birth process as it unfolds. A pouch is not a substitute for human care and advocacy, nor is it a guarantee that you will experience the birth of your dreams. It is there to help keep you centered in yourself, which is the greatest gift you can give yourself or your baby during this powerful transition.

Wicker Box Charm

My (Diane's) fear that my delivery might go wrong was perhaps greater than most because I had a very high-risk pregnancy and I had already suffered many miscarriages. When I packed my hospital bag, to better my chances I also packed a portable altar to focus the Goddess's protection and presence in the delivery room.

I used a tiny wicker box, perhaps three inches square, lined with dark blue satin. I put in a small clay birthing Goddess figure, complete with a tiny removable baby. I filled a small sock kicked off by a friend's newborn with my grandmother's Masonic moon pin and my deceased mother-in-law's pearls. My mother-in-law had saved my husband's baby teeth, so I slipped one in. In went a perfect round black stone from my favorite beach, and an inch-high wooden sheep and lamb that had sat on my desk throughout my pregnancy.

At the hospital I set up my altar on the nightstand, where it stayed invisible for many hours until close to delivery time. "What's that?" my doctor asked.

"My altar," I answered.

For a moment my doctor waited for an explanation, but I just forced a little smile.

"Good idea," she said. We both got back to work.

When we came home I slipped the box under my daughter's crib. It stayed there until my next pregnancy, when I moved it under my bed. Again my portable altar went to the hospital and home, to rest under the newborn's crib. The day my youngest graduated to a bed, I discovered the box dusty and forgotten against the wall when I took the crib apart. Slowly I opened it, fingering each piece before putting the box away. I won't be needing it again.

A Newborn Blessing Ritual

Each participant should bring a bead as a symbolic gift. Parents might provide a bowl of varied beads for those who will inevitably forget. A Goddess-mother and/or Goddess-father should be chosen to hold the child. This person will have a special relationship with the child as he grows, and be one of his primary "aunties."

Ground, center, and create sacred space in whatever way you choose.

Five people should be chosen to call in the blessings of

the four directions and the center on the child. (Or one person can do them all.) For the east, the air, wave incense or sweet-smelling flowers over the baby. For the south, the element of fire, circle the child clockwise with a lighted candle. For the west, for water, sprinkle the child with fresh spring water, ocean water, or Waters of the World (see Brigit Altar). For the north, for earth, gently stroke the baby with flowers or sweet-smelling herbs, or pass him through a wreath of flowers. For center, drum a heartbeat rhythm around the child. Call the names of the child's ancestors as far back as they are known, and then honor the unknown ancestors with thanks for bringing forth a new life. (If the child has been adopted, both biological and adoptive ancestors should be called.)

The Goddess-mother and -father should then call in the Goddess and God to bless the baby. Hold the baby in the center of the circle, and say the Baby Blessing:

> Great Goddess, Giver of Life, we thank you for this precious life that has been given us to tend and nourish. May your blessings follow this young one throughout her life, may she grow in beauty and wisdom, may she learn your ways and know the wonder of your creation. Green One, God of the forest and all growing things, we thank you for the life and vitality of our new baby. We ask you to bless her with good health, good humor, and good sense. Goddess and God, our hearts are full of gratitude. We ask for your guidance as we care for our child, that she might bring as much joy to the world as she has brought joy to the hearts of all of us here. Blessed be.

The parents now come forward and hold an empty bowl. The Goddess-parents direct the people in the circle to hold their beads and meditate on the gifts they wish to offer the child, the qualities they would like to call into his life. "Think about your own qualities," they are told, "about the things you have learned from experience or gained through struggle. Charge the beads with love and protection."

One by one, each person comes forward, drops the bead

We Are a Circle[1]

Words and music by Rick Hamouris

We are a cir-cle with-in a cir-cle, with no be-gin-ning, and ne-ver end-ing.

into the bowl, and names the gift she or he offers. "I give you the gift of love." "I give you the gift of persistence when times are tough." "I give you the gift of making friends easily."

When all the beads are gathered, leave time for people to speak freely, from the heart, about their wishes for the child and the parents. End by singing "We Are a Circle" or a chant of your choice.

Pour out a libation of milk (perhaps laced with breast milk) either onto the ground or, if you are indoors, into a bowl (after the ritual is over, take it out and pour it out onto the earth). Offer new-baked bread to the Goddess and God, and thank the ancestors.

Say thank-you to the Goddess, God, and all the directions, open the circle, and feast. Later, the beads can be strung into a necklace that can be hung over the child's bed and eventually worn when he is old enough to do so safely.

Faery Coverlet Ritual

We call this the Faery Coverlet ritual because it reminds us of how the faeries came to bless Sleeping Beauty with wonderful attributes.

This ritual is especially useful for those who cannot openly engage with their families and friends in Goddess tradition rituals. It can be adapted to almost any kind of gathering, no matter what the spiritual orientation of the group.

Blessing babies with special qualities is ingrained in our culture through faerytales, like that of Sleeping Beauty. Simply presented as a kind of shower party game that allows for our sincere expression of love and good wishes, it does not have to be identified as a part of Goddess tradition.

A coverlet is a blanket made from two pieces of fabric with warm batting placed in between. The three layers are held together by yarn ties, which are left untied for this ritual. Use one of the many craft books to prepare yours. Pass the coverlet from person to person and ask each participant, while holding a pair of the untied yarn ends, to name aloud, or to themselves, a quality they possess and value, and wish for the new baby. "I wish for you my deep pleasure in reading, which has provided me with so much enjoyment in my life." "I wish for you my aptitude for sports, which helped me to think well of myself during some hard times and has kept me healthy." "I wish for you deep friendships, which have given me such pleasure."

As each person finishes her wish, she ties her wish into the blanket with a square knot. The blanket passes around until all the yarn ties are knotted. Now you have a coverlet that wraps the newborn with the blessings of the family and community.

Umbilical Cord Magic

When my (Anne's) first child was born, my husband cut the umbilical cord. He then followed a friend's instructions on preserving the cord:

Cut the cord away from the placenta, close to its base. Over a sink or bowl, squeeze the remaining blood out of the cord, until it is fairly empty and translucent. Lightly oil a small dish or saucer. Starting from the center of the plate, lay the cord down in a spiral pattern. Try not to let the coils of cord touch each other as they dry, or the finished spiral will be stuck together.

Set the dish in an open, airy space for a few days. When it is fully dry, gently pry it off the plate, and you will have a

Cradle Charm

When Margaret's baby came, she invited all of her friends to make small blessing charms. We arrived with a wonderful assortment: embroidered bags filled with special symbols, small herbal sweet-dream pillows, rubber ducks, little woven dolls, and more. Margaret was ready with a grapevine wreath form and wire. We attached all our charms. With our voices and emotions we charged the spells and hung it over baby Jesse's crib, safely out of her grasp.

thin, transparent spiral inside of which you will see the veins that supplied your baby with all its nourishment.

Keeping these relics from our children's births is for us symbolic of our continuing responsibility for raising them to adulthood. We plan on giving each of them their cords in a ritual when they take the step to move out on their own. (Yes, we can tell the umbilical cords apart. They all dried slightly differently.)

Gift of the Goddess: An Adoption Soul Story[2]
by Kate Kaufman Greenway

Each and every adoption family has a unique soul story, just as birth families do. Through creative trancework and focused ritual we can remember these stories. The trauma of abandonment that comes from adoption can be monumental. I believe that this pain can be healed with a spiritual understanding of the soul-to-soul connections that weave throughout many lifetimes, regardless of blood ties.

I have told my son the following story in a variety of ways, over and over again, since he was little. This story is the truth that nourishes and holds our commitment to loving in this lifetime, as mother and son. This story honors our sacred connection. It is the umbilical cord that spiritually links our souls.

Once upon a time a boy and his mother lived happily together, in a cottage deep in the green woods. Once a week the boy and his mother would ride their horses into town with sacks of vegetables, herbs, and cheeses. They loved trading goods at the town market, gathering with their neighbors, and meeting travelers from far away.

As the boy grew, he came to understand how much his

mother was loved and respected by the people who knew her, as she always helped others in need. She knew the ways of magic, and she taught these ways to the boy. They watched the moon change and celebrated the turning wheel of the seasons with special rituals and foods and songs. The boy and his mother lived simply and peacefully, until one day . . .

The boy was on his way home from gathering mushrooms in the woods. Through the trees he saw men on horses riding toward the cottage where his mother was busy dipping beeswax candles. Fear exploded in the boy's throat as he began to run toward the cottage, faster and faster. He heard his mother's voice ring loud inside his body: "Stop! Stay where you are! Climb high in that tree. Become invisible and wait there until the men are gone."

Understanding the urgency in her message, the boy climbed the tree in silence, his body shaking in terror. He watched the men drag his mother out of the cottage and push her into the tiny cart edged with tall, heavy sticks. His mother stretched her energy over to the tree where he was perched. Their eyes linked in sorrow as he felt her speak deep into his soul: "I will never forget you. I will never forsake you." And in that moment, the mother and the boy promised with their hearts to find each other again, to be together again in another time and place, when it was safe for them to live with their magic.

The boy watched with overwhelming grief as the men took his mother away. He knew where they were taking her. He had heard of the prison and the burnings. He had heard of the other women being taken. He didn't understand why these men were afraid of his mother, for she was so good, so wise, so gentle. The boy felt his mother's wise voice flow into his aching spirit: "Go far, far away from this place. Cross the ocean and find a home where you can be free and happy, and safe."

So the boy gathered up his blanket, some food, herbs, and his amulets and left his cottage in the deep woods with tears streaming down his face. In his heart he heard his mother singing, "Everything lost is found again, in a new form, in a new way. Everything hurt is healed again, in a new time, in a new day."

The boy traveled across the ocean and found a new home, a place to be safe. He fell in love. He became a strong and gentle father. His family grew vegetables and herbs and flowers. They sang songs together. And he always wore the amulet his mother had made for him on the day he was born.

Many years and many lifetimes came and went. . . .

In a new time and a new day there was a woman who wanted to become a mother. She felt the pull of another soul in her heart. She felt their kinship, the connection of their love. She felt their story in her blood. She was a peaceful and happy woman, and she was ready to be the boy's mother again. For it was safe now, and it was time for them to be together again and live their magic in the world.

The woman sang to the Goddess each night and day. "I am ready now, please. Help me grow this baby."

She received the seed.

She waited.

She waited and waited.

She took the medicine. She went to doctor after doctor.

She waited and waited and waited. . . .

And still her body did not grow a baby.

She felt the soul of the boy with her all the time. She felt her burning desire to be his mother again.

She cried until her heart was empty. She cried for help.

One day a priestess friend told her that it was time to make a ritual, to call the soul of the boy home again. Together they made the sacred circle and asked the Goddess to hold them as they journeyed together. The woman sang for the soul of her baby to come home. She called, "I am here. I am ready to be your mama. If you are ready, if you want to be my boy, please find your way to me. I will wait for you."

The woman sang her love into the Cauldron of Souls ready to be born. She felt a quickening, a stirring deep in her center. She felt the boy's soul singing back to her. "I am coming soon, Mama. I will find you." The woman smiled then, and she waited. She waited as the wheel turned from Summer Solstice to Samhain. One day very late in October, the phone rang with the news of her baby. He was ready to come home.

The woman cried with joy as she opened her arms to receive her son. He had found his way to her safe embrace. She was mother again, with her special boy, who came as a gift of the Goddess. ❧

Everything Lost Is Found Again[3]

Words and music by Starhawk

Ev - ery- thing lost is found a- gain   in a   new   form, in a   new   way.

Ev - ery- thing hurt is   healed a- gain,   in a   new   time, in a   new   day.

She Changes Everything She Touches[4]

Words and music by Starhawk

She   chan- ges ev - ery- thing she   touch- es,——— and———

ev - ery- thing she touch- es——— chan - ges.——— She chan- ges ev - ery- thing she

touch- es,——— and——————— ev - ery- thing she touch- es——— chan - ges.———

Miscarriages: Misery and Magic

On my way to two successful pregnancies, I (Diane) suffered many, many miscarriages. Each was newly devastating. For one pregnancy, I had tried an eternal light spell, based on my memories of the temples of my childhood. I bought a case of tall votive candles from the local botanica and lit one at the beginning of each week of pregnancy. At nine weeks, I awoke from sleep to a loud crack. The glass candleholder was broken, and wax had spilled everywhere. I stayed up the rest of the night trembling with anxiety, calling my doctor at dawn. A sonogram the week before had shown a steadily beating heart; now there was none.

During these sad times I needed two things: to guide the lost spirit on its journey, and to find comfort for myself. Sometimes I made solitary rituals, others I shared with my group or only with my husband, but each ritual shared certain elements.

Prepare for the ritual by gathering whatever objects you've collected around the pregnancy and that you can let go of. Cast your circle. Call in the directions and the Goddess. I called in Hecate, scythe in hand, who'd gathered the one I mourned back before its birth. Say: *Lady, the reaper, I am empty. You've taken life from my womb, life I wanted, life I invited. Come now to comfort me.*

Talk to the bundle of objects that represented your pregnancy, letting your thoughts and emotions surface. Call on the ancestors of the lost spirit to take it on its journey, to welcome it and care for it until it's ready to try life again. If you're open for it to return to you, say so. Let spontaneous words and songs come. Now is also the time to get angry and sad. Go ahead, you need it. The Goddess can take it! If you cry, let yourself do so freely. Then open yourself to comforting from those around you.

Dispose of your objects. For two miscarriages, I'd bought ornaments that I used as blessings. One was a house, the other was a woman throwing a baby into the air. I tied these to trees. One bundle I put in a coconut shell, which I sent down a stream. Others went off piers or into waves.

If friends and family come, they should bring gifts, or you should get yourself something new to put on your altar and leave there until you're ready to put it aside.

I still commemorate the lost ones on my Samhain altar with a silver pin shaped like a pregnant woman, her womb a big chunk of turquoise. When I go into trance to visit my ancestors, I tell the lost ones that I love them. Each year there are fewer of them under the protection of their ancestors. I suppose the others have gone on to rebirth.

CHAPTER FOURTEEN

Growth

WE SPEND EXTRA attention cultivating toddlers' love of nature. This is the time when children are most open to appreciation of the world. Their constant amazement is one of their most precious qualities. Their wonder and intensity imbue sacredness in much of their play. With very little direction we can include learning about the Goddess, her parts and her whole.

In the Circle of Elements section you will find suggestions for special play with toddlers to develop their relations with each element. But most of all, use your time with toddlers to meander along, small hand in large, noticing thousands of details that usually escape our adult eyes.

Rituals for the Very Young

When my (Anne's) daughter Lyra was three and a half, it was time for her to give up bottles. She was not thrilled with the idea, but we had been gearing up for it for several months, so it did not take her by surprise. She would not hear of actually throwing away or giving away her bottles, so we decided to put them in storage. We found a cardboard box just big enough to fit all the bottles and nipples we could find, and taped it up. Lyra dictated to me the words she wanted written on the box, which we stored in the attic: "Babies need bottles. Lyra doesn't need bottles. Lyra first did, but now she doesn't."

We did not bring her into a circle and formally celebrate the end of her bottle years, for good reason. Throughout early childhood, children need the freedom to move back and forth between the comfort of babyhood and the independence of the older child. Often, as soon as we announce to friends that our child has left a developmental stage behind, she will be right back in the middle of it, sometimes for months. Lyra was not ready for a ritual declaring that she was no longer a baby. She was in the middle of a very long transition period from babyhood into childhood that lasted

until she lost her first baby teeth at age six. The less said about such milestones as toilet training and weaning, the less likely she would be to backtrack.

Yet those early milestones are important for us as parents.

What we have to keep in mind is that we can celebrate the milestones of early childhood for ourselves, without putting our child in the center at every occasion. There will be time enough when she enters school to celebrate her transition into childhood. (See No Longer a Baby ritual for ideas.) Meanwhile, we have our circle of support, whether it be family, friends, a mother's group, or coven, to help us shake out our mantle of motherhood, to let go of the old ways of relating to our child, and to get ready for the next phase to begin.

No More Diapers

The full moon shone high in the sky as I (Diane) carried out my plot. The garage sale was at my friend's house in the morning. I knew if my children saw me taking out their high chair, their bassinet, their baby toys, they would wail and beg and plead, and we were out of space. With luck, they wouldn't miss the items for months, if ever.

The car was full, but I had one more important item to transport: the changing table. Long the focal point of our home, it was about to be replaced by a wooden bookcase. It was after midnight. My husband had gone to bed hours ago. I shifted the other items in the car to achieve another few inches of space. I'd have to hold the table above my head and slide it in just right. Over and over I tried.

From up the hill two women I'd never seen before appeared, out for a late-night walk. They stopped by my car. "Can we help?" one asked. I gratefully accepted. Between the three of us, we easily slid the changing table into place. We stood silently for a moment.

"That's the changing table," I said. "I'm selling it tomorrow. No more diapers in this house."

Suddenly the three of us joined hands and lifted our arms overhead. "No more diapers!" we sang out together, bathed in the moon's white light.

We dropped our hands, and the two women continued down the hill. In a moment I was alone.

"What was that?" I wondered, and went inside to sleep.

Zinna's Birthday Story

The lights go off, and twenty-two silent preschoolers lean forward. Zinna rises from behind the bookcase and places her elbows on the low shelf. She begins: "Four years ago from last Saturday, Brigit's mother didn't look like she does now. She looked like"—Zinna straightens up; her belly is huge—"this!"

Everyone laughs with delight. Brigit begins to glow. "And who do you think was inside?"

"Brigit," everyone choruses. Brigit wiggles. "Then her mommy drove to the hospital, and guess what happened after some work?"

"Brigit got born," the children cry.

Zinna slides out the ball she's been concealing under her shirt. It's a stuffed globe. She holds up a tiny pink baby doll she held hidden in a hand. "And then this tiny little baby Brigit was right here." She holds the baby doll against the California spot on the globe. "But the world didn't stop moving. It turns around the sun, and it takes a whole year." She dances the globe around in a circle. "And when the earth went all the way around the sun, how old was Brigit?"

"One," the children shout. Brigit squeals softly. Her best friend hugs her.

"And what could she do?" Zinna asks.

"Crawl," yells one child. "Cry," several say together. "Play with her rattle," says another. Zinna nods and whirls again. "Then the earth went around the sun again, and then she was . . ."

"Two," everyone shouts.

"And what could she do then?"

"Run, talk," the children call. Zinna whirls again.

"Three," they cheer.

Zinna says, "And then Brigit came to this room and played and learned here. And now . . ." Zinna whirls again. "She's four!"

A shout goes up, candles come out, and "Happy Birthday," the only song the children can sing in tune, rings out. Brigit absorbs the attention like a plant absorbs water, gathers her breath, and blows out the candles with a mighty blow. "I did it," she shouts, hitting her fists into the air.

Tooth Fairy

When Vivian's first tooth came out, I (Diane) didn't think that coins under her pillow would mean that much. So I went to our local bead shop, and there I found enchanting little figures priced between one and two dollars. I bought silver fairies, enameled unicorns, golden suns and stars. For each lost tooth, one charm went under the pillow. In the morning, Vivian and I carefully strung the charm onto a necklace.

When she discovered that the tooth fairy left other children money, I told her that the tooth fairy did different things for different houses. Vivian wouldn't change her charms for any amount of money.

Nighttime Prayers

My (Diane's) children say this nightly prayer:

Bless me, Maiden, Mother, Crone.
[Touching head and feet]
*All between my hands belongs to
the Goddess.*

Lullaby[1]

Words and music by Diane Baker

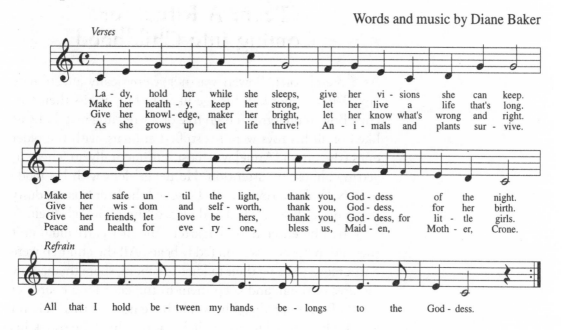

Verses

La - dy, hold her while she sleeps, give her vi - sions she can keep.
Make her health - y, keep her strong, let her live a life that's long.
Give her knowl- edge, maker her bright, let her know what's wrong and right.
As she grows up let life thrive! An - i - mals and plants sur - vive.

Make her safe un - til the light, thank you, God - dess of the night.
Give her wis - dom and self - worth, thank you, God - dess, for her birth.
Give her friends, let love be hers, thank you, God - dess, for lit - tle girls.
Peace and health for eve - ry - one, bless us, Maid - en, Moth - er, Crone.

Refrain

All that I hold be - tween my hands be - longs to the God - dess.

Ocean Lullaby[2]

Words and music by Anne Hill

I'm the bod - y of the o - cean, the roar of the

sea, I can swim with the dol - phins and they sing to

me, and I roll on the waves and I wash through the deep,

as I go to sleep.

No Longer a Baby, Not Yet a Teen: A Ritual for Coming into Childhood

As a preschooler, Bowen was not a physically affectionate boy. Where other kids his age liked to hug or kiss their parents, Bowen preferred a high five or a wrestling match. Least liked of all his toys were his stuffed animals, with the older ones (the ones I [Anne] was most sentimentally attached to) getting almost no attention. He never slept with his teddy bear, Nicholas, so eventually I rescued the bear from its dusty home under Bowen's bed and placed him on a high shelf.

When he entered kindergarten, the first curriculum unit they did in his class was on teddy bears. All the children were encouraged to bring their teddies to school, share them, draw pictures of them, and keep them in the class for a couple of weeks. Bowen, predictably, would have none of this. When I asked if he wanted to bring Nicholas to school, he shook his head in disgust. "There's extras in my class that I can use: the teacher said I didn't have to bring one if I didn't want to."

About a week later, as I left his bedroom with the lights out for the night, a thin wail came from his bunk. He was more upset than he'd been in a long time. I went back to find out what was the matter. "Mama, I can't find Nicholas anywhere and I really miss him and I haven't seen him for *three years*!" He was close to tears, so I reached up onto the shelf and handed him his long-lost teddy. He hugged that bear tight and fell asleep, comforted. He has slept with Nicholas almost every night since.

The change in Bowen—giving and receiving affection freely, taking comfort in the things of his babyhood—was one of the first that marked his transition from insecure toddler and preschooler to self-confident kid. It came just a month after his fifth birthday, and was followed in the next few weeks by many more profound leaps in growth: He wanted to walk to a friend's house by himself, he welcomed the bus rides to and from school, and he asked for chores to do so he could earn money. He suddenly wanted to know about the earth, the stars, Gods and Goddesses, where heaven was; in short, he needed to know about his place in the world, not just his place in our family.

Talking with Charles, a friend from Senegal (see Spring Equinox chapter for his story "The Rainbow and the Antelope"), I learned that in his country it is common to have a ceremony for children at age six, welcoming them as members of the village and imbuing them with new responsibilities. For weeks beforehand, children are taught the customs and stories of their people, schooled in the proper ways to address their elders, then finally accepted through ritual as children of the people. We heard similar stories from other parts of the world, all slightly different, but the main idea was always that of instruction and initiation.

It seemed to my husband, Ross, and me that this process of sacralizing life changes, starting at a young age, could profoundly alter one's life, and might be the most important ingredient in a healthy sense of self-esteem. As Pagan parents, we felt the need to rise to the occasion and create a meaningful ritual for our son as he grew and changed.

Our challenge in formalizing Bowen's passage into childhood was in finding a balance between education and celebration. With his new wide-open curiosity, how much information about the world he was inheriting did he need, and of what sort? How much responsibility should we give him for taking care of his physical needs? Respecting one's elders is a worthy

goal, but in a society where obedience can be twisted into children keeping silent about abuse, what made sense? We also wanted to explore the issue of personal power with him, since he was already being exposed to cartoon violence and fighting on the playground, both examples of power by domination. But was it possible for a five-year-old boy to differentiate between wielding power over others and feeling his own inner power? How could we encourage positive growth without putting down some of his current media choices?

We began by exploring an area of mutual interest: creation myths, heroic legends, and stories of everyday life from as many different cultures as we could find. By reading to him and discussing the stories afterward, we were able to share with Bowen some of the many ways that children grow up, and how spiritual beliefs can change how we live on the earth. This seemed to us a vital education if we wanted him to learn respect for other people and cultures.

We gave Bowen a lot of support for the changes he was already making. When he insisted on walking by himself to his friend's house, we pointed out that as a four-year-old, he had never wanted to do that. He responded by telling us that five-year-olds were braver than four-year-olds. When he came home from school on the bus, I pointed out to him all the things he had successfully remembered: boarding the right bus, bringing lunch box, papers, and jacket home with him, getting off at the right stop with all of his things. He said it was easy for him now that he was five.

One responsibility we gave Bowen was to learn and practice certain social behaviors. At my parents' house, for example, dinner manners are very important, so during relaxed dinners at our house, I would often casually remind him of the difference between how we were eating as opposed to how we would eat at Biba and Papa's house. I practiced with both our children, and they came to see observing manners as a way of respecting other people's customs, not merely as a behavior or discipline issue. I told my mother that Bowen was practicing his manners for dinner at her house, and she was delighted at his effort, and made a point of complimenting him every time we sat down to dinner at her table. A traditional tantrum point had become a positive experience, because we framed it in terms of Bowen's passage into childhood.

Developing chores for him to do was a bit trickier. We knew what he was capable of: He could sweep leaves off the porch with a child-sized broom, pull weeds with us in the garden, feed the cat, and help Ross with his various projects. But when we gave him these chores, he immediately said he couldn't do them. Instead of forcing the issue, we asked for his ideas on chores he could do. He suggested that he take apart Ross's electric shaver—something he did all the time out of curiosity—clean it, and put it back together afterward. This sounded fair to us. We were most concerned that his chores be enjoyable and challenging, so that bound-aries between work and play became less than clear. Over time, what emerged was more of a seasonal chore wheel: He helped peel apples for applesauce in the summer, helped gather acorns for the Spiral Dance in the fall, brought in kindling for the fire in the winter, and helped us with our bee-keeping chores in the spring. From this base of enjoyable yet helpful tasks, we were able to add other chores as he grew older.

We talked a lot about power: power from within, the kind you feel when you are doing something that makes you feel good, and power over others, the kind that most cartoon characters rely on exclusively. Bowen took a series of karate classes with a teacher who emphasized that fighting was not the way to solve problems, only a way to defend yourself when all other options were played out. We let him watch Saturday cartoons but talked to him about what kinds of power his heroes used and why. I learned that he wasn't the undiscriminating sponge I feared he might be, and that in fact he approached his cartoon-watching time with a much broader sense of reality than I remembered having at his age. Through this process, I realized that Bowen's ceremony should be a joyful one, celebrating all the strength and inner resources that our son had gained through his first five years. We decided to make him a "power necklace," as a reminder of all he had learned of his own power from the cultures and situations we had studied. This necklace, as it turned out, was a major focus of his rite-of-passage ritual.

Looking back, I think the key to our

success with the ritual was our discussions with Bowen beforehand. This verbal preparation closely paralleled what I had learned about the process in other cultures, and it created a sense of pride and self-confidence for Bowen. In this way our ceremony became a culmination or fruition of growth, not an introduction to how life would be after the ritual.

In the early stages of ritual planning, I contacted a close friend whose son Corey is about the same age as Bowen. There was also the Mother's Axiom for a Successful Event to consider: If you're having one child there, you may as well have two. I hoped that their shared experience in the ritual would reinforce each boy's sense of accomplishment and friendship.

I wanted to include several good friends in the celebration, and I asked them to find a special bead, rock, talisman, or other item with a hole for stringing, so we could construct special necklaces for the boys. Nine people were able to come, and I collected beads and charms from many others. These beads were meant to convey a sense of protection to the boys, so that when they wore their necklaces they would be reminded of all the people who loved them and sent them good wishes. One friend designed bright beads marked with *B* or *C* so that the boys could tell their necklaces apart. In the end, each boy's necklace had items from a dozen different countries and cultures.

Before the ritual, a friend strung together two vibrant "power necklaces" for Bowen and Corey. We hid each necklace in a different spot in the living room for later that evening.

After dinner, we sent the boys to play while we prepared for the ritual. Lighting candles at the compass points in the room, casting a circle, and invoking the ancestors of Bowen and Corey, we created sacred space. Everyone sat on the floor to be on the same level as the boys. When we brought them in, it was just a short hop from the bedroom door into the middle of the circle. Given different circumstances, I might have made a procession out of the event, but once inside the circle, they felt the change.

We told them this was a time when we celebrated their turning from babies into kids, and that in honor of this big change we would be giving them gifts. Then I brought out crayonlike body paints, and one after the other we all drew pictures or symbols on the boys' bodies, giving them the strength of a tree in their spine, for example, or the speed of lightning in their legs. One friend who had grown up around many exotic animals drew an elaborate animal picture on each boy's chest representing that boy's inherent gifts. The boys weren't the only ones who loved being drawn on. Our three-year-old daughter, Lyra, celebrated herself at the same time by coloring each of her feet different colors. The mood of our circle alternated between solemnity and zaniness, a spontaneous fusion of instruction and celebration.

After the body painting was done, we told Bo and Corey that many people in the world cared about them, prayed for them, and worked to protect them from harm as they grew. As proof of this, we had for each of them a necklace of protection and power, made by their friends, and hidden somewhere in the room. We played the hot/cold finding game, as first one and then the other circled the room in search of his necklace. When both boys had found their necklaces and put them on, we all stood in a circle around them and sang a couple of songs while they danced around as much as they wanted to. Then we sat down again and shared juice and a plate of cookies as the boys fingered the beads on their necklaces and we told them where each had come from.

When the children became fidgety and it was clear the evening was over, we opened the circle, snuffed out the candles, and put the children to bed. The grown-ups then had some time to sit and talk about what we had created. All of us felt positive about the ritual and how enthusiastically Bowen and Corey had responded to it. For many nights afterward, both boys went to bed with their power necklaces on, and have since suggested wearing them on special occasions.

The next fall, I saw our discussions of "inner power" bear fruit. Though he still fought occasionally, he saw his actions in a context that other boys didn't. Many times he remarked that it is a lot harder to think of ways to stop fights than it is to have it out. And shortly after his seventh birthday he told me that he fights when he has to, "But there are other kids who fight all the time. They can't resist it," he said, "because they don't have any inner strength."

CHAPTER FIFTEEN

Coming of Age: Adolescence

Leaving Childhood Behind

MORE THAN ANY of the other stages discussed here, leaving childhood is a physical event. No matter what our inner state,

we physically mature into adulthood. Physical maturity isn't earned, nor is it asked for. It just happens.

For girls this is typically marked by developing breasts and body hair, the onset of menses, and sexual attractions. Boys' voices change, they develop body hair,

Ritual Work and the Elements

Everything we do in ritual can be related to one of the four elements. As you explore and experience each element in preparation for a rite of passage, you might want to include practice of the following components of ritual.

Ritual aspects related to the earth element are: casting a circle and opening it; grounding exercises; altar preparation and cleanup.

Ritual aspects related to air are: invocations; salt-water purification; visualization exercises; reciting blessings.

Ritual aspects related to fire are: raising energy through voice and movement; raising a cone of power; directing and then grounding the energy; finding your place of power.

Ritual aspects of the water element are: scrying; merging energy with trees, plants, candlelight, water, elements, and then returning to self; leaving offerings.

and they experience nocturnal emissions and sexual attractions. These dramatic changes transform children's feelings and needs as well as their bodies. When we acknowledge and celebrate these changes, we can channel their anxieties into a positive pathway into adulthood.

In this section are meditations, activities, and discussions that have particular relevance to this period of a young man's or young woman's life. These practices can be used as needed during your child's teenage years, or they can be woven together into a program of preparation for a rite-of-passage ceremony.

Preparation Exercises

Many of the exercises throughout this book are suitable to help young people prepare for a ceremony that marks their passage into adulthood. To reach this point, adolescents go through a series of experiences designed to strengthen ties to themselves, their families, our society, our planet, and the Goddess. We suggest including work in the areas of element-oriented exercises (see sidebar), spiritual practice, self-knowledge, studying nature, and service to earth and community. The goal is not to complete a certain number of exercises, but to attain usable wisdom and knowledge from each of these areas. The rite-of-passage ceremony then completes the transformation.

Your own ideas for practices can, of course, be incorporated along with those that arise from the child, personal inspiration, peers, your family's spiritual circle, festivals, wisdom writings, and the larger world of Goddess tradition. A final integrating exercise is to create a ritual for your family or community.

Adolescents and Family Ritual

The difference between the roles of younger and older children in my (Anne's) family's rituals is usually that the older children do more. At Beltane, my older daughter helped me welcome the Faeries during our ritual. Others helped make music and kept the dance up better than some of the adults. When the fire for jumping over became coals for roasting marshmallows, we had three adolescents in charge of doling out each of the Triple Goddess aspects: the marshmallows, the graham crackers, and the chocolate bars, which they did with great authority and fairness.

Encouraging teenagers to take on a more active role during rituals can be part of their rite of passage. Not all adolescents will want the challenge of a speaking part in a ritual, of course, but they should understand that the opportunity is there should they decide to take part.

Then there are the family customs, which lend themselves readily to helpers of all ages. Teens can help with cooking projects, altar building, and many other seasonal activities.

The more creative we can be at enlisting the help of our older children and teens in our celebrations, the better-rooted they will be in Goddess tradition throughout their lives. Adolescents who have had experience taking on roles in family rituals will also feel more comfortable creating ritual with their friends, something they may eventually prefer over family rituals.

Beauty

Preparing for the rite of passage is an important time to learn to love our bodies. As we form our adult identities, we are simultaneously pressured to feel inadequate about how we look. With the transition into adulthood just ahead, this is the best time to clear out the debris of social messages and open the paths of strength through delight in ourselves.

A powerful ever-present consumer industry never rests, making sure that unhappy people buy products to change their looks. The standard the beauty industry promotes is unattainable by almost everybody, and often even those who fit the standards don't think they live up to the image. For women, the transition from girl to woman is frequently the start of our feeling bad about our bodies. Girls' angular, thin bodies are glorified, while women's curved and cushioned bodies are seen as unattractive.

The moon, a most potent symbol of womanliness, makes a powerful tool for transforming feelings about our physicality. It swells and thins, reflecting the changes in women's bodies over the course of our lives. As our young bodies mature into round womanliness, we live the dramatic physical transformation the moon accomplishes monthly.

Meditation

This exercise promotes finding joy in yourself, and allows you to discover delight, appreciation, and power in your physicality. Plan to take a full moon cycle to complete this exercise; meditate once or twice a week, fifteen to twenty minutes each time. You're challenging attitudes internalized over many years, so expect inner resistance and slow progress at first.

Ensure some private time, purify, make yourself comfortable, and relax deeply, using your breath to expel tension. Go through your grounding exercises.

Starting from your earliest memories, use mental pictures of yourself to review how you felt in your body during childhood. Review memories when you experienced delight in being physical.

My (Diane's) personal pictures include tremendous joy as I ran as hard as I could until I was drenched in sweat and glowed with heat. I remember the giddy moment when I learned how to swim, my thrill over riding my bicycle on two wheels by myself the first time. Others might capture

these feelings through memories of climbing trees, skating fast, jumping rope hard, playing jacks and making that last tough sweep, or just lying warm and relaxed in the sun. Choose what you respond to most: wild, free moments, or deep, quiet stillness.

Focus on this feeling. Stay with it a long time. Get used to it. Use pictures in your mind to let the feeling become more concrete. Move into those mental pictures, occupying them. This might take many sessions of memory and relaxation, but don't worry. No matter how remote from those times you may be in the beginning, you will begin to capture these sensations in a palpable way.

After you summon up these good physical feelings, take a break, stretching and walking around a bit. Then get back to your relaxed state and visualize yourself right now. Get a good, strong mental image of yourself at this stage in your life. Picture everything from your hair to your toes and solidly establish that visual image.

Now you're ready to start fusing the two. Start by capturing your good childhood feelings of physical contentment. When that's solid, go to your present self-image and hold that image at the same time as you're holding the good feelings. You're mingling a feeling with an image. When you can hold those two together, picture yourself moving through your real-time daily routine, holding the feeling and image together. See yourself getting up, looking in the mirror, and feeling your childhood contentment with your body.

Go on visualizing your morning habits, and work your way through school, the evening, then to sleep. You might want to do this meditation in stages, one part of the day for each session.

You may find barriers in joining good physical feelings to your present self-image. Use your breath to relax more, and keep trying. When your focus gets distracted, quit and start another time when you're fresh. If you really enjoy this exercise, try advancing your age in your thoughts, seeing yourself at age twenty, thirty, and so on, into the three aspects of the Goddess: Maiden, Mother, Crone.

You Are Goddess, You Are God

This exercise is to develop your appreciation that you are part of divinity. In circles, after invoking the Goddess and God, we often turn to each other, exchange a kiss, and say, "Thou art Goddess" or "Thou art God." When doing this, we are reaching out to the divine in each other, from the divine in ourselves.

While our childhood bodies, minds, and emotions make the transition toward full growth, we sometimes hate the stage we're in. How can a face with acne be the face of the Goddess or God? But in that new face, within that new body, the divine lives.

In this exercise you make a mirror for private use and for meditating on the Goddess and God within. It's made from a simple frame constructed around a paper plate. Decorate the frame with the symbols or aspects of the Goddesses and Gods that most attract you. You can add objects as well. If you're drawn to water, for example, you may wish to glue on symbols of water: beach glass, shells, even sprinkles of sand. If you're finding yourself attracted to the aspects of the Green Man, or the Horned One, paint or add leaves, or draw on antlers. If you don't want to draw directly onto the frame, draw on a separate piece of paper, then coat the back with thinned white glue and paste it on.

Cut a hole or any other shape you want in the paper plate,

You will need:

a small round mirror, 8–10 inches in diameter

paper plate

papier-mâché supplies (see Sun Piñata activity in Summer Solstice chapter)

glue or other adhesive

paint and other decorations

varnish (or other clear finishing product)

smaller than the mirror you plan to frame. You may shape the outside of the plate as well, forming sun rays or star points, squaring it or making it into an oval. Pad the paper plate with several layers of papier-mâché, working from the inside hole to the outside edge.

Dry the frame thoroughly, then decorate. While decorating, focus on the qualities represented by each decorative item. Feel the connection with each item. If the connection doesn't happen, put the mirror away and try again later.

Finish the frame with a protective sealant, which will add luster to your work. Glue the mirror to the back of the frame. Keep the mirror on your wall or in a private place, such as under your bed or in a drawer. At least three times a week, take it out and look at your face framed by what you love.

This exercise does not ever have to be finished. New decorations and images can be added and old ones removed whenever you feel the urge.

Altar of the Lost

Entering adulthood means leaving childhood, and much gets left behind, for dozens of reasons. One child may give up drawing because of a bad teacher; another may drop an activity to avoid a label. The coming-of-age period is the time to identify and consider these losses, the time to review life and remember disappointments and decisions.

The purpose of the Altar of the Lost ex-ercise is to take control of your decisions and to realize that the circumstances that caused you to give something up in childhood don't have to follow you into adulthood. Choosing to keep an activity or interest doesn't mean you have to start again soon, or ever. Thirty years after an embarrassing experience, I (Diane) decided to reclaim art. In the same way, leaving something doesn't mean you can never reclaim what you've left.

To prepare for the ritual, spend twenty minutes at a time, three or four days a week for a month, thinking about what you've left behind. A useful device is to think back to your preschool years, then each grade, recalling the teacher, your classmates, friends, and activities. Be visual, see yourself and your surroundings. Then try reawakening memories of your other senses: what you heard, smelled, felt, tasted. Think of what made you feel good and what made you feel bad.

Using this exercise, I remembered when my third-grade art teacher snorted at me, "Why are you drawing lines around the people? People don't have lines around them." I recalled looking at my piece of paper and my crayons, trying to figure out how to draw something without lines around it, feeling more and more desperate, not wanting to look even dumber by asking for help. Many friends report similar stories about singing or sports. What happened to you?

When you've processed your history, make symbols of what you've left behind. The symbols might be a drawing, a sculpture, a small token. Make two piles on your altar: one pile for what shall be left behind, and the second pile for what you choose to bring with you.

Leaving Behind

Ground, purify, and cast a circle. Start with the pile of what's being left. Pick up one object, name it, and then state your initial desire. "I wanted this person to like me because of a great smile and a sense of humor." "I wanted to make the team so I could play ball every day." Feel the original desire.

When the feeling reaches its peak, speak the reason you didn't achieve the desire. "I didn't want to practice the piano long enough to get good." "My throwing arm never got good enough to make the cut." Feel the sadness of not achieving your desire but don't try to hang on to your sadness. Keep your body relaxed, letting the feeling flow through you, down your root, and into the earth. Call on the powers for help.

When those feelings have abated, give your reasons for not bringing these desires into adulthood. "I don't want to spend time waiting for a relationship; I'd rather look for something with available people." "I recognize that I don't want to commit the time it would take to develop my body that much; I'd rather spend my time doing something else." "I can't be the best at that; I'd rather find something where I can excel."

Ask the blessing of the Goddess and God upon your efforts.

Carrying With

Start with the second pile of symbols on your altar. Follow the same steps as in the Leaving Behind.

When the feeling of sadness has passed, speak the reasons for your choice to reclaim these things and carry them into adulthood with you. "I like singing, it makes me feel good, and I can find a place where singing loudly is just fine." "I don't care whether or not I can beat my friend. I'm not in competition with that person, and I think that playing chess might be fun." Ask the blessing of the Goddess and God upon your efforts, and open the circle.

When the work is completed, there are several ways to dispose of articles. If the items can be burned, do so, collect the ashes, and scatter them in the wind or in living water. If they can't be burned, try burying them. If the articles were made from dissolvable clays, sink them in water. If you need to keep them as reminders, fasten them onto a wreath form made of cardboard or wire them onto a hoop.

Sexuality

Pagans love and affirm sexuality, often right up until the moment our teenagers start exploring it! Talking about sexuality can be awkward. The story of Thomas the Rhymer (see Beltane) provides us with the concept of the third road, which can be useful in discussing this issue with our adolescents.

The thorny road of righteousness might be the fundamentalists' attempts to push abstinence as the prime value
taught in sex education classes. The broad road might be our
overriding culture, in which sexuality is used to sell com-
modities, define and judge people, and provide a kind of
numbing drug. But the road that leads to Fair Elfland is the
Pagan understanding of sexuality as sacred—as one of the
ways we encounter the Goddess in her diverse and many
guises. To help our young people find this road, we need to
encourage them in sexual responsibility—toward themselves
and their partners. We must provide them with the information they need to practice safe sex. We must offer them a
supportive environment in which to explore their own desires and awaken their own passions.

What I (Starhawk) would say to our young women and
our young men is this: You are beginning one of the great adventures of life—the exploration of yourself as a sexual being. You're going to be learning about your sexuality until
you're in your grave, and maybe beyond, and as you learn you
will gather personal power that will serve you in all aspects
of life.

But gathering power always involves pain as well as pleasure. You will go through many changes, and you will make
mistakes. Sometimes you'll do things you regret. Sometimes
you won't take opportunities and later wish you had. Your attractions may change, and your needs and desires may transform as you grow. But you are a strong and resilient being,
and you can learn from whatever happens to you.

Unfortunately, at this moment in time some sexual mistakes can threaten your very life—so we want you to have
the information and tools you need to protect yourself. Be
generous and courteous in your encounters. Know that you
have a right to protect your own boundaries—or to let people in. Know that part of the thrill of human sexuality is
sometimes to let ourselves be taken beyond our usual boundaries. Learn to read the energy, and be sensitive to others.
Remember that the Goddess blesses all forms of love. "All
acts of love and pleasure are my rituals," she tells us.

When Not to Have a Ritual

A scene in a friend's short story prompted a discussion with my (Starhawk's) stepdaughters about whether or not a ritual would be appropriate to celebrate a young person's first sexual experience. They were horrified at the idea—as was I when I tried to imagine my mother sending me off with cheers and flowers to lose my virginity. Part of the thrill of sexuality is that your mother is not involved. It's one activity you do without her. To create a ritual for a young woman or man would be to try to claim ownership of their experience. It may, however, be appropriate for parents at this time to perform a ritual of protection and letting go for ourselves.

Youth and Maiden Lovemaking[1]

by Zack Darling-Ferns (age 14)

A lot to being Pagan is being a good lover. My attitude is, why not start sooner than later? So here's a brief lesson on how to be safe, how to be fun, and how to treat your partner well. There are four main responsibilities that you should abide by.

Responsibility number one: Don't get sick. You may hear about STDs (sexually transmitted diseases), and the fact is, the *only* ways to prevent STDs are condoms and outercourse. Outercourse is a fun, safe, extremely erotic way to have sex with someone you like. You are capable of bringing your lover to wonderful climactic pleasures with outercourse. If you don't know exactly what outercourse is, well, it's sex without placing your genitals together, but instead you use things such as your fingers, tongue, etc.

When you get to the age where condoms are needed, and you are worried because they don't fit, don't worry. They *do* make condoms in your size. Two kinds I know of are called Wrinkle Zero and Conjure Snug Fit. Buying condoms may be embarrassing, but it is really worth it. In states where they won't sell them to kids, ask your parents or someone you trust for help.

Responsibility number two: Don't get yourself or your love pregnant. Birth control comes in many forms: pills, diaphragms, spermicides, etc. Condoms are the best way to prevent kids *and* diseases. Outercourse is also another way to prevent kids, and boy, is it fun! [Authors' Note: Spermicidal foam should be used in conjunction with condoms for both disease and pregnancy prevention.]

Responsibility number three: Respect your partner's right to say no. Let's give an example for this one. You've just had a wonderful evening with your partner and you are sitting on your bed, talking. You turn to your partner and ask if s/he wants to make love. Your partner says no. That should be all there is to it. If your partner doesn't want to have sex, don't argue or push them into it. You and your partner should only have sex if *both* of you want to. For all you young men, young women always have the choice. Never push a woman into having sex; it's rude, inconsiderate, and they think less of you if you do. It also takes all the fun out of it for your lover.

Responsibility number four: Respect each other's privacy. What I mean by that is, if you have made love to a beautiful young woman or man, don't go and brag to all your friends about it. What you two did is between you and no one else.

There are many other responsibilities, but those are the four main ones. You should also consider things such as age. If your lover is more than a year younger than you, consider whether it is right for you to be making love with them. If your lover is a year or more older than you, consider whether it's right for them to be making love with you. Young girls may act seductive unknowingly; young men have to be careful and responsible about them and remember that they're young *girls*, not young *women*. In many states the law says that if a minor has sex with someone three or more years younger than them, it is considered an illegal act and you can be taken away from your home for it.

Another thing that you should think about is parents. Now, I know some parents can really give kids a hard time about things in this area, but that's something wonderful about growing up in a Pagan community. Pagan parents are usually more thoughtful on your side about this than parents of other religions. You should also consider your partner's parents. Are they Pagan, strict, or would they not want their son/daughter to have sex? What would happen if they knew? It may seem that they are babbling on about this, but they *do* know what they're talking about.

These are all good guidelines to go by in your quest to become a good lover.

Happy lovemaking!

CHAPTER SIXTEEN

Coming of Age: Rites of Passage

MOVING INTO ADULTHOOD is perhaps the period of life when people are the most needy and open to finding wisdom and life's meaning. Adolescents are desperate to find a way to sort everything out. They are overwhelmed with the urge to be independent, to explore all their new capacities. Adults, knowing that adolescents' judgment hasn't caught up with their other capacities, usually try to put on the brakes. We tell children to "grow up," but we don't tell them how.

If your child is not comfortable working with you on a rite of passage, try to find an adult who's willing to be a sponsor for the process. *Commitment* is the key word here. Many feelings and questions arise when working with these exercises, and a knowledgeable person is needed.

The most successful rites of passage have several ingredients in common: meaningful participation and preparation by the child or adolescent; community involvement; and recognition of the child's, adolescent's, or adult's status by new responsibilities and privileges.

Rites of passage should not be confused with initiation. Rites of passage recognize and facilitate the changes that come with maturation, while initiation is a transformational ceremony of commitment to Goddess tradition. Initiation can be taken on only by adults.

Do not consider any of these rituals a requirement. Families can decide which aspects are worthwhile for them and when each ritual is appropriate. And do not expect to find a one-size-fits-all ritual. A meaningful ritual must be created specifically for each child. These don't have to be elaborate. Successful rites of passage vary from quiet family blessings to major community celebrations.

Other Adults and Rites of Passage

At a festival workshop one year, we (Diane and Anne) heard from single parents about the difficulties of finding other adult Pagans to help bring their sons and daughters through adolescent rites of passage. Especially difficult was the circumstance of one woman who circled only with other women, and needed to help create a ceremony for her son.

One piece of sage advice offered by a mother of several teenagers was to begin cultivating adult friendships for your children early on. Have your children spend occasional afternoons, evenings, or overnights with trusted adults who are willing to be involved in their spiritual education. Find Goddess-parents for your newborn.

Volunteers for a rite of passage must understand that they are taking on a sacred task that might not fit easily into their life. Adolescents, like other humans, have a habit of needing immediate attention at inopportune moments. Both before and after the rite-of-passage ritual, a Goddess-parent should be prepared to respond to crises, questions, and requests for assistance from either the parents or the teen. Though the possibility of inconvenience is always there, the benefits from such a special relationship with a maturing young adult are boundless. It is truly a privilege to participate in a rite-of-passage ceremony, and the bond of trust and friendship established can enrich the lives of everyone involved.

It is critical that we be clear about our expectations. Are we merely asking for someone's attendance at a ritual or help with creating a ceremony? Do we want them to commit to one afternoon per week of preparation with our child? The better we know what we are looking for, the more likely it is that we will find what we want, and the less likely it is that misunderstandings will arise.

Keep in mind that everything that happens during the planning and preparation for a rite of passage has happened for a reason. When we enter the mysteries, mysterious things happen, not all of them predictable or explainable by us. By trusting in the Goddess and our own good intentions, we can let perfect love and perfect trust guide the course of events, and our child's rite of passage will be all the more profound for everyone involved.

My First-Blood Ritual[1]
by Aurora

Before my period came, I was really excited about it. I started bleeding at a friend's house, so I couldn't show how excited I was, but I was so happy!

I couldn't share my feelings with my friends, mainly because most of them aren't Pagan. I only know two other girls I actually talk to about it. But somehow they don't seem interested in any sort of ritual or magic at all. In fact, one of them thinks it's extremely stupid.

My mom and I started planning right away, but since we are no different from any other Pagans, everything was slow. My mom wanted it done in one cycle, but the invitations went out late, and the ritual started late.

You're probably wanting to hear what happened, so I'll tell you. But I must say that I am a young teenager in San Francisco and that most of the people at my school freak when they see my pentacle ring. So I keep my religion a secret and disguise myself as an average Christian teen.

Anyway, first of all on the ritual day a group of women I had chosen from the community came to my house for the Women's Mysteries ritual. We went to a special place by the ocean, where we performed the ritual. At one point my mom and I were bound together and ran around some. Then my grandmother cut the bindings and I ran on my own. I ran down a hill, across an intersection, and into a park, up to an Artemis statue. (That was the worst part, because I was out in public in my funky ritual garb.) There I sat and waited for the other women to come, and thought about my life.

Then they did a little sort of welcoming for me (out by the road with people watching!) and we chanted and I left an offering of flowers by the statue.

Then one woman, Kimchi, used our special magical circle-picker-upper and we all went to the store for some food. Then we drove to my house, ate, and everyone told their First-Blood stories. That was really great. Some of the women's stories were sad because of the way their mothers had reacted to their first periods, but it was also extremely cool because they were open about how they had felt then.

We finished up in a hurry and dashed around like weird people until we were ready to go to the community celebration. That was held in a hall at the Women's Building in San Francisco. We got there late (naturally). Then after a few minutes the ritual started.

My little sister and a boy her age were the gateway. We grounded like always before a ritual, but this was exceptionally good. There were many children there, and as our "grounder" said to feel the energy as fire coming up into our bodies, a little boy exclaimed, "There's no fire in us! If there is, it'll burn us out!"

After that I sat in the middle of the circle with a basket, and each person gave me a bead they had charged with wishes for me. In return I danced for them. (Mostly improv, because I had had only half an hour to work on it that morning.) Then Starhawk led a spiral dance. It was very orderly (unusual for us), with women, then men, oldest to youngest, then youngest to oldest.

At the center, as the cone of power was being raised, suddenly I was picked up by the women and I sat at the top of the cone. It was great! I felt secure, warm, and full of powerful positive energy.

After that we had a gift-giving ceremony. It wasn't really a ceremony, but it was somehow like one. Some of the gifts were three arrows, a very elaborate athame, a crab claw, and lots of jewelry.

After the circle was open, we ate and danced.

The only regret I have is that I wish I had mingled more. Even now as I write I feel like hitting myself for not communicating more. Instead, I sat and talked with two of my friends mostly. All those people were there for me and I was so mean not to talk to them.

Well, after all the ritual and partying was over and everyone had left, except for my family and my three friends, I asked to go out to a movie with my friends. I was so happy when my mom said yeah because it was late and it marked that she trusted me. Now, I won't go into detail about that night because it's not something that I'd like hundreds of people to know about.

Well, that was my First Blood. I'm very glad I had it. I will always remember every part of that day.

I hope that I'm only one of many girls to have First Blood rituals because they are great. Special, powerful, memorable, and something to cherish. Now I'll be expecting to see many First Blood articles in the next few years, so please encourage your kids to have First Bloods, 'cause they are something not to miss. Hell, even ask your neighbor's kids! It's great!

A First-Blood Blessing

Be free, be strong, be yourself, be lucky, be proud to be a woman, be loved and loving. May your body always be a blessing to you, a temple of love and pleasure. May your womb bear fruit at your desire. May you always remember that your power to create is of the body, but not bound by the body. May you bear many different kinds of fruit.

Honor your blood that waxes and wanes with the moon, for it is the living presence of the Goddess. May your blood flow gently, without pain, reminding you that within you lies the circle of birth, growth, death, and rebirth.

Yours is the power to open or close the gates of life, and yours is the responsibility to be a conscious guardian. Open to the embrace of love when you choose, and when you do not choose, may you be inviolable. Care for your body as you would for a sacred grove, and care for those you love. May your life be rich with many forms of love: passion, affection, devotion, compassion, humor and playfulness, wild adventures, and a safe hearth to come home to. May you find lovers, partners, friends, and companions, those who will nurture you and those whom you will nurture. Know that you are unique and precious, that no one else can take your place. Be blessed.

Emrys's Rite of Becoming a Man[2]

by Marylyn Motherbear Scott

It was Beltane morning and the sun shone brightly. I had rested briefly from after dawn to midmorn, then walked with the other women through the woods, carrying buckets of flowers to create the ceremonial gate that we'd erected on our land. Ribbons, some with bells on the ends, now hung from woven branches; roses and other flowers bloomed between twisting stems of manzanita, the gray and oxblood colors of the manzanita in contrast to those of the flowers.

Making a circle, we spoke our intentions to each other. Our hands dug into the mud, preparing the deep place that would receive the maypole. And now the sounds of the men singing and drumming came closer, signaling us that their procession had begun. We dipped our hands into water and shook them off, circling up again and singing our song as we moved once more toward the gate, this time to guard or grant permission to enter.

I had participated in this ritual for many years. Nothing seemed more Pagan than this glorious celebration of fullness, springtime, and fertility. Each Beltane, our community burst into robust and earthy celebration, as colorful and crowded as an overlarge Breughel canvas come to life.

Today's Beltane rite was even bigger than our usual ritual. It was the rite of passage for my youngest son, Emrys, who was almost thirteen years old.

I searched for him as the procession came into sight. The men were singing their song and we women were singing ours, each to our own drums. The men walked on the narrow forest path, on one side and the other of the long fir pole they held between them. When they reached the gateway they waited. The one who was priest said they would ask of us a question. They brought Emrys from the center and asked if we saw him fit to be acknowledged as one who was no longer a child, but becoming a man.

Now he stood, smiling, his long sunlit hair hanging down from beneath a rack of young deer antlers, a deerskin snugged around his shoulders over the top of a handmade ritual robe. Slung over his chest was a handcrafted leather and fur bag for holding his magical objects and tools.

He was questioned by the women, and then he was received through the gate with his Goddess-father opening the way.

Coming-of-Age Blessing for a Young Man

Be free, be strong, be yourself, be lucky, be proud to be a man, be loved and loving. May your body always be a blessing to you, a temple of love and pleasure. May the seeds you plant with awareness take root and grow. May you always remember that your power to create is of the body but not bound by the body. May you sow many different kinds of seeds.

Honor the tides and rhythms of your body, the moments of rising and falling, of hardness and softness, of the swelling of passion and its spilling out, for they are the living presence of the God, and within you lies the circle of birth, growth, death, and rebirth.

Yours is the power to plant the seeds of life, and yours is the responsibility to be a conscious guardian of that power. When you sow seeds, may you tend the new growth and care for the next generation. Open to the embrace of love when you choose, and when you do not choose, may you be inviolable. Care for your body as you would for a sacred grove, and care for those you love. May your life be rich with many forms of love: passion, affection, devotion, compassion, humor and playfulness, wild adventures, and a safe hearth to come home to. May you find lovers, partners, friends, and companions, those who will nurture you and those whom you will nurture. Know that you are unique and precious, that no one else can take your place. Be blessed.

Unrituals: Secrets and Gifts

Adolescence is known for being a difficult and contrary time. We adults may want to guide and bless our children as they face new challenges and pass through new stages, but we have no guarantee that our children will submit to being guided and blessed. We may even feel that the more importance we place on marking our teenagers' passages, the more they resist us.

There are subtle ways, however, of honoring these transitions even when we do not create formal rituals. These unrituals might center around revelations and gifts.

The telling of family secrets can itself become a rite of passage, honoring a child's growing maturity. I (Starhawk) realize now that this is what my mother did for me. Even though we fought all through my adolescence, and she abhorred the idea that I was sexually active, as I grew older she imparted to me one by one the family secrets—that my father had been a Communist in the thirties, that I had an unknown half-sister who was the child of his first marriage, that she had actually slept with the boyfriends she'd had in the ten years since my father died. These revelations were usually made as part of a cozy conversation in her bedroom in an interval between battles, and they helped us sustain a warmth and intimacy that underlay all our fights about control. They marked for me my mother's recognition that I was growing up.

Another simple rite of passage might be the giving of a special gift. When I was sixteen, my mother gave me a zircon ring that her parents had given her when she graduated from high school. To her, the only daughter in a family that valued boys over girls, the ring was precious evidence of their love and esteem. To me, the ring was a mark of her trust—a trust I was not sure I deserved, as I was always afraid of losing the ring. I wore it with both pride and trepidation, and had nightmares in which the ring got lost. But I have it still today, and it is doubly precious to me now that my mother is dead.

An elegant, simple, private unritual can occur during one of those moments of intimacy that just happen when you reveal to your daughter or son something that was secret, and then give a gift that has both intrinsic value and sentimental meaning.

Of course, this unritual presupposes that you have some secrets to share.

Today secrets have a bad name, as we identify them with shame, incest, abuse, and addiction. Those are secrets that destroy families and harm individuals.

But not all secrets are damaging. Some boundaries around knowledge can actually be empowering. A rite of passage requires a mystery, and a rich family life requires a few secrets.

Too much openness can be a burden on children. In Goddess tradition, we have secrets not because we are hiding something we're ashamed of, but because knowledge is useful if it comes at the right time, when one is prepared in the proper way to make use of it.

How do you tell a difficult secret? Today, the secrets my mother so cautiously imparted to me would not be secret at all. We wonder why they were ever hidden. But modern life and technology have presented us with new dilemmas that, while not necessarily a cause for shame, may still be painful or awkward to talk about. When is the right moment to say, "Oh, by the way, your father is not your biological father"? Or "I took fertility drugs in order to have you, I got pregnant with six fetuses, and four of them were 'selectively terminated' "?

Eventually, we all need to know the truth about our origins and our families. There are important medical as well as identity reasons to know who our biological parents are. Subtle distortions creep into any relationship when it is based on concealment.

But truth must be told only when a child is mature enough to integrate it. Had my mother been open about her sex life when I was a young child in the repressed fifties, she would have caused me terrible anxiety and shame. Consider a child's level of understanding, listen to your child's dreams and your own, and meditate on the question. If necessary, do some divination—read the Tarot, the runes, use a pendulum, whatever form you are most comfortable with.

Find the right moment to tell. That moment might come as part of a coming-of-age ritual, or as an informal unritual, as suggested above. Something very personal and perhaps disturbing might better be told privately, in a one-on-one exchange rather than in the midst of a group ritual, so that the child can have space to experience her own emotions untainted by those of other people around her.

Consider whether this truth is best told by the people most intimately involved with your child, or by an auntie, uncle, grandparent, or friend, someone one step removed and perhaps less emotionally involved.

Once a secret is shared with a child, it is no longer a secret. Never burden a child with knowledge she is forbidden to share with others. Never, never, never put a child in the position of having to keep a secret from a parent, sibling, or other person in close relationship.

Make sure your child has ongoing support in the following days and weeks, as he integrates his new knowledge. Make time to be with him, and encourage him to seek out others.

Let your child know that these gifts and revelations are a mark of your trust and recognition of his growth. Whether or not you create a more formal rite of passage, be sure to tell your child that to you, this unritual marks his entrance into a new stage of life.

LaSara's Coming of Age[3]

by Marylyn Motherbear Scott

She was born a child of Faerie, raised on the land. She spent her early years toddling around the high hills of Triple Tree Holt, Greenfield Ranch. Home-schooled from start to finish, she had as teachers the trees and grasses and the dark earth, the starry night sky, the moon through her cycles, the sun as it rose and sat on the near hill, the animals wild and domestic, insects and birds, birth and death.

Now she was crossing another line, this time into the scary place known as adulthood. I wanted to acknowledge this lovely young woman I am privileged to call daughter. Turning eighteen in America was a passage not connected with a particular body change, as her First Blood was. At seventeen, she had still been my legal responsibility. She could not vote and was considered a minor. Suddenly, at eighteen, she was a legal adult. She could vote.

The primary intent of the rite was to celebrate LaSara. On another level, I wanted to join the community in a commitment to continue to protect her. I wanted the community to acknowledge that just as they had played a role in LaSara's growing, they would continue to be an important and responsible part of her life.

It was Beltane, 1989. A large circle formed in a clearing. LaSara stepped into it, her long red hair like flames. A radiance surrounded her crown chakra. She looked like a powerful and lovely Faery Goddess. From the center of the circle she spoke of her love for us. Then members of the circle shared stories of her childhood, telling of the gifts that she had brought to our tribe simply by being.

As we approached the time for her to be birthed into her new relationship with the world, I invited the animal totems of all who were in the circle to attend and bring a gift of their medicine. This symbolized the protection we wished to surround her with. Each person in the circle came forward, offering a story, song, poem, or dance. Some presented her with magical tools and trinkets. Her gratitude and humility shone into the heart of the circle.

I had thought deeply about whether men and children should join the birthing part of the ritual. I decided that the circle of a life, each of its passages, was cocreated by the whole community.

The circle re-formed, each person facing the back of the person before him or her, while LaSara removed her clothes, for we are born naked. She laid herself down and the whole circle gave birth to LaSara as she made her way upon the earth and through the open legs of each man, woman, and child. The labored moaning that day made its own music that became a story that is told and retold.

A radiant Goddess was born and reborn that day to take her rightful place in the grown-up world.

A Family Ritual[4]

by Calla Unsworth

I'm sitting on a hummock of sand on the beach in North Carolina, filled with a deep sense of satisfaction. Yesterday our family had a coming-of-age ritual for Tor, who is leaving home for college this month. I really went out on a limb and had to face a lot of skepticism and resistance to bring the ritual into being. I am the only practicing Pagan in the family, and the only one who felt strongly about having a ritual for Tor. Tor himself was neutral; he likes attention but was afraid of being embarrassed. My partner, Bruce, rolled his eyes but went along with it. Grandma was afraid she would be "required to make a fool of herself."

The only "ritual" that society had provided had been high-school graduation, which in my book is a pretty poor excuse for a ritual. The only cool part is when you get to throw your hat up in the air.

In planning our own ritual, my situation was complicated by the fact that I couldn't priestess it myself. My role was that of a mother letting go. For me to have been running things would have been all wrong, magically. Luckily, my sister was excited and willing to help. She is Pagan-friendly and has powerful energy and good instincts.

So we set to work designing a simple ritual that would be potent without making the family uncomfortable. There would be none of the visible trappings of Paganism, to make people wonder, "What on earth are they doing?" We thought if we mainly allowed the participants to speak for themselves, they would feel safe.

The family group was two grandparents, six parents, and five children ranging in age from three to ten, plus Tor. We asked family members to help out with tasks that we thought they would feel comfortable with. Grandpa would say a blessing for Tor. Grandma would welcome each person into the circle. The kids would welcome the elements. My sister-in-law agreed to "dragon," to deflect any curious passersby.

And my sister would serve as priestess. We decided to hold the ceremony on the beach at four o'clock in the afternoon.

On the morning of the ritual, we asked the children to help us prepare the ritual space by creating a circle of seashells on the beach. (Hurricane Felix had just passed by, leaving the beach blanketed with beautiful shells.) But the grandparents decided at the last moment that this was the day to take the kids on an all-day field trip to another island, assuring us that they would return by three-thirty.

I felt annoyed and disappointed, afraid that everyone would return exhausted and cranky, with no energy for the ritual. It made me feel that they didn't value or take seriously what was being planned, which was true. But I also saw that my anger was connected to letting go of Tor. So I let go of my resentment and stayed on track.

In the morning my sister, brother-in-law, and I prepared the space without the kids. We marked out a generous circle in the sand and lined it with big white shells, one right next to the other. It was gorgeous. Then we went up to the house, ate, and napped.

At three-thirty the grandparents returned. As I had feared, the kids, who had been very excited about the ritual before, were exhausted and whiny, demanding a lot of attention. I stayed anchored, trusting that everything would work out. Together, we walked the long path down to the beach.

Grandma went into the shell circle first and beautifully welcomed each person. My sister cast the circle with words alone, talking about the circle of family and our bonds of commitment to each other. Her partner grounded us by asking us to imagine and feel the earth under our feet. Then the children welcomed the elements. The older ones said, "Welcome to the ocean," and "Welcome to the sky." Then the little ones caught on and chimed in, and we got a lot more than we bargained for. People laughed, and it was perfect.

Then, passing around a beautiful conch shell to serve as a talking stick, each person shared a reflection or favorite memory of Tor and our family, and wishes for his future. The memories were funny and heartwarming. It was wonderful to hear each person's experiences. There were tears in our eyes and lumps in our throats along with the laughter.

When everybody had spoken, Bruce and Tor and I went into the center. Bruce tied a silver rope onto his wrist and then Tor's. He spoke beautifully about what it had meant to be Tor's parent. Then I tied a silver rope onto my wrist and onto Tor's. I talked about changing his diapers and taking care of him. I was crying by this point.

Tor took a pair of scissors and cut the ropes. It was an incredible moment. You could hear the indrawn breath of the whole group. He was supposed to say some words about becoming an adult, but we were all beyond words at that moment. So we just held each other.

We rejoined the circle, and Grandpa said his blessing over Tor. Then Tor went back into the center alone. Grandma gave each child a bell to ring. The little kids ran around and around Tor, ringing the bells to seal the blessings, which made everyone laugh again. We opened the circle, and snacked, and everyone went body-surfing before dinner. I was very happy. I had really stuck my neck out to bring this to pass. And what had happened turned out to be important for the whole family. When I went to bed that night, I felt more solid, somehow.

CHAPTER SEVENTEEN

Life Transitions

New Home Ritual

CHILDREN, WITH THEIR dependence on adults for mobility and access to the world, feel moves very keenly. This ritual not only acknowledges the transition a family makes between homes, but celebrates the new home as a place of sanctuary, stability, and peace.

Gather drawing materials, cornmeal, a trowel if there's a yard and the season is appropriate for planting, a pot with earth if there isn't a yard, and seeds of some easily grown plant, or a potted plant. Prepare a site for burning paper.

Just when you've arrived in the new place, find some un-hurried time and put out paper and the drawing materials. Invoke the directions, showing the children the directions in their new space. After casting and invoking, have each person draw a picture about what he or she wants from the new house.

Talk while you draw: "I'd like to plant some flowers." "I'd like my bedroom to be blue." Also encourage talk about what you and the children would like to happen in the new house. "I'd like to find a friend my age in the neighborhood." "I'd like to stop feeling sad about moving." "I'd like to see Daddy more." Invite the children to write words on their pictures. Act as scribe for the nonwriters.

Give each person a handful of cornmeal, tuck the draw-ings into your pockets, and go outside. Walk clockwise around the building or, if you have to, around the block. Don't be shy about looking odd to the neighbors. Remember that being in sacred space makes you partially invisible.

While walking, sprinkle a thin circle of cornmeal that en-tirely surrounds the building. Use your outside hands, so you are walking within the circle. Talk to each other about the life you'd like to have in your new home. "I'd like to play a lot of games in this home." "I'd like to do better in school in this new home, and enjoy my homework more." "I'd like to have enough hot water in this home for a bath at night." Mix the mundane with loftier aspirations, the serious with the silly. When you've completed the circle, share a hug and wish each other happiness.

If your child is willing, burn the pictures, mix the ashes into the soil at your planting site, then sow the seeds or your chosen plant. For children who don't want to burn their pic-tures, ceremoniously hang their picture in their chosen spot.

Divorce Rituals[1]

by Vibra Willow

As we approach the turn of the century, there is no question that the nature of marriage as a social institution has changed, for economic and many other reasons. No longer are we expected to fall in love as starry-eyed teenagers, marry the boy or girl next door, and live happily ever after. Now not only do we get divorced, so do our parents and grandparents! Yet we all keep getting married again. And, truth be told, most of us who do decide to end a marriage feel that we have somehow failed; that something precious, even sacred, has been irretrievably lost, not just from each of our lives, but from our collective life.

In our culture, divorce is a legal process that happens away from the sight of the community, almost in secret. There is no public witness, by friends and family, to the unfastening of the bonds; the couple is not required to stand among their loved ones and declare their intention to live apart.

We know that ending a marriage is often a creative and positive act, one that benefits both the couple and their children. It can provide relief from daily tension, from open and covert conflict, from pretense. Divorce calls on the wisdom of the Crone—the power to cut off what is unhealthy, so that new life may grow. It is also an act of personal courage, requiring deep honesty and moving from the known to the unknown.

Through a divorce ritual that includes the couple, their children if they have any, and their community, we can lessen the pain and confusion and hasten the healing. We may even be able both to grieve and to celebrate.

In a divorce ritual we literally hold the couple and their children within the larger circle of our community, while they open the smaller circle that has been their marriage. Their children can experience an affirmation of continuing love and commitment to them, by their parents and their community.

The following two rituals are based on the one that David and I did when our marriage ended. We wanted to release each other from the sacred vows we had made. Only during and after the ritual did we come to understand how important it was to our friends and family to be able to take part in our divorce, which they perceived as a change in their lives as well.

The form of these rituals also reflects my belief that marriage vows—like any vow made by a Witch, especially—are powerful, sacred, and binding; we cannot simply pretend we never said them. Otherwise, our word becomes meaningless, and our power to act with integrity and intention is seriously weakened. Thus, to be free of a marriage in which we have made promises, we must be honorably released from our vows.

Ritual of Release for a Couple in Community

Before the ritual, choose one person or more, trusted by both of you, to help plan the details of the ritual, and to act as priestess or priest. Separately take some time to reflect on what you want to discard, and what you want to honor and to keep alive from your marriage. Gather small stones or pebbles to represent these things. Take the stones that represent the things you want to release, and toss them away, preferably into the ocean or the running water of a river or stream. The other stones, representing what was good and healthy between you, you will bring to the ritual. You might choose something positive from every year of your relationship or marriage, letting that memory represent all that you want to keep from a particular year. Or you might choose any number of positive memories.

Invite your covens, close friends, and family to come to the ritual. Children may want to invite a close friend or two.

Bring your ritual tools plus your stones or pebbles and ritual brooms. Remember tissues, for expected tears.

Create the circle and invoke the deities.

The priestess or priest will then walk to the center of the circle and mark a large circle, big enough for the two of you to stand in. This can be done by sprinkling anything harmless and of a contrasting color onto the ground—lime or birdseed on grass, sand or soil on cement, flowers or potpourri indoors or on any surface. This circle represents your marriage, and you are about to step into it together for the last time.

Enter the circle together and face each other. Each of you carries the pebbles or stones you gathered. Greet each other as you wish. Then take turns speaking aloud. First, tell each other what you believe was good about your marriage and worth keeping—and exchange the stones that represent these things.

Next, ask to be released from your vows. You may want to make short remarks about this change in your life. If you do, be careful to talk about your own life and your own decisions, and not to include accusations or recriminations, because this is the moment you are *letting go* of each other. Of course, your own regrets, sadness, or sense of loss may naturally be expressed.

Conclude by saying: *When we were married [joined, handfasted] I promised* [include here the actual vows you made]. *I ask you now to release me from those vows.*

The other should respond, *Yes, I do now release you from those vows.*

Then each of you should say in turn, *You are no longer my husband [wife, partner]; I am no longer your wife [husband, partner].*

Both of you then use the brooms to sweep away the circle. You will simply be standing as individuals inside the circle of the community. Your children can be invited to come into the center with you, if they want to. This would be a good time for each of you to embrace each of them.

The priestess or priest can now invite anyone present to speak to either or both of you, to talk about what your marriage and your release ritual have meant to them, to offer blessings and good wishes. The children, of course, are welcome to participate in this. If either of you has anything you want to ask of or say to the community, now is the time to do so. You may also want to affirm what you will continue to offer to each other. Be prepared for a lot of emotions to be expressed, and for anybody/everybody to cry. Maybe everyone would like to sit down for a while. The two of you will simply blend in, taking your places as individuals among all the members of the community.

Now the priestess or priest can help to raise energy using chanting or a spiral dance. Raising a cone of power will at once release both of you from your married status within the community and shower you with blessings and empowerment for your newly separate lives. Ground the energy when it falls.

Bless and share food and drink. Thank and dismiss the deities and the directions, and open the circle.

Ritual of Release for an Individual in Community

It may be that only one member of a couple wants a ritual. Work the same way, gathering stones, inviting help and company. After casting a circle, go into the circle alone and speak to your community, as in the ritual before through the restatement of your vows.

Then say:

Today, standing here with my family and community, and calling on the wisdom and power of the Goddess, who lives in my heart, I now declare my release from those vows and ask all of you to witness what I have done.

The circle responds together:

We have witnessed what you have done. You are released. So mote it be.

You can then say,

[Name] is no longer my [husband, wife, partner], and I am no longer [his, her] [wife, husband, partner].

And the community will respond, *Blessed be.* You may then sweep away the circle in which you have been standing.

Your children may come into the center with you as you listen to the people gathered express to you what your marriage and decision to end it have meant to them, as well as their blessings and visions for your future. As in the couple ritual, raise energy and open the circle.

The Story of Winter and Summer

a divorce story retold by Starhawk

Circle round, and I'll tell you a story from Scandinavia, about the Goddess of Winter and the God of Summer. . . .

One day, as the Gods and Goddesses were feasting in their hall at Asgard, a young Goddess marched into their hall and pounded on the floor with her gleaming spear. Her eyes were cold with rage, yet she was so beautiful in her silver armor, white hunting dress, white fur leggings, and snowshoes that all had to admire her.

She walked directly up to the high table and faced Father Odin himself. "You have killed my father," she said, her voice as sharp as the winter wind. "I am Skadi, Goddess of Winter, and my father was Thiazzi, the Frost Giant you destroyed. I demand the life of one of the Gods in return."

"We will pay you gold in return for your father's life," Odin answered. "For we have indeed killed him, because he stole from us Idun of the Golden Apples. Her apples keep us young, but he kidnapped her and would have let us all die. We had no choice but to take her back. Still, he was your father, and we are willing to pay you something to ease your loss."

Skadi's eyes glittered fiercely, and her mouth curled in scorn. "I don't want your gold," she sneered. "Only blood will satisfy me."

Redheaded Loki, trickster and troublemaker, winked at his brother and sister Gods. "Maybe I can put her in a better mood," he whispered. He began to make faces, tell jokes, and perform a series of tricks with a goat he tied to himself with an invisible cord. Everything Loki did, the goat repeated, and the sight was so funny that soon all the Goddesses and Gods were rolling on the ground with laughter, and even Skadi had to smile.

As soon as they saw she was no longer quite so angry, the Goddesses and Gods pointed to the sky, where two stars gleamed. "There are your father's eyes," said sweet Freya, the

Goddess of love. "We have set them there as a sign of honor. Now, let go of your thirst for revenge, and take any of the Gods you wish to be your husband. Then you may have a child, and in that way receive a life in return for your father."

Skadi looked around her and saw the glowing face of Baldur, God of Light, the handsomest of all the Gods. "He would make a fine husband for me," she thought. "Maybe I should accept their offer."

"Yes, listen to Freya," Odin urged. "Where else will one as beautiful and proud as yourself find a mate, if not among the Gods?"

"There is only one thing," Freya said. "You must choose your future husband by looking only at his naked feet. Then I will bless your union."

Skadi was blindfolded so that she could only see downward. The Gods stood around her in a circle, and she looked at their feet. One pair of feet was so perfectly formed that she was sure they must belong to Baldur.

"I choose you," she said. But when the blindfold was removed, she saw that she had picked not Baldur but Niord, the God of the Summer Shore.

Skadi was disappointed, but Niord was thrilled at his luck. He treated her with such kindness and honor that she soon forgot the appeal of Baldur's handsome face. One moon they spent in Asgard, where all the Goddesses and Gods devoted themselves to pleasing Skadi. Then Niord took her to his home by the sea.

The days were long, the sun shone, the ocean sparkled blue and green, and the waves were full of fish. Skadi loved Niord, and she tried to be happy, but the light reflecting on the ocean was too bright, and the seagulls' cries woke her out of her sleep. She grew more and more tired and grumpy, until finally she said to Niord, "I can't live here! Take me back to my home among the beautiful mountains. Let us live there."

Niord was devoted to Skadi, so he agreed.

"I will live among your cold mountains for nine nights out of every twelve, if you will spend the other three here with me," he said.

So they journeyed back to Skadi's home among the stark, rocky crags and the ice fields of the glaciers. Skadi was happy, for she loved the crisp mountain air and the high peaks, but Niord grew more and more unhappy. At night he was kept awake by the howling of the wolves and the roar of the wind. By day he shivered as snow and hail pelted down. The nine nights he spent in the abode of winter began to seem unbearably long, and the three nights on the Summer Shore far too short.

For many years they continued to try to live together. But Skadi grew more and more unhappy with each visit to the Summer Shore, and Niord became more and more miserable in the winter cold.

"This cannot go on," he finally said one day when the winds howled and the fire kept going out. "Skadi, I love you, but soon I will begin to hate you if I must live here any longer."

"I know," she agreed. "I can hardly bear the thought of returning to that gull-ridden shore. We had better part while our love is still strong, rather than remain together until love turns to bitterness."

And so Niord returned sadly to the Summer Shore, and Skadi remained alone in her mountain realm, hunting and traveling. Those who must journey in the winter cold call on her for protection. And some say she later married and bore a son who became the first king of Norway, giving her name to Scandinavia. Others say she found a husband more to her liking in Uller, the God of Winter. And Niord lived on the warm beaches of the Summer Shore, blessing the months of summer, the crops, and the time of flowers.

And so it is, sometimes, that even those who love each other cannot live together without losing themselves.

Handfasting as a Family

When we become handfasted or remarry, the ritual transforms our child's life as much as our own. Include children old enough to know what is going on in the ritual. One or more of the following suggestions may feel right for your ceremony.

⊚ After you and your partner say vows to one another, both turn to each child and express your love and devotion, assuring each of your intention to take care of him and work together to keep his best interests in mind.

⊚ Have your new partner and your child work out pledges to speak to one another during the ceremony. This is especially useful for older children.

⊚ If rings will be exchanged, consider also exchanging a bracelet, ring, charm, or other token that identifies all of you as being in the same family.

⊚ Place an empty vase on the center altar. Each family member should hold a flower. During the ceremony, have each person place his or her flower into the vase, which symbolizes the family unit. Those who can should state their intention to keep their family bonds sacred and strong, or express their feelings about the family changes as best they can.

⊚ Have all the family members drink from the same cup, or eat from the same bread, after a blessing has been said over it.

Bringing a Child into Your Family

Bringing another child into your family, whether a relative, friend, or a local youth in need, is a tremendous shift that affects your entire family, especially if the arrangement will be long-term. Fostering, especially in adolescence, is a time-honored tradition in Pagan cultures. There is nothing quite so rewarding as having a direct positive effect on a young person's life. And yet, integrating another child into your family does not happen overnight. It takes a lot of work and commitment from everyone involved, and the adjustment period for your family may take months. Depending on your situation, you may want to have a ritual welcoming the child into your family at some point during the adjustment period.

The Family Candelabra

This is an excellent way to ceremonially bring your foster child into the family, and can be used for ongoing work with family dynamics. Find a candelabra with as many candlestick holders as there are members of your family. Then find tapers of the same length to fill the candelabra. You may want the tapers all the same color as well, or perhaps let each family member pick one in their favorite color. Other things you will need are thin sheets of colored beeswax for decorating candles (available through mail-order catalogs or at specialty stores), a table spread with newspaper, and a few small, dull knives.

Gather the family together and explain that each person will decorate a candle for the family candelabra. Demonstrate how to use a knife to cut pieces of the beeswax and place them on the candles. The process is very easy, though younger children may need help cutting the exact shape they want. Emphasize that the design they choose is not important; they are free to be creative. This is something that will be on display in the house, however, so they should try to make something that they will like looking at often. Caution them against putting on the decorating wax very thick, unless your candelabra has deep trays to catch the drips.

While children (and adults) are working on their candles, you can answer the inevitable questions about why you are doing this. Explain that lighting a candle is like saying a prayer or making a wish. People use candles to meditate and pray with all over the world, sending their hopes and wishes and questions to the Gods and Goddesses. When you decorate a candle, you are putting more of your energy into the candle, and that can make your prayer or meditation stronger. When a family decorates candles and then puts them into a candelabra all together, all their spirits and prayers are joined in a way. Each individual's candle contributes to the strength of the whole family's spirit, and having the family candelabra lit also strengthens each individual spirit. That's what it is like to be in a family, too. Explain that now, because a new child has joined the family, it is important that the family have a candelabra big enough for all of you.

When the candles are complete, light the candles and see what a beautiful sight you have created together. Say:

> *Great Goddess, we give thanks today for our family, and each person in it. Please watch over us and protect us, and hear our prayers. And for [name of new child], who has just joined our family, help him feel welcome, help him feel our love and caring, as we are all loved and cared for by you. Goddess, we ask your help to keep our family strong. Help us listen to each other and talk from our hearts. Thank you for bringing us together, Goddess, and thank you for this good life. Blessed be.*

Your family candelabra can be used on special occasions and during family ceremonies as you see fit. Place it on the family altar or in a prominent spot in your home. Have your family decorate new candles to replace the old ones as they burn down, and may your family's health and spirit always burn strong and bright.

Talking to Children About Death

Everything that lives dies in its turn to make room for new things to come into life. And we die so that our spirits can rest and grow young again and return to life with more wisdom. The Goddess does not die. The Goddess is the whole circle of birth, growth, death, and rebirth. She never goes away from us, and when we die, we go to her.

There are no pat answers for the complex question of why people die, though young children might be satisfied with the simple, poetic explanation of death above. Others may find comfort reading the stories in the Samhain section, about death and the ancestors. See Notes for a recommended book on children and death.

When Tragedy Strikes

There are times when, for all our action, concern, and vigilance, we cannot stop tragedy from entering our lives. Hurricanes, earthquakes, fires, and floods show us the incredibly fierce and destructive side of nature. There are also many human-caused tragedies that we guard against and hope won't happen to anyone, let alone to our family. Yet even if it is beyond our control to prevent some terrible situation, we still need to attend to the effects of the incident, especially as they impact ourselves and our children.

Here are some suggestions for things to do:

⚭ Use your altar to send energy to victims of tragedy. If you are concerned about missing children, cut out their pictures from flyers, milk cartons, or grocery bags, and light a candle for them at your altar.

You can set up an altar to the lost ones—runaway, kidnapped, injured, or missing children. Along with pictures and drawings, you might add symbols of love and comfort (teddy bears, baby blankets, and so on), as well as symbols of strength and courage (scissors to break bonds, a flashlight for finding the way home, herbs for healing). This simple but powerful act creates a place where we can grieve as well as pray to alleviate their suffering or hasten their return.

⚭ Donate money or needed articles to related organizations. Coins in a coffee tin at the supermarket may mean very little to us, but it is a good example for our children of how people work together to solve problems. Pass a hat for the cause at rituals and other events, or let the children bundle up pennies from your change jar to donate.

⚭ Take steps to minimize the damage of any future tragedies. Talk to your children about basic personal safety, and make sure they know their address and phone number by heart. Consider enrolling them in a child self-defense course. Keep emergency food supplies, extra blankets, and a store of drinking water on hand.

⑥ Sometimes the only thing we can do is pray. If your children say nightly prayers, suggest they add a line asking the Goddess to send comfort to those in need.

⑥ Join in public mourning or remembrance rituals. Even if you don't attend with your children, be sure to do your own grieving.

⑥ Help your children understand the ways different cultures and traditions cope with tragedy and loss by telling them stories and myths about death. Stories from your own family history or circle of friends can be especially powerful and healing for your children to hear.[2]

A Young Boy's View of Death

Bowen's (Anne's son) view of death, which he had pondered over for some months, is that after you die, a black stretch limousine from the Faery Taxi Service comes to your door and picks you up for a ride. Inside the limo, you can watch video games and read comic books while snacking on any of the wide variety of foods in the fridge.

Once the limo makes it up to the Gates, the guy at the Gates asks for your ID. If your ID isn't approved, you have to leave. If your ID is approved, you are escorted to the waiting room while the deity of your choice pores through his or her file cabinet to find out where you get reincarnated. The waiting room has a big, squishy couch and any type of magazine you want to read.

Then the Faery Taxi Service picks you up again. If you've been especially good, you can go to the paradise of your choice, but if you've been just normal, you are taken to your next incarnation.

Deceased Pet Ritual

Losing a pet can be very traumatic, especially for children. This ritual can help them express their feelings and gain an understanding of the natural cycle of life and death and renewal.

If you live in the country, it might be possible to bury the pet on your property. If burial of the pet is prohibited, a grave can still be dug and the ritual held without the body. For those without a yard, a pot filled with earth will suffice as a memorial.

Create a coffin of wood or cardboard in which to bury the pet. Or simply wrap the pet in a favorite blanket or use a pet bed. Gather the pet's special toys or treats, or special tributes such as poems, pictures, or drawings. Cleanse and consecrate the burial or memorial site. Take turns digging the grave. Talk about special memories of good times with the pet.

Place the animal's body and/or mementos in the grave. Say, *Fellow traveler, trusted friend, may your journey be peaceful, happy, and free. As you join in the great dance of creation, we thank the Goddess for your time with us, and we will hold you forever in our hearts.* Take turns filling the grave. Sing "Fur and Feathers and Scales and Skin."

Fur and Feathers and Scales and Skin[3]

Words and music by Patricia Taylor

Fur and Feath-ers and scales and skin, diffe-rent with-out but the same with-in.

Man-y a bod-y but one the soul, by all crea-tures are the Gods made whole.

Plant a small tree or plant on the grave or in the pot. Talk with your children about how the pet's body, which it no longer needs, will nourish the tree or plant and help it grow. Explain how all of life and death is a circle, and leave a small circle of stones around the tree or plant. Leave a larger stone as a marker, perhaps with the name of the pet written on it.

When Children Ask About Dying

We (Diane and family) climbed under the hot sun, the two children a little ways ahead. They stopped to wait for us. As my husband and I reached them, one asked, "What happens when we die? I mean, I know we go to the Isle of Apples, but what do we do there?"

These questions never come at good times. My husband got very quiet. This was my department.

"We rest and grow young again," I began.

"Do we eat apples?" the other interrupted.

"Yes. Everytime we eat an apple we grow younger, but as we grow younger, we go backward through our lives. We finish everything that didn't get done. If we had a fight with someone, we resolve it. If we needed to say I'm sorry, we say it. If we forgot to tell someone that we loved them, we tell them. Then we're just a spirit. The Goddess puts us into her cauldron of rebirth, and we get mixed in with all the other spirits. And when she has a new life, she dips in and pours out a new spirit. We don't become ourselves all over again. Everyone gets a brand new spirit made up of this mix."

The children nodded. I watched their faces. They were satisfied, and it was enough for now.

PART FOUR

CIRCLE OF ELEMENTS

Earth My Body

Earth my bo - dy, Wa - ter my blood, Air my breath and Fire my spi - rit,

The Elements of Life

In the Goddess tradition, as in many other earth-based traditions, the elements that sustain life are sacred. The four elements of air, fire, water, and earth form a circle, with the fifth element, spirit, in its center. Each of the first four elements represents one of the four directions. For us, air is the east, fire is the south, water is the west, and earth is the north. In your circles, you must work with the correspondences that feel right to you.

The elements teach us about ourselves. Air, fire, water, and earth represent our minds, our energy, our emotions, and our bodies. When we face a problem or a challenge, we can ask ourselves whether we've looked at it from the point of view of each element. What do we think? What energies do we notice? What feelings do we have? How are our bodies affected? What does our inner spirit tell us? The circle of the elements helps us remember to consider the whole, not merely one part, of any question or decision.

When these four elements are present and in harmony, the fifth element, spirit, or center, is created. Spirit is what we call conscience, character, intuition, or the small voice inside. In Goddess tradition, this is the place where our acquired knowledge and our innate wisdom meet and are touched by the Goddess to form an inner spirit, a sense of direction that steers us away from harm and toward our life's purpose.

In the task of raising children in Goddess tradition, we find that just as the four elements earth, air, fire, and water connect to make the sacred circle, these elements, when translated into human attributes, make the child a whole, vibrant person.

Our goal, as people who are rooted in the world view of Goddess traditions, is to raise children who are empowered. Empowerment is that combination of self-confidence, independent thought, intuition, and engagement with the world that enables us to live by our principles and stand up for what we believe in. By creating an environment that empowers our children and ourselves, we strive to create a culture based on concern and compassion, rather than apathy and indifference.

In the following sections we discuss each of the five elements and their primary associated qualities as they relate to child rearing. We focus on realistic goals and commonsense strategies that we all can draw from, regardless of our personal preferences on a number of parenting issues.

CHAPTER EIGHTEEN

Air

EVERY MOMENT OF our lives, we must breathe in order to survive. Air carries sounds and scents, and its clarity allows light to pass through so that we can see. Air is invisible, except when other things move in response to its motion, when the wind makes branches dance and leaves fly, or bends the grasses down as it passes.

We share breath with all of life. Like other red-blooded creatures, we breathe in oxygen and expel carbon dioxide, which is used by plants and trees to transform the pure energy of the sun into food for all living things. Plants and trees give off oxygen, which we breathe in, and so a balance is sustained. We honor air as the breath of the Goddess and the gift of our most ancient fellow living creatures.

In our tradition, we associate air with the east, the direction of dawn and sunrise. Because air is invisible, we identify it with the parts of ourselves that are important but cannot be seen: our mind, our vision, our thoughts, and our dreams. Air represents knowledge and understanding, which we gain by looking closely at what is around us.

Air is connected with springtime, the dawn of the year. The animals of air are, of course, birds and all flying insects, such as dragonflies and butterflies. Air's colors are pale pinks, yellows, and whites.

Some of the Goddesses of air are Iris, the Greek Goddess of sunrise and the rainbow, and Oya, Yoruba Goddess of the whirlwind and sudden changes. Boreas is the Greek God of the wind; Hermes is the power of thought and communication. Elegba, the Yoruba trickster, translates human language into that of the *Orishas*, the great powers of the universe. All could be invoked for the gifts connected with air.

Symbols of air to place on your altar might be feathers, incense or other good-smelling things, fans, pinwheels, or kites. In our tradition the tool of air is the athame, the Witch's knife. It stands for the power of the mind to separate things, to say: "I am me and you are you and we are not the same." Clearly, a knife is an inappropriate tool for young children. Substitutes might be a pair of scissors or a pen (the pen is mightier than the sword).

Breathing with Children

Breath training is a basic tool with many uses, and children age four and up can learn and use breath effectively. Start by practicing these exercises yourself. When you've experienced the benefits and feel confident with the techniques, it's time to teach the children. Bedtime, when the children are relaxed and quiet, works best.

Begin by explaining that there's more to breathing than taking in air, that there are "special breaths." Establish a working knowledge of breath. Show them where the lungs are; talk about breathing through the nose and mouth. Have the children breathe from their chests, making their chests rise with inhalation and fall with exhalation. Explain how the diaphragm muscles lift the space between the chest and belly. Ask them to make their stomach expand when they breathe, like a balloon. Have them breathe fast, then slow, back and forth a couple of times. Point out how fast breathing comes from the chest and slow breathing comes from the stomach. Help them realize that we breathe from the chest when we're crying or scared. Then show how deep breathing from the stomach makes us feel calm and courageous.

Belly Breath

Teach deep diaphragm breathing by having your child put her hands on the stomach just below the navel, fingers barely touching. Have the child picture sucking air all the way to the bottom of her lungs, lifting the stomach and making her fingers move apart. Then ask her to blow all the breath out, bringing the fingers back together.

In a separate exercise, have the child move her belly up and out, letting the breath rush into her lungs. Then compress the diaphragm, pushing the air out. After your child is comfortable with this exercise, try it in stages. Let the air fill the belly, then the spaces behind the lower ribs, ribcage, collarbones, and clavicle. Reverse on the exhalation.

Counting Breath

Have the child breathe in while counting to three slowly, and breathe out while counting to three slowly. Then join in, so you are breathing and counting together. This exercise is especially useful for dealing with a child who can't stop crying or screaming. When the adult starts breathing and counting, the child will catch the rhythm and join the breathing pattern.

Grounding Tree Breath

Have the child find a comfortable position. Ask her to picture the earth and all the things growing from the earth. Then have her imagine herself as a tree, with roots going deep into the earth, drawing up energy from the earth with each inhalation. Describe the energy going up all the rootlets into the main roots, into the trunk (which is like legs and the body), shoot out the top of the branches (which are like hands and a head), then fall to the earth and sink back in. Explain how the earth is the source of all energy, and we may share as much of it as we need, whenever we want, always returning what we can't use back to the earth.

Nature Breathing

While outdoors, invite children to breathe with different natural objects. Get close enough to the object of choice so they breathe in the air that surrounds it.

For earth breathing, lie on the ground and visualize the earth as a living body. Try to detect the earth's breath and join with it. Picture our breath being absorbed by trees and plants, and see their exuded oxygen entering our bodies. For sun breathing, while lying in the sun, picture breathing in the very rays of the sun. Imagine warm tendrils of light spreading from the lungs down to arms and legs, into hands and feet, fingers and toes, ears and chin.

Breathing Through Emotion

When a child gets stuck in any strong emotion, such as fear, anger, or sorrow, help him establish a deep breathing pattern. Ask him to feel his emotions and to blow them out, a little at a time, with each breath. In a panic situation, watch his breathing pattern and coach him verbally at inhalation and exhalation points: "in a little longer" or "out a little longer." When his breath starts stretching out, join the breathing and start counting.

Air Play for Toddlers

Blow bubbles. Blow up balloons and let them float in the house. Fly a kite. Make a pinwheel, a wind sock, or wind chimes. Tie ribbons to trees and let children watch them flutter in the breeze.

Pinwheel

Make a pinwheel using plain paper, a pin, and a pencil with an eraser. Follow the diagram for cutting (see illustration 1), and make a pinhole on each dot. Fold the paper over until all the pinholes are lined up over the central pinhole (see illustration 2). Spear with the pin and firmly plant the pin's point into the pencil eraser.

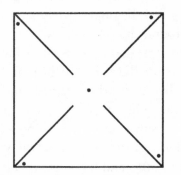   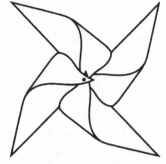

ILLUSTRATION 1   ILLUSTRATION 2

Windsock

Decorate a piece of construction paper, then tape the long sides together to form a tube. Make three equidistant holes about ½ inch from the top. Run a length of thread through each hole and tie the threads together about 9 inches from the holes. Cut the other end of the paper tube into fringes. Fasten the thread handle to a stick and wait for the wind.

Wind Chimes

Cut off the bottom of a large plastic bottle, leaving 3 inches of the side. Make a hole in the middle of the bottom and run a thick thread with a large knot at the end through the hole. Punch holes around the sides and suspend items: old silverware, keys, shells, whatever makes noise.

Dreams

Almost all children go through episodes of frightening dreams. This visualization technique may help them cope.

Ask your child to picture herself in the dream. Acknowledge how scary the dream seems and remind her that you're right with her. Encourage her to tell you what she is seeing. Don't move ahead before the whole image is formed. If the child has trouble getting the image, help out with concrete questions: "Picture your feet. Are you wearing shoes? Which ones?" Slowly move up the body. When the child has a firm mental self-image, ask what she can use to keep her safe from the things in her dream that scare her.

In Goddess tradition, there are the traditional tools of the athame, wand, cup, and pentacle. If your child has trouble thinking of a tool, provide descriptions. For example, a cup could pour out an ocean that would block whatever is chasing her, or a wand can transform enemies into friends. My (Diane's) children have their own preferred tools. For Brigit, spunky and assertive, the tool of choice is a sword. Vivian, caught up in her inner world of rainbows and unicorns, likes a wand.

After the child has named the tool, help her visualize it as vividly as possible. Ask how the tool feels in her hand and how she will carry it. With Vivian, I told her, "Look down and see your hand. Your hand starts feeling a little warm and tingly, and you can see sparkles. These are forming together into a wand in your hand. You can curl your hands around it. Can you feel it?" She answered yes. I asked her whether it was heavy or light. She said it was light. When I asked her

Dream Life

I (Anne) try to use the terms *waking life* and *dream life* when talking to my children about their dreams, instead of comparing dream life with "real life" or "reality." This helps remind us that the dreamworld is every bit as important as the world we inhabit once we get out of bed.

what color it was, she told me it was gray. Then I asked whether it was long or short, wood or metal, fancy or plain. It turned out to be long, metal, and plain.

"What can it do?" I asked.

"I can wave it and sparkles will come out and stop the trolls." From there she decided that she needed a crown, a dress, and shoes, and she drifted into a dream, well dressed and supplied with an arsenal of magical troll-fighting tools.

Your child can use you and other beloved people as a tool in dreams. Let her know that if she calls a person in her dreams, that person's dream self will come. Have your child describe what actions that person could do to help. If she doesn't have solutions, make suggestions, like shrinking or slowing down what is feared until it is no longer a threat.

Take as much time as you need, but don't turn this into a full-blown fantasy production. The goal is to revise the dream, not to create a new adventure. Encourage permanent vanquishing or containment, like turning trolls into bushes. Finish with a hug and a kiss.

Revisiting a dream is best done just after the child has woken up from the dream or early the next morning, but never before bedtime, as it might trigger fears and block the child's focus.

Judging Dreams

It is difficult to remain nonjudgmental about the images from our children's bad dreams. We may find ourselves assuming that dragons and snakes are bad, for instance, when it may simply be an action done by the beast that triggers our child's fear, not the fact of its existence.

When my (Anne's) daughter Johanna was two, she went through a phase of dreaming about scary monsters. After listening to each dream, I would exclaim that the monsters were bad and that they should go away and not bother her.

One morning as we sat together eating breakfast, Johanna started to tell me about the previous night's monster dream. "Monsters eat me! Monsters going to kill me!"

I decided to change tactics and not assume that being killed in one's dream is a bad thing. In an interested and not worried voice, I asked, "Oh? What happened then?"

There was a pause, then she answered, "Monsters brushed my hair." And after that the monsters painted her hair and gave her a haircut, both of which pleased Johanna and had her giggling.

Twice more that week she told me her dream of being killed by monsters, and both times I asked what happened next. She told me the story of their hair-design party, laughing at how silly and thoughtful those monsters were in the end.

Dream Journals

I (Anne) have started dream journals where I write down every dream I can remember my children telling me, beginning when they were very small. They may not choose to look at their dreams in depth now, but when they are older and are ready, they will have a valuable record to refer to.

For the morning rush, when there's little time to share and write down dreams, I have a microcassette recorder. I simply hand it to the children, and they recite their dreams into it while they're still in bed or sometimes in the car on the way to school. Later, I transcribe the dreams into the journals.

A Wishing Custom

My (Diane's) daughters practice this wishing custom. They catch floating seed pods and whisper wishes to the seed. Then they release the seed back into the air. If the seed finds good ground and ends up taking root and growing, their wishes will come true.

A Trip to the Museum

Visit a museum to see artistic and historical tributes to Goddesses and Gods. Antiquities collections are often filled with hundreds of hand-sized Goddesses and Gods that were formed for sacred use.

Point out that these were not considered works of art at their creation, but part of every person's daily life. Be prepared with your mythology and your storytelling skills. Don't be afraid to criticize or differ with the way a myth or deity is presented; we argue with movies or books, so why hold back with art?

Try guessing who made these statues, where they were kept in the house, and how they were used. For example, my (Diane's) children guessed that statues with pointed ends instead of feet were stuck in the ground or sand outside and kept people company as they pounded grain or wove cloth. They also decided that especially tiny God and Goddess figures belonged to children, perhaps tied up with string and worn as a necklace, or put into a tiny bag. The idea that children like themselves played with figures similar to Goddess dolls makes a deep impression.

After seeing the myriad Gods and Goddesses our ancestors sculpted, try making some of your own from clay. The library is full of books with pictures of Goddesses dating from Neolithic times and covering many different cultures. Make lots of figures and leave them out for others to find. Cradle them in the crooks of trees, tuck them onto library shelves, or leave them on park benches.

CHAPTER NINETEEN

Fire

ALL LIFE ON earth depends on the energy of the sun. Plants can use that energy directly to live and grow. Animals must eat plants or other animals. But directly or indirectly, we are all sustained by the sun.

In the Northern Hemisphere, the sun is brightest and hottest when it shines at high noon from the south. Therefore south is the direction we associate with fire.

Fire is also the element that warms our houses and cooks our food. The hearth fire is sacred in every earth-based tradition, for fire is the living heart of the home. Before television, people would gather before a fire to tell tales and sing songs during the long nights of winter. We still love to sing around a campfire or chant over a ritual fire in the center of our circles.

Fire is also dangerous. Like all things of power, fire demands respect. A curtain wafting across a candle can burn down a home. The summers are dry where we live, and a careless match or stray spark can ignite a wildfire that may burn thousands of acres and hundreds of homes. Learning to know fire means learning how to use fire safely and how to put a fire out. Fire reminds us that we are all responsible for each other's safety.

Fire is the symbol of human energy as well as the sun's energy. Health, strength, enthusiasm, and passion are qualities of fire. When we direct our energies, when we focus on a goal, we use our will, one of the powers we find in this element. Fire is connected to all the forms of magic that direct energy, especially healing and protection.

The time of day connected to fire is, of course, high noon, just as its season is high summer. The colors of fire are red, orange, and bright golden yellow. The lion, because of its bright golden color and wild, dangerous power, is often seen as a symbol of fire. So is the dragon, with its fiery breath. Legends tell us that salamanders could live in fire—but don't test the myth with any of the ones you may find!

Brigit, of course, is the Goddess of the sacred flame of poetry, healing, and the forge. Pele is the Hawaiian Goddess of the volcano. Hestia is the Greek Goddess of the hearth. Lugh is the Celtic sun God. Wayland Smith is the ancient God of the forge. Set is the ancient Egyptian God of the hot desert sun. There are many more Goddesses and Gods of fire.

On our altars, a candle flame brings the presence of fire to our rituals. The tool of fire in our tradition is the wand, which is used to direct energy, and wands are often made of wood, which burns. You can make a wand of your own by cutting (with adult help) a small branch from your favorite tree. Be sure to ask the tree's permission, and leave an offering.

Fire Play for Toddlers

Let your toddler blow out a candle as many times as she wishes. The trick is to light two candles. Keep one burning and use it to relight the other so you don't end up using all your matches.

If you have a fireplace in your home, light a fire, turn off all the lights in the house, and let this be your evening's entertainment. If you don't have a fireplace, plan to camp or picnic where you can make a fire.

Kitchen Memories

Share your most memorable childhood cooking, eating, or kitchen memories with your child while creating a meal together. Or recall a kitchen experience with your child when he was much younger.

If you are creating food for a special occasion, try telling the seasonal story that you know best to your child. Older children can be reminded that the energy we bring to food is the energy we get out of the food. If you have a kitchen Goddess or God figure, say a prayer or ask a blessing during preparation. I (Anne) have inherited lots of kitchen utensils from both my grandmothers, and feel their presence with me whenever I use them. My children like hearing stories of their great-grandmothers as we cook together (fortunately, at least one was a good cook).

Protection Blessings

Keeping children safe is a powerful primal urge. Our concern tinges every parting, just as our gratitude infuses every reunion. Fear's presence is subtle but constant: the pause at the door to hear gentle breathing, the quick inventory of new friends' homes for hazards. So start protection blessings early, do them often, and try not to worry too much.

Four Elements Blessing

This blessing asks each of the great powers to protect our children. Many parents from Goddess tradition create a newborn ceremony for their children that dedicates them to the Goddess and God and asks for safekeeping. The Four Elements Blessing may be combined with that ceremony, or performed separately.

Renew your blessing as your child reaches new developmental stages, such as walking to school or driving a car.

To prepare, spend time thinking about the elements. Gather a symbol for each and charge them as charms to offer to the elements. Hang it in a tree for air, burn it for fire, throw it into living water, and bury it in earth.

For the ritual, create sacred space. Taking extra time in the purification process, focus on each element as you work. Do the same while casting the circle, informing each element that you will be asking for help and protection.

Using visualization, dance, or whatever method works for you, mesh with the qualities of the element, naming it, feeling it, and making the offering. Then name the child or children and ask for each element's blessing and protection.

Don't catalog every peril possible from each element. That is an impossible task. If you've noted a particular vulnerability, name it and ask for a special blessing. Do the same for any of your particular fears for the child. For example, Brigit is irresponsible around water, so I (Diane) added this entreaty: "Brigit does not understand the dangers of water. Help her and protect her from dangers while I keep teaching her respect and caution for you."

The following invocations and requests are provided only as examples to help you craft your own special ritual.

Air: I come before you asking favor and protection for my daughter, a deeply wanted and loved child. Grant her your wisdom and let her mind have your quicksilver thoughts for action whenever danger is near. Share your clear eye for seeing, your way of discerning.

May all the breaths of her life be of clean, wholesome air. Let her blood flow red with your oxygen. Move her breath freely and easily until the peaceful end of a long and healthy life. When in your realm, may she fly with the grace of the migrating bird, and always return safely to earth. Bless her eyes and her lungs. Bless her thoughts, so that she may think clearly and find her mind a source of pleasure and joy.

Fire: *Sacred flames, I bring you my daughter, longed for and treasured. I ask your favor and protection. Let her know your abundant vitality and energy through strength and courage in herself. Shield her from fire's destruction; spare her from the firepower of guns, from war, from harm powered by hatred and flame combined. Let the blaze of her heart bring warmth, not burning; let the flames of transformation bring her growth, not destruction. May her passions bring her fulfillment.*

Water: *Holy water, I bring to you my daughter, long sought and dear. May she never thirst. May she always swim through earth's water with strength and safety. Let feelings flow through her without injury; let her learn the art of change from your many forms. May she navigate relationships with insight, tact, and integrity. Let her always find nourishment for her spirit in your presence. Be for her a source of comfort and peace.*

Earth: *Sacred body, I bring to you my daughter, our hopes and love come to life. Let her body be whole and strong; let no harm come to her from your creatures. Let health be her birthright; may she know little pain. In sickness, let your wise medicines heal her. May your powers of renewal be within her. May her body be a source to her of joy and pleasure and her hands make good work in the world.*

Short Protection Spells

⑥ When the children go out by themselves, visualize a bubble around them that keeps out any harm.

⑥ Before trips, visualize a circle around the car or airplane, and see your family arriving safely at your destination. On your first night away from home, thank the Goddess for your safe arrival, and upon getting back home, give thanks for your safe return.

⑥ If I (Diane) ever get an intuitive feeling that my children need a little more protection, I try to figure out the reason: Don't I trust the driver? Have I forgotten to tell my child something? After taking care of

Going-Away Blessing

Don't forget to bless yourself. Our children and other loved ones need us whole and strong. I (Diane) say this little spell to my car when I go out for an evening.

Carry me well,

Carry me true,

Carry me away

and back to you.

identifiable doubts, I may pack a little charm into their backpacks.

֍ When traveling away from your children, bring something of theirs with you: a lock of hair or pictures. Send protective blessings to your children through these items.

֍ When accidents and injuries do happen, try to remember that perhaps, without the Goddess's protection, worse things might have happened. There was the time when Vivian (Diane's daughter) fell out of a tree because she thought an ax stuck in the upper trunk was a branch she could grab. She took a nasty fall, but the ax didn't fall on top of her!

Healing Rituals for Illness

The attention sick children get is a ritual in itself. Treats like ice cream or ginger sodas for sore throats or sick tummies, being read to in bed, and watching television in the afternoon make children feel they are in a special space. Adding a real healing ritual that combines touch and visualization promotes recovery, helps soothe children, and teaches kids techniques to use for themselves and others.

Begin by either holding the child in your lap or putting your hands on where the child is suffering pain or discomfort. Describe what you're doing with simple words: "I'm using my thoughts to make pictures of my roots going deep into the earth to the warm healing center, the same heat that turns our compost pile into fertile soil. Now I'm letting the energy flow up my roots, just like plants suck up moisture from the ground. I feel the energy flowing into my hands, and through my hands into your body. I feel the healing energy. It's like the refreshing rains, the winds that blow away smog, the heat-making power of fire, the growing life of earth. It flows through me into you."

Match your visualization to each ailment. For an achy flu, you might say: "I see this energy making where I'm touching feel less sore. It's melting the pain and soothing your stomach." For fever: "I feel my hands taking in the heat and sending down the germs to the earth, where the germs will be cleansed and transformed." For a cold, try envisioning warmth breaking up the congestion and drying up the sniffles. You can send energy on a search mission to find all the germs and infuse them with a healing glow. Guide your child to focus on each part of her body in order to locate and dissolve germs. Help your child see herself as feeling good again, free of illness and doing whatever she loves most.

Invoke Brigit, the Goddess whose many aspects include healer, to watch over a sick child while you're not there. Charging medicine also helps. Hold the bottle or the pills and describe what you're doing: "I'm pulling up the healing powers of the earth, the power that makes seeds sprout, that makes kittens chase balls, that makes bread rise, and letting it flow into this medicine, so that every time you take this, you get a dose of Goddess-healing, and my love, too."

Tree of Life Meditation for Healing

When my (Anne's) eight-year-old daughter had a bad bicycle accident, her wounds required dozens of stitches in and around her mouth. In addition, two permanent teeth were knocked out. After getting home from the hospital, we asked all of our friends to send her healing energy. And I worked with Lyra on receiving the energy being sent to her.

We began with a Tree of Life grounding exercise (see A Basic Structure for Ritual). I told her to imagine being her favorite tree. She sent her roots down into the soil and felt them take hold firmly. We extended our grounding to imagine the roots of her teeth regenerating with vitality in their sockets.

Then we moved up to the branches of her tree. I told her to feel how all of the prayers and good wishes being sent to her were like a warm, gentle wind that helps the tree grow.

She responded that there was a nest of birds living in the tree, and that whenever a good wish came floating by on the breeze, one of the birds would fly up, grab it, and bring it down into the tree branches.

We spent a bit more time with the whole feeling of being a tree, sustained by the energy of the earth and sky, effortlessly receiving the healing energy sent by others. I reminded her that though this was an easy exercise, it was very powerful, and the more she practiced it, the better. We came up with all sorts of times when she might use her meditation: lying in her bed before or after sleep, riding on the bus to and from school, whenever she was bored or worried about how her healing was going. I made it a point to ask her every so often how her practice was going. Judging from how fast and fully her wounds healed, I think her self-healing work has been incredibly successful.

CHAPTER TWENTY

Water

LIFE BEGAN IN water, in the currents of the primeval ocean, and living things need water to survive. Our bodies are mostly water, and our blood is similar to seawater in its chemistry. Water carries nutrients to all the cells of our bodies and cleanses our wastes. Clean, sweet water is sacred to all people who honor life.

Water moves in a great cycle around the globe. Rain falls on the earth, bringing life to plants, soaking into the soil or collecting in streams and rivers that flow to the sea. The great tides and currents of the ocean sustain sea life from the tiny plankton to the great whales, influencing the weather, wearing away the shore. Water evaporates from the surface of the waves, forming clouds that bring the rain, and so the cycle begins again.

The summers are very dry where we live, so the first rains of winter are especially sacred. Suddenly new life appears. Seeds sprout, and grasses begin to grow. Our winters are often very wet, and rain comes down for days and days. Dry streams spring to life and rivers widen their flow. In flood years, we see the immense power of water to break through obstacles and carry away anything that blocks its flow. In drought years, water becomes extremely precious to us, and we learn to guard every drop carefully.

Water also represents our feelings and emotions. After all, our feelings flow and change like water. We can bathe each other in love and appreciation, but we can also rage and storm like the ocean waves crashing against the shore. When we honor all our feelings, the ones we think of as positive and those we think of as nega-tive, we can choose how to act so that our emotions feed life. When we know our anger, we can choose to act peacefully. When we admit our fear, we can choose to act with courage.

For us, water is in the west, the direction of the ocean and the rain. Its time of day is the gray twilight, and its season is autumn, when the rains return. The colors of water are blue, blue-green, and gray. All water animals—all fish and sea creatures, including dolphins, whales, and the wise salmon—are symbols of water.

Tiamat, the ancient Babylonian sea serpent Goddess, was mother of all the Gods. Aphrodite, Greek Goddess of love, is also Goddess of the sea. Brigit carries the power of the holy well along with the sacred flame. Oshun is the Yoruba Goddess of the river and of love, art, and culture. Yemaya is the Mother Goddess of the ocean. Ba'al is the Canaanite God of storms and the returning rains of winter. Tlaloc is the Toltec God of rain. Mananan mac Lir is the Welsh God of the sea, while Poseidon is the Greek ocean God, whose horses are the wild waves.

On the altar, the symbol of water and the traditional tool is the cup or chalice. Seashells, water-smoothed stones, and images of water creatures can also be used.

Water Play for Toddlers

Take a walk after a rain and splash in puddles. Find a running gutter or tiny stream and float leaves or twigs out to sea. (We like to put in goldfish crackers to "swim out to sea.") Water all your plants. Suck on an icicle.

Sacred Bathtime

Try keeping a plant near the bathtub or shower. When warming up the water at the beginning of your child's bath, save a little in a cup and let your child feed the plant. Say: *Water to clean, and water to feed; water runs through our bodies and back to the earth. May you never thirst.* Or keep a plastic spray bottle nearby and let your child mist the leaves as part of the bathing ritual.

If you use scented oils or salts in the bath, look for ones with seasonal or family significance. My (Anne's) great-grandmother was Pennsylvania Dutch, and her rose garden was her pride and joy. When I add rose oil to my daughters' bath, I remind them of this heritage and of how generations in their family have cultivated rose blossoms.

Sacred Water

All water is sacred, and there is nothing wrong with using tap water or bottled water for offerings. But if you want to get fancy and learn more about the water that keeps you alive, collecting your own Waters of the World is a good way to start.

As with most magic, the more you know about what you are doing, the better you will be at it. So as you pour your own tap water into a jar, recite to yourself what you know of where that water comes from. What river or lake, spring or reservoir did it come from? Was it piped to your house over large distances, or is it from a well outside your back door? If this water had not been piped into your house, which direction would it go, and where would it eventually flow into the ocean?

Get in the habit of bringing a small jar of your water with you when you go different places. Do you have a friend you visit in another city? Collect some of the water there, and try to find out where it comes from. Does your family visit the ocean, or drive across a bridge over a river? There are all sorts of ways to collect water. Remember, it takes only a drop or two of water from each source to add the essence of that waterway to your Waters of the World. And as you collect a bit of water, give thanks to the water for its strength and life-giving powers. Then give something in return—a piece of food for the spirits of the water, or maybe a drink from the water you have brought with you. It is important, if you intend to use your Waters of the World for offerings and other magical purposes, that you collect it respectfully from its source.

Rain Hat

You will need:

9- or 10-inch paper plate

narrow ribbons of rainbow colors

glue

cotton balls

glitter, paint, markers

Draw a circle inside the paper plate, leaving a 2-inch rim around the outside of the plate. Divide the inner circle pie-style into eight equal parts. Working from the center out, cut along these pie lines, being sure you don't cut into the outer edge. Bend the resulting triangles up to form sun rays. Color or paint these rays bright yellow and add glitter. Paint the rim sky blue or rain gray.

Punch holes around the rim, about $1/2$ inch in from the edge, and hang ribbons for rain. Glue on fluffed cotton balls for clouds. For extra decoration, cut out a rainbow shape from heavy white paper and color.

Weather: Changing Attitudes, Feeling Gratitude

One day after a drought here in California was finally ended by the arrival of blessed rains, my (Diane's) children, much to my dismay, came home chanting, "Rain, rain, go away, come again another day." Carefully I took them through the loop of life, how rain meant food, healthy trees making

Rain Song[1]

Words and music by Diane Baker

Wel- come back to the rain, rain, rain, We're glad the wa- ter's com- ing down a - gain, The seeds are born in the storm, Wel- come back to the rain.

healthy air, water for birds and frogs. We slipped on our rain boots and went for a splash walk, getting soaked in spite of our umbrellas and raincoats.

I improvised a song:

It's raining, raining, raining, raining, raining, raining down on me. On the grass, and on the bushes, on the plants and on the trees. It rains on streets and rains on houses, on umbrellas and on me, bringing life, and bringing drinks, and bringing baths for all who need.

We played with the second and third lines, the girls adding whatever they could think of that was being rained on. While other pedestrians huddled under canopies and made mad dashes across the street, we took our time, singing and celebrating, and agreeing that we're happy to be a family that likes rain. On our return we took a hot bath, reveling in the pleasures of being able to use more water, then drank hot chocolate, thinking about the sweet, fresh grass the cows would have.

Keep looking for ways to celebrate rain. Select beautiful umbrellas. Create a special "rain cupboard" or rain box, complete with books about rain, and indoor games and art supplies, to be used only on rainy days.

Rain Ritual

Rain, rain, stay around!
Don't go to another town!

My kids and I (Anne) yelled our new chant as we dashed through the first downpour of the season. Earlier in the day, I had taken our nearly-two-year-old on errands, purposely leaving the umbrellas at home so she could know the joys of having rain pour down her face. By the end of the day, when her sister and brother got home from school, she was holding her head and screeching with delight along with them.

Running, dancing, leaping, and yelling for joy in the first rain seems the proper response here in sun-parched California. As soon as the rains start, I set a large bowl outside to collect rainwater for a ritual.

To perform your own rain ritual, gather for your altar things that need the rain, such as mosses, plants, a bowl of earth, and a handful of seeds. Also add things that look lovely in the rain, like pebbles, leaves, and spiderwebs. When the bowl of rainwater is filled, bring it in and place it in the center of the altar.

To begin the ritual, cast a circle. Raise the bowl of rainwater and say:

Holy rainwater, you who came from the sea and the sky to feed life on earth, we bless you and thank you for coming to us again. May you reach to the very least of us. May all life on the earth be renewed and refreshed by you. As you water the branches, may you water the roots. As you water the blossoms, may you water the seeds. May all that has been thirsting be replenished by you, beloved rain. Fall on our children, the leaves and branches of our tree; may they never thirst. Fall on us, the trunk of our tree; penetrate through the bark of the days; may we never thirst. Fall on the ground; reach to our ancestors, the roots of our tree, those who hold us all and support us even though we do not see them; may they live on. May all life thrive in the blessed rain!

Pour a bit of water onto every plant in the room, and place the bowl in the middle of the circle. One by one, the children and adults can take something from the altar and put it in the bowl of water for a blessing, or dip their fingers in it, or sprinkle it onto something they want to give energy to. Pass around cups of tea and a plate of cookies and close the circle.

CHAPTER TWENTY-ONE

Earth

THE EARTH—ROCKS, minerals, and the living soil beneath our feet—is the mother of all life. Plants draw energy from the sun, but they are nourished by the earth. Seeds are planted beneath the ground to begin their lives. The dead bodies of animals and plants are taken back to the soil to feed new life.

We think of the earth as a solid thing, but soil is amazingly complex. A square foot of good garden soil is like an underground city full of spaces, caverns, crystalline arches, and mineral bridges, all teeming with life. Soil contains air, so that the life within can breathe, and carries water to sustain billions of soil creatures and feed the roots of plants. When we truly understand the marvelous world below us, we can protect the soil from erosion by wind and water, and learn to help build new, rich soil where plants can grow. Gardening, tending trees and plants, and caring for animals are all ways to honor and protect the sacred earth.

The earth is the element that stands for our bodies. Our physical bodies are sacred, and we must take care of ourselves as we take care of the earth. All the food we eat, all the things we make and do and use, are part of this element.

Because good soil is often dark, the color of earth is black and its time is midnight. The green of living plants and growing things is also a good earth color. Its direction is north, the one quarter of the sky where in the Northern Hemisphere the sun never travels, and its season is winter, the time of darkness when seeds sleep beneath the ground. Plants, trees, and all land animals, especially big ones such as bulls and bears, are symbols of earth.

Gaia (GUY-yuh) is the ancient Greek Goddess whose name means "earth." Demeter was the Goddess of grain and agriculture. Eriu was the Irish Goddess who gave her name to the land itself. In many Native American stories, Corn Mother is the sacred being whose body feeds the people. Cernunnos is the Celtic Horned God, the God of animals. The Green Man in all his aspects is the God of plants and trees. Ogun is the Yoruba Lord of the Forest. Robin Hood is an old English forest God. There are many, many more Goddesses and Gods of earth, of particular plants and animals, and of sacred places.

Symbols of earth for the altar can be stones, crystals, rocks, or living plants. Leaves, grain, fruits, flowers, and vegetables can also be used. The traditional tool of earth is the pentacle, a five-pointed star in a circle, often inscribed on a plate or made of metal. Its five points stand for the four elements, plus the fifth, spirit. They also stand for the five senses, for our five fingers and toes, and for the human body with legs apart and arms uplifted to invoke the Goddess. The circle around it stands for the wheel of life. For us, the pentacle is a symbol of wholeness and balance, and of the ancient mysteries of our tradition.

Earth Play for Toddlers

Taking a leisurely walk with no destination is one of the nicest ways to share time with a toddler. Instead of cramming everyone's pockets with objects picked up during walks, make a bracelet of masking tape, sticky side out, and stick on found items. For the more ambitious, cover a piece of cardboard with two-sided sticky tape. Fasten larger found items and display as a collage.

Take a mud walk, squishing mud between your toes.

If your area has clay soil, dig some up to make little figures. Dry them in the sun and hide them around the neighborhood, behind rocks and in trees.

Create little rock piles in the areas you visit frequently.

Gardens for the Yearly Cycle

One of the greatest gifts we can give our children is a love of gardening, of working in the sacred earth, making flowers bloom and vegetables ripen in abundance. Having said that, the question arises: Just how do we bestow this wondrous gift on the reluctant youngster who hates vegetables and thinks dirt is yucky, bugs are creepy, and physical labor is something to be avoided at all costs?

It has been our experience that children don't take naturally to gardening. They enjoy digging, to a certain extent, and most seem to like cutting things down, hacking things up with sharp-edged tools, and picking flowers, but sustained, systematic work is often beyond them. Fortunately, there are ways to encourage them to garden.

Give them their own piece of the garden, even if it's only a pot on a fire escape. Encourage them to plant something easy and rewarding, and to enjoy the fruits of their labors, to give gifts from the garden, and to contribute the leaves, flowers, vegetables, and fruit they've grown to rituals and celebrations.

Here are a few examples of some easy, magical things to grow:

Sacred Garden Time

When entering a garden, have your children take a moment to breathe deeply, send their roots down into the ground, and feel deeply connected to the earth.

Say a prayer like:

Spirits of the plants, green ones, brothers, sisters, cousins, I greet you today on this bright patch of soil. I ask your permission to pick what I need to feed my family in body and soul; may you guide my hands to pick enough and not too much. May our mother the earth be well and healthy, and may all the children of the earth thrive and be happy. May we meet and part in peace.

⚘ Herbs make great seasonings, are pest-resistant because of their volatile oils, and can be used in various craft projects. In a mild climate like ours, rosemary grows into hedges and lavender becomes enormous; help the children harvest and dry these herbs for dream pillows (see Summer Solstice crafts). Mint grows almost everywhere, in fact, it can take over a garden, so confining it to a pot might be a good idea. Children can pick it for tea, offer it to a friend with a tummyache, or weave it into a wreath for a festival. Mugwort has silvery leaves and also spreads easily. Scented geraniums are fun to sniff and also lovely in wreaths. Pineapple sage has beautiful red flowers that hummingbirds love. Sage comes in several colors and variations that can make lovely, low-care patterns. Borage reseeds itself in a sunny spot, and the cheerful blue flowers are fun to pick for salads.

⚘ Find out the native plants in your region, and plant some in your yard. Natives are by definition perfectly adapted to your area, and they can provide valuable food and habitat for birds, insects, and small animals. Plants that attract butterflies and hummingbirds will make the garden a fascinating place for children to see something of the natural world.

⚘ Simple, reblooming flowers such as daisies and cosmos give children something to pick for bouquets all summer long. Avoid fussy plants like (alas!) roses, which need pruning and feeding to do best—or plant a tough variety like Cecile Brunner, the sweetheart rose.

⚘ Bulbs are almost care free. Find out what grows without fuss in your climate. In our area, tulips need to be refrigerated before planting, but daffodils will naturalize, and lilies come back year after year. Bulbs also lend themselves to designs; you could plant a pentacle of narcissus or spell out your child's initials in crocuses.

⚘ Flowering shrubs and berry bushes are easy once established. I (Starhawk) still remember picking raspberries from my grandmother's garden, and the wonderful scent of her lilacs. Hydrangeas grow to be huge, tolerate shade, and produce flowers all summer long. Currants have lovely flowers and delicious fruit. Again, pick varieties that like your growing conditions, and stand back.

When choosing what to plant, have your child give some thought to producing food, flowers, herbs, and fruit for rituals throughout the year.

Samhain: Pumpkins, of course. The vines need space to wander, but can be grown up a trellis or tied up onto a fence. Marigolds are a traditional flower for El Dia de los Muertos, and we use them on our Samhain altars. Also, grow any special flowers or vegetables that your own beloved dead enjoyed. Rosemary is called the herb of birth and death, and a cup of mugwort tea will make for special dreams on Samhain night.

Yule: Seeds from poppies grown in the summer can be saved and sprinkled on cookies. Jam made from summer fruit can be eaten on Yule bread. Paperwhite narcissus, started in a dish just after Samhain, should bloom at Yule as a symbol of rebirth.

Brigit: A handful of wheat or barley from a health-food store can grow a small stand of grain, enough for making a Brigit doll. Bulbs forced to bloom early can symbolize the return of spring.

Eostar: Early-blooming bulbs symbolize spring. Barley and poppies can be saved and dried to honor Demeter. Or plant a garden for Persephone of roses, lilies, narcissus, hyacinths, and crocuses.

Beltane: In our mild climate, roses are beginning to bloom. Plant lots of flowers for wreaths; sow grain to dry to decorate the Goddess figure on the maypole. If you live in a cold climate, make your wreaths out of fresh-smelling herbs and flowers from spring bulbs.

Eating

Respect for food is a product of respecting our earth and the people who work the earth to support our species. Banish the phrase "I hate . . ." from the table. Instead, a child may say that she doesn't like or doesn't want to eat a food. Give her a reminder: "The earth spent her energy making this food for people to eat, and many people spent their time and work so that this food could be on our table, so if you don't like it, say so, but this isn't deserving of hatred. Save hate for what hurts you."

Summer Solstice: It's true roses take work, but what would summer be without them? Asiatic lilies bloom in June, and plant lots of fun flowers to pick for bouquets and wreaths.

Lughnasad: Sunflowers are easy and fun for children to grow, and would be perfect for the Lammas altar. If you plant even a small patch of grain, cut some for this holiday.

Mabon: Plant vegetables to make the harvest rainbow, and gourds to decorate the altar (see Mabon Activities).

Your children might also want to explore some special gardens of their own. Besides Moon Gardens (see Moon Cycle), consider also:

Faery Garden: Attract faeries with plants and flowers associated with them—thyme, foxgloves, primroses, snapdragons, the Faery rose (an easy-care shrub with sprays of small roses), and many others.

Healing Garden: Mint, comfrey, sage, mugwort, borage, feverfew, lemon balm, and fennel are all easy, safe, and fun to grow.

Garden of Good Smells and Fun Things: Honeysuckle to pull apart and taste, rose geraniums, lamb's ears to stroke, buddleia to attract butterflies, lady's mantle to collect dewdrops, morning glories that open and close, scarlet runner beans for red flowers and spotted magic beans, sweet peas for bouquets.

Food Garden: Many catalogs offer special seed collections of easy-to-grow varieties for children. Radishes are great for quick results. Cherry tomatoes are fun to eat right off the bush, and they ripen more quickly than the big ones.

Whatever you do, don't let the garden become a burden, a constant reproach, or a power struggle. Make sure both you and your children enjoy the garden, and you will be giving them skills and understandings that can last for life.

Growing: A Story
by Diane Baker

Terry woke up. She felt snug in the warm dark. A worm wiggled by. "Hello," said the worm.

"Hello," said Terry. "What are you?"

"I'm a worm," the worm said.

"What's a worm?" Terry asked.

"I dig under the ground to keep the earth soft so seeds can grow."

"What's a seed?" Terry asked.

"Why, you're a seed! Don't you know?"

"No, I don't know."

"Seeds lie in the ground and then they grow up to be plants."

"What is grow?" asked Terry.

"Growing is getting longer and deeper," said the worm.

"How do I do that?" asked Terry.

"Try stretching," suggested the worm, and wiggled away.

Terry stretched first one way and then another until *pop!* Out of her bottom came a little white fuzzy root. All that stretching made Terry feel hungry. Just then, Terry's root started taking in water and other good things. Terry felt bigger and bigger until *pop!* A little stem came out her top and pushed through the soft dirt above her. Terry felt air all around and something else, bright and hot.

A ladybug landed right next to Terry.

"Hello," said the ladybug.

"Hello," said Terry. "What is that warm, bright feeling?"

"That's the sun," said the ladybug.

"It feels nice. What are you?"

"I'm a ladybug. I fly around and eat little bugs," she answered.

"I'm a seed," Terry told her.

"You're not a seed anymore," she told Terry. "You're a tiny new plant, still curled up."

"What's a plant?" asked Terry.

"A plant can be a lot of things," said the ladybug.

"What kind of plant am I?" Terry asked.

"Maybe you're a blade of grass. You'll stand straight and grow next to a lot of other blades. You make the ground soft for animals to walk on."

"That sounds nice. Maybe I'm a blade of grass," Terry said as the ladybug flew away. Terry thought about being a blade of grass and tried to stand up tall. Sure enough, Terry's little curly top uncurled. Terry stood up straight.

Along came a buzzing bee.

"Hello," said Terry. "What are you?"

"I'm a bee. I fly around and make honey," the bee told Terry.

"I think I'm a blade of grass," said Terry to the bee.

"You don't know?" the bee asked.

"No, not really," Terry said.

"Maybe you're not a blade of grass. Maybe you're a flower," the bee suggested.

"What's a flower?" asked Terry.

"A flower is a plant with beautiful colored petals. Bees drink its nectar and make honey."

"That sounds nice. Maybe I'm a flower," Terry said as the bee buzzed away.

Terry thought about flowers. "I'd better grow up so I can get my petals." Terry stretched and stretched again. *Pop!* Out came two leaves from the top of her stem. "How fine this growing is," Terry thought as she spread her new leaves in the warm, bright sun.

Slipping slowly along, a snail came up to Terry.

"Hello," said Terry. "What are you?"

"I'm a snail. I slide slowly along the ground and live in my round shell. What are you?"

"I think I'm a flower."

"You think you're a flower, but you don't know for sure?"

"No, I don't."

"Maybe you're a bush, then," the snail said slowly.

"What's a bush?" Terry asked.

"A bush grows up tall and big around. It has lots of branches and leaves to hide snails and other animals, like rabbits and mice."

"That sounds nice. Maybe I'm a bush."

"Maybe you are," the snail called back as it slid away from Terry.

"If I'm a bush, I need lots of leaves and branches," Terry thought, and decided to try growing again. Terry stretched and stretched. Her stem grew longer. Her roots grew deeper, then *pop!* Out came two more leaves on beautiful branches. Terry let her new leaves and branches move back and forth gently in the wind. "I'm getting quite big," Terry thought proudly. "Soon I'll be a bush."

Just then, a little bird flew down and sat next to Terry.

"Hello, I'm a bird. I fly and sing. What are you?"

"I think I'm a bush."

"Too bad you're not a tree," said the bird.

"What's a tree?" Terry asked.

"A tree grows a very long time and gets really tall, taller than anything else. It has deep roots that go way down, and a trunk that goes straight up. Trees make shade and air for everybody. Sometimes they make fruit and nuts for us to eat. Birds and squirrels live in them."

"That sounds wonderful. Maybe I am a tree," Terry told the bird.

"If you are, I'll come back to build my nest," the bird said, flying away.

Terry thought it would be wonderful to be taller than anything else, so she stretched and stretched, and could feel herself growing higher and higher. She stretched again and felt her roots growing deeper and deeper. As she grew, she saw a girl kneeling next to her.

"What are you?" Terry asked.

"Hello. I'm a big girl. I run and jump and play, and my mommy helped me plant you in my garden."

Terry looked at her. Running and jumping and playing sounded like a lot of fun. She wished that she were a girl, too.

"Is a girl a plant?" Terry asked hopefully.

She laughed. "No, a girl is a person. You're a plant, you're a tomato plant."

"What's a tomato plant?"

"You'll grow up and make nice, juicy red fruits that I'll pick and eat."

Terry was worried. "Will that hurt me?"

"No, not at all. You'll just make more tomatoes," the girl told Terry.

"What will happen to my fruit?"

"That will become part of me," she explained.

"Does that mean I'll be a girl like you?"

"Well," said the girl, thinking hard, "it means that part of you will be me, at least a little bit of me."

"Does that mean that I'll get to run and jump and play?"

"Oh, yes, and lots of other things, too. You'll get to read stories, and go on swings, and ride my bicycle, and see everything from the car."

"What's a car?" asked Terry.

"You'll learn all of that later," said the girl. "Now it's time for me to water you."

She poured fresh, cool water over Terry. It felt wonderful. Terry could feel her roots growing wider and deeper as they drank up the good water.

The days and weeks passed. Terry grew bigger, with strong branches and lots of leaves that opened toward the sun. She grew flowers and the flowers changed into tomatoes, which were green at first and then red. The girl came to visit her every day.

Finally the day came when the girl's mother said, "This tomato's ripe. You can eat it now."

Terry gave her one of her tomato fruits. It didn't hurt at all. Before she ate the tomato, the girl cut it open and scooped out the seeds, which she put on a plate to dry. As the girl ate, Terry felt a part of herself moving through the girl's body, and when the girl ran to play, a part of Terry did, too. How wonderful it was to run with legs, to have hair to toss, and to have eyes to see everything!

The next day, the girl carefully put Terry's seeds away where they slept, warm and safe in the dark, waiting to wake up next spring. ⚮

Honoring Trees

No thealogy, no ritual can do as much to teach children to love nature as a friendship with a real tree. A fruit tree in your backyard, a favorite climbing tree, a host to a bird's nest, or a newly planted sapling can become a source of joy and connection for your child. I (Starhawk) still remember the tree my friend Barry and I most loved to climb when I was nine years old. I still mourn the magnificent sycamore I could see from our kitchen window that our neighbors cut down years ago.

To have a real relationship with a tree means to care for it—to make sure it has sufficient water in its early years, to prune away dead branches, to learn what companions growing at its feet will make it happy and healthy. Horticultural instruction is beyond the scope of this book, but I encourage you to ask for help and advice. Trees are forgiving of mistakes, and I have come to believe that simply by giving them concentrated attention and observation, you will help them thrive. In fact, they will most likely survive whether you prune them or not, feed them or not, carefully thin and pick their fruit or let it fall to the ground to rot.

Deforestation is occurring all over the world at an alarming rate, contributing to erosion, the loss of species, and global climate change. As an act of faith and magic to help the healing of the earth, plant trees!

Plant Trees Together

Make tree planting a family ritual to mark special occasions: the birth of a child, a graduation, a special accomplishment. Even a small backyard can accommodate several dwarf or espaliered fruit trees. If you have no space at all, perhaps you know someone who owns land that could benefit from another tree. Or donate a tree to a city park or a hospice.

Ritual for Planting a Tree

When you plant the tree, you may wish to ground and create sacred space, or you may simply gather round the tree and say the following blessing:

Tree, we plant you here to mark our joy at [name the special occasion]. As you grow strong and flourish, may you remind us of this moment. As we tend and care for you, may we remember that love must also be nurtured. As we enjoy your shade [blossoms, fruit] in future years, may we continue to enjoy happiness. Blessed be.

Pass a chalice of spring water or fruit juice clockwise around the circle. Each person pours out a few drops as a libation to the tree and has an opportunity to speak of her own feelings about the occasion. When all are done, pass the chalice around again and give each person a sip. Open the circle if you have cast one. If not, you might end with the "Tree Wassail" song in this chapter.

A Birth Tree

When a child is born, a family may save the placenta and plant it beneath a tree. Follow the ritual instructions for planting a tree, using the following blessing:

Tree, we plant you here to honor the birth of our child, [name]. May you be fed by the placenta that fed her. May you grow strong, tall, and beautiful as she grows. May you teach her to love and care for all things in nature. As she tends you, may she learn that love must also be nurtured. As she enjoys your shade [blossoms, fruit], may she enjoy many sorts of happiness. Blessed be.

As libations are poured, each person should speak a wish for the child.

What happens if your special tree dies? Don't panic. This is not an omen of disaster; it may simply be bad luck or bad weather. It may have "taken a blow" for your child, averting misfortune. Give it a funeral, use its wood in some way (if only to kindle a special fire), and plant another.

A Memorial Tree

Trees can also be planted to mark a death or a loss. Again, follow the ritual instructions for planting a tree. If the person has been cremated, the ashes can be scattered under the roots. Or the tree can simply be a memorial. Use this blessing:

> *Tree, we plant you here to mark the passing of our beloved* [name]. *As you grow strong and tall, may your branches become a welcoming home for his spirit. As we tend you, may we nurture our sweet memories of him. As we enjoy your shade* [blossoms, fruit], *may the pain of our grief be eased. As your seeds drop to earth and are buried to grow again, so may* [name] *in time come to be reborn. Blessed be.*

As the libations are poured, each person should share a memory of the deceased.

A Wassail Ritual

An ancient custom in the British Isles was the Wassail. At Samhain or Yule, families would take a pail of hard cider out to the orchard, dip the branches of the oldest or best-bearing apple tree in the cider to give it a drink, sing traditional Wassail songs, and then pour what was left on the ground as an offering.

If you are lucky enough to have some fruit trees of your own, adapt this custom using nonalcoholic cider or juice in a bowl or chalice. Let your children help dip the branches, pour out the juice at the base of the tree, and then refill the bowl and drink as you sing the Wassail song. If you don't have apple trees, adapt the words to fit your trees.

Tree Wassail[1]

Words by Starhawk, music by Anne Hill

1. We praise the trees, strong may you grow,———— we
2. May win-ter's cold to you be kind, May you
3. We thank you for your blos-soms sweet,———— We

praise your roots that down-ward go, we praise your bran-ches————
blos-som in the spring sun-shine, May gen-tle rain in its
thank you for the fruit we eat, Re-ceive our thanks for————

reach-ing high,———— bear-ing leaves that touch the sky, *Chorus:*
sea-son fall, May you be loved by one and all. In the
all you give,———— Grow in joy, long may you live!

spring, with blos-soms crowned,———— In fall, ap-ples ripe and

round, Bless the flower and bless the seed,———— And

bless the fruit of eve-ry tree.————

Tree Friends

A family in my (Diane's) neighborhood includes the trees on their lot as part of their circle of friends. They've named them, selected birthdays for them, and had parties for them during which they hang home-strung beads on the branches. They give presents to these trees on gift-giving holidays, including worms they release among the roots, and bows they tie onto the branches.

Tree Alphabet

In Celtic traditions, a specific tree corresponds with a specific letter of the alphabet (see Celtic Tree Alphabet). Sometimes secret messages are conveyed by a handful of leaves from different trees. When the leaves are read as letters, the words of the message can be understood. Many of those trees grow in a wide variety of climates. Can you find any of these trees near where you live?

Collect a leaf from as many of the trees in the Tree Alphabet as you can find nearby. You can even try creating a tree alphabet unique to your area by substituting native trees and shrubs for the trees that don't grow where you live. Then with a friend, try passing messages back and forth with leaves. It is not necessary to spell out each word of the message. Select certain phrases or words that you use a lot, and assign a tree or shrub to each. That way you will be able to say quite a lot with a handful of leaves!

Learning from Trees

One of the best ways for adults and children to tune into the place where they live is by observing the yearly changes in the local trees. You can start by noticing what kind of trees live near you. Are they evergreens, or do they drop their leaves in the fall? Are they all the same kind of tree, or are many species represented?

Collect a leaf or two from each different tree you can find, and paste them on a special Tree Chart or in a Tree Book. Using books from the library, or a neighbor knowledgeable about local trees, identify each tree you have found.

Then, as the seasons pass, write down your observations about the changes each tree goes through. In which month does it leaf out? When does it flower, bear fruit, or drop its seeds? Is it native to the region, or was it imported from somewhere else?

Celtic Tree Alphabet

Letter	Tree	Celtic Name
A	Fir	Ailm
B	Birch	Beith
C	Haze	Coll
D	Oak	Duir
E	Aspen	Edhadh
F	Alder	Fearn
G	Ivy	Gort
H	Hawthorn	Huath
I	Yew	Ido
L	Rowan	Luis
M	Vine	Muin
N	Ash	Nion
nG	Broom	nGetal
O	Furze	Onn
Q	Apple	Queirt
R	Elder	Ruis
S	Willow	Sail
St	Blackthorn	Sraibh
T	Holly	Tinne
U	Heather	Ur

If the trees are in a natural setting, such as a park, broaden your study to the plants that grow around each tree. Does the tree support a variety of plant life, or do conditions around the tree make it difficult for plants to grow there?

Walk Ideas

Plan theme walks or walks with a special purpose. Try a rain walk or a water walk, following the course of a stream. For "magnifying" walks, arm each person with a magnifying glass. On a "dried things" walk, gather dried flowers, grasses, and seed pods to take home for making wreaths.

Studying Nature Is Learning Divinity

One of my (Diane's) primary goals as a parent is to help my children revere earth, and discover the powerful correlation between loving nature and loving the Goddess. My personal motto, "Studying nature is learning divinity," is at the heart of my family's weekly nature hikes.

Turning my children into hikers was not easy. We started with short walks in parks close to home. Even then, the children hated everything about the excursions and complained. Eventually I hit on the device of telling them a story while we were walking, stopping every time we rested. Judiciously administered treats also helped. Our walks started going faster and longer. Whining decreased. In better moods, the kids started making discoveries along the trails. After three months, they stopped demanding a story.

For the "study" part of my personal creed, we sometimes take field guides, binoculars, magnifying glasses, and sketch books. We're learning to identify birds, trees, rocks, flowers, and insects. We speculate about how the places we visit fit together, and we draw. We also try to revisit the same places each season and mark the changes.

Nature Notebook

Nature teaches a wonderful lesson about the mystery of life: that everything changes and everything stays the same. Tracking our local environment by keeping a nature notebook brings children nose to nose with this wondrous cycle.

Supply a child with a nice notebook with blank pages so they're not limited by lines. Include a set of colored pencils, a decent sharpener, and an art eraser. Stock your personal library with guides to the local birds and plants.

Your children are ready to stalk their neighborhood. Challenge them to identify seven local birds, trees, flowers, and bushes. Encourage them to draw pictures in as much detail as possible. Select two or three sites in your area, perhaps a corner of a local park and a favorite nearby tree. Visit them at least four times a year, taking detailed notes about the changes you see with the seasons. For nonwriters, take their dictation. If your child refuses to draw, try photographs. Press leaves into the book, dissect a flower, describe seeds and how they travel. You might measure new plantings or follow the fate of seedlings.

For city people, find bits of nature in your neighborhood; she leaves no place untouched. You may want to include people and our habitats as part of your natural urban environment. Note awnings going up and down with the seasons, how the local produce selection shifts, how the weather affects people's transit patterns. Measure rain- and snowfall. All this, noted and checked again the following year, brings a sense of time's circular nature.

Record what stays the same as the cycles go around: the trees blooming in the same order, the light casting a certain shadow just like last year, the birds returning to the same nesting sites, the snow runoff following the well-worn culvert. We are the watchers of change and stability, the two constants that are always with us.

Making Your Mark

While we frown on graffiti, we delight in leaving small messages about our love of nature. And we appreciate others who have done the same. Recently, at a local state park, we (Diane's family) came across dozens of charming rock piles, complicated little structures that were carefully balanced and shaped. The girls decided that the largest pile was a priestess and created little rock people to help her. Since then, we've joined the fun, leaving rock piles to mark where we've passed.

Here are other ideas: Place rocks in a circle. Gather twigs and feathers into bundles and hang them from trees. Scoop up clay from streambeds, shape them into animals, and set them on stumps to dry in the sun and melt in the rain. Weave wreaths with sticks and fill them with leaves. Form long kelp stalks into spirals along the beach, or make little altars of shells under shelves of rocks.

When we make our nature mark, we are saying, "We are here, we're all around, and this world is our home."

CHAPTER TWENTY-TWO

Spirit

WE HAVE GONE around the wheel of the elements and visited all four directions. Now we come to the center, the place of that mysterious fifth element we call "spirit," although we could just as well call it "mystery." The center is the place of change and transformation, and this element is not so much a physical presence but the sense of connection that puts us in touch with the great powers of life and death. Spirit might also be called "relationship," as the center is the place where we connect with the Goddess and God, with our traditions, and with prayer, blessings, meditation, and personal practice. Another name for this section might be "core values," for here we contemplate ethics, right and wrong, and our responsibility to be healers, peacemakers, and protectors of the earth and her peoples.

Spirit is timeless. It corresponds to the whole cycle of day and night, the whole wheel of the year, and the realm beyond time. Its color is clear—or the rainbow, which contains all colors. All the Goddesses and Gods can be considered as aspects of the center.

The traditional tool of the center is the cauldron, the magic soup pot that combines the earth/metal of the container, the fire below and the air to feed it, and the water within to bring about transformation. The drum, which holds the heartbeat of a circle and keeps a large group unified, is also a tool of center. Many symbols can be used on the altar to represent spirit. One of our favorites is a mirror, for our connection to the sacred must be found inside each one of us.

The Ethics of Goddess Tradition

Do as Thou Wilt and Harm None

Goddess tradition offers a basic ethical creed: "Do as thou wilt and harm none."

"Do as thou wilt" celebrates our physicality, acknowledging desire as the wellspring of life and creativity. We view pleasure— eating, lying in the sun, dancing, enjoying humor and merry company—as partaking of the divine body of the Goddess. At the same time, we protect this gift of physicality and existence that has been entrusted to us by taking care not to degrade ourselves or others with harmful behaviors.

"Harm none" tells us to value and respect diversity in humanity and in our environment. We protect future generations by using our planet's resources wisely and avoiding greed and wastefulness that exploit people and our planet.

This does not mean that nothing or no one ever gets hurt. The balancing act between personal desire and harm to others will always be with us. Although the creed gives guidance, it does not simplify decisions.

The Morals of Magic

Goddess tradition does not end our obligations to each other with the creed of not doing harm. In Goddess tradition we have a maxim: "Everything you send shall return three times over." Known as the threefold return, these words but describe how all energy works, for benefit or detriment, for justice or injustice. Every place we focus our energy is affected by the threefold return.

The threefold return is not the same as getting what you deserve. Everyone's energies merge and mingle. One or many bad actions might not come back to you directly. Fate has notoriously bad aim. But our cumulative bad actions end up affecting our communities and all of its members. The few who pollute our water make everyone's children ill. One abused child who is not rescued may grow into a social danger. The threefold return lays the responsibility upon us not to just avoid harm, but to work for the benefit of our planet and community. Declining to act has as much power as any other decision. Our job is to help children grasp how important they are as individuals, and how their actions and decisions affect the entire web of life. By understanding the threefold return, children understand this innate connectedness, their personal significance, and their part in our community.

Pagan Family Values

Goddess tradition functions with an organic worldview based on observation of nature, including human nature. Our enduring values arise from our knowledge that people and community are one. From the sole to the whole, the importance of each person and all life is intertwined. We do not focus on individual salvation, but on the welfare of the community in its broadest definition and consider each entity as precious and sacred.

For children to internalize morals, it is crucial to develop the basic components for establishing character and maintaining values. These are: empathy, self-worth, creativity, whole thinking, and spirit. Like every other part of human nature, they are measured out in different doses to each child, but they can be developed and nurtured in each person, some more easily, some with more difficulty.

In order to develop character and morality in our children, we are obliged to create certain conditions in our homes that will encourage their acceptance of our values. These are not so different from the efforts of good parents from any other spiritual tradition, but they are important enough to include here regardless.

We provide both emotional and physical security, so our homes are a safe place where children can depend on care and love. We respect our children by accepting who they are as individuals and protecting their integrity. We extend our protection and support in spiritual ways as well. We try to help them realize their potential, encouraging their interests and talents and making their development and progress among our highest priorities. And we work on making the world a safer, saner, healthier place as part of our commitment to raising children.

Nobody will ever know us better than our children, not our parents, not our spouses, not our best friends. Our children make a study of us in a way no one else ever will. If we don't act according to our own values, they will know. Being parents is our incentive to live up to our own expectations.

Manners

We believe in teaching children manners—that is, forms of behavior which reflect our values, smooth social interactions, and exhibit kindness and concern for others whether or not these sentiments are actually felt at any given time. We want to help our children live in the real world, to be able to go with us to visit people, to share joyful and memorable occasions and to know how to make friends. In Goddess tradition, there are three principles of good manners.

Kindness toward others is the essence of good manners: Making people feel welcome, valued, and comfortable, and apologizing when we do something that harms others.

Balance is another basic principle behind our conception of manners: We appreciate what we're given, give back something for what we receive, and are generous, not boastful, about what we have.

Equality is our third principle. All people are of equal worth and value, and deserving of respect, so we don't order people around or take advantage of those who are smaller and weaker.

Adapting the Traditions We Were Raised In

Few of us who are raising Pagan children were ourselves raised as Pagans. Most of us were born into some other religion, and may still feel a deep pull and strong ties to the culture and spirituality of our origin. Those of us who are Jewish, like myself (Starhawk) and Diane, or who come from African, Native American, Asian, Central or South American, or Pacific Islands ancestry may feel a strong sense of responsibility to the generations that suffered and struggled to preserve a culture and sense of peoplehood against persecution, conquest, and genocide. We cannot abandon our ancestors, even when we come to the painful realization that we cannot simply accept what we have received from them, either.

Goddess tradition encourages us to honor our ancestors by carrying on their traditions, reinterpreting them if necessary so that they accord with our beliefs today. Although fundamentalists of every stripe maintain that theirs is a divinely inspired, unchangeable tradition, the truth is that every religion alive today reflects a long and continuing process of reinvention and reinterpretation. Nobody practices Old Testament Judaism, original Christianity, or the untempered teachings of the Buddha. When we adapt and reinvent, we are not diminishing the traditions of our origin, but expanding them.

In my collective household, for example, we light the Chanukah menorah around the time of Winter Solstice. As we add one candle each night, we both speak of the symbolism of the Solstice and the return of the light and recount the story I learned in Hebrew school about the Macabees' revolt against religious oppression and the miracle of the oil that burned for eight days. My husband and housemates are devoted to their childhood custom of decorating an evergreen tree—topped with a sun or Goddess doll, perhaps, instead of a Christmas angel. The Yule tree, the lights, and most of our Christmas customs are Pagan to begin with—all we need to do is remove the thin shell of Christianity that coats them. Even Santa Claus most likely derives from an ancient Nordic sun god.

We encourage you to keep the traditions that have meaning for you, and to let go of those that strike you as harmful or destructive. There can be many reasons for continuing a practice. For example, I (Starhawk) fast on Yom Kippur not because I believe Yahweh is judging me, but as a way of keeping a connection to my ancestors. My friend Thorn keeps Lent as a way of focusing her own spiritual development. And at my house, we hang up stockings for Santa to fill, simply because it's fun!

Here are a few suggestions for answering the questions of children in the Devastatingly Logical phase of child development:

- I was taught this custom means _____, but to me it means _____.

- We do this to honor our ancestors, who did _____ because they believed _____.

- Your grandma doesn't do this, but we do because we believe _____.

Facing Prejudice

Children challenge us. I (Starhawk) remember when my youngest stepdaughter, Juliana, who at the time was ten years old, had a battle with her mother who was attempting to impress upon her that it was not wise to tell everyone at school that she was a Witch. Raised by political activists, encouraged all her life to speak truth to power, Julie was outraged at the idea that she should be silent in any way. "Look at this!" she said, waving a dollar bill in righteous anger, pointing at the printed phrase IN GOD WE TRUST. "How come they get to put their god on the money, and we can't even talk about ours?"

As adults, we have the life experience and ego strength to face prejudice without internalizing it. We have resources for mobilizing support and taking action.

But our children are not yet adults. Unlike us, they did not choose to be Pagan, except perhaps insofar as we choose our parents before birth. They do not have the resources we do, and they are naturally susceptible to the judgments of others. Not only that, children are logical. If something is good, we should be able to talk about it openly. If children can't talk openly about what is normal to them, they will begin to feel abnormal.

Our children have the right to talk about their religion in school without fearing ridicule or reprisals. Our children deserve the same kinds of opportunities and resources children of other traditions have. It's up to us to provide them. The beginning of that struggle is the understanding of our history. We must know the origins of the prejudice against us in

Refrigerator-top Altar

Reverence for our ancestors can be extended to remembering them at mealtimes. Some families have a permanent shrine to their ancestors; we suggest the top of the refrigerator for this altar. It is close enough to the middle of the house so your ancestors won't feel neglected, yet high enough and out of the way so that small children, cats, and visitors won't knock it over accidentally. A portion of any meal can be set aside in a small bowl and placed on the altar, to keep the ancestors well fed. A candle lit at mealtimes, and perhaps a photograph or fresh flowers, completes this simple shrine to those who came before.

order to counter it effectively. Here is a suggested explanation to share with your children:

There are many different names for our religion. We call it the "Old Religion" because respect for the living earth is the earliest spirituality. Pagan, another name we use, originally meant the people who lived in the countryside, close to the earth, who held on to the old ways longest. Some of us also call ourselves by a name that is a very old word for healer, for someone who can use magic to make things change. That word is *Witch*.

Why do people believe silly or terrible things about Witches?

In Europe, the late 1400s through the 1600s were a time of great change. New ideas, new science, and discoveries challenged the churches and their beliefs. They needed scapegoats, someone to blame, so they accused the Witches and the traditional healers of casting evil spells and worshipping the Christian Devil.

When somebody was accused of being a Witch, they were thrown in prison and tortured in horrible ways. Many couldn't stand the pain and confessed to things they had never done. Others refused to confess and they were killed, hanged, or even burned alive. All their money and property were given to the Church, so greedy people often accused others in order to enrich themselves.

Hundreds of thousands, possibly millions of people, were murdered during the Burning Times. Probably many of the people who suffered and died weren't Witches or Pagans at all. The Witch persecutions attacked women who were strong and independent, and they also murdered lesbian women and gay men. Jewish people, Christians who practiced a form of worship that differed from the official Church, early scientists, and atheists were also murdered for their beliefs.

During those same years, Europeans were capturing African women, men, and children and bringing them to the Americas as slaves. Millions died along the way. The native peoples of this land were also attacked, and many were slaughtered, enslaved, or died of European diseases. Their ancient earth traditions were banned and called Devil worship.

This was a terrible time in human history. Yet this horrible history can teach us an important lesson: that we must respect other people's traditions and differences, even when we disagree with them. Every religion, even ours, includes people who live their best ideals, and others who cloak greed and cruelty in religious symbols. We know that Christianity at its best teaches love and caring, and we honor the many Christian women and men who truly practice its teachings.

During the Burning Times, in order to save themselves and still go on practicing their religions, people had to worship in secret. They could not tell the truth about what Paganism meant for many, many years, or defend their native or tribal traditions. Not until the 1950s did anyone write books about the Old Religion as a living practice.

Many people still believe the lies about

Witches that were told during the Burning Times. Many people still do not respect religions that say the earth is sacred. If they did, they could not make money by cutting down ancient forests or digging mines into sacred mountains. We would have to change the way we live, and change makes some people afraid. When people are afraid, they often get mad, so they may get very angry at people who talk about being Witches or Pagans. Or they may simply make fun of us.

Why do we call ourselves Witches and Pagans, then, if these words make people angry? We do because we believe it is important to tell the truth. People don't like to remember the Burning Times, or to admit the terrible things that were done to other tribal peoples. But unless we remember, we cannot understand the way the world is today. And if we do not remember how cruel people can be to each other, we may go on being that way. For cruel things did not just happen long ago. As we look around the world today, we can see how easy it is for people to hate and fear others who are different. Many people still suffer from war and persecution.

We also don't think it's fair that we should have to hide who we are. In this country, we are supposed to be free to practice any religion we choose. To keep that freedom alive, we must use it. If we are afraid to tell people who we are, then we are not free. If we speak out honestly, then we strengthen our freedom. Unfortunately, people still have a lot of prejudice against Witches and Pagans. *Prejudice* means "prejudge": to already have your mind made up

about somebody before you know them or learn the facts about them. People can be prejudiced against other people because of their beliefs, or their name, or the color of their skin, or the way they dress or speak. But our religion teaches us that prejudice is wrong. All people are sacred, and the differences in how we look and speak and talk and think are the different puzzle pieces we need to see more of the whole.

Because of prejudice, it often is not safe to tell other people about our religion. This is wrong. It is against what we believe, and it is against the freedom of religion that our Constitution guarantees.

Many, many grown-up Witches and Pagans are fighting this prejudice. We write books, give talks, go on radio and TV, write letters, and teach people the truth about our religion. But there is still a great deal of work to do.

The need to tell the truth is strong, but so is our need for safety. We never say that somebody else is a Witch without first asking their permission. This is a rule that comes from the Burning Times, when known Witches were condemned to death.

Your family may be open about their beliefs or keep them secret. Only you and your family know what the right way is for you. Talk about your ideas and fears honestly together. You may not want other kids to know about your religion. Or you may want to talk to them and teach them the truth about what we believe. Either way, only you and your family can decide what is right for you.

Whatever you decide, be proud of who

you are. Our religion is very beautiful and loving, and has many important things to teach the world. When we feel angry, or sad, or hurt because other people do not understand us, we can become more determined to change the world so that people of all religions and families can be free.

Educating the Public

When we speak to the media, or engage in dialogue, we are often asked to give simple answers to complex questions. Here are some "Sound Bites" to prepare yourself with:

Q: What do we worship?

A: We worship Mother Nature.

We worship Mother Nature and the God of Growing Things.

We worship the sun and the moon and the earth.

Q: What does it mean to worship something?

A: It means to love and protect it and give it energy. But often, instead of saying we worship a Goddess or God, we'll say we work with a Goddess or God—because we believe that we are partners with the Goddesses and Gods, and that they need our help to create abundance and happiness.

Q: What is a Witch?

A: A Witch is someone who has made a deep commitment to the Goddess, the great powers of birth, growth, death, and rebirth.

Q: What is a Pagan?

A: A Pagan is someone who belongs to a sacred earth tradition of spirituality.

Q: How many Witches and Pagans are there in the United States?

A: Nobody knows. We have no slot on the census, and no national registry. All we know for sure is that the movement has grown tremendously in the last twenty years. We estimate that we number somewhere in the hundreds of thousands.

Q: Do Witches have supernatural powers?

A: All people have powers of intuition and imagination. Witches train and develop ours.

Q: Do Witches practice magic?

A: We practice true magic, the art of changing consciousness at will. Real magic is learning to use your mind and all of your senses. Real magic is training your imagination.

Q: Do Witches and Pagans believe in the Bible?

A: We believe the Bible is full of wisdom and many important teachings, but it is not our holy book.

Q: What is your holy book?

A: We believe in learning from nature. Books can help us, but our sacred teachings come from what we observe in the natural world.

Q: Do Pagans believe in Jesus Christ?

A: We believe Jesus was a great teacher and healer, and the world would be a better place if more people practiced what he actually preached. But he is not our Saviour.

Q: Don't Witches worship the Devil?

A: No. We worship the powers of life. Like other religions, our tradition teaches us to be honest, kind, compassionate, and caring, to protect the earth and all of her living beings. We have no Devil in our tradition. The Devil is a Christian concept, and Satanism is a Christian heresy that has nothing to do with us.

Q: How do you know your Goddess is not evil? How do you know you aren't calling on forces that might appear to be good but actually serve the powers of evil?

A: The same way you know you're not eating chocolate ice cream when you ordered vanilla. Evil has a different taste and flavor than good. Evil leads to actions that harm others—and evil acts can be carried out in the name of any religious tradition. We must always look at our actions and their consequences, not just at the symbols we use or the names we call upon.

Q: You may think your religion is good, but how do you know that when you get to the higher levels, you won't be forced to commit evil acts?

A: First of all, there are no higher levels. We have no hierarchy that extends beyond the small groups called covens. No ethical Witch or Pagan will ever ask anyone to do something that contradicts her or his own sense of right and wrong. Any group that uses coercion or force of any kind is acting against our tradition. Should you encounter such people, we encourage you to leave their group and seek support elsewhere.

Q: Do Witches ritually abuse children?

A: No. Abuse of children is one of the worst violations of our core values that we can imagine. It contravenes our responsibility to care for the next generation. It destroys the love and trust that are the foundation of our tradition. Sexual abuse denies the sacred aspect of sexuality. Should you encounter any abusive situation where children are involved, we urge you to report the matter to Child Protective Services.

Charges of child abuse have been used against unpopular religions and groups for thousands of years. We must beware of believing every horrifying account of ritual abuse without evidence. In the name of protecting children, serious miscarriages of justice have occurred.

Q: Do Witches cast spells? For what?

A: We use the focused power of the mind to bring about change. We might work on healing someone who is sick or injured, or on protecting someone we love, or on improving our luck. We don't hex or curse, as we believe that what we send out magically returns on us three times over.

Tree of Life Meditation

This grounding meditation is an excellent, safe practice that can be used daily, and is especially helpful in times of stress or transition. For younger children, use a shorter version (see A Basic Structure for Ritual).

Find a quiet spot, away from observation or distraction. Start by taking three deep breaths. On the first two breaths, concentrate on drawing in energy from all around you and collecting it in your belly. As you exhale the third time, push that ball of energy right down through your pelvic floor, letting it take the shape of a big tap root working its way into the ground beneath you. Take a few more breaths, and with each exhalation, continue to push that root down through the soil, letting your feet also sprout roots that join and intertwine with each other as they sink effortlessly deeper into the earth. Let your roots travel down, finding hidden pockets of minerals, crystal caves, deep stores of water underground, the rocks and bones that make up the earth's crust. All that nourishment can feed you; it rises up through your roots like sap every time you inhale.

Now as you breathe in, feel all of the riches of the earth, all of the energy of our planet that you need, rising up through your roots, entering through your feet, legs, and pelvis, rejuvenating every system in your body. Feel the earth's energy helping the flow of your digestion; feel it bringing oxygen into your bloodstream. If there is a place in your body that needs healing, let the earth's energy go to that place and begin the work of healing. And if you find anything that you don't need—any unwanted energy, any thoughts or habits that are harmful to your body—send it down through your roots on each exhale, letting it drop deep within the earth and be transformed.

Now you have made a living circuit between your body and the earth below you. As you breathe in and out, feel the interchange through your roots: fresh energy in and old energy out. Let that swirling motion fill your entire body, your chest, arms, neck, and head, until you are pulling the earth's energy up through the top of your head like a crown of leafy branches above you. Feel those leaves unfurl in the warmth of the sun, let them gently rustle in the breeze, and when you're ready, try breathing in oxygen, sky energy, from above you.

Trust that that your breath is bringing you all the power, clarity, energy, and sustenance you need, keeping you in balance with the earth below and sky above. When you can feel that effortless circuit of bringing in and letting go, when you feel rooted in the ground and open to the sky, open your eyes and look around you with clear sight. Blessed be.

Place of Power Meditation

A place of power is a spot where we feel good: strong, safe, powerful, and fully alive. It can be an actual physical location or a place we go to only in our imagination. When I (Anne) was a girl, my place of power was a large rock on the hillside next to our house. It felt magical to me, and every time I sat on it I felt instantly more centered, my troubles receded, and I was filled with a deep peace and calm. When we bring a problem or question to our place of power, we can work with it using the tools of magic there. Standing in our power in a sacred place, we open ourselves to greater possibilities and potentials than we normally have at our disposal.

In a place of power meditation we use trance and visualization techniques to visit our own magical place. A technique to help you enter a trance state is called an "induction," and may take the shape of an imaginary journey (like the one here). At the end of the meditation we come back the way we came, by taking the induction journey again in reverse. It is important to remember to take the journey back into your body after being in a trance, because it makes the transition between trance and waking consciousness much smoother. There are many different trance inductions, and with practice you will find that some work better for you than others. (For short inductions, see Visualization and Trance in Tool Chest section of Chapter 2.) Once you become skilled at going to your place of power, you may find that it takes very little induction to get there. For now, though, find a comfortable place, sit or lie down, close your eyes, and take three deep breaths.

Imagine yourself standing by a hole in the ground. There is a staircase descending into the hole, stone worn smooth by generations of footsteps. Take the first step onto the stairs, which now look **red.** As you descend, you notice that the red light seems to be coming from all around you. The walls on either side are glowing red, and on your tongue is the taste of raspberries, or maybe pomegranate juice.

Keep walking down, breathing deeply, and notice how the light is slowly changing to **orange,** a deep orange that colors the stone and your arms as they swing to your sides. You are walking down the spiral staircase through orange, with the taste of oranges on your tongue and the air humming an orange tune around you.

Now you feel the shift around and within you to **yellow,** your yellow feet on yellow stones walking down, through the yellow air that smells of fresh lemons. Keep walking down, as the passage hums now of **green,** and the stones beneath your feet are covered in green moss, and as you take deep breaths you notice the air smells moist, like the green earth.

You keep breathing and descending until the light around you changes once again, this time to a beautiful sky **blue.**

Using the Meditations

You may want to tape-record these meditations, leaving pauses between each sentence. Then play the tape to help you practice the meditations, so that you don't have to worry about remembering the whole thing while you are doing it. When the visualization has become familiar to you, try practicing without the tape. Let yourself experiment with other images that feel right to you. If you know an adult experienced in Goddess tradition, and especially if you are using these exercises to prepare for your rite of passage, don't hesitate to ask questions or get help when you need it.

You look around and notice blue light coming from the stones, and the sound of birdsong in the air about you. Breathe in the blue, let it fill your body with cool breezes and open spaces, and keep walking down, down, where the blue turns to **indigo,** the color of the twilight sky, a deep, dark blue. Let that glowing light into your body, and notice how the stairs are still easy to see as you descend deeper into the earth.

Now the light around you shifts once again, turning the stairs beneath your feet to **purple,** sending a hum of purple through your body, leaving you with the taste of dark plums on your tongue.

Breathe again as you reach the last step and come to a large wooden door set in the stone wall. You push the door open and find yourself in a place that is new, yet familiar. Do you recognize this place? Take a few steps, look around you at the landscape. If you have been here before, is there anything different from the way it was before? If this is a new place, does it remind you of someplace you knew before? Is there a part of this place that draws you toward it? Find the area here that makes you feel the safest, that is full of good magic for you, and go to it. This is your place of power.

Breathe deeply, and take a few moments to make yourself comfortable here. When you are ready, turn to the **east.** What lies in the east for you? Is it a feeling? A scene? Is there someone here to greet you, maybe an ally from the plant or animal world? These are the gifts and challenges to you from the powers of the east.

Take some time here, remembering to breathe deeply, and do anything you feel called to do.

When you are finished, thank the east for its gifts and turn toward the **south.** What do you feel? Do you hear or sense anything? Open your senses to the south, and see what gifts and challenges lie here for you. Notice how your body responds, what emotions are stirred here. When you are ready, thank the powers of the south and turn to the west.

Facing the **west,** what do you notice? Is there a different feeling to the landscape here? Do you hear different sounds or see different things? Is this direction harder or easier for you to be comfortable in than the east or south? What gifts and challenges does the west have for you right now? Take a few moments, remembering to keep breathing. When you are done, thank the powers of the west and turn once more to the north.

As you face the **north,** once again notice how you feel, what you see, what sounds come to your ears. Are there allies here for you? What gifts and challenges are here for you in the north? Again, take the time you need here, and when you are finished, thank the powers of the north. Feel how you yourself are the center of this circle, the dynamic point of motion in the center of your own place of power, and know that you can come back anytime. You know the way here, and your place of power will be waiting for you whenever you choose to return.

Now say goodbye to your place of power, go back to that door in the stone wall nearby, and open the wooden door. Take a deep breath and start walking up the purple steps on the spiral staircase. As you walk slowly up the stairs, take two or three deep breaths with each color, from purple to indigo to blue, on to green, then yellow, orange, and finally red. Take the time you need to bring yourself up the spiraling stairway of color, until you can see sunlight overhead. Walk those last few steps through the hole in the ground, back to where you are right now, in your body, feeling relaxed and rejuvenated. When you are ready, open your eyes and say your name aloud three times. Welcome back! Blessed be.

Blessing Beads

(adapted from Donald Engstrom's idea)

Collect or make special beads to represent: the four elements; the Goddesses and Gods you feel closest to; your family; your own helpers; the things you care most about; the things you are working on or hoping for.

String the beads, and when you want to be calm, or before you go to sleep at night, hold them in your hand and run them through your fingers, saying "Blessed be . . ." at each bead. For example: "Blessed be the earth, blessed be the air, blessed be the fire, blessed be the water, blessed be spirit, blessed be the Goddess, blessed be the God, blessed be my mother, blessed be my father, blessed be my cat, Paw, blessed be Brigit, blessed be Lugh, blessed be the redwoods, blessed be my soccer team, blessed be me when I'm learning not to lose my temper all the time."

The beads can also be a traveling magic circle. Start with a grounding bead, follow with one for each of the four directions, the center, the Goddess, the God, ancestors, and special helpers, and then a series of beads for special blessings. Then make a second string of beads arranged in reverse order. As you go through the first string, then the second one, you cast a circle, work magic, and devoke.

Sand Beads

Mix sand and glue together. Roll into balls the size of marbles or smaller. Make holes by pushing a toothpick through the bead. Leaving toothpick in place, let dry on wax paper for a day; twist toothpick a couple of times during that period to keep it from becoming stuck. When you remove the toothpick after bead is dry, rub off the lip that may have formed around the holes.

Tip: If you rotate the toothpick slightly as you gently push it through, you will minimize deformation of the bead. When the toothpick is in place, pat bead back into shape.

Salt Dough Beads

Use the salt dough recipe in the Tool Chest, and follow instructions for making Sand Beads. Salt dough beads can be decorated before drying. To imprint a design, simply press material, like leaves or shells, against the bead. Try embedding small objects, such as colorful bits of glass (with no sharp edges!) or tiny stones. These objects are more likely to stay on if you dot white glue on their back before imbedding. For color, knead a few drops of food coloring into the salt dough. The color will turn a lighter shade as the bead dries.

Making Large Beads from Salt Dough

Form aluminum foil into the desired shape; it should be slightly smaller than the actual size of the bead you want. Roll salt dough into a sheet ½ inch thick. Cover the foil with the dough and smooth dough with your hands. Pierce with toothpick. Bake like salt-dough figures (see Tool Chest), turning toothpick occasionally. Rotate bead once. After pulling out toothpick, file the lip smooth using sandpaper or a nail file. Paint or decorate.

Tip: Use as little foil as possible. The denser the foil bead, the harder it will be to pierce.

Papier-Mâché Beads

Papier-mâché is perfect for making beads that are larger (1 inch or more in diameter) and yet are light and easy to decorate. Form aluminum foil into the size and shape bead you want. Tear small bits of white paper and soak in liquid laundry starch. Cover foil bead with soaked paper, using at least two layers of paper. Smooth the surface, then pierce with toothpick. After bead hardens, decorate with paint or markers.

Rose Petal Beads

Mix the flour, salt, and water until it forms a stiff dough. Crush the rose petals into a wet mass in your palm, then knead in as much as the dough will absorb and still remain pliable.

Roll the dough into small beads and pierce with toothpicks. Let dry on wax paper. Before beads harden completely, remove toothpicks and smooth beads.

Note: All these beads will melt on contact with water, so keep dry!

You will need:

1/3 C flour

1 T salt

2 T water

3 C rose petals, torn into very small pieces

toothpicks

The Environment, Peace, and Justice

Our children are growing up in a world very different from the one we would design for them. We want our children to love nature and care for the earth, yet we sometimes wonder if there will be any nature left by the time they grow up. Every day, species are disappearing, ancient forests are being clear-cut, and the natural environment is being destroyed and degraded all around us. We teach our children to respect differences and honor diversity, yet we raise them in a world full of hatred, misogyny, racism, homophobia, and prejudice of all kinds. We expect them to value fairness in a world of injustice, to value peace when violence surrounds them and war is always on the horizon.

The three of us (Anne, Diane, Starhawk) have been active throughout our adult lives in issues of ecology, peace, and social justice, yet the world today seems grimmer, more violent, more restricted, and less hopeful than it did when we were growing up. How can we help our children cope with issues that overwhelm adults? How can we raise empowered children when we ourselves often feel powerless, fearful, or hopeless?

Our primary human responsibility is to

pass on to the next generation a world at least as viable as the one we inherited. For our children's sake, we cannot close our eyes to the environmental disasters our society is creating, nor can we ignore the human suffering that surrounds us. But we must not become overwhelmed by the dimensions of the problems we face. The children in our lives obligate us to hold hope for the world, to work actively on changing what is wrong rather than simply complaining or despairing.

We must also consider carefully how to share information about these issues with children. Too often, even political movements that in theory wish to empower people use fear as a motivator in reality. "If we don't stop the deployment of this weapons system, we will have a nuclear war." "If we clear-cut this forest, nothing will be left." "No woman is safe walking down the street; any man might be a rapist."

Fear is a powerful motivator, but not an empowering one, even for adults. Whether or not the fears are realistic is not the issue; the point is, children need to be protected from such fears while being taught appropriate caution. Small children, especially, need to believe in their parents' power to protect them. When we discuss difficult issues with children, we need to phrase our concern in terms of our positive values: "We want to stop nuclear testing because we love Mother Earth, and the tests hurt her and can hurt too many other people and creatures." "We want to save this forest because it is an ancient, sacred, special place and because trees are our friends and teachers." "We want to

teach everybody to respect and honor women—and men, too—as we do because we love the Goddess. We want the cities and streets to be safe for everybody."

Especially in the years of early childhood, we need to exert some control over what children are exposed to in the media. They may inevitably hear of kidnappings and murders, but they don't need to see footage of the bodies or hear all the grim details. They might need to know that the Gulf War is happening, but they don't need to watch hours and hours of CNN footage of the same bombings repeated over and over again. (Do adults? That's another question!)

As children grow and can handle more complex information, we can share with them more and more of our own responses to world events. We can find appropriate actions to take so that our children see us "walk our talk." We want them to know that, yes, the world has many serious problems, yet those problems can be solved, and children can be part of the solution.

Raising children consciously requires enormous faith and deep compassion. We must believe that healing is possible—for ourselves, for our communities, for the earth. Or at least we must choose to act as if we believe that the world can still be saved. We must refrain from blanket condemnation of any group, however they might have historically oppressed us, in order to hold the hope of change. We must face our own guilt, fear, and shame, whether for our own complicity in destruction or for the deeds of our ancestors.

Most of all, we must believe that we have a right to be, that human beings are not a blight on the planet, as some environmentalists seem to believe, but are capable of learning to contribute to the health, diversity, wisdom, and joy of Mother Earth.

We must also face our children's questions. If we have succeeded in raising them to intuitively love and honor the earth, then the acts that seem wrong to us will seem incomprehensibly strange, misguided, and even stupid to them. What can we say when they ask, "Why are they cutting the trees?" "Why are we having another war?" "Why does the Goddess let this happen?"

We have no easy responses to suggest. What I (Starhawk) might say to a child is this:

"The Goddess and God are not all-powerful. They depend on us to work with them to heal the earth and create justice and peace. In fact, we are part of the Goddess. The Goddess gave us the freedom to use our minds in any way we want. At one time, human beings learned to use our minds in a certain way that let us build machines and do a lot of things we couldn't do before. We gained many wonderful powers and inventions, but we forgot the most important thing of all: that everything is interconnected. And so we have made some terrible mistakes. Now we must learn to use our minds differently, in ways that may be easier for children than for a lot of grownups. Changing our way of thinking about things and doing things is not easy. Some people will always resist because they're afraid, or because they benefit a lot

from the old way of doing things. But change will come. Just as we learned to hurt the earth, we can learn how to heal her."

In dealing with political and social issues, we urge you to follow one basic principle: Put your child's needs first. Children are not bumper stickers; they should not be used to publicly display your beliefs. Some of the most unhappy children I (Starhawk) have known were the daughters and sons of activists who never had time to spend with them because they were always too busy supporting the Starving Children of Somewhere Else. It is difficult to balance community activism with a healthy family life, especially when there are few others to take on the many projects that need doing, but remember that raising children well is itself a political act. In the end, it is how well you can enjoy life while doing important work that will impress your children, not how harried you are for the cause.

Let the seasons suggest times of activity and withdrawal from political work. I (Anne) find that I naturally have more energy for community work between spring and fall, where the light is at its fullest. During the winter months, I want to hibernate and enjoy the sound of rain on my roof. Respect these cycles in your children as well, and don't panic if they lose interest in a project for a while. It is consistency over the long term that is the most important thing, not staying busy when your instincts tell you to take a break.

Action is the best counter to hopelessness—but your child's safety and inner security must come first. There are many actions that children can safely take to stand up for the ideals and act on their concerns. Cultivate their enthusiasm by starting out small, with clearly defined goals. Here are some suggestions for nurturing a sustainable commitment toward the Earth, and a healthy connection to spirit.

Children can:

⚕ Write (or dictate) letters to elected officials, newspapers, and television stations, expressing their opinions.

⚕ Conserve, turn off lights, be careful with water, take responsibility for recycling.

⚕ Make compost.

⚕ Garden, and donate surplus produce to a local homeless shelter or soup kitchen.

⚕ Plant trees.

⚕ Carry a plastic bag to the beach or park to pick up garbage.

⚕ Save money to donate to a cause of their choice.

⚕ Learn about the environment.

⚕ Participate in community cleanup days. (As an extra plus, there is often free food at these events, always a draw for my own kids [Anne's].)

⚕ Speak out when they encounter untruths, unfairness, prejudice, or intolerance. We can all be an example to our children by doing so ourselves.

⚕ Learn about the history, mythology, and current struggles of their own people as well as people from different places and ancestries. Our children will be strong justice-bringers when they are grounded in love and true pride in being who they are.

⚕ Create rituals. During our seven-year drought, Deborah and her Goddess-daughter Katie set up a rain altar. On it they put a blue cloth, symbols of water, shells, bowls, and pitchers. Together they asked the Goddess to bless us with rain. Running Deer, a counselor at an inner-city high school, encouraged the students to set up a traditional Dia de los Muertos/Day of the Dead altar in the main hallway for their peers who had died of violence. For the first time in that place, a shared public space was created where gang members, straight-A students, and at-risk teens of many different backgrounds and cultures could mourn their friends and acknowledge the pain of the everyday violence that surrounds them.

⚕ Participate in marches, demonstrations, and political actions, with due consideration for the children's safety. If you have any reason to believe the situation might involve police violence or physical danger, don't expose a child.

Finally, remember to celebrate. The greatest counter to despair is to win a few good victories. Much has been lost, but we are still alive. The world has not yet been destroyed in nuclear war. Nelson Mandela, at this writing, is president of an apartheid-free South Africa. Pelicans wing their way over the bay, and many rivers run cleaner than before. All these gains were achieved by the efforts of many people over long periods of time. Often, political victories come so long after our actions that we lose the sense of connection between ourselves as cause and our effects. Claim credit anyway. Throw a victory party, share a feast, shout hurrah! Teach your children that change is possible, that mistakes can be overcome, that the world can truly be made a better place. If you have ever acted to protect the earth; if you have ever stood up for human decency, compassion, and interconnection; if you have ever spoken out for freedom—then congratulate yourself for every struggle won, every life saved, every tree that still stands rooted and green.

The Rainbow Circle
by Starhawk

Circle round, and I'll tell you a story about time....

Long, long ago, when the world was still new, all the people who lived on the earth knew that they were children of the Goddess. They loved their Mother, for she was very beautiful, with her high, snow-capped mountains, her deep, blue oceans, her wide plains of grass, her broad deserts, and her forests of great trees. She gave them everything they needed to live, and they delighted her with their songs, their dances, and the curious things they invented.

More and more people were born, and they spread out over the earth. As they traveled, they began to live differently from one another. The forest dwellers learned to live among the great trees; the people of the plains learned how to follow the herds on the great prairies. Some people became sailors and fisherpeople; others learned to plant crops along the great rivers. They called the Goddess by different names and made new songs and stories. And the Mother was happy, for she was never bored. People were always thinking up something new that delighted her. Although she was their Mother, she left them free to grow and change—

because only when people are free can they invent new things. And the Goddess loves surprises.

But time passed. As people grew more different from one another, some of them began to become afraid. In fortunate lands life was easy and rich; in other places it was harsh and difficult, and some people became jealous of others. They began to fight with each other, to try to take away what other people had. They turned their imaginations to making better and better weapons of war. They forgot that they were children of the Mother. Instead, they invented new Gods and tried to make people forget the names of the Goddesses and Gods that reminded them of the Circle of Life.

The Mother became very sad. She loved surprises—but not bad ones! She hated to see her precious children hurt each other. She cried when they suffered and died.

But the Mother was also wise. She knew that if her children were to be free, they would make mistakes. And if they were to grow up, she would have to let them learn from their mistakes—even if it took them thousands of years. And maybe, even from their mistakes, good things might yet grow. So she kept quiet, even when people forgot her and did things that hurt the earth herself.

Not all the people forgot her. In every land, among every race of people, many remembered the old ways. They were teachers and elders, wise priestesses and priests, or powerful magicians, and they were also ordinary people who never stopped loving the earth, the trees, the animals and birds. They knew that thousands of years might

go by before human beings learned from their mistakes and began to love the Mother again, but they found ways to keep her memory from disappearing. Many taught their children the ways of healing, or buried images of her for people to find in later times. They continued to do their rituals in secret. And when they died, many of them pledged to be reborn in the time when the memory of the Goddess would reawaken, and to bring back the knowledge that people would need.

Now that time has come. Now more and more children are born into this world who remember the Circle of Life, and who bring with them the knowledge that we need to help heal the Mother and teach people how to live happily with each other again.

So right now is a wonderful time, because all of us who are alive right now can help to heal the hurtful things that have been done to the earth and to people. That may seem like a lot of work, but it can also be a lot of fun. For the things that heal the Goddess are often the things we love to do best—dancing, singing, doing kind things for people, planting gardens, and cleaning up our garbage. Whenever you think of something new, or draw a picture or make up a story, the Goddess laughs with delight. And the more she laughs, the stronger she gets, and the more people will hear her voice and remember that we are the children of the Mother. So once again human beings, in all our different lands and with all our different ways, can live in the same circle, stretching around the earth like a rainbow.

Notes

1, p. 6. For a full discussion of the various Wiccan traditions, see Margot Adler's *Drawing Down the Moon* (New York: Viking Penguin, 1997).

Chapter 1: Goddess Tradition and Children

1, p. 14. Used by permission of Diane Baker.

2, p. 15. Diane's story is an interpretation for young children of our current scientific understanding of the origin of the cosmos. When nature is sacred, there need be no conflict between science and religion.

3, p. 17. "The Goddess Dances the World Awake" is the Pelasgian (pre-Indo-European) creation myth adapted from the version that appears in Robert Graves's *The Greek Myths* (New York: Penguin, 1990).

4, p. 18. Used by permission of Starhawk.

Chapter 2: Handing Down Our Traditions

1, p. 22. © 1984, 1989 words and music by Sarah Pirtle. Discovery Center, BMI. Used by permission.

2, p. 23. Used by permission of Andras Corban Arthen.

3, p. 24. Used by permission of Serpentine Music Productions.

4, p. 25. Used by permission of Diane Baker.

5, p. 36. See Anne Carson, ed., *Spiritual Parenting in the New Age* (California: The Crossing Press, 1989) for her wonderful description of making shadow boxes with her children.

Chapter 3: Moon Cycle

1, p. 58. Used by permission of Serpentine Music Productions.

2, p. 60. Used by permission of Serpentine Music Productions.

Chapter 4: Sun Cycle

1, p. 69. Used by permission of Steven W. Posch.

Chapter 5: Samhain

1, p. 77. Many, many versions of this traditional tale exist. This version is my (Starhawk's) own telling that comes out of work we have done at Reclaiming Witch camps. I have long wondered why so many faerytales involve a wicked stepmother and two stepsisters. Of course, envy is a potent theme in human life, but this threefold constellation occurs so often that I began to suspect it might be a code for some lost mystery. There may have once been an initiation tradition for young girls in which they were placed in the care of a surrogate mother for testing and training. I experimented with writing the story from that perspective, trying not to lose its fearful quality, which seemed integral to its power.

While working intensely with the story one summer, I awoke one morning with the voice of the Baba Yaga in my head, saying "Once I had a beautiful face." That was all—but my understanding of the mysteries she reveals to Vasalisa came from that one visitation.

For an alternative reading of the story, I highly recommend *Women Who Run with the Wolves: Myths and Stories of the Wild Woman Archetype* by Clarissa Pinkola Estes (New York: Ballantine, 1992).

2, p. 89. Used by permission of Ellen Klaver.

3, p. 90. This recipe was adapted courtesy of Bobbi Salinas, *Indo-Hispanic Folk Art Traditions II* (California: Pinata Publications, 1988), a wonderful book devoted to teaching the customs and activities of the Indo-Hispanic culture.

4, p. 94. Ibid.

Chapter 6: Yule/Winter Solstice

1, p. 101. Used by permission of Diane Baker.

2, p. 101. The story of Mother Winter is originally the German tale of Frau Holle, whose name is associated with the root of English words such as *holy* and *holly*. In other words, Holy/Holly/Winter Woman. She is also associated with the elder tree, which in German is called *Hollunder*.

In this version, I (Starhawk) have taken the liberty of making her house a gingerbread house. The gingerbread house is always associated with this season in spite of the horrors of the Hansel and Gretel story. I felt it deserved to be represented in a more positive tale, as it so strongly represents the House of Abundance, the House of the Goddess.

Teenagers and older children might want to note the similarities and differences with the tale of Vasalisa. Both are initiation stories—about going to the Goddess for learning and gifts, and receiving transformation. Mother Winter is a gentler aspect of the Goddess than Baba Yaga, but both are teachers and keepers of mysteries. And both require us to clean house!

3, p. 114. Used by permission of Serpentine Music Productions.

4, p. 120. Used by permission of Starhawk.

5, p. 121. Meringue tips are courtesy of Alice Medrich, author of *Chocolate and the Art of Low-Fat Desserts* (New York: Warner Books, 1994) and *Cocolat: Extraordinary Chocolate Desserts* (New York: Warner Books, 1990).

Chapter 7: Brigit

1, p. 125. We learned of this charm from *Celtic Gods and Celtic Goddesses* by R. J. Stewart (London: Blanford, 1990), p. 99.

2, p. 126. Used by permission of Starhawk.

3, p. 128. Used by permission of Diane Baker and Serpentine Music Productions.

4, p. 133. Used by permission of Diane Baker

Chapter 8: Eostar/Spring Equinox

1, p. 151. The story of Demeter and Persephone is an old myth, full of rich associations and perplexing mysteries. In ancient times, the myth formed the basis for the Eleusinian mysteries, one of the ceremonies that preserved elements of Goddess tradition in ancient Greece. This is one of the major stories we use in working with adults today.

My (Starhawk's) version of the story has, of course, been changed. In the classical myth, Persephone is carried off and raped by Hades. Most likely, the rape reflects the political takeover of the older Goddess-worshiping people of Greece by patriarchal invaders, who eventually developed classical Greek culture. I felt a story of rape is not an appropriate myth for Pagan children. In fact, in working with adults in trance and ritual, we never tell the story as one of rape. I believe the abduction is an overlay on an earlier tale of initiation, of voluntary descent into the Underworld.

Nevertheless, there is some emotional truth in the image of abduction, of being carried away into the dark. Perhaps a descent into the Underworld is never wholly voluntary. We may start down there, thinking we can easily return, but then we are caught. As we go through life, we suffer periods of loss and grief, moments when all the structures of life fall apart. This story teaches us that those descents can become initiations, can awaken new life and creativity. Yet I know of no one who joyfully welcomes the abyss when it opens under our feet. So in this telling of the tale, I have tried to retain some of that feeling of surprise and helplessness. Kore initiates her own descent, but she doesn't realize what she is getting herself into. And once begun, her descent has its own momentum, which she cannot resist.

In working with the story, it is important to remember that it is not a simple moral tale. Every element in it is fraught with ambivalence. Kore grasps for the flower, and her desire to pluck and possess it opens the chasm beneath her. And yet without this mistake, this wrong act, she would not ever fully become herself. Demeter loves her daughter, grieves for her, threatens to ruin the world because of her loss. Yet if Kore had not been lost, she would never have become a power in her own right.

2, p. 157. Used by permission of Serpentine Music Productions.

3, p. 157. Used by permission of Diane Baker and Aaron Joseph Feldman.

4, p. 158. Used by permission of Charles Dabo.

Chapter 9: Beltane

1, p. 175. The story of Thomas the Rhymer is one of many tales that record encounters between people of this world and the inhabitants of Faery. The story is a tale of initiation into contact with the great powers that underlie earth life. We choose it as a Beltane story because Beltane is the holiday that speaks of the embracing of all life. The story teaches us that the road to fair Elfland is always the Third Road, the one that transcends dualities, that will not accept narrow choices. If we live in a world of black and white, we will never come to the Twilight.

I (Starhawk) am indebted to both R.J. Stewart and Francesca De Grandis for insights into this story.

2, p. 183. Used by permission of Carol Lee Sanchez.

3, p. 187. Used by permission of Serpentine Music Productions.

4, p. 195. Used by permission of Diane Baker.

5, p. 197. See Note 5 in Chapter 6 for a list of dessert cookbooks by Alice Medrich.

Chapter 10: Summer Solstice

1, p. 202. Used by permission of Diane Baker.

2, p. 204. Used by permission of Serpentine Music Productions.

3, p. 205. "The Twelve Wild Swans" is a powerful, disturbing tale of the challenges we face when we undergo a process of initiation. Told in hundreds of different versions from all over Europe, it is an old and widespread tale full of Goddess symbolism. The Queen wishes for a daughter whose colors are red, black, and white—the full, the dark, and the new moon. The twelve wild swans are the twelve months of the year, with Rose as the thirteenth lunar month. Spinning and weaving are crafts that are sacred to the Goddess. Shirts are souls.

When we use this story with adults, we often hear complaints from people reacting to the sur-

face level of the tale. "It's another story about a woman sacrificing herself for men!" "Why does Rose have to keep silent? Why can't she be empowered to speak her truth?"

We urge you to see this story as we believe it is meant to be seen: as an initiatory tale. Fulfilling challenges, facing fears, and refusing to be daunted by pain, misunderstanding, or persecution are some of the ways we grow in personal power. Keeping silence is one of the abilities basic to all magical discipline. Rose becomes a shaman and healer, one who has the power to retrieve lost souls.

This story is especially appropriate to use with older children who are preparing for their Rite of Passage.

4, p. 214. Used by permission of Rafael Jesús González.

5, p. 218. Used by permission of Sparky T. Rabbit.

6, p. 220. Used by permission of T. Thorn Coyle.

7, p. 224. Used by permission of Pandora Minerva O'Mallory.

Chapter 11: Lughnasad/Lammas

1, p. 251. Used by permission of Diane Baker and Serpentine Music Productions.

Chapter 12: Mabon/Fall Equinox

1, p. 256. Originally I (Starhawk) tried to extract only the visit to the elder animals from this story, making it a tale of wisdom-seeking and liberation, uncluttered by giants, Oedipal dilemmas, head-chopping, and menus offensive to vegetarians. However, in telling the story to children, especially to small boys only recently emerged from the Klingon warrior phase of child development, I realized that I had left out the best parts. Now they're back in, and while the tale becomes less morally and spiritually correct (and cluttered with more difficult-to-pronounce Welsh names), it's a much more lively tale.

This story is surely one of the most haunting and mysterious of our traditional tales. It is a small incident in the larger saga of Kyllwch and Olwen found in the fourteenth-century Welsh compilations of tales that have become known as Mabinogion. Although written down in medieval times, they contain elements that refer back to the pre-Christian era. This tale seems to be a remnant of some older legend, dating back to the times when heroes were truly Sons of the Mother. In fact, the archaic nature of Mabon is one of the themes of the story.

The Arthur of this story is not the historical king, nor the head of Mallory's Round Table but more akin to the ancient Pagan God. The supernatural powers of a deity are embodied in his companions, his aspects.

The tale as it has come down to us leaves us with many unanswered questions. It is less about Mabon himself than about the process of finding him, and what it does tell us is that to find the Imprisoned God we must go back and back and back, seeking ever older knowledge until we find the Salmon of Wisdom himself. But who was Mabon? Why was he taken from his mother, and why when he was three nights old? Who was keeping him in prison and why? Why can he be freed only by fighting? The answers are lost somewhere in the past, behind the deletions and distortions of Christian monks and the breaking of old traditions of knowledge.

2, p. 261. Used by permission of Tala Divinia.

3, p. 266. Used by permission of Diane Baker and Aaron Joseph Feldman.

4, p. 279. Used by permission of T. Thorn Coyle.

Chapter 13: Beginnings

1, p. 294. Used by permission of Rick Hamouris.

2, p. 296. Used by permission of Kate Kaufman Greenway.

3, p. 298. Used by permission of Starhawk.

4, p. 299. Used by permission of Starhawk.

Chapter 14: Growth

1, p. 305. Used by permission of Diane Baker.

2, p. 305. Used by permission of Serpentine Music Productions.

Chapter 15: Coming of Age: Adolescence

1, p. 319. Reprinted by permission of Zack Darling-Ferns and *How About Magic?* "Youth and Maiden Lovemaking" originally appeared in Volume 1, Issue number 4, of *How About Magic?* in 1990.

Chapter 16: Coming of Age: Rites of Passage

1, p. 323. Used by permission of Aurora.

2, p. 326. Used by permission of Marylyn Motherbear Scott.

3, p. 329. Used by permission of Marylyn Motherbear Scott.

4, p. 331. Used by permission of Calla Unsworth.

Chapter 17: Life Transitions

1, p. 336. Used by permission of Vibra Willow.

2, p. 347. For a more extensive discussion of children and death see Starhawk, M. Macha Night-Mare and Reclaiming, *The Pagan Book of Living and Dying* (San Francisco: HarperSanFrancisco, 1997). Our on-line resource section also has a number of suggested books for children and adults on coping with death at <www.circleround.com>.

3, p. 348. Used by permission of Patricia Taylor.

Chapter 20: Water

1, p. 375. Used by permission of Diane Baker.

Chapter 21: Earth

1, p. 389. Used by permission of Starhawk and Serpentine Music Productions.

Resource Section

For an extensive listing of recommended books covering all the topics presented in this book, a calendar of Circle Round workshops and events, and many other resources for Goddess tradition families, please visit our website at:
<www.circleround.com>.

Books for Families to Enjoy

Cohen, David, ed., *The Circle of Life: Rituals from the Human Family Album*, San Francisco: HarperSanFrancisco, 1991. This incredible coffee-table photography book chronicles the stages of human life through initiations, rites, and ceremonies from around the world. A treasure.

Edwards, Carolyn McVickar, *Sun Stories: Tales from Around the World to Illuminate the Days and Nights of Our Lives*, San Francisco: HarperSanFrancisco, 1995. Sun tales from around the world—mostly from earth-based traditions but including also the Christmas and Chanukah stories in versions readable for Pagan children. Highly recommended! Also, her book, *The Storyteller's Goddess: Tales of the Goddess and Her Wisdom from Around the World*. A wonderful multicultural collection of Goddess tales.

Frasier, Debra, *On the Day You Were Born*, New York: HBJ & Co., 1991. A beautiful picture book to tell young children of their beginnings and their place in the world.

Hoffman, Mary, *Earth, Fire, Water, Air*, New York: Dutton Children's Books, 1995. Hoffman mixes nature, history, spirit, and myth from many cultures, connecting them with lyrical explanations. The illustrations are whimsical, powerful, and very attractive to children.

Kraul, Walter, *Earth, Water, Fire, and Air: Playful Explorations in the Four Elements*, Edinburgh: Floris Books, 1984. From toddlers to teens, there are toys to make, games to play, and all sorts of fun to be had by mucking about with the elements.

Luenn, Nancy, *Mother Earth*, New York: Atheneum Books, 1992. Diane's children's favorite, with its lyric intertwining of earth and life: "Trees and plants her living hair. . . Animals her fingers."

McFarlane, Marilyn, *Sacred Myths: Stories of World Religions*, Portland: Sibyl Publications, 1996. This collection has sections on Christianity, Hinduism, Judaism, Buddhism, Native American, and Sacred Earth (Goddess) traditions—a great way for children to see our tradition included on equal footing with others! Also a good way to introduce them to some of the common cultural stories from other traditions.

Waldherr, Kris, *The Book of Goddesses*, Hillsborough, OR: Beyond Words Publishing, 1995. A gorgeously illustrated picture book of thirteen Goddesses from around the world.

Wirth, Victoria, *Whisper from the Woods*, New York: Green Tiger Press, 1991. We follow the trees in their turning cycles, a compassionate early introduction to these ideas.

Goddess Tradition Periodicals, Organizations, and Websites

PanGaia: Living the Pagan Life. Subscriptions $18/year (4 issues). *SageWoman Magazine.* Subscriptions $21/year (4 issues). Both magazines are at P.O. Box 641, Pt. Arena, CA 95468. 707-882-2052. Email: info@sagewoman.com. For more information, check out their beautiful website: <www.sagewoman.com>.

Reclaiming Quarterly. Subscriptions $20–$50/year sliding scale (4 issues). P.O. Box 14404, San Francisco, CA 94114. For more information on the Quarterly or Reclaiming's many projects and events, go to <www.reclaiming.org>.

Green Egg Magazine. P.O. Box 488, Laytonville, CA 95454. 707-984-7062. Subscriptions $28/year (6 issues), sample issue $6.00. Email: gemagazine@aol.com. For more information about *Green Egg*, its children's magazine *How About Magic*, and the Church of All Worlds, which publishes both, visit their website at <www.caw.org>.

Covenant of the Goddess (COG) is an international Wiccan organization with local councils in most regions of the U.S. For information on COG activities and local area groups, send e-mail to info@cog.org or write: COG, Correspondence Officer, P.O. Box 1226, Berkeley, CA 94701. Among their resources for Goddess tradition families is the Hart and Crescent Award, a merit badge program for youth eleven and older of Wicca and other nature religions. The adult version, the Distinguished Youth Service Award, is also available. For information, please send a SASE to: Hart and Crescent Award, c/o Amber K, P.O. Box 1107, Los Alamos, NM 87544. COG also has an extensive on-line listing of recommended books for parents, young and older children. The COG website is at <www.cog.org>.

The Pagan Parenting Web Site, created by Jaz Gordon, has articles, rituals, songs, and stories, an updated resource list, organizations, and publications for teens, homeschooling resources, forums, and much more. While there are many sites of interest to Goddess tradition families on the World Wide Web, this one is worth checking out first <www.pagan.net/~jaz/pparent/>.

Sources for Books and Music of Goddess Tradition

Chinaberry Book Service. The mail-order company of choice for many Pagan parents, with books, games, and treasures for all ages. 800-776-2242. 2780 Via Orange Way, Suite B, Spring Valley, CA 91978.

Serpentine Music Productions. The complete source for music of Goddess traditions, with many titles appropriate for children, plus videos and songbooks. Many of the chants and songs in this book are available through their free catalog. P.O. Box 2564, Sebastopol, CA 95473. 707-823-7425. Or visit them online at <www.serpentinemusic.com/serpentine>.

HearthSong Catalog. Has a wonderful selection of toys, games, books, and projects for families. 800-325-2502. Or write to request a catalog at P.O. Box 1773, Peoria, IL 61656-1773.

About the Authors

Starhawk is a writer, teacher, activist, and Witch who has been a long-term leading voice in the Goddess movement. She is the author of *The Spiral Dance: A Rebirth of the Ancient Religions of the Great Goddess* (San Francisco: HarperCollins, 1979, 1989), *Dreaming the Dark* (Boston: Beacon, 1982), *Truth or Dare: Encounters with Power, Authority and Mystery* (San Francisco: Harper-Collins, 1987), *The Fifth Sacred Thing* (New York: Bantam, 1992), *Walking to Mercury* (New York, Bantam, 1997), and coauthor of *The Pagan Book of Living and Dying* (San Francisco: HarperSanFrancisco, 1997). She travels widely in North America and Europe teaching and lecturing. She is a founding member of the Reclaiming, a network of communities committed to linking Goddess spirituality and work for social change, and writes a regular column for the *Reclaiming Quarterly*.

Starhawk collaborated with director Donna Read on the Woman and Spirituality series for the National Film Board of Canada. She and Donna Read are currently working on a film biography of Marija Gimbutas, the archaeologist who did groundbreaking work on the Goddess cultures of old Europe.

Starhawk has four grown stepdaughters, all of whom are a credit to their upbringing, although she can claim very little of that credit for herself. She has two step-grandchildren and has lived collectively for over fifteen years, participating in the joys and cares of the lives of many Goddesschildren.

She lives most of the time now in a small hut in the woods, which only occasionally revolves on chicken legs and is not, alas, made of gingerbread.

Information on her schedule, travels, and projects can be found through the Reclaiming website at http://www.reclaiming.org/cauldron/starhawk/welcome.html.

Diane Baker is a writer, attorney, and hearing officer specializing in children's issues, mental health, and housing. In 1980 she co-founded the Reclaiming collective with Starhawk. She is a librarian and has published articles in many magazines, including *FamilyFun* and *Parenting*. She lives in Berkeley, California, with her husband and two children.

Anne Hill is a teacher, writer, musician, and entrepreneur. Her writing and music have been published most recently in *Cyborg Babies: From Techno-Sex to Techno-Tots* (New York: Routledge, 1998) and *The Pagan Book of Living and Dying* (San Francisco: HarperSanFrancisco, 1997). She has also had essays and poetry published in several periodicals, including *Mothering* and *New Age Journal*. She has worked with the Reclaiming collective since 1986, teaching classes and workshops and producing music CD's. She is a student of aikido and the owner of Serpentine Music, a distribution and production company for music of Goddess tradition. She and her partner are raising their three children, niece, and nephew in Sebastopol, California.

We (Starhawk, Diane, and Anne) invite you to share your experiences in raising children in Goddess tradition, whether as parents, teachers, or friends. We're maintaining a web site and hope to start a newsletter. Contact us at <www.circleround.com> or via mail: Circle Round, 2625 Alcatraz Avenue #423, Berkeley, CA 94705.

Index